THE SOUL-BODY PROBLEM AT PARIS, CA. 1200-1250
HUGH OF ST-CHER AND HIS CONTEMPORARIES

ANCIENT AND MEDIEVAL PHILOSOPHY

DE WULF-MANSION CENTRE
Series I

XLII

Series editors

Gerd Van Riel
Russell L. Friedman
Carlos Steel

Advisory Board

Brad Inwood, University of Toronto, Canada
Jill Kraye, The Warburg Institute, London, United Kingdom
John Marenbon, University of Cambridge, United Kingdom
Lodi Nauta, University of Groningen, The Netherlands
Timothy Noone, The Catholic University of America, USA
Jan Opsomer, Universität zu Köln, Germany
Robert Pasnau, University of Colorado at Boulder, USA
Martin Pickavé, University of Toronto, Canada
Pasquale Porro, Università degli Studi di Bari, Italy
Geert Roskam, K.U.Leuven, Belgium

The "De Wulf-Mansion Centre" is a research centre for ancient, medieval, and Renaissance
philosophy at the Institute of Philosophy of the Catholic University of Leuven,
Kardinaal Mercierplein, 2, B 3000 Leuven (Belgium).
It hosts the international project "Aristoteles latinus" and publishes
the "Opera omnia" of Henry of Ghent and the "Opera Philosophica et Theologica" of
Francis of Marchia.

THE SOUL-BODY PROBLEM AT PARIS, CA. 1200-1250

Hugh of St-Cher and His Contemporaries

MAGDALENA BIENIAK

LEUVEN UNIVERSITY PRESS

Leuven University Press / Presses Universitaires de Louvain / Universitaire Pers Leuven
Minderbroedersstraat 4, B-3000 Leuven (Belgium)

ISBN 978 90 5867 802 7
D / 2010 / 1869 / 36
NUR: 732

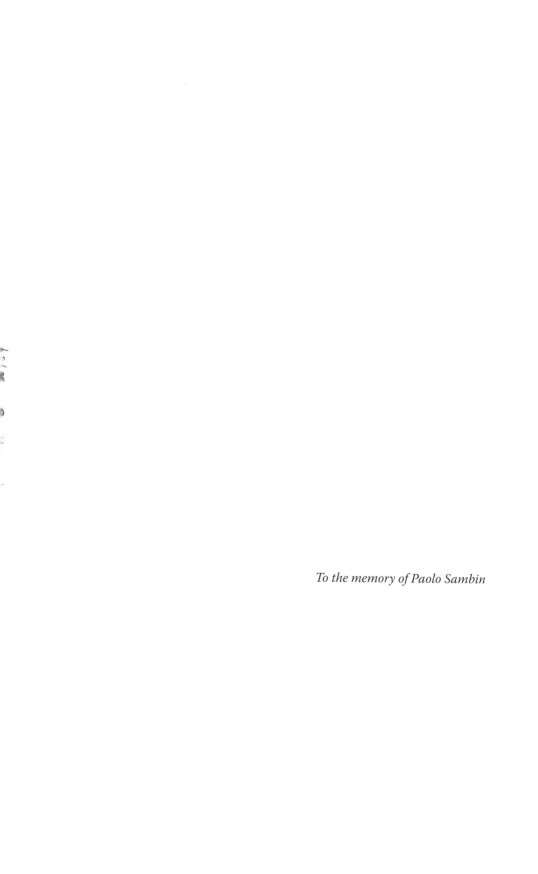

To the memory of Paolo Sambin

TABLE OF CONTENTS

ACKNOWLEDGEMENTS

A well-known American proverb reads as follows: "If you see a turtle sitting on a fencepost, he had help getting there". This study was only possible thanks to those scholars who generously offered me their time and their qualified competence. Above all, I am grateful to Prof. Riccardo Quinto (Padua), who has been advising me for over six years with his untiring patience and expertise. I also wish to thank Prof. Ruedi Imbach (Paris), my doctoral supervisor in France, for his kindness and valuable advice. My special thanks go to Prof. Francesco Bottin (Padua), without whose help this work would not have been realized. Thanks to Russell Friedman (Leuven) for his help with the publication of the book and especially the English version of the text. I am also sincerely grateful to the eminent members of the Leonine Commission, who allowed me to use their facilities in Paris, in particular Adriano Oliva (O.P.), who often guided me through the intricate labyrinth of research work; Zbigniew Pajda (O.P.), to whom I am particularly indebted for helping me to master information technology; and Paweł Krupa (O.P.) and Fabio Gibiino (O.P.), companions in long and not only philosophical discussions. I gratefully remember Louis-Jacques Bataillon (O.P.). I give my special thanks to Prof. Zénon Kaluza (Paris), always willing to provide his precious help. My stay in Paris would not have been possible without the support offered by Prof. Nicole Bériou, who helped me in particular to cope with practical problems; my grateful thanks to Prof. Irène Rosier-Catach (Paris) and Prof. Olivier Boulnois (Paris) as well, whose lessons were a source of inspiration for me. Particularly significant help was provided by Prof. Bernardo Carlos Bazán (Ottawa), whom I sincerely thank for his advice and support. I am also grateful to Prof. Sten Ebbesen (Copenhagen), Barbara Faes de Mottoni (Rome), Luisa Valente (Rome), Patricia Stirnemann (Paris), Gregorio Piaia (Padua), Ilario Tolomio (Padua), Giovanni Catapano (Padua), Mikołaj Olszewski (Warsaw), Paul Bakker (Nijmegen), Marc Clark (Santa Paula, California), Henryk Anzulewicz (Bonn), Valeria de Fraja (Padua), Hilary Siddons, Massimiliano Lenzi (Salerno), Beatrice Cillerai (Pisa), Monica and Dragos Calma (Paris) and, last but not least, Stephen Chung (Paris), who provided very valuable suggestions on the concept of *unibilitas*. Finally, this work would not have been completed without the support given by Marcin, my parents, Elisa, Ilaria and Luca, who carried me through the hard moments, and without many other people who helped me during the past three years. I am sincerely grateful to all of them.

INTRODUCTION

This research originates from an edition and a study of a short disputed question written in the first half of the 1230s by Hugh of St-Cher and entitled *De anima*.[1] The question is part of a collection of a very large number of *quaestiones disputatae* and other texts compiled in the Paris environment between the end of the twelfth and the second half of the thirteenth century. This manuscript collection is preserved in Codex 434 of the Bibliothèque Municipale of Douai and consists of three volumes, the first two of which contain 572 *quaestiones theologicae* and the third of which about forty different texts.[2] This collection is a precious witness to the theological debates that took place in Paris during the first decades of the thirteenth century,[3] at the very beginning of the reception of Aristotle's *libri naturales* and *Metaphysics* on the one hand, and, on the other, of new Hebrew and Arabic philosophical sources, in particular Avicebron's *Fons vitae* and Avicenna's *De anima*. These works were translated around the middle of the twelfth century[4]

---

[1] Cf. M. Bieniak, "Una questione disputata di Ugo di St.-Cher sull'anima. Edizione e studio dottrinale", *Studia antyczne i mediewistyczne* 2 [37] (2004), pp. 127-184.

[2] Cf. *Catalogue général des manuscrits des bibliothèques publiques des départements de France. Bibliothèque de Douai*, Douai 1878, vol. IV, pp. 246-249; O. Lottin, "Quelques *Questiones* de maîtres parisiens aux environs de 1225-1235", RTAM 5 (1933), pp. 79-81; P. Glorieux, "Les 572 Questions du manuscrit de Douai 434", RTAM 10 (1938), pp. 123-152, 225-267; V. Doucet, "A travers le manuscrit 434 de Douai", *Antonianum* 27 (1952), pp. 558-568; Bieniak, "Una questione disputata", pp. 127-131; regarding the third volume in particular, see R. Quinto, "Il Codice 434 di Douai, Stefano Langton e Nicola di Tournai", *Sacris Erudiri* 36 (1996), pp. 233-361.

[3] J.-P. Torrell, *Théorie de la prophétie et philosophie de la connaissance aux environs de 1230. La contribution d'Hugues de Saint-Cher*, Louvain: Spicilegium sacrum Lovaniense, 1977, pp. V-XI.

[4] Cf. Ch. H. Haskins, "A list of text-books from the close of the twelfth century", *Harvard Studies in Classical Philosophy* 20 (1909), p. 92; M. Grabmann, *Forschungen über die Lateinischen Aristoteles - Übersetzungen des XIII. Jahrhunderts*, Münster: Aschendorff, 1916 (B. G. Ph. M., 17. 5-6), pp. 19-27; L. Minio-Paluello, "Nuovi impulsi allo studio della logica: la seconda fase della riscoperta di Aristotele e di Boezio", in ed. CISAM, *La scuola nell'Occidente latino dell'alto medioevo*, vol. II, Spoleto, 1972, pp. 743-766; G. Diem, "Les traductions gréco-latines de la Métaphysique au Moyen Âge: Le problème de la Metaphysica Vetus", *Archiv für Geschichte der Philosophie* 49 (1967), pp. 7-71; L. Minio-Paluello, "Le texte du «De anima» d'Aristote: la tradition latine avant 1500", in id., *Opuscula. The Latin Aristotle*, Amsterdam: Hakkert, 1972, pp. 250-276; F. Van Steenberghen, "L'aristotélisme", in *Introduction à l'étude de la philosophie médiévale*, Louvain: Peeters, 1974, pp. 488-490; B. G. Dod, "Aristoteles Latinus", in *The Cambridge History of Later Medieval Philosophy*,

and aroused considerable interest among Latin medieval thinkers. In particular, these texts strongly influenced the previously existing conception of man. This impact, however, did not constitute a mere acceptance of certain doctrines, since the new philosophy was compared with the edifice of theological knowledge built up over the previous centuries, and was possibly integrated into it. Indeed, the peculiar character of medieval thought, notably that of the thirteenth century, may be seen as a blend of different elements.[5] Philosophical interest was not the only engine of psychological research: in several cases, the decisive factors were dogmatic requirements and traditional interpretations of patristic authorities. Moreover, historical circumstances – together with factors of a doctrinal nature – sometimes played an influential role too, for instance when a particular kind of heresy arose, thus inciting Christian theologians to use new arguments to defend the revealed truths endangered by heterodox doctrines. In order to provide a thorough analysis of early thirteenth-century anthropological thought and to understand its developments as well as the exigencies it was based on, it is necessary to consider all these factors. For this reason, the aim of the present study is not only to cast light on the influences exerted by Aristotle and other philosophical authorities on early thirteenth-century theologians, but on many occasions to focus on the other elements that led to the development of certain theological doctrines. Special importance is attached to the religious dogmas that in most cases gave direction to anthropological thought.

The present study is centred on the problem of determining the nature of the union between the human soul and the body.[6] In the twelfth and thirteenth centuries, in the Latin West, the debate concerning this theme was mainly character-

---

ed. N. Kretzmann - A. Kenny - J. Pinborg, Cambridge: Cambridge University Press, 1982 (EL 45.1), pp. 74-78; L. Bianchi, *La filosofia nelle università: secoli XIII-XIV*, Firenze: La nuova Italia,1997, pp. 11-14. On the reception of the new Aristotle, see also M. Grabmann, *I divieti ecclesiastici di Aristotele sotto Innocenzo III e Gregorio IX*, Roma 1941.

[5] On the problem of the definition of medieval philosophy, see for instance P. Schulthess - R. Imbach, *Die Philosophie im lateinischen Mittelalter: ein Handbuch mit einem bio-bibliographischen Repertorium*, Zürich: Artemis & Winkler, 1996, pp. 17-24; R. Imbach, "La philosophie médiévale", in id., *Quodlibeta. Ausgewählte Artikel - Articles choisis*, Freiburg: Universitätsverlag, 1996, pp. 17-36; R. Quinto, *"Scholastica". Storia di un concetto*, Padova: Il Poligrafo, 2001, pp. 329-411.

[6] Among recent works devoted to this problem, we should mention in particular C. Casagrande - S. Vecchio (ed.), *Anima e corpo nella cultura medievale. Atti del V Convegno di studi della Società Italiana per lo Studio del Pensiero Medievale, Venezia, 25-28 settembre 1995*, Firenze: SISMEL edizioni del Galluzzo, 1999; T. W. Köhler, *Grundlagen des philosophisch-anthropologischen Diskurses im dreizehnten Jahrhundert: die Erkenntnisbemühungen um den Menschen im zeitgenössischen Verstandnis*, Leiden – Boston: Brill, 2000; M. Lenzi, *Forma e sostanza. Le origini del dibattito sulla natura dell'anima nel XIII secolo*, Ph.D. thesis, supervisor A. Maierù, Università di Salerno, 2004-2005.

ized by a tension between two contrasting needs: on the one hand, the need to protect the unity of the human being and, on the other, the need to defend the immortality of the soul, since it may seem that a dominance of the latter naturally leads to a dualist conception of man. However, it would be wrong to define this conflict as a clash between the requirements of dogma and those of philosophy. Both the faith in the immortality of the soul and the belief that man forms a unity – as posited, for example, by the concept of *persona*, faith in the resurrection, and the dogma of the incarnation of the Word – have their own place in Christian doctrine. Hence, both theological and philosophical arguments were involved in support of these needs.

The tension between the two polarities mentioned above is the interpretative thread leading us through the theological texts written in the first four decades of the thirteenth century. The text is therefore divided into two main sections. The first section traces the evolution of anthropology from the dualist perspective, which had prevailed in the early Middle Ages,[7] towards a unitary conception of man. This section focuses on those dynamic forces that put greater emphasis on some unitary aspects of the conception of man and that were not necessarily related to Aristotelian thought: indeed, the greater attention paid to these aspects was partly preceded and partly accompanied by the assimilation of Aristotle's *De anima*.

The first part of this section will deal with a doctrine typical of Hugh of St-Cher's anthropology and taken up again by several later authors, namely the doctrine of the *unibilitas substantialis* of the human soul in regard to the body. In order to provide a thorough analysis of this theory we will first describe the doctrinal frame it resulted from; then we will examine those writings in which the *unibilitas* theory appears for the first time, beginning with William of Auxerre's *Summa aurea* and Hugh of St-Cher's question *De anima*; finally, we will consider the implications of this doctrine from the 1230s up to Thomas Aquinas.

Secondly, we will analyse the debate over whether the human soul is a person. This problem is closely related to the doctrine of *unibilitas substantialis* and certainly represents one of its sources. Reconstructing the controversy over the soul-person will necessarily include a study of a number of works produced in the twelfth century, in particular the *Commentaries* by Gilbert of Poitiers on Boethius' *Theological Treatises* and Alan of Lille's *Summa "Quoniam homines"*. Just as in the case of the *unibilitas* doctrine, so the analysis of the debate on the soul-person will include some texts produced in the second half of the thirteenth century.

---

[7] Cf. I. Tolomio, *L'anima dell'uomo: trattati sull'anima dal v al ix secolo*, Milano: Rusconi, 1979, *passim*.

The second main section of the present work concentrates on the aspects of early thirteenth-century anthropology that involved a dualist conception of the human being. These aspects emerge most clearly from the debate on the powers of the human soul, particularly in relation to their ontological status. Indeed, in the first half of the thirteenth century, the doctrines concerning the powers of the soul are consequences of the general ontological view of the human being and clearly reveal the difficulties, incongruous elements and even aporias characterizing the anthropology of that time. At the same time, the debate concerning the powers of the soul, which was fuelled by different trends of thought, shows in a paradigmatic way the discordances between the anthropological sources used in the early thirteenth century.

We will first examine the doctrines concerning the rational powers, and secondly the doctrines concerning the vegetative and sensitive powers. The debate on the ontological status of the first type of powers represents a continuation of the debates that had started in the twelfth century: indeed, it coincides with the debate on the problem of whether the soul is identical to its powers. As regards this debate, it should be noted that the impact exerted by the new philosophical sources on the positions held by early thirteenth-century Parisian masters was very limited.

By contrast, in the first decades of the thirteenth century, the debate on the vegetative and sensitive powers of the soul was mostly fostered by the reception of Avicenna's *De anima* and of other sources newly translated into Latin. The chapter devoted to the vegetative and sensitive powers deals with two main themes: first, the problem of the intermediary powers between the rational soul and the body; second, the question of whether the inferior powers survive after the separation of soul and body. As regards the doctrine of the intermediary principles between soul and body, the doctrinal contribution provided by some philosophical sources, in particular Avicebron's *Fons vitae* and Avicenna's *De anima*, accords easily with the doctrines elaborated in the twelfth century. By contrast, the problem concerning the survival of the sensitive and vegetative powers of the human soul finds different solutions in the texts that mainly follow the theological tradition, on the one hand, and in those that are more influenced by the new philosophical sources, on the other.

The final part of our analysis will concern a power that may be classified both among rational faculties and sensitive faculties, namely human memory. The debate on the ontological status of this power is particularly complex, but the subject is of great importance, in particular because it is related to the problems concerning the separated soul and the resurrection of man.

This work partly rests on the study of unpublished texts, notably some disputed questions preserved in the aforementioned collection in ms. Douai 434 and Hugh of St-Cher's *Commentary* on the third distinction of book I of Peter Lombard's *Sentences*. An edition of these texts is given in the appendix to the present monograph.

Part One
Towards the Unity of the Human Being

1.1
ACCIDENTAL UNION OF THE SOUL WITH THE BODY
AND *UNIBILITAS SUBSTANTIALIS* OF THE HUMAN SOUL

The center point of the present study is Hugh of St-Cher's anthropology.[1] It is the center point, although not a privileged one: it is central because reconstructing the opinions of this theologian is our primary purpose; it is not privileged because these opinions must be seen and evaluated within a broader context. Indeed, Hugh is not a revolutionary author, but a reconstruction of his contribution to the anthropological debate allows us to analyze some important philosophical developments which until now have not received sufficient attention from scholars. What is more, Hugh's thought has exerted some influence and therefore is not to be neglected.

---

[1] Hugh was probably born about 1190, in 1224/1225 he entered the Order of Preachers; during the years 1230-1235 he taught at Paris; in 1244 he became the first Dominican cardinal. He died in 1263. Concerning Hugh's life and works, see J. Fisher, "Hugh of St. Cher and the Development of Medieval Theology", *Speculum* 31 (1956), pp. 57-69; Th. Kaeppeli, *Scriptores Ordinis Praedicatorum Medii Aevi*, Roma: Ad Sanctae Sabinae - Istituto Storico Domenicano, 1970, vol. II, pp. 269-281; W. Principe, *Hugh of Saint-Cher's Theology of the Hypostatic Union*, Toronto: Pontifical Institute of Medieval Studies, 1970, pp. 14-21; A. Paravicini Bagliani, *Cardinali di curia e 'familiae' cardinalizie dal 1227 al 1254*, Padova: Editrice Antenore, 1972, vol. I, pp. 257-259; A. M. Landgraf, *Introduction à l'histoire de la littérature théologique de la scolastique naissante*, Montréal: Institut d'études médiévales, 1973, pp. 175-177; Torrell, *Théorie de la prophétie*, pp. 88-90; A. Ghisalberti, "L'esegesi della scuola domenicana del sec. XIII" in *La Bibbia nel Medio Evo*, Bologna: ed. G. Cremascoli, Edizioni Dehoniane, 1996, pp. 291-304, pp. 293-294; *Hugues de Saint-Cher († 1263), bibliste et théologien*, L.-J. Bataillon, G. Dahan et P.-M. Gy (ed.), Turnhout: Brepols, 2004, *passim*; J. Bartkó, *Un prédicateur français au Moyen Age: les Sermons modèles de Hugues de Saint-Cher (1263)*, Veszprém: Pannon Egy. K., 2006, *passim*. It seems that Thomas Aquinas was able to start studying at Paris as a bachelor under Albert the Great thanks to Hugh's intercession when the latter was already a cardinal; cf. Guill. de Tocco, *yst. S. Thom.*, c. 15, ed. Le Brun Gouanvic, pp. 120-121: "Post hec autem cum frater Thomas sic mirabiliter in scientia et in uita proficeret, et magistro Alberto ex commissione reuerendi patris fratris Iohannis de Vercellis, magistri ordinis, incumberet ut Parisiensi studio de sufficienti baccellario prouideret, magister predicti sui discipuli preuidens uelocem in doctrina profectum persuasit per litteras predicto magistro ut de fratre Thoma de Aquino pro baccellario in predicto studio prouideret, describens eius sufficientiam in scientia et in uita. Quem cum non statim duceret acceptandum adhuc sibi in gratiis predictis ignotum suasu dompni Vgonis cardinalis eiusdem ordinis, cui erat de ipso per litteras intimatum, predictus magister ipsum in predicti studii baccellarium acceptauit, scribens ei ut statim Parisius se conferret et ad legendum Sententias se pararet".

Hugh's question *De anima* presents an interesting doctrine that urges us to reconsider the opinion – still widespread among scholars – that the beginning of the thirteenth century constitutes an age marked by a rather homogeneous anthropological dualism. According to Hugh, the ability to be united with the body, which is called *unibilitas*, belongs to the human soul in a substantial way and represents its specific difference with respect to the angel. This ability remains in the soul even after its separation from the body and prevents the human soul from being a person.

The present chapter aims at analysing this doctrine by reconstructing its sources and comparing it with other contemporary anthropological theories. Moreover, we will see the response aroused by the doctrine of the *unibilitas substantialis* in the literature of later decades. Finally, we will try to give an answer to the question concerning the connection between this theory and a doctrine mainly inspired by Avicenna, i.e. the doctrine of the "double consideration" of the soul.

1.1.1   THE ACCIDENTAL UNION OF THE SOUL WITH THE BODY

1.1.1.1   Avicenna and early Avicennianism

Avicenna's *De anima*[2] is certainly one of the works that most influenced the psychology of the first decades of the thirteenth century. As recently demonstrated by Nicolaus Hasse, this influence mainly concerns the classification and description of the powers of the soul: no other Avicennian doctrine is quoted so extensively and for such a long period.[3] But also the way in which the Arab philosopher addresses the question of the ontological status of the soul and of its essence is taken up quite often by thirteenth-century authors. It is useful, therefore, to dwell for a moment upon the main features of the Avicennian approach.

In his *Liber de anima* as well as in his *Metaphysics*, Avicenna adopted an Aristotelian language and was thus considered a peripatetic philosopher by the Latin masters.[4] However, the *Liber de anima* clearly conveys an anthropological view which is imbued with Neoplatonism, especially as concerns the question of the ontological essence of the human soul.[5] For in Avicenna's view the human being

---

[2] Regarding the reception of the *Liber de anima*, see especially N. Hasse, *Avicenna's De anima in the Latin West*, London: The Warburg Institute, 2000. An interesting reconstruction of the influence exerted by Avicennian anthropology on thirteenth-century authors has been recently presented by Lenzi, *Forma e sostanza*, pp. 155-233.

[3] Cf. Hasse, *Avicenna's De anima*, p. 228, pp. 236-314, especially pp. 242-253.

[4] Cf. Hasse, *Avicenna's De anima*, p. 227 ; G. Verbeke, *Le «De anima» d'Avicenne. Une conception spiritualiste de l'homme*, in Auic., *de an.*, IV-V, ed. Van Riet, pp. 3*-4*.

[5] Verbeke, *Le «De anima» d'Avicenne*, p. 11*: "Qu'on se rappelle la définition aristotélicienne de l'âme: elle est la première entéléchie du corps; Avicenne reste fidèle à cette

must be primarily identified with his soul: this point of view is clearly expressed in the famous hypothesis of a flying man.[6] The being of the soul, as well as its essence, is independent of the corporeal dimension. Indeed, according to Avicenna, if we consider the soul in its relation to the body, we may define it as a "perfectio prima corporis naturalis instrumentalis habentis opera vitae".[7] This definition, however, does not concern the proper essence of the soul. If considered in itself, the *psyche* is an immaterial and independent spirit capable of knowing itself and destined to an eternal life outside the body.[8] Avicenna thus presents a theory of the "double consideration" of the soul: on the one hand, it is seen in itself, i.e. as regards its essence; on the other hand, it is seen in relation to the body, i.e. in its relational aspect.[9]

What is the basis of the connection between the soul and the human body? According to Avicenna, the human soul has a natural tendency in itself that urges it to perfect a particular corporeal substance. Indeed, the soul is oriented towards one body, not towards any body. At the same time, this tendency constitutes its principle of individuation. Therefore the human soul is not individuated thanks to the body, i.e. through the impression on matter, but has in itself the ability to be-

---

optique: pour lui, le corps fait partie de la définition de l'âme comme l'oeuvre fait partie de la définition de l'artisan. Mais, pour connaître l'essence de l'âme, pour savoir ce qu'elle est en elle-même, Avicenne estime qu'une autre recherche est nécessaire: ceci ne s'inscrit plus dans l'optique aristotélicienne, mais dépend d'une psychologie dualiste d'origine néo-platonicienne. Si l'on peut étudier l'essence de l'âme sans tenir compte de sa relation au corps, c'est que l'âme subsiste en elle-même en dehors de sa relation au corps et ne se sert de l'organisme corporel que comme d'un instrument".

[6] Auic., *de an.* i, 1, ed. Van Riet, pp. 36-37; cf. Hasse, *Avicenna's De anima*, pp. 80-87; M. Sebti, *Avicenne. L'âme humaine*, Paris: Presses Universitaires de France, 2000, p. 19; B. C. Bazán, "Pluralisme de formes ou dualisme de substances?", *Revue Philosophique de Louvain* 67 (1969), p. 40.

[7] Auic., *de an.* i, 1, ed. Van Riet, p. 29$^{62\text{-}63}$.

[8] On the question of resurrection in Avicenna, see J. R. Michot, *La destinée de l'homme selon Avicenne. Le retour à Dieu (ma'ad) et l'imagination*, Leuven: Peeters, 1986, *passim*.

[9] Cf. Auic., *de an.* i, 1, ed. Van Riet, pp. 26^{27}-27^{30}: "Hoc enim nomen "anima" non est indictum ei ex substantia sua, sed ex hoc quod regit corpora et refertur ad illa, et idcirco recipitur corpus in sui diffinitione". A similar doctrine appears in several thirteenth-century authors; cf. Ioh. Blund, *tract. de an.* 2, 1, ed. Callus - Hunt, pp. 5$^{32\text{-}63}$; Philipp., *sum. de bon.*, ed. Wicki, p. 281$^{40\text{-}41}$; Rol. Crem., *sum.*, ms. *Paris, Bibliothèque Mazarine 795*, 87ra; Ioh. Rup., *sum. de an.*, ed. Bougerol, pp. 116^{44}-117^{57}; Alb. Magn., *sum. theol.*, ii, tr. 12, q. 69, art. 2, ed. Iammy, p. 350a. A very similar theory is also expressed in *De spiritu et anima*, 9, PL 40, p. 784; cf. Alex. Halen., *q. ant.* xviii, 1, ed. PP. Collegii S. Bonaventurae, vol. i, 297^{18}-21. As regards the history of the theory concerning the dual consideration of the soul, see Lenzi, *Forma e sostanza*, pp. 115-233; P. Bernardini, "La dottrina dell'anima separata nella prima metà del xiii secolo e i suoi influssi sulla teoria della conoscenza (1240-60 ca.)", in *Etica e conoscenza nel xiii e xiv secolo*, ed. I. Zavattero, Arezzo: Dipartimento di Studi Storico-Sociali e Filosofici, 2006, pp. 29-30.

come individuated. In order to fulfil this ability, the soul needs the body; yet, when the two substances are separated by death, the soul remains individual in act. According to Avicenna, the union with the body is necessary in order that souls may become distinguished from one another; nevertheless, the natural tendency towards the body, which for the soul represents the true principle of individuation, is not an essential property for it, but is "aliquid ex accidentibus spiritualibus".[10]

In the Avicennian perspective, the relation with the body exerts no influence at all on the essence of the soul: it is a purely accidental union.[11] For the corporeal organism does not constitute the proper location of the soul nor its ultimate destination, where its complete beatitude will be accomplished, but just an ephemeral instrument, a temporal abode and a sort of garment.[12] The psychophysical union thus constitutes an extremely weak and instrumental composition occurring between two real substances. Indeed, Avicenna not only insists on the autonomy of the soul as spirit which is perfect in itself, but also postulates some degree of com-

---

[10] Auic., *de an.* V, 3, ed. Van Riet, p. 106[49-53]: "Inter animas autem non est alteritas in essentia et forma: forma enim earum una est. Ergo non est alteritas nisi secundum receptibile suae essentiae cui comparatur essentia eius proprie, et hoc est corpus. Si autem anima esset tantum absque corpore, una anima non posset esse alia ab alia numero", p. 111[19-27]: "Ergo anima non est una, sed est multae numero, et eius species una est, et est creata sicut postea declarabimus. Sed sine dubio aliquid est propter quod singularis effecta est ; illud autem non est impressio animae in materia (iam enim destruximus hoc); immo illud est aliqua de affectionibus et aliqua de virtutibus et aliquid ex accidentibus spiritualibus, aut compositum ex illis, propter quod singularis fit anima, quamvis illud nesciamus"; cf. Sebti, *Avicenne*, pp. 25-33.

[11] Cf. also Auic., *de an.* I, 1, ed. Van Riet, pp. 15[77]-16[84]: "Et id a quo emanant istae affectiones dicitur anima, et omnino quicquid est principium emanandi a se affectiones quae non sunt unius modi et sunt voluntarie, imponimus ei nomen «anima». Et hoc nomen est nomen huius rei non ex eius essentia, nec ex praedicamento <...> in quo continebitur postea; nunc autem non affirmamus nisi esse rei quae est principium eius quod praediximus, et affirmamus esse rei ex hoc quod habet aliquod accidens. Oportet autem ut, per hoc accidens quod habet, accedamus ad certificandum eius essentiam et ad cognoscendum quid sit".

[12] Cf. Auic., *de an.* V, 4, ed. Van Riet, p. 144[54-56]: "Si autem hoc est eis (i.e. animae) accidentale, non substantiale, tunc destructo uno illorum, destruetur relatio quae accidit alteri et non destruetur ad destructionem alterius, quamvis sic pendeat ex eo"; *ibidem* V, 7, ed. Van Riet, pp. 160[36]-161[39], pp. 162[57]-163[64]: "...quae autem exercentur instrumento, coniunguntur in principio quod coniungit eas in instrumento, quod principium procedit ab anima in instrumentum (...). Haec autem membra non sunt vere nisi sicut vestes; quae, quia diu est quod adhaeserunt nobis, putavimus nos esse illa aut quod sunt sicut partes nostri; cum enim imaginamur nostras animas, non imaginamur eas nudas, sed imaginamur eas indutas corporibus, cuius rei causa est diuturnitas adhaerentiae; consuevimus autem exuere vestes et proiicere, quod omnino non consuevimus in membris: unde opinio quod membra sunt partes nostri, firmior est in nobis quam opinio quod vestes sint partes nostri"; Sebti, *Avicenne*, pp. 18-19; Verbeke, *Le «De anima» d'Avicenne*, p. 11*.

pleteness in the body itself, since corporeity, which is proper to the body, is not due to the rational soul, but to an intermediary form, the corporeal form.[13]

Such doctrine seems hardly compatible with the Aristotelian theory of the soul. Further, it should be observed that, in the Latin translation of Avicenna's *Liber*, the soul is defined as 'perfection', rather than 'form' or 'entelechy'. On this point, the Latin translation exactly reflects the Arabic text: and in fact the Arabic version of the Aristotelian definition adopts the term 'kamāl', which, as explained by Meryem Sebti, literally means 'perfection'.[14] This change is not merely cosmetic. Avicenna actually rejects the Aristotelian conception that the soul is the form of the body with which it constitutes one substance.[15] In his view, the soul constitutes a substance which is complete as such and does not need the body to complete its essence. Moreover, the soul does not give the form to prime matter but is just a principle of further perfection for a material body somehow prepared to receive it. Avicenna thus introduces a deep difference between 'form' and 'perfection': only the latter of these terms can be referred to the human soul. The specificity of Avicennian anthropology lies above all in the fact that the term 'perfection' does not describe the substance of the soul but a mere relational and operational – or, in other words, accidental – aspect of it.[16]

The Arabic definition of the soul as perfection of the body enters the Latin West not only through Avicenna, but also thanks to Costa Ben Luca's treatise *De differentia spiritus et animae*. It is through the latter that the definition is assimilated into the first Latin work influenced by Avicenna, i.e. the *De anima* by Dominicus Gundissalinus:[17]

---

[13] Cf. Auic., *metaph.* II, 2, ed. Van Riet, pp. 78-79; cf. Sebti, *Avicenne*, pp. 22-23.

[14] As well as in Avicenna's *Liber*, this term appears in Qusta ibn Luqa's and Averroes' treatises: cf. Cost., *diff. an. et spir.* 3, ed. Barach, p. 134; Auer., *in De an.* II, 7, ed. Crawford, p. 138$^{2-3}$; see also Sebti, *Avicenne*, p. 16; Lenzi, *Forma e sostanza*, pp. 123-124, adn. 21.

[15] Cf. Sebti, *Avicenne*, pp. 16-17: "Il établit – contre l'acception véritable d'Aristote – que la notion de perfection et celle de forme sont distinctes et ne relèvent pas du même ordre: définir l'âme comme la forme d'un corps revient à la caractériser comme l'un des deux composants de toute substance première; cela permet à Aristote de déduire que l'âme est une substance, parce qu'elle est la forme d'un corps. C'est précisément cette conséquence qu'Avicenne récuse".

[16] Cf. Bazán, "Pluralisme de formes", pp. 38-39; id., "The Human Soul: Form *and* Substance? Thomas Aquinas' Critique of Eclectic Aristotelianism", AHDLMA 64 (1997), pp. 103-104. Regarding the soul-body relation in Avicenna, see also M. T. Druart, "The Human Soul's Individuation and its Survival after the Body's Death: Avicenna on the Causal Relation between Body and Soul", *Arabic sciences and philosophy* 10.2 (2000), pp. 259-273.

[17] Dom. Gund., *de an.*, ed. Muckle, p. 40$^{13-15}$. The treatise, which includes a large number of passages copied verbatim from Avicenna's *Liber*, was written about 1170-1175; cf. R. C. Dales, *The Problem of the Rational Soul in the Thirteenth Century*, Leiden - New York: Brill, 1995, p. 13; E. Gilson, "Introduction", in Dom. Gund., *de an.*, ed. J. T. Muckle, *Mediaeval Studies* 2 (1940), pp. 23-27.

Aristoteles autem sic definivit animam dicens: "Anima est prima perfectio corporis naturalis, instrumentalis, viventis potentialiter".

A similar definition appears in John Blund's *Tractatus de anima*, written at the very beginning of the thirteenth century:[18]

A natura est preparatio in corpore organico ut ipsum sit convenientius ad animam rationalem recipiendam quam ad aliud recipiendum; sufficienti autem preparatione corporis et appropriatione existente ut anima ei infundatur, a primo datore formarum ei infunditur anima, et ita nature ministerio precedente subsequens est a prima causa perfectio, scilicet anima que est perfectio corporis organici viventis potentialiter.

This is not the only point of contact between John Blund's *Tractatus de anima* and Avicenna's *Liber*. Indeed, according to John too, the term 'perfection' does not describe the soul in its essence, but merely denotes an accident of its substance, i.e. its relation with the body.[19] John openly refuses to call the human soul a 'form' because, in his view, this would prejudice its immortality, since a form is necessarily dependent on its matter and becomes corrupt with the corruption of the latter.[20] We might therefore conclude that in John Blund's treatise too the concept of form and the concept of perfection acquire two different meanings. Actually, whereas the concept of substantial form is always strictly connected with matter,

---

[18] Ioh. Blund, *tract. de an.* 25, 2, ed. Callus - Hunt, pp. 98^{24}-99^5; cf. R. W. Hunt, "Introduction", in Ioh. Blund, *tract. de an.*, ed. Callus - Hunt, p. xi.

[19] Ioh. Blund, *tract. de an.*, 2, 1, ed. Callus - Hunt, pp. 5^{32}-6^3: "Hoc nomen anima designat rem suam in concretione. Significat enim substantiam sub quodam accidente in relatione ad corpus organicum in quantum ipsum animatur et vivificatur per ipsam, et gratia illius accidentis dicitur esse perfectio ipsius, eo scilicet quod ipsa ipsum animat". A convincing interpretation of John Blund's position is provided by Massimiliano Lenzi, *Forma e sostanza*, 126 (in English translation): "The recourse to the category of 'relation', and to what might be defined as its peculiar foundation, i.e. the *quoddam accidens*, that is the corporeal and functional tendency of the soul to animate the body, is here referred to a typically substrative and categorial theory, according to which a differently characterized *res* – in the case at hand a spiritual substance – possesses a further determination, i.e. its inclination to animate and vivify the body, that disposes and qualifies it in relation to something else".

[20] Ioh. Blund, *tract. de an.*, II, 1. 15, ed. Callus - Hunt, p. 5$^{16-22}$: "Sed obicitur. Forma dat esse, et materia in se est imperfecta: unde omnis perfectio est a forma. Ergo cum perfectio corporis organici habentis vitam in potentia sit anima, anima est forma. Sed nulla forma est res per se existens separata a substantia. Ergo cum anima sit forma, anima non habet dici res per se existens separata a substantia. Ergo anima non potest separari a corpore, sed perit cum corpore".

a perfection may denote a merely accidental reality, thus not touching the essence of substance and not endangering its independency.

1.1.1.2 Philip the Chancellor's *Summa de bono*

Philip the Chancellor († 1236) belongs to the first generation of Parisian theologians influenced by Avicenna's philosophy. It is certain that his main theological work, the *Summa de bono*, was already produced after the first version of William of Auxerre's *Summa aurea*,[21] although the exact date of its composition remains uncertain.[22] Moreover, viewed from our perspective, the *Summa de bono* is particularly significant because it is the primary source of Hugh of St-Cher's disputed questions.

Philip and Hugh knew each other. When the Dominican began teaching at the Faculty of Theology in Paris (1231), Philip was already a highly reputed master, mainly known as one of the most esteemed preachers of his time.[23] We also know that he had close relations with the Parisian Dominicans, and this is why many of his sermons express praise towards the Order of Preachers. Again, it was Philip who granted the *licentia docendi* to Roland of Cremona.[24] Hugh and Philip were thus members of the same milieu in the same period: one may easily deduce that they knew each other, which is also attested by the fact that in 1235 they both took part in the dispute on the plurality of benefices.[25]

The close kinship between Hugh's question *De anima* and the *Summa de bono* had already been pointed out by Odon Lottin.[26] Subsequently, Jean-Pierre Torrell demonstrated that the question *De prophetia*[27] too contains several borrowings from Philip's *Summa*.[28] The question *Quomodo anima uniatur corpori* – practi-

---

[21] For dating the *Summa aurea*, cf. *infra*, p. 20.

[22] The *Summa* was commonly dated to between 1228 and 1236 (death of Philip the Chancellor), but the editor proposes a decidedly earlier date, i.e. the years 1225-1228; cf. N. Wicki, "Introduction", in Philipp., *sum. de bon.*, ed. Wicki, pp. 63*-65*.

[23] Cf. J. B. Schneyer, *Die Sittenkritik in den Predigten Philipps des Kanzlers*, Münster: Aschendorff, 1962-1963 (B. G. Ph. Th. M., 39. 4), pp. 115-119.

[24] Wicki, "Introduction", pp. 26*-27*.

[25] Cf. F. Stegmüller, "Die neugefundene Parisier Benefizien-Disputation des Kardinals Hugo von St. Cher OP.", *Historisches Jahrbuch* 72 (1953), pp. 179-182; Ch. de Miramon, "La place d'Hugues de Saint-Cher dans les débats sur la pluralité des bénéfices (1230-1240)" in ed. Bataillon, L.-J. , Dahan, G., and Gy, P.-M., *Hugues de Saint-Cher (†1263), bibliste et théologien,* Turnhout: Brepols, 2004, pp. 341-386.

[26] Cf. O. Lottin, "Un petit traité sur l'âme de Hugues de Saint-Cher", *Revue neoscolastique de philosophie* 34 (1932), pp. 468-475.

[27] This question too is preserved in the ms. *Douai 434* and bears n. 481, following the classification made by P. Glorieux, "Les 572 Questions du manuscrit de Douai 434", RTAM 10 (1938), p. 239. It has been published by Jean Pierre Torrell; cf. *Théorie de la prophétie*, pp. 1-58.

[28] Torrell, *Théorie de la prophétie*, pp. 73-87.

cally a compilation of passages from the *Summa de bono* – should be added too
to this list.[29] In the case of the question *De anima*, the material drawn, either verbatim or with small variations, from the *Summa* amounts statistically to about
sixty percent of the text. Evidently, Philip's anthropology was determining for the
thought of Hugh of St-Cher; it is thus advisable to dwell on a few aspects of the
scientia de anima as it is expounded in the *Summa de bono*.[30]

Philip the Chancellor addresses the theme of the human soul in the first part
of the *Summa de bono*, which bears the title *De bono nature*. After discussing
problems related to angels and corporeal creatures, Philip devotes a long section
to psychology and divides it into nine questions concerning eighteen different
problems. Among these, let us point out a chapter entitled *Quid sit anima*. More
than a *quaestio*, this is a short introduction to the anthropological section. While
answering the question advanced in the title of the chapter,[31] Philip quotes the definition of the soul given by six authorities, among whom figure Seneca, Calcidius,
the text *De motu cordis* ascribed to Aristotle, Augustine, Nemesius of Emesa[32] and
the author of *De spiritu et anima*. The listed definitions, however, do not include
Aristotle's treatise *De anima*. This omission is significant:[33] unlike Aristotle, all
the cited authors describe the soul as an autonomous substance or a rational spirit.
This fact too shows that Philip, like Avicenna, does not consider the union with the
body as something decisive for the essence of the soul. Yet, this does not mean that
he ignores or totally rejects the anthropology elaborated by the Philosopher. This
is confirmed by the fact that the Aristotelian definition, cited in its Arabic version,
appears in another place in the *Summa de bono*:[34]

> Primus actus anime est quod sit "perfectio corporis naturalis organici" etc.,
> secundus actus est operari; sicut in ense primus est figura et forma, secundus
> secare, et secundus actus non est sine primo.

---

[29] Cf. *infra*, pp. 183-186.

[30] The anthropology expressed in the *Summa* has been recently expounded by N.
Wicki, *Die Philosophie Philipps des Kanzlers: ein philosophierender Theologe des frühen
13. Jahrhunderts*, Fribourg: Academic Press, 2005, pp. 79-144; cf. also R. Zavalloni, *Richard
de Mediavilla et la controverse sur la pluralité des formes*, Louvain: Éditions de l'Institut
supérieur de philosophie, 1951, pp. 407-409; Lenzi, *Forma e sostanza*, pp. 177-184.

[31] Cf. Philipp., *sum. de bon.*, ed. Wicki, p. 156.

[32] Nemesius was called "Remigius" by Philip and other contemporary authors; cf. I.
Brady, "Remigius - Nemesius", *FS* 8 (1948), pp. 275-284. On Nemesius's anthropology, see
B. Motta, *La mediazione estrema. L'antropologia di Nemesio di Emesa fra platonismo e
aristotelismo*, Padova: Il Poligrafo, 2004.

[33] Cf. Bazán, *The Human Soul*, p. 110; Wicki, *Die Philosophie Philipps des Kanzlers*, pp.
80-81.

[34] Philipp., *sum. de bon.*, ed. Wicki, p. 231[24-26].

The *Summa* certainly contains several quotations from *De anima* and other works of the "new" Aristotle. But Philip is an acute thinker, conscious of the difference between an anthropology based on the matter-form relation and the traditional Augustinian and Neoplatonic view.[35] The role assigned to the notion of form or perfection[36] is thus significantly reduced. According to Philip, the soul cannot be defined as a form: for the notion of form is inseparably connected to dependency on matter, hence it necessarily implies corruptibility.[37]

The human soul, however, resembles a form in a way. This is why the body needs the soul in order to receive its ultimate perfection: the role that the soul performs towards the organism is thus analogous to that performed by a form as united to matter. Yet, the human soul, in its essence, is chiefly a substance and a spirit: hence its essential independence from matter and incorruptibility. The human soul must therefore be defined as a substance resembling a form, not the converse.[38]

It is further to be noted that Philip, like Avicenna, introduces an intermediary form between soul and body. This *forma prima*, that Philip calls "corporeity", prepares matter to receiving the soul. The body is therefore a substance even before

---

[35] Indeed, there are passages in the *Summa* that suggest that Philip possessed a thorough knowledge and a clear understanding of the Aristotelian principles; cf. Philipp., *sum. de bon.*, ed. Wicki, p. 283[70-74]: "Aut enim <anima> unitur ut substantia aut ut forma. Ut forma non, quia forma se ipsa unitur cum materia et non alio principio extrinseco, quia unum et ens idem dicunt. Ergo idem est quo est ens et quo est unum. Sed omne ens compositum ex materia et forma est ens per formam; ergo per eam est unum, essentialiter dico"; cf. Lenzi, *Forma e sostanza*, p. 180.

[36] Unlike Avicenna, Philip does not seem to assign two different meanings to these terms and uses them as if they were synonyms, for instance: "non est forma tantum sive perfectio"; Philipp., *sum. de bon.*, ed. Wicki, p. 281[40].

[37] With the exception of celestial bodies; cf. Philipp., *sum. de bon.*, ed. Wicki, p. 287[186-189]; Philipp., *sum. de bon.*, ed. Wicki, p. 281[6, 16-18]: "Primo autem ostendetur quod anima nullo modo sit in corpore. (...) Item neque ut forma in materia, quoniam ad destructionem materie sequitur destructio forme tam substantialis quam accidentalis in esse", p. 282[27-30]: "Neque est per impressionem; impressum enim non subsistit sine eo cui fit impressio, et non est tota forma in qualibet parte eius cui imprimitur, sed commetitur se secundum partes. Item neque est ut coniunctio materie et forme, nam a materia non separatur forma, a corpore autem separatur anima".

[38] Philipp., *sum. de bon.*, ed. Wicki, p. 281[40-41]: "Solutio. Dicendum est quod anima, sicut dictum est, non est forma tantum sive perfectio, sed et substantia. Unde duplicem habet comparationem sicut dicetur", pp. 281[54]-282[60]: "Nec est contra illud Augustini qui dicit quod non est in corpore sicut forma in materia. Intelligendum est quod non est sicut forma in materia secundum omnem modum, quia separatur a corpore secundum quod substantia. Potest ergo proportionari duobus, scilicet forme vel perfectioni secundum dictum modum, et etiam radio luminis perficientis aera, quia ille radius separabilis est ab aere et remanet aer licet non illuminatus; sic anima separabilis a corpore, et remanet corpus, licet non in sua perfectione".

receiving the soul. Consequently, Philip defines the soul as an "ultimate form",
i.e. that form or perfection which completes a being that was already prepared by
other forms, such as the form of corporeity.[39] The soul proper to the human being
thus represents the ultimate form, or rather "is like a form" (*ut forma*).[40] Hence,
the relation between the human soul and the form can be described as a type of
analogy. For this reason, as stated by Philip himself, the union of soul and body
represents a markedly weaker union in comparison with the hylomorphic conjunction.[41]

   Philip's theory was assimilated rather indiscriminately by the anonymous author of the so-called *Summa Duacensis*.[42] It is thus significant that this *Summa*,
besides repeating all the typical elements of the "analogical" conception presented
by Philip, explicitly states that the relation between soul and body is a relation of
an accidental kind. For the function that the soul performs in its body does not
coincide with the soul's intrinsic nature, but rather depends upon an accidental
feature of the soul.[43]

   Such a view might also be attributed to Philip. Indeed, in approaching gnoseo-
logical themes, Philip dwells on the role of sensible knowledge with respect to

---

   [39] Cf. Zavalloni, *Richard de Mediavilla*, pp. 407-408.

   [40] Philipp., *sum. de bon.*, ed. Wicki, p. 284[89-102]: "Ad hoc respondeo quod anima secundum quid unitur per modum forme, secundum quid per modum substantie; utrique
enim est proportionalis. Quod autem opponitur quod forma unitur se ipsa, quare anima
se ipsa, secundum hoc dicendum est quod sunt quedam forme prime, quedam ultime,
quedam medie. Prime forme cum prime sint, absque medio materie coniunguntur, ut est
corporeitas. Ultime forme per medium coniunguntur, et quia ultime non sunt media neque
dispositiones materiales ad aliarum coniunctionem. Ultima autem forma naturalium est
anima. Medie autem et per medium coniunguntur quandoque et quandoque sunt media
et quasi materiales dispositiones; verbi gratia potentia sensibilis per medium coniungitur
suo subiecto, scilicet mediante ut dispositione materiali potentia vegetabili; et hoc quando
est ultima perfectio. Quandoque autem ipsa eadem in nobiliori subiecto est medium et
quasi dispositio materialis, scilicet comparatione anime intellective. Manifestum est igitur
quod, licet sit ut forma, non tamen per se corpori necesse est coniungi".

   [41] Philipp., *sum. de bon.*, ed. Wicki, p. 287[185-193]: "Post hec queritur cuiusmodi unitas sit
secundum unionem anime ad corpus. Et dicendum est quod est triplex unitas. (...) Tertia
est in illis in quibus aliqua duo coniunguntur ita quod alterum separabile est ab altero, ut
anima a corpore et corpus ab anima, et hec est minima. Et per hec deprehenditur quod
minima unitas est in homine".

   [42] N. Wicki, "Introduction", in Philipp., *sum. de bon.*, ed. Wicki, pp. 49*-62*; cf. P. Glorieux, "La «Summa Duacensis»", *RTAM* 12 (1940), pp. 104-135.

   [43] *Sum. Duac.*, 5. 1, ed. Glorieux, p. 40: "Quare in medio iam restant tales due res spirituales quarum una sit incorruptibilis secundum suam substantiam et erit tamen corruptibilis secundum suam virtutem; et talis est anima. Ipsa enim anima ab accidente habet
quod animat. Unde secundum talem effectum habet cessare; et ita quoad hunc est corruptibilis. Essentia tamen sua incorruptibilis est"; cf. Lenzi, *Forma e sostanza*, p. 179.

the human soul. Unlike the angel, the human soul is able to know *per speciem extractam* because it is joined to the body. The substance of the soul, however, is in no way affected by this conjunction: for the death of a human being changes the way of acquiring knowledge but has no influence on the soul as concerns substance.[44] We may thus conclude that according to Philip too the union with the body is not essential for the soul but constitutes something accidental for it.

1.1.2 THE *UNIBILITAS SUBSTANTIALIS* OF THE HUMAN SOUL: HUGH OF ST-CHER AND HIS CONTEMPORARIES

1.1.2.1 William of Auxerre

William of Auxerre strongly influenced Hugh of St-Cher's theology,[45] just as he influenced most thirteenth-century theologians.[46] His main work, the *Summa aurea*, although written already during the 1220s, perhaps represents one of the most important links between the theological thought of the twelfth century and the thought of the following century. Indeed, it is a great synthesis, inspired both by the main theological currents of the twelfth century and by the philosophical works made available by the new translations. This is why the sources of the *Summa* comprise both the Victorines and Gilbert of Poitiers and his school; the structure of the *Summa* and William's method are mostly inspired by Peter Lombard's *Sentences* and Alan of Lille's writings; visible influences also come from Praepositinus of Cremona, Peter Cantor, Stephen Langton's *Theological Questions*[47] and Godfrey of Poitiers' *Summa*, just to name a few authors.[48] It is also evident that William knew Aristotle's *libri naturales* (including *De anima*)[49] and John

---

[44] Philipp., *sum. de bon.*, ed. Wicki, pp. 268[163]-269[168]: "Intellectus autem hominis ideo cognoscit per speciem extractam, quia coniunctus est; sed intellectus angeli inconiunctus est et in se incorruptibilis; quare et intellectus hominis, nisi hoc ipsi contingat gratia coniunctionis. Set gratia coniunctionis non habet nisi modum differentem intelligendi, et substantia non mutatur. Igitur non attinget corruptio nisi modum intelligendi et non substantiam".

[45] The *Summa aurea* represents the main source of Hugh's Commentary on the *Sentences* of Peter Lombard; cf. Landgraf, *Introduction*, p. 175.

[46] Cf. J. Arnold, *Perfecta Communicatio. Die Trinitätstheologie Wilhelms von Auxerre*, Münster: Aschendorff, 1995 (B. G. Ph. Th. M., N. F. 42), pp. 15-24.

[47] J. Gründel, *Lehre von den Umständen der menschlichen Handlung im Mittelalter*, Münster: Aschendorff, 1963 (B. G. Ph. Th. M., 39.5), p. 342.

[48] Cf. Arnold, *Perfecta Communicatio*, pp. 24-35.

[49] Gründel, *Lehre von den Umständen*, p. 334; Arnold, *Perfecta Communicatio*, pp. 35-38.

Damascene's *De fide orthodoxa* translated by Burgundio of Pisa.[50] The influence exerted by Avicenna's *Metaphysics* is rather limited and that exerted by Avicenna's *De anima* remains uncertain; even less probable is that William knew Averroes' commentaries.[51]

The story behind the *Summa*'s composition appears to be extremely complex.[52] Most probably the work traces its origins back to some questions discussed by William at Paris over the course of a rather long period.[53] The work is preserved in over one hundred and thirty manuscripts which transmit different versions of it; there are, in addition, several abridgements compiled by other authors. The re-daction history of book II, where William deals with the soul, is particularly com-plex. To simplify, we shall refer to two redactions of the *Summa aurea*: the first – hereafter called redaction 'A' – was written between 1215 and 1226 and contains a "short" version of all four books, whereas redaction 'B' presents a long version of the first two books and dates from a later period, probably the years 1226-1229.[54]

In order to understand William's doctrine on the human soul it is necessary to consider that the various questions composing the *Summa aurea* may have been drawn up with considerable time in between. The same questions are sometimes solved in very different ways in the two redactions of the work. This applies to the problem of the soul as well.

On two occasions William deals with the following problem: what is the basis of the substantial difference between soul and angel? In other words: why do angel and soul belong to two different species? The question is first posed in redaction A, in the third chapter of book II. First of all, William states that the intellect of the angel and the intellect of the soul do not differ as to species. For this reason, the soul cannot be identified with its intellect;[55] if it were so – i.e., if both types of spiritual creatures could be identified with their rational power – they would not differ as to species.[56] Hence, the specific difference between soul and angel cannot

---

[50] Arnold, *Perfecta Communicatio*, pp. 31-32.

[51] Arnold, *Perfecta Communicatio*, pp. 36-37.

[52] The history of the transmission of this work has been reconstructed by J. Ribaillier, "Introduction", in Guill. Altissiod., *sum. aur.*, ed. Ribaillier, *passim*; see especially pp. 31-33, pp. 297-298.

[53] Cf. Ribailler, "Introduction", p. 16; Arnold, *Perfecta Communicatio*, p. 9.

[54] Cf. Arnold, *Perfecta Communicatio*, pp. 13-15; see also Ribaillier, "Introduction", p. 16; V. Doucet, "Prolegomena", in Alex. Halen., *sum. theol.* III, Quaracchi: ed. PP Collegii S. Bonaventurae, 1948, p. 132b; Gründel, *Lehre von den Umständen*, pp. 329-330.

[55] Such a solution would have been rejected by Hugh. And indeed, as we shall see, the Dominican thinker affirms the essential identity of the soul with its rational powers; cf. *infra*, chap. 2.1.2.3.

[56] Guill. Altissiod., *sum. aur.* II, 1, c. 3, q. 3, ed. Ribaillier, p. 261[86-93]: "Et ego loquor de perfectionibus quibus nate sunt perfici intelligentia angelica et anima rationalis; et quia

rest on their rational faculty. William designates another ability as the source of the substantial distinction between the two types of spiritual creatures: it is the language faculty.[57] For the angel is able to form an intelligible language through which it can convey illuminations to other angels and to souls. By contrast, even when separate from their bodies, souls can only avail themselves of the sensible language.[58]

In interpreting William's solution, the following question arises: if the specific difference of the soul consists in the sensible language, then wouldn't it be correct to say that, basically, the distinction between soul and angel lies in the connection between the soul and the human body? William definitely rejects this hypothesis: according to him, the fact that a substance becomes joined to something else does not bring any essential change to it.[59] Consequently, the union with the body cannot constitute the cause of the specific difference between soul and angel.[60]

This theory, which William asserts very clearly in redaction A of his *Summa*, undergoes a radical transformation in redaction B of book II. Speaking about the dignity of the two spiritual creatures, William confirms once again that the ra-

---

irrefregabiles videntur nobis huius rationes, ideo concedimus eundem specie intellectum angeli et hominis; et hinc potest sumi argumentum ad destruendum istam opinionem, quod anima est sua potentia. Nam si anima est suus intellectus, et angelus suus, et intellectus anime et angeli idem sunt secundum speciem, sicut probavimus, et angelus et anima idem sunt secundum speciem; quo nichil absurdius".

[57] Guill. Altissiod., *sum. aur.* II, 1, c. 3, q. 4, ed. Ribaillier, pp. 263[60]-264[70]: "Aut hoc erit secundum diversitatem linguarum, de quibus loquitur Apostolus: *Si linguis hominum loquar*, inquit, *et angelorum*. Quod autem debeat sic esse, videtur per supra dictam auctoritatem Damasceni, qui dicit quod tradunt angeli aliis angelis et animabus sanctis illuminationes suas, scilicet sermone intelligibili, non sono vocis formato; anime vero sermone sensibiliter formato suas illuminationes communicant. Et hoc concedimus, quod penes huius modos formandi sermones suos sive penes ydiomata sua, id est penes potestates a quibus sunt huius linguagia actualia et actuales formationes sive traditiones, differunt substantialiter".

[58] Guill. Altissiod., *sum. aur.* II, 1, c. 3, q. 5, ed. Ribaillier, p. 266[42-47]: "Et ad hec omnia respondemus secundum ea que predicta sunt, quod anime neque exute a corporibus neque in corporibus manentes habent usum formandi sermonem intelligibilem intelligibiliter, quia non ipse ministrant spiritualiter. Prelatus enim ministrat sensibiliter inferiori, et anima prelati animabus subditorum ministrat sensibiliter. Sed intelligibile ministerium tantummodo est angelorum".

[59] Guill. Altissiod., *sum. aur.* II, 1, c. 3, q. 4, ed. Ribaillier, p. 262[23-29]: "Et sunt alii qui dicunt quod angelus substantialiter differt ab anima in eo quod ipse per se est stans, corporis unitione aut amixtione non egens, quemadmodum anima. Et hoc non videtur verum esse. Nam quod dico «per se stans», in privatione sonat; quod patet si resolvas. Sed negatio sive privatio, cum nichil sit, quomodo dabit alii esse aut diversitatem secundum esse, quod proprium est substantialis differentie?".

[60] Cf. Bieniak, "Una questione disputata", p. 152.

tional quality[61] cannot constitute the specific difference between soul and angel.[62] However, when it comes to designating positively the cause of the specific difference between the two spiritual substances, William, instead of speaking of the differing languages, concludes that the human soul is substantially different from the angel because of its ability to sustain the body:[63]

> Substantialiter autem differt anima ab angelo eo quod apta est nata vivificare corpus et ei misceri. Angeli autem differentia ab anima rationali est impermissibilitas sive abstractio absoluta a corporea substantia, qua aptus est angelus stare in se et per se sine aliqua dependentia ab aliqua inferiori substantia. Homo vero dicitur factus ad ymaginem et similitudinem Dei, quia hec est eius dignitas extrema super omnia bruta animalia.

In redaction B of his *Summa*, William thus embraces the same opinion he had previously rejected. Inevitably, his position arouses questions. First of all, in redaction A William defines the substantial difference as "diversitas secundum esse".[64] Is it possible that such a difference consists in a simple power? We should remember that William refuses to identify the essence of the soul with its powers. Otherwise, this *"aptitudo"* or *"dependentia"* would be something more than a power: in fact, it would be the very essence of the soul. On the one hand, we cannot exclude this hypothesis; on the other, we should not forget that in redaction A William establishes that the specific difference between soul and angel depends on a power, i.e., on the ability to produce a determinate kind of language. In any case, we should conclude that the *aptitudo* or *dependentia* of the soul in regard to the body cannot constitute a mere accident: otherwise, the difference with the angel would not be

---

[61] See, for example, Alex. Halen.(?), *q. ant.*, Appendix II, 1, ed. PP. Collegii S. Bonaventurae, III, p. 1456[5-8]: "Item, differentia specifica debet accipi ab actu summo speciei vel potissimo. Sed summus actus vel potissimus in anima et angelo est intelligentia, et haec non est eadem specie in anima et angelo; ergo non sunt idem specie. Quod concedimus".

[62] Guill. Altissiod., *sum. aur.* II, appendix 19, ed. Ribailler, p. 751[34-47]: "Unde videtur quod intelligentia angeli melior sit quam intelligentia hominis, quia naturaliter est amplior, cum sit naturaliter a sensibus abstractior. Unde in hoc videntur differre specie angelus et anima humana. Aliam enim differentiam substantialem difficillium esset assignare. Sed credimus quod non propter hoc sint diversarum specierum angelus et anima rationalis, propter duas causas: prima, quia eadem est perfectio ultima intellectus angeli et intellectus anime rationalis, scilicet cognitio Dei sive virtus, scilicet intellectus, sapientia et prudentia. Secunda ratio est, quia intellectus anime rationalis amplificabitur secundum mensuram intellectus angeli (...). Et per hoc patet quod propter amplitudinem intelligentie non differunt substantialiter angelus et anima rationalis sive intellectus eorum".

[63] Guill. Altissiod., *sum. aur.* II, appendix 19, ed. Ribailler, pp. 751[48]-752[53].

[64] Cf. *supra*, p. 21, n. 59.

substantial but just accidental or numerical. This possibility is clearly rejected by William.

Where are the roots of William's new doctrine to be found? His argumentation would seem to lead us to the Aristotelian anthropology. But it should be noted that book II of the *De anima* is never mentioned in the *Summa aurea*: this omission does not seem to be inadvertent. Nevertheless, William knows and makes use of Aristotle's *De anima*; some Aristotelian influence is thus not to be excluded. However, the language used by William still more recalls the theological sources. Indeed, the tendency of the soul towards the body already appears in Augustine's thought.[65] The Church Father holds that the human soul, unlike the angel, possesses a "naturalis appetitus corpus administrandi": this doctrine was certainly known to medieval authors too.[66] Hence, the Augustinian theological tradition already contains two important elements: first, the relation of the human soul with the body is not purely extrinsic, but has a correlation in the nature of the soul; second, the natural desire towards the body is present in the soul but not in an angel; consequently, the relation between the soul and its body is different from the relation subsisting between the angel and the body temporarily assumed by it.

Certainly, the solution proposed by William recalls the Augustinian doctrine, but the two theories are not equivalent. Indeed, as William acknowledges, a specific difference must be based on a diversity "secundum esse", hence on a substantial difference: it follows that making the specific difference depend upon the connection with the body has important ramifications.

Finally, one may ask whether William is the first author to hold that the substantial difference between soul and angel consists in a certain dependency on the body. In my own research, I could not find any work antecedent to the *Summa*

---

[65] Aug., *gen. ad litt.* XII, 35. 68, ed. Zycha, CSEL 28. 1, pp. 432^{15}-433^{1}, PL 34, 483: "Sed si quem movet, quid opus sit spiritibus defunctorum corpora sua in resurrectione recipere, si potest eis etiam sine corporibus summa illa beatitudo praeberi; difficilior quidem quaestio est, quam ut perfecte possit hoc sermone finiri: sed tamen minime dubitandum est, et raptam hominis a carnis sensibus mentem, et post mortem ipsa carne deposita, transcensis etiam similitudinibus corporalium, non sic videre posse incommutabilem substantiam, ut sancti Angeli vident; sive alia latentiore causa, sive ideo quia inest ei naturalis quidam appetitus corpus administrandi; quo appetitu retardatur quodammodo ne tota intentione pergat in illud summum coelum, quamdiu non subest corpus, cujus administratione appetitus ille conquiescat"; cf. Alex. Halen., *q. ant.* XVI, d. 1, ed. PP. Collegii S. Bonaventurae, I, p. 228$^{11-16}$: "Item, anima per naturam unibilis est corpori, angelus autem non; hanc autem differentiam ostendit Augustinus inter animam et angelum, XII *Super Genesim* in glossa. Et propter hanc unibilitatem compatitur anima corpori patienti; unde Damascenus: "Anima, corpore inciso, ipsa non incisa, condolet et compatitur"". Alexander writes his questions between 1220 and 1236; cf. "Prolegomena", in Alex. Halen., *q. ant.*, ed. PP. Collegii S. Bonaventurae, vol. I, p. 5*.

[66] Cf. *infra*, p. 72, n. 194.

aurea maintaining this theory. But we should not forget that in redaction A of book II, William cites – and rejects – the opinion held by some contemporary authors ("sunt alii qui dicunt") that the soul differs from the angel in a substantial manner because of the union with the body.[67] We do not know if these authors really existed; actually, they might be a mere rhetorical device.[68] But although the invention of this doctrine cannot be definitely ascribed to William, we may certainly affirm that it was through William's *Summa aurea* that the theory of the substantial difference based on the psychophysical connection was assimilated by the thinkers belonging to the oldest Dominican school, namely, Hugh of St-Cher and Roland of Cremona.

1.1.2.2   Hugh of St-Cher's question *De anima*

Hugh of St-Cher formulated his disputed question *De anima* at Paris in the first half of the 1230s, after he had commented on Peter Lombard's *Sentences*.[69] The three articles of the question are chiefly based on the *Summa de bono*.[70] Moreover, it is known that Hugh had a deep knowledge of the *Summa aurea* as well,[71] which he had employed as a manual when he was commenting on the Lombard's *Sentences*. Further, Hugh's commentary also included a certain number of passages inspired by Avicenna's *De anima*.[72] As previously seen, the latter denies that the union with the body plays a determining role for the essence of the soul, but rather tends to consider this conjunction as something accidental. This tendency appears in the first version of the *Summa aurea* too, whereas in the other version the theory of the accidental union is subjected to doubt. What is Hugh's attitude in the face of such a heritage?

---

[67] Cf. Guill. Altissiod., *sum. aur.* II, 1, c. 3, q. 4, ed. Ribailler, p. 262[23-25]. The attribution proposed by the editors of the *Summa aurea* is rather misleading because they refer to the following passage of Dominicus Gundissalinus' *De unitate*, ed. P. Correns, Münster: Aschendorff, 1891 (B. G. Ph. Th. M., 1.1), p. 9: "Et propter hanc diversitatem formae unitatis non uno modo, sed pluribus dicitur aliquid esse unitate unum. Unum enim aliud est essentiae simplicitate unum, ut deus. Aliud simplicium coniunctione unum, ut angelus et anima, quorum unumquodque est unum coniunctione materiae et formae"; cf. Bieniak, "Una questione disputata", pp. 151-152.

[68] William might refer to Alan of Lille's doctrine too; cf. *infra*, pp. 71-72, although Alan does not – at least explicitly – define the difference of conjunction as a substantial difference.

[69] Cf. Bieniak, "Una questione disputata", pp. 133-135.

[70] Cf. Bieniak, "Una questione disputata", pp. 135-150.

[71] Cf. K. L. Lynch, *The Sacrament of Confirmation in the early-middle scholastic period*, I, New York: St. Bonaventure, 1957, p. 144; Landgraf, *Introduction*, p. 175.

[72] Cf. Hasse, *Avicenna's De anima*, p. 37, pp. 241-257, p. 278. Though, it remains uncertain whether Hugh had a direct knowledge of Avicenna's work or knew it exclusively through the works of his Parisian colleagues.

In the first article of the question *De anima*, Hugh intends to identify the essence of the soul and point out the kind of difference existing between the latter and the angel. Initially, the article seems to indicate Philip the Chancellor's position. Indeed, Hugh starts his exposition by enumerating the same definitions of the soul that appear in the chapter of the *Summa de bono* entitled *Quid sit anima*.[73] The soul is defined as an incorporeal substance and a spirit: Hugh embraces this point of view and certainly does not deny the substantial character of the soul.

But the exposition adopts a different tone when the Dominican presents his solution to the central problem of the article, i.e., whether the difference between the human soul and the angel is accidental or substantial.[74] In contrast to Philip's chapter, the Dominican master integrates the Aristotelian definition at the crucial point of his exposition. The quotation seems directly drawn from the translation of the *De anima* made by James of Venice,[75] but the translation of the word "endelichia" given by Hugh is rather Avicennian: for the soul is not '*forma*', but rather '*perfectio*'. The term '*perfectio*' replaces the Aristotelian '*forma*' in all the three articles of the question; however, although Hugh uses an Avicennian term, his conception of the connection between the soul and the body conflicts with that held by Avicenna. Indeed, in Hugh's mind, the soul's orientation towards the body does not constitute an accident of the soul but an intrinsic character of its substance. Consequently, it is the *unibilitas substantialis*[76] that constitutes the

---

[73] Cf. *supra*, p. 16.

[74] Hugo de S. Caro, *q. de an.* I, ed. Bieniak, p. 169[38-46]: "Item. Per hoc quod est substantia incorporea, non differt ab angelo; reliquum autem accidit animae, quod patet quia potest esse sine illo; ergo anima solo accidente differt ab angelo. (...) Solutio. Dico ad primum quod anima et angelus differunt substantialiter, non numero tantum, sicut duo homines, ut quidam voluerunt, sed specie, ut homo et asinus. Conveniunt autem in genere remoto quod est substantia et in genere propinquo quod est spiritus. Sed anima est spiritus unibilis, angelus vero spiritus omnino non unibilis, unde angelus ita est substantia quod non perfectio, anima vero ita substantia quod perfectio alterius, scilicet corporis organici, ut dicit Philosophus quod est "endelichia corporis organici potentia vitam habentis". Haec autem unibilitas inest animae naturaliter et substantialiter per quam differt ab angelo (...)".

[75] Cf. Bieniak, "Una questione disputata", pp. 155-156.

[76] As previously seen, the pair '*substantialiter*'-'*accidentaliter*' is already employed in a similar context by William of Auxerre; nevertheless, in the contemporary usage this formula chiefly belongs to Christological language; see for instance Guill. Altissiod., *sum. aur.* III, c. 2, ed. Ribailler, p. 14[33-38]. The word *unibilitas*, which starts to be employed only in the 1220s-1230s, appears in questions concerning both the hypostatic union and human psychology; cf. Alex. Halen., *q. ant.* XV, disp. 1-2, ed. PP. Collegii S. Bonaventurae, I, pp. 193-207, especially p. 203[26]: "respondeo quod in spiritu angelico et humano ex parte superiori est simplicitas similis, scilicet secundum intelligentiam, in utrisque; sed ex parte inferiori, secundum quod anima unibilis est ad corpus, est maior compositio in anima quam in angelo", p. 200[7-12], p. 195[12-14]: "unibile duobus modis dicitur: vel quod habet potentiam activam, vel quod habet potentiam passivam vel materialem".

specific difference between soul and angel. At the crucial point of his exposition, Hugh abandons Philip's anthropology and the Avicennian tradition.

The solution of the first article of the question *De anima* quite probably reflects the B redaction of the *Summa aurea*.[77] Inspired by William of Auxerre's solution, Hugh presents a theory of the *unibilitas substantialis* that plays a central role in his exposition. However, from the lexical standpoint, the term *'unibilitas'* is probably derived from the *Summa de bono*. Indeed, in order to explain why souls were not created at the beginning of time like angels, Philip argues that souls, unlike angels, are "unitable" because they constitute the perfections of bodies.[78] By joining *'unibilitas'*[79] to the term *'substantialis'*, derived from the *Summa aurea*, Hugh creates a new formula promptly taken up by later authors. And indeed, the *unibilitas substantialis* theory reappears, slightly changed, in the works of John of La Rochelle, Albert the Great, Bonaventure and Thomas Aquinas.

The doctrine of the *unibilitas substantialis* presents some typical features. First, a "substantial" or "essential" property[80] is clearly contrasted with an accidental property: indeed, if *unibilitas* were for the soul a mere accident, then the difference between the human soul and the angel would be merely accidental or, in other words, numerical. In addition, in Hugh's view, *unibilitas* probably consti-

---

[77] Guill. Altissiod., *sum. aur.* II, appendix 19, ed. Ribailler, pp. 751[48]-752[50]: "Substantialiter autem differt anima ab angelo eo quod apta est nata vivificare corpus et ei misceri"; cf. *supra*, pp. 21-23.

[78] Philipp., *sum. de bon.*, ed. Wicki, p. 260[68-74]: "Preterea, videtur ostendi per simile. Sic est de substantiis spiritualibus que sunt angeli, quod omnes sunt create simul; pari ergo ratione videtur de spiritualibus substantiis que sunt anime rationales. Non enim esse earum dependet a corpore cui coniunguntur, sicut esse anime sensibilis aut vegetabilis. Ad aliud vero quesitum dicendum est quod non est simile de angelis et animabus, quia angeli sunt substantie non unibiles corporibus, anime vero sunt corporum perfectiones. Convenit ergo ut idem sit tempus perfectionis et perfecti. Cum enim sint quedam que ita sunt substantie quod non perfectiones, ut intelligentie angelice quedam que ita perfectiones quod non substantie, ut perfectiones impresse corporibus, quedam medio modo se habent simul et substantie et perfectiones, et in quantum perfectiones, idem tempus perfectionis et perfecti".

[79] Hugh could find this term in Alexander of Hales' questions as well; cf. Alex. Halen., *q. ant.* XV, disp. 2, ed. PP. Collegii S. Bonaventurae, I, p. 200[15-23]: "Sed maior est compositio in humana natura quam in angelica; et adhuc in anima humana, quia ibi compositio est secundum vires, et preterea comparando ad unionem cum corpore. Item naturalis appetitus est in spiritu humano ut uniatur corpori, qui non est in spiritu angelico. Relinquitur ergo quod maior est compositio in spiritu humano, et ita minor similitudo, et ita minor convenientia eius ad divinam [naturam]; et ita videtur quod minor sit unibilitas".

[80] It should be noted that the terms *substantia* and *essentia* were mostly considered as interchangeable; cf. Hugo de S. Caro, *in I Sent.*, d. 25, ed. Breuning, p. 386, n. 189; cf. also O. Lottin, *Psychologie et morale aux XIIe et XIIIe siècles*, Duculot, Gembloux 1942, vol. I, pp. 486-487.

tutes something more than the simple ability to move and provide the body with senses. The difference between soul and angel consists in the fact that the soul, besides performing these functions, also constitutes the perfection of the body it is united with, whereas the union between the angel and a body assumed by it is purely operational and instrumental. According to the Dominican master, these are two relations of a different kind because the former is intrinsic (*regimen intrinsecus*), whereas the latter is extrinsic (*regimen extrinsecus*).[81]

As already seen, *unibilitas* – which means the ability to sustain the body – is an essential feature of the soul, and elsewhere Hugh also calls it *aptitudo naturalis*. *Unibilitas* as such remains in the human soul even after the separation from the body.[82] Finally, substantial *unibilitas*, as an *aptitudo* belonging to the nature of the soul, is closely related to the fact that the human soul, unlike an angel, is not a person.[83]

Here one may ask whether the theory of the *unibilitas substantialis* advanced by Hugh can still be defined as a dualist doctrine. Considering the presuppositions, the answer must be positive: for such a conception can only arise if one regards the human soul as a substance and a species. Undoubtedly, in Hugh's case, these two points are not questioned. However, wishing to determine the definition of the human soul on the basis of the first article of the question *De anima*, we should conclude that it consists in *unibilitas*: indeed, according to Hugh, the ability to be united with the body determines the specific nature of the soul.[84]

As to the content, Hugh's question *De anima* basically brings nothing new; nevertheless, its exposition provides significant help in making the step taken by William of Auxerre fully explicit. Indeed, for the first time, the very essence of the soul is defined in relation to the body: the Avicennian theory of the accidental union of soul and body is thus left behind.

---

[81] Hugo de S. Caro, *q. de an.*, 1, ed. Bieniak, p. 170[76-81]: "Ad primum ergo dico quod diffinitio Remigii convenit angelo, sed duplex est regimen corporis: intrinsecus quod attenditur secundum perfectionem et motum et sensum, aliud extrinsecus quod attenditur secundum motum solum. Primo modo anima est regitiva corporis, movet enim et perficit et sensificat illud. Secundo modo angelus: non enim angelus perfectio est corporis quod assumit, sed motor eius, et quod dicunt aliqui, angelos habere corpora aeria, non est verum, sed est contra sanctos".

[82] Hugo de S. Caro, *q. de an.*, I, ed. Bieniak, p. 170[82-85]: "Ad secundum, quod anima et angelus differunt accidente solo etc., dicendum quod «regens» non dicit actum, sed aptitudinem, secundum quam anima apta est naturaliter regere corpus illo triplici regimine quod diximus, et hanc aptitudinem habet anima etiam separata. Haec enim est illa unibilitas de qua supra diximus".

[83] Cf. Hugo de S. Caro, *q. de an.*, I, ed. Bieniak, p. 170[64-65].

[84] This interpretation is confirmed by the meaning associated with the word '*substantialiter*' in other contexts too; cf. *infra*, chap. 2.1.2.

1.1.2.3   Roland of Cremona

Like Hugh of St-Cher, Roland of Cremona († 1269) is strongly influenced by the *Summa aurea*. By contrast, the literary interdependence between Hugh's works and Roland's works is more difficult to establish. We know that Roland had taught theology at Paris in the years 1229-1230, that is before Hugh became regent master at the same faculty.[85] Hugh replaced him because, after teaching for just one year, the Dominican *magister* left Paris for Toulouse, where he continued the academic activity until 1233-1234, when he finally moved to Italy.[86] Roland was therefore an elder colleague of Hugh. And yet, after comparing Roland's *Summa* with Hugh's *Sentences Commentary*, Odon Lottin concluded that it was Roland who had been inspired by Hugh's text, not the converse. This hypothesis appears to be supported by the limited diffusion of the *Summa* in the Parisian circles, due to the fact that Roland wrote his work after leaving Paris, perhaps when he was already in Italy.[87] Lottin's hypothesis, however, cannot be considered conclusive also because it rests on comparisons between very short passages from the two texts: consequently, the similarities between the two texts may be due to the use of a common source, i.e. William of Auxerre's *Summa aurea*, rather than to their mutual dependence.[88]

Earlier studies allow us to conclude that quite probably Hugh did not know Roland's *Summa* when he wrote his *Sentences Commentary*. Yet, we know that his disputed questions are subsequent to his first theological work;[89] as to the questions, the problem concerning the relationship with the *Summa* must therefore be examined anew. Actually, even if Roland wrote his work already in Italy, we cannot totally exclude the possibility that Hugh had known the *Summa* before composing his questions.

Hugh's question *De anima* and Roland's *Summa* have an important point in common. Indeed, while discussing the punishment of purgatory, Roland dwells upon the difference between the human soul and the angel. Whereas the angel, since it is a separate substance, acquires its perfection outside the body – he

---

[85]   Indeed, Roland was the first Dominican master to teach theology at Paris; cf. E. Filthaut, *Roland von Cremona O.P. und die Anfänge der Scholastik im Predigerorden*, Vechta i.O.: Albertus-Magnus-Verlag der Dominikaner, 1936, pp. 20-27; O. Lottin, "Roland de Crémone et Hugues de Saint-Cher", RTAM 12 (1940), p. 136.

[86]   Cf. Filthaut, *Roland von Cremona*, pp. 20-27.

[87]   Cf. Lottin, "Roland de Crémone", p. 143; Hasse, *Avicenna's De anima*, p. 36.

[88]   Cf. R. Quinto, "Le Commentaire des Sentences d'Hugues de Saint-Cher et la littérature théologique de son temps", in *Hugues de Saint-Cher († 1263), bibliste et théologien*, pp. 314-315, footnote 41.

[89]   Cf. Bieniak, "Una questione disputata", pp. 133-135.

writes – the human soul can receive its ultimate perfection only in the resurrected body: for the soul somehow depends upon its body.[90]

Here Roland includes an objection similar to that reported by William of Auxerre in the A redaction of the *Summa aurea*. Even though the soul and the angel, owing to the union with the body, are different, nevertheless this difference cannot constitute their specific difference because the relation with the body represents just an accident.[91] Roland accepts this objection: angel and soul do not differ as to species by virtue of the soul's current state of conjunction. According to Roland, the difference goes deeper: indeed, since the creation, the soul possesses an intrinsic dependency on the body, a dependency which is not merely accidental but is defined as substantial (*substantialis*).[92]

Roland's exposition can be explained simply on the basis of William of Auxerre's *Summa aurea*. Indeed, it appears that Roland knew both redactions of the *Summa*: that in which the substantial difference between soul and angel is such that it depends upon the language of spiritual substances, as well as that in which the same difference is explained by the psychophysical connection. Consequently, his argumentation is but an attempt at reconciling the two positions held by William. The manoeuvre is effective: for Roland draws a distinction between the *state*

---

[90] *Paris, Bibliothèque Mazarine 795*, f. 102va: "Vnde dixerunt philosophi quod anima humana creata erat perfectibilis secundum scientias et uirtutes ita ut hic recipiat aliquam perfectionem, postea autem ultimam, et ideo satis rationabiliter dispositum est ut anima non possit mereri nisi hic; perfectam autem perfectionem non habebit anima donec uerum resumat corpus in resurrectione, quia quodam modo anima dependet a corpore, et ideo sancti clamant in Apocalipsi <6, 10> «usque non uindicas sanguinem nostrum», quia sancti uolunt habere corpora sua ut anime ipsorum magis perficiantur. Vnde apparet hic ipsa differentia inter animam et angelum quia anima perficit se in corpore mediantibus uiribus que dependent a corpore; angelus autem perficit se extra corpus, ut dicunt magistri". A similar argument is used by Hugh as well, *De anima*, ed. Bieniak, p. 170[66-69]: "Tertia est differentia quia angelus ordinatus est ad beatitudinem percipiendam in se tantum, anima vero in se et in corpore. Iustum enim est ut sicut anima in corpore meruit, ita in corpore remuneretur dotibus eius; angelus vero quia corpus non habuit nec in corpore meruit, dotibus eius carebit". This passage is transcribed verbatim from the *Summa de bono*; cf. ed. Wicki, pp. 157[58]-158[62].

[91] This reasoning recalls – besides William's *Summa* – Avicenna's position too: indeed, according to Meryem Sebti's interpretation, Avicenna defines the relationship with the body as an accident of the soul, more precisely the accident of relation; cf. Sebti, *Avicenne*, p. 14.

[92] Rol. Crem., *sum.*, ms. *Paris, Bibliothèque Mazarine 795*, 102va: "Set contra: talis differentia non est nisi accidentalis, intra corpus et extra corpus; set angeli et omnes anime differunt secundum speciem, ergo per aliud, quod concedimus. Differunt enim ab inuicem quia anima creatur cum dependentibus a corpore, et hec est substantialis differentia, angelus autem non"; cf. C. R. Hess, "Roland of Cremona's Place in the Current of Thought", *Angelicum* 45 (1968), p. 438.

of being united and the *disposition of the soul to be conjoined*. This distinction enables us to affirm both that the presence of the body represents an accident for the soul and that the ability to form such a union is an aspect of its very essence: this is the basis underlying the *unibilitas substantialis* theory.

Roland's position is very close to that of Hugh, but this closeness can be explained by their common use of William of Auxerre's *Summa aurea*. The mutual dependence between the two Dominican masters is improbable for other reasons too. On the one hand, when Hugh started his teaching activity, Roland was already in Toulouse. Further, the question *De anima* probably had no large circulation outside Paris, as indicated by the fact that it has been preserved in only one manuscript. On the other hand, it is certain that Hugh attended Roland's lessons in Paris; yet, as already said, the *Summa* was composed when Roland had already left Paris. It follows that probably Hugh and Roland elaborated their solutions independently.

In addition to the influence exerted by the *Summa aurea*, Roland's *Summa* clearly reveals the influence of the Avicennian psychology.[93] Indeed, even though Roland knew Aristotle's *De anima* well, in his *Summa* – like in Hugh's question – the term *'entelechia'* is regularly replaced by the word *'perfectio'*. As previously seen, however, Roland leaves behind the Avicennian view that the union of soul and body is accidental. It also appears that, in Roland's perspective, the presence of two "perfections" in one thing is impossible: for the being of a substance depends upon the perfection; hence, in man there is only one being and only one perfection. In actuality, Roland's interpretation reveals a new receptiveness toward the Aristotelian anthropology as well as a certain independence from the Avicennian perspective.[94]

In spite of this, Roland's *Summa* also contains a passage that radically contradicts his theory of the substantial difference between the human soul and the angel. Indeed, in a question entitled *De intentione necessaria in baptismo*, i.e. outside a strictly psychological context, Roland states that the soul, after its separation from the body, becomes a spirit that cannot even be called 'soul': the separation brings about the abandonment of the relation with the body, thanks to which the soul receives its name.[95]

---

[93] Cf. Hasse, *Avicenna's De anima*, pp. 36-42.

[94] Filthaut, *Roland von Cremona*, p. 100; Zavalloni, *Richard de Mediavilla*, p. 387.

[95] Rol. Crem., *sum.*, ms. *Paris, Bibliothèque Mazarine 795*, 86va-87ra: "Item. Sacramenta non sunt nisi ecclesie, ergo non existente ecclesia non erint sacramenta (...), sicut anima exuta a corpore non est anima, quamuis sit spiritus, quia per separationem a corpore amisit illam comparationem qua dicitur anima, ergo non est baptismus non existente ecclesia neque aliquod sacramentum"; cf. Hess, "Roland of Cremona's Place", p. 438.

By contrast, the question *De anima* excludes such a theory. For – according to Hugh – the inclination toward the body remains in the soul after death too. In fact, if *unibilitas* is to be conceived of as something substantial, then it is necessarily independent of the actual presence of the body: otherwise, it would be a purely accidental characteristic. On this point, Hugh's question seems to preserve greater coherence than Roland's *Summa*.[96]

1.1.2.4 William of Auvergne

Among the theologians who were active in the years when Hugh and Roland wrote their works, William of Auvergne (†1249) surely deserves special attention because his *De anima* represents one of the most extensive psychological writings of the time. William probably wrote his treatise in the second half of the 1230s, when Hugh's question *De anima* was already completed;[97] however, considering that William began to teach at Paris already about 1223, we should examine his opinion as regards the connection between the human soul and the body.

The text written by the bishop of Paris and Hugh's question appear to possess some convergence. Indeed, in the chapter devoted to the way in which the human soul is infused into the body, William repeatedly affirms that the ability to sustain the body constitutes a *virtus essentialis* for the soul and that the latter is present in the body in an essential way (*essentialiter*).[98]

---

[96] The question *De anima* departs from the *Summa* in other respects too. Indeed, whereas Roland maintains that souls and angels are composed of matter and spiritual form, Hugh devotes a whole article of his question to rejecting such a theory; cf. Rol. Crem., sum., *Paris, Bibliothèque Mazarine 795*, 21vb; Hess, "Roland of Cremona's Place", p. 438; Hugo de S. Caro, *q. de an.* III, ed. Bieniak, pp. 176^291-184^580. Similarly, whereas Hugh asserts the identity of the rational soul with its powers, Roland states the opposite; cf. Hess, "Roland of Cremona's Place", p. 440; *infra*, pp. 102-106.

[97] Cf. J. Kramp, "Des Wilhelm von Auvergne *Magisterium Divinale*", *Gregorianum* 1 (1920), pp. 559-562; R.-A. Gauthier, "Notes sur les débuts (1225-1240) du premier 'Averroisme'", *Revue des sciences philosophiques et théologiques* 66 (1982), p. 360; Hasse, *Avicenna's De anima*, p. 43.

[98] Guill. de Alv., *de an.*, 4, 40, ed. Le Feron, p. 200b: "Anima enim humana velut rex, et rector quidam est totius corporis humani. Quod si dixerit quod creatio vel constitutio regis non facit debere esse regem in qualibet parte regni cui creatur rex, aut praeficitur, et propter hoc creatio animae humanae juxta similitudinem istam non debet facere, neque cogere animam humanam esse in qualibet hujusmodi partium corporis sui. Respondeo in hoc quod creatio vel electio regis non dat regi ut per semetipsum sive per essentiam suam dominetur, aut praesit regno, vel partibus regni, neque potestas regia potestas est quae sit regi ex se, vel per se, sed per obedientiam solam, et voluntatem subditorum et forsitan potestas regia non aliud est apud regem hujusmodi, nisi voluntas aut obedientia subditorum. Hoc autem manifestum est quia cessante vel sublata prorsus voluntate vel obedientia subditorum sublata est omnino ab eo potestas regia et propter hoc nihil potest in subditos, vel in alios in quantum rex sit, sed in quantum homo tantum, et hoc est dicere ex naturalibus

And yet, what is the precise meaning of the word '*essentialiter*' within the exposition made by the theologian? In order to establish if William and Hugh attribute the same meaning to this term we should first of all examine the context where William situates it. Indeed, the purpose of the passage is to answer the question concerning the way in which the soul is present *per se* in all parts of the body: "qualiter in qualibet parte corporis humani creetur anima humana".[99] William explains the modality of this presence by using an analogy. According to him, the soul sustains its body as a king rules his kingdom: "Anima enim humana velut rex et rector quidam est totius corporis humani".[100] However, the limbs of the body do not obey the soul by virtue of themselves, as do citizens when they obey their king: for the human body performs a fully passive role and all his operations depend just upon the soul. For this reason, William states that the soul is in the body *essentialiter*, namely, in the same way in which God is in the world.

'*Essentialiter*' has thus a double meaning. On the one hand, the term expresses the perfect passivity of the body and the perfect activity of the soul in their state of conjunction. William insists on this point repeatedly. Indeed, according to our theologian, the soul alone constitutes the subject of all human operations: the different powers belong uniquely to the soul, whereas the body is but an instrument.[101]

---

viribus suis, et intendo si fortitudine, et viribus prevalet adversus illum vel illos quemadmodum leo potest in oves, vel alia animalia. Potestas autem creatoris qua rex est dominantissimus omnium saeculorum non est aliunde vel a foris, nec dependet ullo modorum ex voluntate vel obedientia cujuscumque, vel quorumcumque. Nec potest creator omnipotentissimus quicquam per alios vel alia a se: quin potius alia nihil possunt nisi ipso, vel per ipsum: et propter hoc ubicumque potest ibi et est, cum nihil possit alicubi nisi per se. Et ad hunc modum licet multum distante similitudine, anima in totum corpus cui praeficitur potest per semetipsam, non per obedientiam membrorum non exhibetur ei nisi propter ipsam, et ipsa obedientia membris est ex animae potestate naturali sive essentiali eidem. Quapropter quemadmodum si rex aliquis praeficitur regno alicui, et partibus ejus ita ut virtute sua propria, et non aliena possit in totum illud, et in singulis partes ipsius, dubitari non potest quin esset essentialiter sive personaliter in toto regno, et singulis partibus ipsius. Quia igitur sic se habere de anima humana manifestum est ipsam sua virtute propria, et essentiali, sive naturali totum corpus, et partes ejus quas praedixi, propriaque virtute essentiali, seu naturali posse in totum illud, hoc est et in singulis partibus viventibus istius. Manifestum est ipsam esse essentialiter sive principaliter in toto corpore, et singulis partibus ejus. Non enim est aniame humanae potestas movendi et regendi corpus et membra singula ipsius ab illo, vel ab illis, quia nec ipsis est virtus hujusmodi, aut potestas qua ipsa se moveant: sed animae ipsi est virtus hujusmodi essentialis et imperium naturale super illi, cui necesse habent naturaliter obedire pro posse et viribus suis".

[99] Guill. de Alv., *de an.*, 4, 40, ed. Le Feron, p. 200a.
[100] Guill. de Alv., *de an.*, ed. Le Feron, p. 200b.
[101] Guill. de Alv., *de an.*, 4, 23, ed. Le Feron, p. 149: "Cujus est potentia, ejusdem est et actus, videre autem nullo modo oculi est, igitur nec potentia videndi, sive virtus visibilis. (...) Manifestum est igitur tibi per hoc quod virtus videndi sive potentia apud animam est, et in ipsa".

All the powers thus remain in the human soul even after a man's death.[102] It follows that when William states that the soul sustains the limbs of the body in an essential way, he intends to stress that the ability to sustain the body only belongs to the essence of the soul and not to the essence of the body, because the latter has a uniquely passive role: "ipsa obedientia membris est ex animae potestate naturali sive essentiali eidem". Further, it should be noted that William, unlike Hugh, does not contrast the word "essentialiter" with the word "accidentaliter": indeed, William's purpose is not to establish the way in which the ability to sustain the body belongs to the soul, i.e., to establish whether it belongs to the soul as an accident or as its specific difference. His purpose is only to show that this ability fully belongs to the essence of the soul and does not depend upon the body because the body is totally passive.

On the other hand, William states that the soul is present in its body in an essential way, that is to say with all its substance or essence in all the limbs: "Manifestum est ipsam esse essentialiter sive principaliter in toto corpore, et singulis partibus ejus".[103] In this case too, the meaning that the bishop gives to the word 'essentialiter' is quite different from that given to the same word by Hugh of St-Cher or by Roland of Cremona.

Furthermore, as concerns the ontological character of the connection between the soul and the body, William's view is not very far from that of Avicenna. Indeed, William states that the soul can know itself and that its *esse* does not depend at all on the body.[104] As Bernardo C. Bazàn observes about William's exposition, the union between the soul and the body can be defined as purely operational and accidental, having no influence on the proper character of the human soul. For William states that the relation between the spiritual substance and the human body resembles the relation between a rider and his horse or between a house and its inhabitant.[105]

---

[102] Cf. *infra*, chap. 2.2.2.5.

[103] The word *substantialiter* acquires a similar meaning in the *Summa "Quoniam homines"* by Alan of Lille. Indeed, Alan wonders whether demons go *substantialiter* into human bodies, i.e., whether they go into the bodies "with their substance"; cf. Alan. de Ins., *sum. quon.*, n. 136, in P. Glorieux, "La somme *Quoniam homines* d'Alain de Lille", AHDLMA 20 (1953), pp. 273-275.

[104] Guill. de Alv., *de an.*, 4, 9, ed. Le Feron, p. 165: "Quod propter mortem corporis nihil de esse ipsius animae deperit. (...) Amplius cum anima humana propter corpus non sit nec propter vires quibus operatur in corpus et per corpus, nisi forsitan secundario et in parte; cum alie vires sint in ea principales".

[105] Guill. de Alv., *de an.*, 3, 11, ed. Le Feron, pp. 101b-102a: "Attende autem diligenter exempla quae tibi posita sunt de equo et equite, de domo et inhabitatore, de instrumento et operatore, de veste seu vestimento atque vestito; et apparebit evidenter quod rationabilius est, et sermonibus nostris, usuique loquendi consonantius ut corpus dicatur pars hominis

Hence, whatever was the relation between the question *De anima* by Hugh of St-Cher and the text written by William of Auvergne, they evidently differ on an important point. Indeed, although both theologians use the term '*substantialiter*', it seems that the *unibilitas substantialis* conception is basically foreign to William's anthropological view.

***

In order to evaluate the anthropology of the decades 1220s-1230s, we may adopt two different perspectives. On the one hand, we may compare it with Aristotle's or Aquinas's thoughts, thus adopting the perspective of an anthropological view denying the substantial character of the human soul. If we consider the *unibilitas substantialis* theory from this perspective, we must conclude that it is an eclectic doctrine which is still close to the traditional anthropological dualism. For the human soul is defined as a substance and a spirit of its own species; moreover, in the case of Hugh and Roland, the term 'form' is systematically replaced with that of 'perfection' emanating from the Arabic tradition, in which the Aristotelian philosophy is extensively reinterpreted through the categories of Neoplatonism. On the other hand, we may compare the thought elaborated by William of Auxerre and the early Dominican masters with that elaborated by the most influential authors of their time, such as Avicenna, Philip the Chancellor or William of Auvergne. In this respect, the *unibilitas substantialis* represents an interesting novelty. Indeed, at that time, the inclination of the soul to be united with the body was always defined as an accident of the soul, hence the same human composite was characterized by a merely accidental unity. By contrast, according to this new conception, the ability or inclination to become united, called '*unibilitas*', can no longer be a mere accident because this feature represents a substantial property of the soul, so that it becomes that which distinguishes it from the angel, i.e., a substantial difference. Hence, the very essence of the soul is designated through its *unibilitas* which takes the features of an essential or substantial inclination.

As we shall see later in this study, the *unibilitas substantialis* theory continued to play an important role in the second half of the thirteenth century.

---

quae cadit in rationem hominis in quantum hominis, quemadmodum equus in rationem equitis in quantum equitis. Ipsae enim operationes quae fiunt per corpus, ut ostensum est tibi in praecedentibus, ipsius animae humanae verissime ac propriissime sunt, sicut est loqui, disputare et etiam, quamquam indignetur Aristoteles, texere et aedificare"; cf. Bazán, "Pluralisme de formes", p. 47.

1.1.3 *UNIBILITAS SUBSTANTIALIS* AFTER HUGH OF ST-CHER

1.1.3.1 John of La Rochelle

John of La Rochelle († 1245) wrote his *Summa de anima* a few years after Hugh's question *De anima* was composed. Probably written by the Franciscan master in the second half of the 1230s,[106] the *Summa de anima* is chiefly based on Philip the Chancellor's *Summa de bono* and in many respects adopts the perspective found in the Avicennian anthropology. In particular, the structure of the first part of the *Summa*, which is devoted to the substance of the soul, derives directly from the conception presented in Avicenna's *De anima*. Indeed, John distinguishes between the consideration of the soul in itself, i.e. in respect to its essence, and the consideration of the soul in relation to the body. As explicitly announced by John himself, these two types of approaches are expounded in two separate sections.[107]

Like Philip the Chancellor, John uses the terms 'perfection' and 'form' interchangeably. However, unlike Philip, John reiterates that the ability to be united with the body belongs to the human soul in a substantial way and that this ability represents its substantial difference with the angel. The terms used by John to express this doctrine clearly resemble those used by Hugh:

> Primo ergo queritur an anima corpori uniatur per medium, an sine medio; et cum unibilitas non sit accidentalis anime sed essencialis et sit illud quo essencialiter differt anima racionalis ab angelo, sicut dictum est prius.[108] Unitur anima corpori per suam unibilitatem: ergo unitur per suam essenciam; ergo sine medio. - Item, cum anima uniatur corpori ut forma et perfectio ejus, forma autem unitur per se materie, ergo anima unitur per se corpori; ergo sine medio.[109]

---

[106] The editor proposes to date it around 1235-1236, but the only certain *terminus ante quem* is the year of John's death; cf. J.-G. Bougerol, "Introduction", in Ioh. Rup., *sum. de an.*, ed. Bougerol, p. 12; Hasse, *Avicenna's De anima*, p. 47.

[107] Ioh. Rup., *sum. de an.*, ed. Bougerol, p. 80[1-6]: "Dicto de anima quantum ad fieri, consequenter dicendum est de ea quantum ad esse; et hoc duobus modis: quantum ad esse absolutum et quantum ad esse comparatum ad corpus. Quantum uero ad esse absolutum anime, ostendenda sunt ista: quod anima sit substancia; quod incorporea; quod simplex; quod una in tribus potentiis, scilicet vegetabili, sensibili, racionali; quod ymago Dei".

[108] Cf. Ioh. Rup., *sum. de an.* ed. Bougerol, p. 71[88-92]: "Et dicendum ad obiecta, quod cum dico spiritum unibilem hoc quod dico unibilem facit differenciam secundum speciem, et non solum differenciam secundum modum essendi; nam unibile facit speciem hominis esse animam, non unibile uero in angelo facit angelum spiritum esse tantum"; *ibid.*, p. 70[75-85].

[109] Ioh. Rup., *sum. de an.*, ed. Bougerol, p. 115[1-7].

All the typical elements of the *unibilitas substantialis* doctrine are present in the passage from the *Summa de anima* quoted above. First of all, John – just like Hugh and Roland of Cremona – contrasts accidental inherence with a substantial, namely essential, property. The *unibilitas* characterizing the human soul is substantial: the soul must therefore be immediately (i. e. without any intermediaries) united with the body, just as a form or a perfection is united with matter.[110] Furthermore, a typical feature is that John considers the notion of '*unibilitas*' as having an affinity to that of 'perfection' or 'form'. Moreover, in another passage from the *Summa*, John states that the soul, owing to its *unibilitas*, is not a person.[111]

The similarities between Hugh of St-Cher's question *De anima* and John's *Summa* are so evident and numerous that we are spontaneously induced to speculate about their mutual dependence. As affirmed by the editor of the *Summa*,[112] John's work mainly reflects the psychological doctrines elaborated at Paris in the first half of the 1230s: this was the period in which Hugh taught at the Parisian faculty. John may have read Hugh's question *De anima* or attended his teaching. Moreover, considering the similarity between the formulas used in the text, it clearly appears that the dependence of the Franciscan master upon Hugh's writing is highly probable, unless both availed themselves of a different source that remains unknown to us.

---

[110] Nevertheless, the solution to the problem of the union between the soul and the body which is adopted in the *Summa de anima* is more complex. As it is unitable, or alternatively, as it is a form or perfection, the human soul is united directly with its body. However, John holds that the human soul is above all a substance: for a spiritual substance, ontologically very distant from the corporeal substance, needs intermediary powers to be united with the body. It is unclear how John intends to reconcile the two perspectives. Cf. Ioh. Rup., *sum. de an.*, ed. Bougerol, pp. 116⁴⁴-117⁵⁷: "Respondeo. Anima racionalis unitur corpori secundum duplicem modum: unitur enim ut forma sue materie siue ut perfectio suo perfectibili; unitur eciam ei ut suo organo siue instrumento per quod operatur, duplex est ergo racio unionis. Secundum primum modum unitur anima corpori sine medio: corpori dico in ultima disposicione se habenti secundum quod est in corpore, sicut materie necessitas ad forme susceptionem scilicet anime, sicut lignum in ultima disposicione se habens calefactionis et siccitatis: cum scilicet est summe calefactum, se habet immediate ad susceptionem forme igneitatis. Secundum uero secundum modum unitur anima per medium, et medium istud est potencia siue uis eius secundum enim quod anima unitur corpori ut suo organo per quod operatur est comparacio anime sicut artificis operantis per instrumentum quia secundum hunc modum se habet anima ad corpus".

[111] Ioh. Rup., *sum. de an.*, ed. Bougerol, p. 70⁸⁴⁻⁸⁵: "Quoniam angelus per hoc quod separatus est, habet esse persona; anima per hoc quod unibilis, habet esse forma et perfectio et non persona: ergo differens est esse hinc et inde secundum speciem".

[112] Cf. Bougerol, "Introduction", p. 13.

1.1.3.2 Albert the Great

The first theological works of the acclaimed Dominican master Albert of Cologne († 1280) probably date from the first half of the 1240s. The fact that Hugh and Albert belonged to the same Order and probably came into personal contact with each other[113] does not allow us to affirm that the question *De anima* left clearly recognizable traces in the works written by the *doctor universalis*. Yet, *unibilitas* is part of the philosophical terminology used by Albert. The term especially appears within the context of the discussion on the problem of the difference between the soul and the angel. Albert addresses this problem at least three times, first in the *Commentary* on book II of the *Sentences*, then on two occasions in the *Summa de homine*; a discussion on this subject also appears in the *Summa theologica* ascribed to Albert.[114] Although Albert's anthropological view undergoes some changes over the course of time, nevertheless, in the three passages mentioned above, *unibilitas* constitutes for Albert the main cause of the specific difference between the rational soul and the angel.

First of all, in the *Commentary* on the *Sentences* of Peter Lombard, when speaking of the ability of the soul to be united with the body, Albert contrasts a substantial characteristic, which is the cause of the specific difference, with an accidental characteristic, i.e., an extrinsic relation that represents just an accident for the soul. Moreover, as it occurs in Hugh's question *De anima*, *unibilitas* is defined as an irremovable characteristic of the human soul, that remains in the latter even after a man's death.[115]

A similar solution is proposed later on, in the chapter *De differentia angeli et animae* of the *Summa de homine*. On this occasion, Albert mainly emphasizes the condition in which the human soul is created, and considers the immediate

---

[113] Cf. *supra*, n. 1.

[114] The *Summa* also contains a whole question entitled *Utrum anima humana unibilis sit corpori*; cf. Alb. Magn., *sum. theol.* II, vol. 13, q. 77, ed. Borgnet, pp. 68b-71a. As regards the attribution of the *Summa* to Albert, see A. Fries, "Zur Problematik der «Summa theologiae» unter dem Namen des Albertus Magnus", *Franziskanische Studien* 70 (1988), pp. 68-91; id., "Zum Verhältnis des Albertus Magnus zur «Summa theologiae» unter seinem Namen", *Franziskanische Studien* 71 (1989), pp. 123-137; R. Wielockx, "Zur «Summa theologiae» des Albertus Magnus", *Ephemerides Theologicae Lovanienses* 66. 1 (1990), pp. 78-110.

[115] Alb. Magn., *In* II *Sent.*, d. 1, a. 13, ed. Borgnet, p. 22b: "*Ad aliud* dicendum, quod unio fundatar super naturam animae quia ipsa naturaliter dependet ad corpus, et hoc patet quia in comparatione ad corpus diffinitur, et ideo non dicit solam relationem, sed etiam differentiam specificam: sed quia specificae differentiae ultimae frequenter sunt nobis incognitae, ideo nominamus eas per signa conuenientia, et quandoque per duas remotiores differentias coniunctas conscribimus unam. *Ad aliud* dicendum, quod licet separabilis sit, tamen adhuc per proportionem unibilitatem habet ad corpus; et cum separata est a corpore, non separata est ab unibilitate"; cf. also id., *In* III *Sent.*, d. 5, a. 16, ed. Borgnet, p. 116; *infra*, p. 87.

infusion of souls into the bodies as a proof of the existence of the *dependentia unibilitatis* in the soul.[116]

Finally, the same elements reappear in the *Summa theologica* ascribed to Albert. The text underlines that *unibilitas* to the body does not depend upon the powers of the soul, but on the very essence of the soul. Further, the text confirms that *unibilitas* remains in the soul after a man's death and makes souls different from angels both as to species and as to genus.[117]

1.1.3.3   Bonaventure

In general, scholars have not focused their attention on the concept of *unibilitas substantialis.* Certainly, in some cases the term *unibilitas* is noticed;[118] yet, the role associated with this term is rather marginal. In most cases, the concept is compared to the "wish of union" present in Augustine's thought or to the "inclination" toward the body asserted in Avicenna's *De anima*: but studies are silent on the problem of the essentiality of *unibilitas.*

Against this background, the essay written by Thomas Osborne represents a real exception. The title of the article is significant: *Unibilitas: The Key to Bonaventure's Understanding of Human Nature.*[119] Mainly resting on some passages

---

[116] Alb. Magn., *de hom.* I, q. 30, a. 2, ed. Borgnet, p. 501b: "Et preterea substantialis differentia animae est, quod ipsa est unibilis corpori, non ut forma tantum habens esse in materia, sed ut forma et substantia mouens et regens corpus ut nauta nauem. (...) Et quod ita sit, scilicet quod anima dependentiam unibilitatis habeat ad corpus, patet ex hoc quod etiam creator non creat eam nisi in corpore"; id., *Über den Menschen*, H. Anzulewicz and J. R. Söder (ed. and transl.), Hamburg: Felix Meiner Verlag, 2004, p. 56: "Solutio: Dicendum secundum supra determinata de angelis quod substantialis differentia animae et angeli est in hoc quod anima inclinatur ad corpus ut actus, angelus autem non. Et ideo dicimus substantiale esse animae quod sit actus corporis"; cf. S. Lipke, "Die Bedeutung der Seele für die Einheit des Menschen nach De homine", in W. Senner, *Albertus Magnus. Zum Gedenken nach 800 Jahren: Neue Zugänge, Aspekte und Perspektiven*, Berlin, 2001, pp. 207-219.

[117] Alb. Magn., *sum. theol.* II, vol. 2, q. 9, ed. Borgnet, pp. 140-141: "Solutio. Dicendum, quod anima rationalis et Angelus, et specie, et genere differunt. Est enim animalis anima intendens in delectabilia corporis: et sic differt genere. Angelus autem spiritus, et ad delectabilia carnis non respiciens. Differunt etiam specie: anima enim rationalis secundum seipsam et secundum totum affectum unibilis est corpori. Per hoc patet, quod ipsa est actus corporis organici physici potentiam vitae habentis. Et hoc non est per potentias tantum, ut quidam dixerunt, sed per essentiam suam, sic enim nisi essentialis forma esset hominis, homo non esset homo. (...) Et si objicitur, quod secundum hoc anima separata non differt ab angelo. Dicendum quod falsum est: quia etiam anima separata, propter hoc quod secundum esse unibilis est corpori, affectum et intentionem retinet ad corpus, in tantum quod etiam a contemplatione retrahatur".

[118] Cf. E. Gilson, *History of Christian Philosophy in the Middle Ages*, New York: Random House, 1955, p. 361; H. Wéber, *La personne humaine au XIIIe siècle*, Paris: Vrin, 1991, p. 88, p. 102; Lenzi, *Forma e sostanza*, pp. 173-174, pp. 208-218.

[119] *Journal of the History of Philosophy* 37. 2 (1999), pp. 227-250.

from Bonaventure's († 1274) *Commentary* on book II and III of the *Sentences*, Osborne concludes that *unibilitas substantialis* constitutes the central concept of Bonaventure's anthropology. Indeed, the *unibilitas* conception allows Bonaventure to consider the human soul as a spiritual substance and at the same time as a part of a more complete substance, i.e. man.[120] The author of the essay emphasizes the following points: first, *unibilitas* assures the specific difference between soul and angel; second, the concept exclusively describes a substantial union, such as that subsisting between a perfection and its matter, not an accidental or operational union, such as that between the angel and the body it assumes;[121] moreover, a "unitable" soul is conjoined to its particular body through its essence, with no mediation;[122] the ability to be united always remains in the human soul, also after a man's death;[123] finally, owing to its *unibilitas*, the human soul is not a person, not even when it is separated from the body.[124] To my mind, Bonaventure's text fully confirms Osborne's interpretation.[125]

Secundo circa hoc quaeritur, quae sit illa differentia, per quam Angelus et anima differunt. Quod autem differant essentialiter per hoc quod est unibile, videtur primo sic. (...)

Item, esse unibile convenit animae rationali: aut ergo essentialiter, aut accidentaliter; sed non accidentaliter, constat: quia tunc ex corpore et anima non fieret unum per essentiam: ergo essentialiter hoc convenit animae. Sed quaecumque differunt in aliquo modo essentiali, differunt specie: ergo anima et Angelus etc.

Item, pars suum esse completum non habet, nisi secundum quod est in toto: ergo cum anima rationalis sit pars hominis, suum esse completum non habet, nisi secundum quod est in suo toto, scilicet in homine, ut pars. Sed non est pars hominis, nisi secundum quod est unibilis: ergo in unibilitate ad corpus consistit complementum animae. Sed per illud habet unumquodque essentialiter differre sive distingui ab aliquo, in quo consistit eius complementum: ergo etc.

Illud ergo, quo anima est unibilis corpori, tale dicit quid essentiale respiciens, quod est nobilissimum in anima; et ita penes illud recte sumitur specifica differentia, secundum quam differt anima a natura angelica. (...)

Quod obiicitur ultimo, quod differentia essentialiter adhaeret; dicendum, quod esse unibile adhaeret inseparabiliter, quia aptitudo semper inest, quamvis

---

[120] Osborne, "Unibilitas", *passim*, especially p. 228.
[121] Osborne, "Unibilitas", p. 229.
[122] Osborne, "Unibilitas", p. 231.
[123] Osborne, "Unibilitas", p. 230.
[124] Osborne, "Unibilitas", pp. 246-248.
[125] Bonav., *in* II *Sent.*, d. 1, p. 2, a. 3, q. 2, ed. PP. Collegii S. Bonaventurae, p. 49a, p. 50b, p. 51.

non semper insit actus, sicut patet in rationabilitate et gressibilitate. Et sicut gressibilis truncatur, et rationalis anima stulta efficitur non natura, sed propter defectum naturae; ita quod anima separatur, hoc est in poenam peccati. Et ideo esse separabile non sic assignatur differentia animae, sicut esse unibile.

As previously seen, all these elements already appear in the question *De anima* by Hugh of St-Cher and in the *Summa de anima* by John of La Rochelle. The similarity is not incidental: evidently, Bonaventure, who was a pupil of John's, had extensive recourse to John's *Summa*.[126] By contrast, as regards Hugh's question, quite probably it did not exert a direct influence on Bonaventure's *Commentary*; nevertheless, it should be noted that from a textual point of view there are important similarities between the ways they argue. First of all, both texts lay emphasis on the opposition between the terms *accidentaliter* and *essentialiter* (or *substantialiter*): indeed, solely the substantial *unibilitas* can form the basis of a specific difference, whereas an accidental virtue can only originate a numerical difference. Secondly, the term *unibilitas* is paralleled by the concept of a natural *aptitudo*, i.e. a natural and intrinsic inclination or ability to be united. Lastly, in Hugh's and Bonaventure's texts, perhaps more than in Albert the Great and John of La Rochelle himself, *unibilitas substantialis* performs a really central role, because the whole solution to the problem of the specific definition of the soul rests on this concept. As we shall see more deeply in the next chapter, the same concept plays an important role also in the question of the personal character of the soul.[127]

1.1.3.4   Thomas Aquinas

There exists abundant literature concerning the difference between Thomas Aquinas's anthropology and the anthropology elaborated by his predecessors: here we do not intend to summarize what has been said previously.[128] At the beginning of this short section it should be observed that the purpose of my research is not

---

[126]   Wéber, *La personne humaine*, pp. 90-103; Osborne, "Unibilitas", p. 234.

[127]   Cf. Bonav., *in* III *Sent.*, d. 5, a. 2, q. 3, ed. PP. Collegii S. Bonaventurae, p. 136a: "Preterea, unibilitas sive aptitudo uniendi cum corpore non est animae accidentalis, sed est ipsi animae essentialis, et ita non potest ab ea separari vel circumscribi, salva ipsius natura, sicut superius in secundo libro ostensum fuit"; cf. *infra*, chap. II.

[128]   See especially Bazán, "Pluralisme de formes", pp. 30-73; id., "The Human Soul", pp. 95-126; cf. also A. Masnovo, *Da Guglielmo d'Auvergne a S. Tommaso d'Aquino*, Milano: Vita e pensiero, 1945; S. Vanni Rovighi, *L'antropologia filosofica di San Tommaso d'Aquino*, Milano: Vita e pensiero, 1965; A. C. Pegis, "The Separated Soul and Its Nature in St. Thomas", in *St. Thomas Aquinas: 1274-1974. Commemorative Studies*, edited by A. A. Maurer, Toronto: Pontifical Institute of Medieval Studies, 1974, vol. I, pp. 131-158; A. C. Pegis, *St. Thomas and the Problem of the Soul in the Thirteenth Century*, Toronto: Pontifical Institute of Mediaeval Studies, 1983; Wéber, *La personne humaine*, pp. 146-187; M. Sweeney, "Soul

to argue that Aquinas's anthropology was no different from the thought elaborated by theologians in the first half of the thirteenth century. In fact, I shall here consider Aquinas's thought just insofar as it assimilated a concept elaborated in the previous decades, i.e. the concept of *unibilitas substantialis*, but I shall not evaluate the personal contribution given by Aquinas to the development of anthropology.

Aquinas writes his *Commentary* on Peter Lombard's *Sentences* in the middle of the 1250s, i.e., very near in time to the composition of Bonaventure's *Commentary*. The Franciscan theologian had discussed the *unibilitas* doctrine in the question about the specific difference between soul and angel, when commenting on the first distinction of book II and while dealing with the personal character of the soul after the body's death in the *Commentary* on the fifth distinction of book III of the *Sentences*. Aquinas considers the same questions when he comments on the third distinction of book II and, like Bonaventure, on the fifth distinction of book III. It is precisely here that Aquinas refers to the *unibilitas* concept.

Unlike Bonaventure, Aquinas does not assign a fundamental role to this term.[129] Aquinas is inspired by the argumentation of his predecessors and does not reject the *unibilitas* concept as such, but clearly reduces its role. Indeed, in Aquinas's view, *unibilitas* does not form the foundation of the substantial difference between soul and angel, but just the first of its consequences. On this ground, in the *Commentary* on book II of the *Sentences*, Aquinas states that soul and angel belong to different species; yet, their specific difference does not correspond to any of the features commonly indicated by the *quidam*, but to the degree of possibility (*gradus possibilitatis*). This does not mean that *unibilitas* is not a difference between soul and angel; and yet, it is not the essential or specific difference, but just the most important consequence of the essential or specific difference.[130]

---

as Substance and Method in Thomas Aquinas' Anthropological Writings", AHDLMA 66 (1999), pp. 143-187.

[129] Osborne, "Unibilitas", p. 229.

[130] Thom. de Aquino, *in* II *Sent.*, d. 3, q. 1, a. 6, Edizioni Studio Domenicano, III, pp. 188-196: "Si diceres, quod distinguitur penes unibile corpori et non unibile: contra. Quidquid consequitur rem habentem esse completum, non distinguit eam essentialiter a re alia: quia omnia huiusmodi quae sic consequuntur rem, sunt de genere accidentium. Sed unio ad corpus est quaedam relatio quae consequitur animam habentem in se esse completum ad corpus non dependens; alias sine corpore esse non posset. Ergo hoc quod est unibile corpori, non distinguit essentialiter vel secundum speciem animam ab angelo. (...) Et ideo tertia opinio communior est, cui assentiendum videtur, quod anima et angelus specie differunt. Quibus autem differentiis specificis distinguantur, diversimode assignatur. Quidam enim assignant eas specie distingui, per hoc quod est unibile corpori et non unibile. Alii vero per hoc quod est rationale et intellectuale esse. (...) Nec est mirum quod sic diversimode Angeli et animae differre assignantur: quia differentiae essentiales,

The solution to the problem of substantial difference between soul and angel proposed by Aquinas in his *Commentary* on book ii of the *Sentences* is also reflected in the question relating to the personal character of the separated soul which is dealt with in the *Commentary* on the fifth distinction of book iii:[131] indeed, here too, the role assigned to *unibilitas* is markedly smaller than that we have observed in Bonaventure's *Commentary*. Nevertheless, this concept is used repeatedly in this context too; in addition to it, we meet the term *aptitudo naturalis*, a phrase already familiar to us from Hugh of St-Cher's question *De anima*.

The term *unibilitas* does not disappear from Aquinas's writings after the *Sentences Commentary*. We meet it again in the works commonly considered as the most significant ones with respect to his anthropology, i.e. in the *Disputed questions on the soul* and in part I of the *Summa theologiae*.[132] In the *Summa*, Aquinas brings forward the question whether soul and angel belong to the same species (*Utrum anima et angelus sint unius speciei*), but his answer is different from that given in the *Sentences Commentary*: the soul cannot differ from the angel in a specific way because the soul without the body does not belong to any species. Yet, despite this difference in the solution, *unibilitas* preserves its role since it is regarded as the most important consequence of the essential nature of the soul:[133]

> Ad tertium dicendum quod corpus non est de essentia animae, sed anima ex natura suae essentiae habet quod sit corpori unibilis. Unde nec proprie anima est in specie; sed compositum. Et hoc ipsum quod anima quodammodo indiget

quae ignotae et innominatae sunt, secundum philosophum designantur differentiis accidentalibus, quae ex essentialibus causantur, sicut causa designatur per suum effectum; sicut calidum et frigidum assignantur differentiae ignis et aquae. Unde possunt plures differentiae pro specificis assignari, secundum plures proprietates rerum differentium specie, ex essentialibus differentiis causatas; quarum tamen istae melius assignantur quae priores sunt, quasi essentialibus differentiis propinquiores. Cum ergo substantiarum simplicium, ut dictum est de Angelis, sit differentia in specie secundum gradum possibilitatis in eis, ex hoc anima rationalis ab Angelis differt, quia ultimum gradum in substantiis spiritualibus tenet, sicut materia prima in rebus sensibilibus, ut dicit Commentator in 3 de anima. Unde quia plurimum de possibilitate habet, esse suum est adeo propinquum rebus materialibus, ut corpus materiale illud possit participare, dum anima corpori unitur ad unum esse: et ideo consequuntur istae differentiae inter animam et angelum, unibile, et non unibile, ex diverso gradu possibilitatis. Item ex eodem sequuntur aliae differentiae (...). Ad tertium dicendum, quod unibilitas non est propria differentia essentialis; sed est quaedam designatio essentialis differentiae per effectum, ut dictum est".

[131] Thom. de Aquino, *In* iii *Sent.*, d. 5, q. 3, a. 2, Edizioni Studio Domenicano, v, pp. 336-340.

[132] The composition of the questions (1266-1267) precedes that of the *Summa theologiae*; cf. Bazán, "The Human Soul", pp. 96-97.

[133] Thom. de Aquino, *sum. theol.*, Ia, q. 75 a. 7 ad 3, EL 5, p. 207b.

corpore ad suam operationem, ostendit quod anima tenet inferiorem gradum intellectualitatis quam angelus, qui corpori non unitur.

Such argumentation is also presented in the *Questions on the soul*, within the framework of the discussion concerning the problem of the individuation of the soul:[134]

> Manifestum est autem, ex hiis que supra dicta sunt, quod de ratione anime humane est quod corpori humano sit unibilis, cum non habeat in se speciem completam, set speciei complementum sit in ipso composito. Vnde quod sit unibilis huic aut illi corpori multiplicat animam secundum numerum, non autem secundum speciem, sicut et hec albedo differt numero ab illa ex hoc quod est esse huius et illius subiecti.

On the basis of these texts, we may conclude that the term *unibilitas* not only is deeply rooted in Aquinas's terminology, but also appears in the passages that are most important for his anthropology.[135]

* * *

As Thomas Osborne observes,[136] the easy assimilation of the term *unibilitas* into Aquinas's thought suggests that this word cannot be univocally situated in the frame of a dualist anthropology. In fact, Aquinas, like previous authors, conforms this term to the context of his anthropological view. Nevertheless, we should above

---

[134] Thom. de Aquino, *qq. de an.*, q. 3, ed. Bazán, pp. 27³⁰⁵-28³¹⁶; cf. Thom. de Aquino, *resp. de art.*, q. 108, ed. Verardo, p. 240b, n. 935: "Sicut igitur corpus non est tota causa animae, sed anima secundum suam rationem aliquem ordinem ad corpus habet, cum de ratione animae sit, quod sit unibilis corpori, ita corpus non est tota causa individuationis huius animae; sed de ratione huius animae est quod sit unibilis huic corpori, et haec remanet in anima etiam corpore destructo".

[135] The term is also assimilated by Aquinas's commentators and critics; see for instance Thom. de Vio (Caietanus), *in Sum. theol.* Ia, EL 5, p. 207b: "Sed esset hic alia difficultas: quomodo unibilitas est de essentia animae, ut s. Thomas hic dicit"; Guill. Mar., *correct.*, a. 30, in P. Glorieux, *Les premières polémiques thomistes: Le Correctorium Corruptorii "Quare"*, Kain: Le Saulchoir, 1927, p. 126: "Si dicas quod animae separatae distinguuntur et individuantur unibilitate vel aptitudine uniendi ad tale corpus; contra: esse distinctum vel individuatum est esse actuale; unibilitas vel aptitudo uniendi dicit potentiam vel aliquid ad minus in potentia quia dicit dispositionem quamdam essentiae animae quae dispositio naturali ordine praecedit potentiam animae; potentia autem non dat esse actuale; ergo illa uniendi aptitudo non dat animae separatae esse individuatum"; cf. A. Aiello, "La conoscenza intellettiva dell'individuale: note alla soluzione di Guglielmo de la Mare", *Acta philosophica* 9 (2000), p. 21.

[136] Osborne, "Unibilitas", p. 229: "In fact, unibility has a variety of uses which depend upon the context of its appearance and the thought of the one who uses it".

all consider that this concept is not without a history. First of all, it does not take
its rise from the Avicennian philosophy but rather from the Christian theological
tradition. Secondly, since its first appearance in the anthropological speculation,
unibilitas appears to be related to the theory of the substantial difference between
soul and angel. Hence, it would be wrong to hold that this concept involves the
idea of the accidental union between soul and body: on the contrary, it expresses
the effort made in order to get beyond this kind of conception. This is the reason
why *unibilitas substantialis* is not related to the – typically Avicennian – theory
of the dual consideration of the soul, where the soul is taken, on the one hand, in
itself, on the other hand, in relation to the body. Indeed, according to the Avicennian doctrine, the soul's definition makes no mention of the soul-body connection, i.e. the human soul is defined as a spiritual substance which is complete and
independent as such; by contrast, its function of animating a body represents just
an accident for it and does not affect its essence, since it is exclusively an extrinsic
relation. Otherwise, if we were to define the soul's essence in a way when considered in itself and in another way when considered in its relation with the body,
then we would necessarily fall into a contradiction. For this reason, the theory of
the dual consideration of the soul involves, at least in Avicenna's case, the theory
of accidental union. By contrast, the *unibilitas substantialis* theory constitutes
an attempt at taking the reference to the body into the very essence of the soul.
Certainly, one might object that theologians of the first half of the thirteenth century – for example Roland of Cremona or John of La Rochelle – maintain both the
theory of the dual consideration of the soul and the *unibilitas substantialis* theory.
In my view, however, on a strictly theoretical level, these positions cannot be easily
reconciled. Their contrast becomes evident when John of La Rochelle states that
the human soul is united with the body without intermediaries because it is unitable, but requires the presence of intermediaries because it constitutes a spiritual
substance:[137] this is a clear contradiction. On the one hand, this difficulty derives
from the imperfection of the *unibilitas substantialis* theory itself: it is unclear,
just to give an example, whether *unibilitas* denotes an ontological incompleteness
of the soul or constitutes a power of it. Furthermore, should it be a power, then
it would be necessary to determine the type of powers *unibilitas* belongs to.[138] As
we shall see in the second section of this study, many of Hugh's contemporaries

---

[137] Cf. *supra*, pp. 35-36.
[138] In the *Quaestiones antequam esset frater*, in a dispute concerning the hypostatic
union, we find an attempt to clarify the notion of *unibile*; cf. Alex. Halen., *q. ant.* XV, disp.
1-2, ed. PP. Collegii S. Bonaventurae, I, p. 195[12-14]: "Unibile duobus modis dicitur: vel quod
habet potentiam activam, vel quod habet potentiam passivam vel materialem. Hanc autem
non habet divina natura, sed humana hanc habet ut uniatur cum divina, quia recipit perfectionem in hac unione".

distinguish between three or even four genera of powers which differ from one another on an ontological level. On the other hand, it should be noted that John of La Rochelle incorporates into the *Summa de anima* various doctrines deriving from trends of thought that cannot always be easily reconciled, such as traditional Christian theology and Avicennianism.[139]

In any case, the *unibilitas substantialis* theory, considered in its roots, does not depend upon the dual consideration of the soul. In order to reconcile the immortality of the soul with the *unibilitas* theory, or with the hylomorphic conception of man, it was necessary to introduce another distinction: indeed, it was necessary to draw a clear distinction between the actual presence of the body and the ability to be united with the body, or that which gives the soul the ability to be united. This distinction will enable thirteenth-century thinkers to assert both that, on the one hand, the actual presence of the body may come to an end and, on the other, that the soul without the body is not conceivable because it is the relation with the latter that defines the soul's essence. As we shall see in the next chapter, this distinction is the result of a slow conceptual evolution antecedent to the beginning of the thirteenth century.

---

[139] Let us mention, for example, two radically different views concerning the condition of man after death: on the one hand, the Christian faith in the resurrection of the body; on the other, the negation of corporeal life in the afterworld according to Avicenna; cf. Michot, *La destinée de l'homme, passim*. The question of the incarnation of the Word too was totally foreign to the Arab philosopher.

1.2
THE HUMAN SOUL AND THE CONCEPT OF PERSON

1.2.1 "THE HUMAN SOUL IS NOT A PERSON". THE *SENTENCES COMMENTARY* OF HUGH OF ST-CHER

The substantial and immortal ability to be united with the body represents the main feature differentiating the human soul from the angel. The first article of Hugh of St-Cher's question *De anima* centres around this doctrine. Nevertheless, the reason why Hugh adopts this position is not totally clear; indeed, the question contains no justification for this theory. The *Summa aurea* offers no better explanations: indeed, William of Auxerre too makes no mention of the reasons why he adopts the theory of the substantial difference between soul and angel which is based on the union with the body. Hence, what is the origin of the *unibilitas substantialis* conception?

In the question *De anima*, in addition to the first difference between the two spiritual substances, Hugh mentions a second distinction too: whereas the angel, like man, is a person, the soul is devoid of the character of person.[140] The connection between the two differences does not explicitly appear in the text of our question. Yet, the link becomes evident if we turn to Hugh's *Commentary* on Peter Lombard's *Sentences*. In his commentary on at least three distinctions, the Dominican master insists that the human soul is not a person, and each time he justifies his position extensively. Indeed, although the soul is a substance having a rational nature, owing to the fact that it is united with the body it lacks the character of individuality; moreover, even when the composite dissolves due to death, nevertheless the soul is not a person, because "being a part" belongs to its nature independently of the presence of the body. Indeed, according to Hugh, the soul is never individual, because it was not created to subsist separately, but begins to exist at the very moment of infusion. The soul's destiny is inseparably linked to the totality of the human being; for this reason, after death, the souls of the saints wish to be reunited with their bodies.[141]

---

[140] Hugo de S. Caro, *q. de an.* 1, ed. Bieniak, p. 170[64-65]: "Et hec est secunda differentia anime et angeli quod angelus est persona et non anima sed homo <est persona>".

[141] Hugo de S. Caro, *in* III *Sent.*, d. 5, ed. Breuning, pp. 351[353]-352[382]: "Magister Hugo de Sancto Victore: Anima, inquantum est spiritus rationalis, ex se et per se habet esse personae, et quando ei corpus associatur, non. (...) Sed magister Hugo et etiam Magister in

The natural and immortal wish to be united with the body – about which Hugh writes in his *Commentary* on book III of the *Sentences* – recalls another expression contained in the question *De anima*, i.e. '*aptitudo*', that is, a suitability for union that remains in the separated soul:[142]

> Ad secundum, quod anima et angelus differunt accidente solo etc., dicendum quod "regens" non dicit actum sed aptitudinem secundum quam anima apta est naturaliter regere corpus illo triplici regimine quod diximus, et hanc aptitudinem habet anima etiam separata. Hec enim est illa unibilitas de qua supra diximus.

Indeed, *unibilitas substantialis* seems to be related to the characteristics of the human soul enumerated in the *Commentary* on book III of the *Sentences*, namely: the lack of individuality and of the character of person; the desire of the soul for its body; the condition of "being a part" which is engraved in its nature; finally, the body as the proper place of the soul. Hence, in order to understand the origin of the substantial *unibilitas* theory, we should above all reconstruct the genesis of the soul-person doctrine. This doctrine refers to Boethius' *Theological Treatises* and even more to the interpretation of the latter given by Gilbert of Poitiers. Hence, this chapter is intended first of all to be a search for the literary sources of Hugh's texts and, secondly, an attempt at reconstructing the evolution leading from the assimilation of Boethius' definition up to the denial of the personal character of the separated soul.

1.2.2 EVOLUTION OF EXPRESSIONS

Among all the treatments dealing with the question whether the human soul is a person, let us identify a number of texts influenced by the *Commentary* written by Gilbert of Poitiers († 1154) on Boethius' *Contra Eutychen et Nestorium*.[143] I have examined six authors living in the twelfth century and in the first half of the thirteenth whose works are evidently dependent on one another. In addition to Gilbert's commentary, my analysis will concern the pertinent passages from

---

littera videntur falsum dicere, quod anima separata sit persona. Anima enim creata est in corpore, non extra corpus per se. Et ita creata est non ut ipsa pro se esset aliquid unum, sed ut unita corpori faceret aliquid per se unum. Et animae sanctorum naturaliter appetunt incorporari. Ergo anima separata non est persona".

[142] Hugo de S. Caro, *q. de an.* I, ed. Bieniak, p. 170[82-85].

[143] The *Commentary* was written between 1144 and 1148; cf. N.-M. Häring, "The Commentary of Gilbert, Bishop of Poitiers, on Boethius' *Contra Eutychen et Nestorium*", AH-DLMA 21 (1954), p. 244.

the *Summa "Quoniam homines"* by Alan of Lille († 1202), the *Summa* by Simon of Tournai († 1201), the *Sentences Commentary* and the question *De persona* by Stephen Langton († 1228), the *Summa aurea* by William of Auxerre († 1231) as well as the aforementioned texts by Hugh of St-Cher, i.e., his commentary on three distinctions of the *Sentences* and the disputed question *De anima*. An analysis of the terminology used in the various expositions has allowed me to establish the relations of dependency existing among the texts written by these six authors. These relations are schematically laid out in the following diagram:

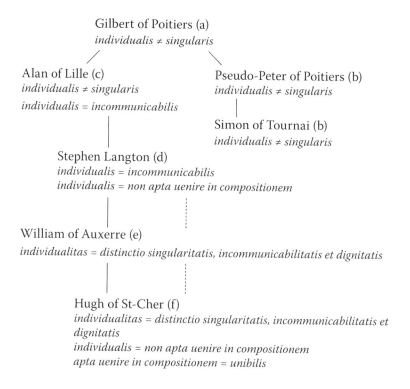

Gilbert of Poitiers (a)
individualis ≠ singularis

Alan of Lille (c)
individualis ≠ singularis
individualis = incommunicabilis

Pseudo-Peter of Poitiers (b)
individualis ≠ singularis

Simon of Tournai (b)
individualis ≠ singularis

Stephen Langton (d)
individualis = incommunicabilis
individualis = non apta uenire in compositionem

William of Auxerre (e)
individualitas = distinctio singularitatis, incommunicabilitatis et dignitatis

Hugh of St-Cher (f)
individualitas = distinctio singularitatis, incommunicabilitatis et dignitatis
individualis = non apta uenire in compositionem
apta uenire in compositionem = unibilis

1.2.2.1 Gilbert of Poitiers

Gilbert of Poitiers' argumentation centres on the distinction between the terms 'individual' and 'singular'. For the human soul is singular but not individual, because all its properties belong to another individual, i.e. man. The soul, as part of something else, may be defined as a single thing, but not as an individual. Individuality constitutes a *sine qua non* for being a person; consequently, the human soul is devoid of the character of person.[144]

---

[144] Gilb. Pict., *in C. Eut.*, ed. Häring, pp. 272-273, PL 64, 1371 D - 1373 A: "Persona est nature rationalis indiuidua substantia. Secundum hanc diffinitionem humana anima uidetur esse persona. Non enim, sicut quidam dixerunt, est endilichia - hoc est forma - sed

1.2.2.2   Pseudo-Peter of Poitiers and Simon of Tournai

There is a strong resemblance between Gilbert's text and the *Gloss* on the *Sentences* of the so-called pseudo-Peter of Poitiers, probably written between 1167 and 1175.[145] The anonymous theologian takes up Gilbert's reasoning without adding new elements. Subsequently, about 1200,[146] Simon of Tournai copies verbatim and inserts in his *Summa* the passage from the *Gloss* of Pseudo-Peter. Both authors may have had direct access to Gilbert's text; evidently, however, Simon availed himself especially of the *Gloss*:

potius substantia i.e. subsistens habens in se formas et diuersorum generum accidentia. Et est nature rationalis. Intelligit enim atque discernit - et separata a corpore et in corpore posita - usque adeo quod homo, qui ex anima constat et corpore, sicut proprio corporis statio distenditur ita propria anime potentia discernit. Est etiam cuiuslibet hominis anima - sub genere spiritus et anime specie - sua, qua ab omnibus que non sunt illa anima diuiditur, proprietate indiuidua. Sic igitur anima, que hominis est pars constitutiua, uidetur recte esse persona. Hoc tamen impossibile esse per hoc intelligitur quod nulla persona pars potest esse persone. Omnis enim persona adeo est per se una quod cuiuslibet plena et ex omnibus, que illi conueniunt, collecta proprietas cum alterius persone similiter plena et ex omnibus collecta proprietate de uno uere indiuiduo predicari non potest: ut Platonis et Ciceronis personales proprietates de uno indiuiduo dici non possunt. Tota uero anime Platonis proprietas, id est quidquid de ipsa naturaliter affirmatur, de ipso Platone predicatur (...) Hac igitur ratione Platonis tota forma - nulli neque natura conformis- uere est indiuidua. Omnis uero pars eius singularis quidem est: non autem uere indiuidua quoniam multis est saltem natura conformis. Itaque anima eius, cuius tota forma pars est forme Platonis, non uero nomine dicitur "indiuidua". Ideoque quamuis ipsa sit rationalis nature substantia, nequaquam tamen potest esse persona. Et generaliter, sicut dictum est, nulla cuiuslibet persone pars est persona quoniam partis eius ex omnibus, que ipsi conuenire intelliguntur, collecta proprietas naturaliter est diuidua".

   [145] This dating refers especially to the gloss on book I; cf. P. S. Moore, *The Works of Peter of Poitiers, Master in Theology and Chancellor of Paris (1193-1205)*, South Bend, 1936, pp. 148-151. Regarding a partial edition of the first two books of the *Gloss*, see K. Emery, "*Quaestiones, Sententiae* and *Summae* from the Later Twelfth and Early Thirteenth Centuries: The Joseph N. Garvin Papers", *Bulletin de philosophie médiévale* 48 (2006), pp. 60-63. See also M. L. Colish, "The Pseudo-Peter of Poitiers Gloss", in *Mediaeval Commentaries on the Sentences of Peter Lombard. Vol. 2*, ed. P. Rosemann, Leiden: Brill, 2010, pp. 1-33.
   [146] Cf. J. Warichez, *Les* Disputationes *de Simon de Tournai: texte inédit*, Louvain: Spicilegium sacrum lovaniense, 1932, p. XXI, n. I.

GILBERT OF POITIERS[147]

PS-PETER OF POITIERS[148]

SIMON OF TOURNAI[149]

Persona est nature rationalis indiuidua substantia. Secundum hanc diffinitionem humana anima uidetur esse persona. Non enim, sicut quidam dixerunt, est endilichia- hoc est forma- sed potius substantia i.e. subsistens habens in se formas et diuersorum generum accidentia. Et est nature rationalis. Intelligit enim atque discernit - et separata a corpore et in corpore posita - usque adeo quod homo, qui ex anima constat et corpore, sicut proprio corporis statio distenditur ita propria anime potentia discernit. (...)
Hoc tamen impossibile esse per hoc intelligitur quod nulla persona pars potest esse persone.
Omnis enim persona adeo est per se una quod cuiuslibet plena et ex omnibus, que illi conueniunt, collecta proprietas cum alterius persone similiter plena et ex omnibus collecta proprietate de uno uere indiuiduo predicari non potest: ut Platonis et Ciceronis personales proprietates de uno indiuiduo dici non possunt.
Tota uero anime Platonis proprietas, id est quidquid de ipsa naturaliter affirmatur, de ipso Platone predicatur.

Boetius in libro De duabus naturis et una persona Christi personam describit, dicens: "Persona est racionabilis nature individua essencia". Secundum hanc diffinitionem humana anima videtur esse persona. Non enim, licet quidam dixerunt, est endelichia, id est forma, sed pocius substancia habens in se fomas et diversorum generum accidencia. Est etiam anima nature racionabilis. Intelligit enim atque discernit et separata a corpore et in corpore posita.

Sed quia nulla persona est pars persone, anima autem est pars persone, anima ergo non est persona. Licet enim sit substancia nature racionabilis, non tamen est individua individuali proprietate, ab omni alia re diversa sed singularis. Omne enim individuum est singulare et omnis forma individualis forma est singularis sed non convertitur. (...)
Anima vero Platonis nullius proprietatis participio differt a Platone. Omnis enim proprietas partis est tocius sed non quevis tocius statim partis intelligitur esse.

Boethius in libro De duabus naturis et una persona Christi personam describit dicens: "Persona est naturae rationalis individua substantia". Secundum hanc definitionem humana anima videtur esse persona. Non enim, licet quidam dixerint, est entelechia, id est forma, sed substantia potius habens in se formas et diversorum generum accidentia. Est etiam naturae rationalis. Intellegit enim atque discernit et separata et in corpore posita usque adeo, quod homo, qui ex corpore constat et anima, sicut distenditur spatio corporis, ita propria animae potentia discernit. Sed quoniam nulla persona pars personae, anima autem personae pars, anima non est persona. Sed anima, licet sit substantia naturae rationalis, tamen non est individua, sed singularis.
Refert enim inter singulare et individuum, inter singularem proprietatem et individualem, cum omne individuum singulare sit, sed non convertitur. (...)
Anima vero Platonis nullius proprietatis participio differt a Platone. Omnis enim proprietas partis est totius. Nam quidquid est in parte, et in toto.

---

[147] Cf. *supra*, p. 49, n. 144.

[148] Ps. Peter of Poitiers, *Glossa* in I *Sententiarum*, 9, 1, in J. N. Garvin, *Papers*, University of Notre Dame Archives, CGRV 4/6, pp. 105-106; *Paris, Bibl. Nat. lat. 14423*, f. 49[ra-rb].

[149] Sim. Torn., *sum.*, n. 2, ed. Schmaus, pp. 60-61. On the conception of person in Simon, see M. Schmaus, "Die Trinitätslehre des Simons von Tournai", *RTAM* 3 (1931), pp. 373-396, especially pp. 376-377.

1.2.2.3 Alan of Lille

Alan of Lille too is inspired by Gilbert's *Commentary*. Indeed, in his *Summa* he
writes that the soul does not constitute an individual of a species, although – as a
single thing – it belongs to a species. For this reason, we should not confuse that
which is individual with that which is single, because all individual things are also
single, but if a single thing is a part of an individual, then the thing itself is not individual. The distinction between '*singularis*' and '*individualis*' reappears in Alan
too. Yet, his exposition adds some new elements to those found in Gilbert's *Commentary*. In particular, the summa *Quoniam homines* contains the term '*natura
communicabilis*'. According to Alan, the soul is "communicable" since its nature
is part of the human individual; in other words, the nature of the soul is totally
included in another nature, hence it is a part. For the soul has a natural tendency
to be united with the body in order to form the human being; therefore it is not
individual. Actually, in Alan's view, the concept of individuality is part of the definition of 'person' to exclude those realities that are *communicabilia* in fact or by
nature. The soul is an example of a reality of this kind.[150]

---

[150] Alan. de Ins., *sum. quon.* I, n. 34-35, in P. Glorieux, "La somme Quoniam homines d'Alain de Lille", *AHDLMA* 20 (1953), pp. 172-174: "Per hoc quod sequitur «individua»
removetur ab eis que comunicabilia sunt, id est que non sunt per se sed sunt de alio, ut
anima. (...) Unde anima cum veniat in constitutione hominis, non est individua, id est valde
divisa cum sit de alio; nec proprius eius status potest dici individuum cum non valde di-
vidat animam ab omni re, quia natura partis est natura totius; quoniam sicut substantia
anime cedit in substantiam hominis, ita omnis natura anime in natura totius. (...) Ergo cum
proprius status anime sit etiam status hominis, eam non dividit ab omni re. Itaque nec
ipse proprie potest dici individuum, nec anima proprie individua. Que quamvis post dissolutionem separetur a corpore, tamen natura communicabilis est; et ita non est individua;
quamvis enim separetur actu, tamen eius natura exigit ut uniatur corpori; unde et naturaliter desiderat unionem corpori. Per hoc ergo quod persona dicitur individua, separatur
ab eis que sunt actu vel natura communicabilia, ut ab anima. Per hoc vero quod sequitur
«nature rationalis», separatur a non rationali. (...) Sunt tamen qui dicunt animam post dissolutionem esse personam. Quod sic probatur: anima post dissolutionem est res per se una,
quia ulli unita. Ergo res individua. Ergo cum sit nature rationalis, est persona. (...) Item si
anima modo est persona et prius non erat persona, accidentale est anime esse persona. |
Item in natura anime est ut non sit per se sed de alio; et ita anima natura non est individua;
et ita natura non est persona. Ergo si est persona, contra naturam est persona. (...) Prem-
issis rationibus ducti, dicimus quod anima nec unita nec separata a corpore est individua
vel persona. (...) Tercie vero respondentes dicimus quod hec anima non est individuum
alicuius speciei, quamvis sit singulare alicuius, nisi forte individuum summatur pro singulari. Et secundum hoc erit instantia in equivoco si dicitur: est individuum alicuius speciei; ergo est individua; ut si dicamus cathinus est genus thebanorum; ergo est genus. Ad
quartum vero opinionem respondimus quod in natura hominis est ut sit persona, quia non
est ut sit persona, quia non est natura communicabilis; et ideo cum homo per se existat et
non sit de alio, debet iudicari persona. Anima vero non, cuius natura exigit unionem". The

1.2.2.4 Stephen Langton

Alan's *Summa* strongly influenced the work of Stephen Langton. The latter approaches the problem of the soul-person in at least two writings,[151] namely, the *Commentary* on book I of the *Sentences*[152] and a disputed question entitled *De persona*.[153] In Langton's texts there are some typical features clearly deriving from

Summa was probably written between 1159 and 1180; cf. R. Quinto, "Alanus de Insulis" in *Grundriss der Geschichte der Philosophie (Begründet von Friedrich Ueberweg). Die Philosophie des Mittelalters, Band 2: 12. Jahrhundert*, ed. R. Imbach et T. Ricklin, Basel: Schwabe, forthcoming; L. O. Nielsen, *Theology and Philosophy in the Twelfth Century. A Study on Gilbert Porreta's Thinking and the Theological Exposition of the Doctrine of the Incarnation during the Period 1130-1180*, Leiden: Brill, 1982, pp. 342-343, n. 227; M.-T. d'Alverny, *Alain de Lille, Textes inédits, avec une introduction sur sa vie et ses oeuvres*, Paris: Vrin, 1965, p. 64.

[151] On the concept of 'person' within a Trinitarian and Christological context, see also Langton's *Summa* in S. Ebbesen - L. B. Mortensen, "A Partial Edition of Stephens Langton's Summa and Quaestiones with Parallels from Andrew Sunesen's Hexaemeron", CIMAGL 49 (1985), pp. 124-134; L. O. Nielsen, "Logic and the Hypostatic Union: Two Late Twelfth-Century Responses to the Papal Condemnation of 1177", in S. Ebbesen - R. L. Friedman (ed.), *Medieval Analyses in Language and cognition. Acts of the symposium; The Copenhagen School of Medieval Philosophy, January 10-13, 1996*, Copenhagen: Det Kongelige Danske Videnskabernes Selskab, 1999, pp. 251-277. The passage from the *Summa* is clearly composed later than the theological question because on two occasions it refers to it using the formulas «alias dictum est» and «alibi dictum est»; cf. Steph. Langt., *sum.*, ed. Ebbesen - Mortensen, pp. 124; 129; Bieniak, "La place d'Étienne Langton", forthcoming. There exists another text about the person, which is part of an anonymous *summa* one of whose manuscripts attributes the text to Stephen Langton, but which is certainly spurious, i.e. the *Summa "Breves dies hominis"* (*Bamberg, Staatsbibliothek, Patr. 136*, 1rb-2rb; *Oxford, Bodleian Library, Laud. Misc. 80*, 117vb-118ra). The *summa* was probably composed by a contemporary of Peter of Poitiers before 1210, or perhaps before 1177, and does not rely on Langton's texts; cf. R. Quinto, *"Doctor Nominatissimus". Stefano Langton († 1228) e la tradizione delle sue opere*, Münster: Aschendorff, 1994 (B. G. Ph. Th. M., N. F. 39), pp. 43-53. The *summa* does not mention the anthropological aspect of the concept of 'person'. I am grateful to Riccardo Quinto for allowing me to consult the transcription he made of this passage.

[152] Steph. Langt., *in* I *Sent.*, d. 26, ed. Landgraf, pp. 26-27. The *Commentary* was written before 1215, perhaps even before 1207; cf. *ibidem*, XXXIII-XXXIV. As regards the dating, see also the contributions of Claire Angotti and Riccardo Quinto in the volume *Étienne Langton. Predicateur, bibliste et théologien, Colloque international 13-15 septembre 2006, Paris, Centre d'études du Saulchoir*, EPHE-CNRS, ed. L.-J. Bataillon - N. Bériou - G. Dahan - R. Quinto, Brepols, Turnhout, forthcoming, as well as the contribution of Riccardo Quinto in *Mediaeval Commentaries on the Sentences of Peter Lombard. Vol. 2*, ed. P. Rosemann, Brill, Leiden, 2010 pp. 35-78.

[153] Cf. *infra*. The theological questions probably date from Langton's later teaching years, which came to an end in 1206; moreover, as Sten Ebbesen points out, some of the questions were written before 1195, since they exerted an influence on Anders Sunesen's *Hexaemeron*; cf. Ebbesen - Mortensen, "A Partial Edition of Stephen Langton's Summa",

Alan of Lille's argumentation, among which is included the term '*incommunicabilis*'. A person, i.e. an individual substance, must be *incommunicabilis*, namely, it cannot be "apta uenire in compositionem". Indeed, to be individual does not only entail not being a part of something else, but entails above all the lack of an *aptitudo*, i.e. of the tendency to be a part of a composite to form something else.[154] Furthermore, it should be noted that Stephen Langton leaves out the opposition between '*individualis*' and '*singularis*', which was fundamental for the argumentations elaborated by Gilbert, Pseudo-Peter of Poitiers and Simon.[155]

1.2.2.5 William of Auxerre

Langton's work, in its turn, exerts an influence on William of Auxerre's *Summa aurea*.[156] William makes a synthesis of the doctrines elaborated by his predecessors.[157] Indeed, in his *Summa*[158] he writes that in order for a substance to be indi-

pp. 25-26. The dating of the theological questions has been studied by Riccardo Quinto as well, "La constitution du texte des Questiones", in *Étienne Langton. Predicateur*, forthcoming; cf. L. Antl, "An Introduction to the *Quaestiones Theologicae* of Stephen Langton", FS 12 (1952), p. 170. Some typical features of the question *De persona* reappear in Andr. Sun., *hexaem.* II, ed. Ebbesen - Mortensen, pp. 106[1023]-107[1061]; cf. S. Ebbesen, "Addenda to Gertz Commentarius", in Andr. Sun., *hexaem.*, ed. Ebbesen - Mortensen, pp. 445-449.

[154] On the '*persona*' problem in Langton's question, see M. Bieniak, "La place d'Étienne Langton dans le débat sur le concept de 'persona'", in *Étienne Langton. Predicateur*, forthcoming; R. Heinzmann, *Die Unsterblichkeit der Seele und die Auferstehung des Leibes*, Münster: Aschendorff, 1965 (B. G. Ph. Th. M., 40.3), pp. 137-138.

[155] Steph. Langt., *de pers.*, ed. Bieniak, pp. 100[170]-101[101]: "Magister tamen in Sententiis dicit quod anima dum est in corpore non est persona, set dum est extra corpus est persona, quia tunc, ut dicit, est substantia indiuidua; quod non concedimus, quia hoc nomen 'indiuidua' in illa descriptione non solum priuat actum componendi, set etiam aptitudinem, et ita cum anima extra corpus posita sit apta uenire in compositionem, non est tunc substantia indiuidua, quare nec persona, nec esse potest»; cf. id., *in* I *Sent.*, d. 26, ed. Landgraf, 26-27: «Et <hoc nomen 'substantia'> secundum quod ponitur in descriptione hac <Boetii>, convenit cum omnibus rebus primi predicamenti. Per hoc 'rationale' dividitur ab aliis rebus primi predicamenti, que non sunt rationalia. Per hoc 'individua' ab animabus, que sunt substantie rationales, set non sunt individue, quoniam non incommunicabiles, et ideo non sunt persone. Communicantur enim eo modo, quo communicatur pars a toto. (...) Et nota quod hoc nomen 'individua' notat aptitudinem in actum, id est non communicabilem. Et hoc dico propter animam, que est communicabilis, ut pars a toto".

[156] The *Summa* probably dates from the first half of the 1220s and was certainly composed before 1226; cf. J. Arnold, *Perfecta Communicatio. Die Trinitätstheologie Wilhelms von Auxerre*, Münster: Aschendorff, 1995 (B. G. Ph. Th. M., N. F., 42), pp. 10-16.

[157] Cf. Heinzmann, *Die Unsterblichkeit*, pp. 144-146.

[158] Guill. Altissiod., *sum. aur.* I, 4, c. 1, ed. J. Ribaillier, Editiones Collegii S. Bonaventurae ad Claras Aquas Grottaferrata, Roma 1982, pp. 81[81]-82[98]: "Item videtur, quod anima secundum huius diffinitionem sit persona, quia anima est distincta substantia suis accidentibus, et ita substantia individua. Et constat, quod est rationalis naturae. Ergo anima

vidual, it must possess three characteristics: *distinctio singularitatis*,[159] *distinctio incommunicabilitatis*[160] and *distinctio dignitatis*.[161]

1.2.2.6 Hugh of St-Cher

The threefold distinction made by William, i.e., the distinction of singularity, incommunicability and dignity, became classic for all thirteenth-century authors. Among them was also Hugh of St-Cher. The overwhelming influence exerted by the *Summa aurea* becomes evident in Hugh's commentary on almost all the distinctions of the *Sentences*.[162] In this respect, the discussion about the person is no different: indeed, Hugh, in his commentary on distinction 25 of book I of the *Sen-*

---

est rationalis naturae individua substantia. Ergo est persona. Contra: Anima non est per se una. Ergo non est persona. Solutio: Ad praesens notandum est, quod duplex est distinctio. Est enim distinctio singularitatis, quae opponitur universalitati. Quae distinctio constat ex proprietatibus, quas in nullo alio est reperire. Et hanc distinctionem vocat hoc nomen substantia, positum in illa diffinitione. Est etiam distinctio incommunicabilitatis, qua aliquid non potest communicari ut pars. Ex hoc patet, quod non est ibi repetitio eiusdem, quoniam alia est distinctio, quae notatur per hoc nomen individua. Primam distinctionem habet anima, secundam non. Ipsa non est substantia individua, secundum quod nomen individua sumitur in illa diffinitione. Et ita patet, quod anima non est persona. Est etiam tertia distinctio, quae notatur per hoc nomen individua. Quae impedit, ne Christus secundum quod homo sit persona»; cf. *ibidem*, III, 1, c. 3, q. 8, ed. Ribaillier, 36[53]-37[69]: «Solutio. Dicimus quod re vera Ihesus in quantum Ihesus non est persona. Ad hoc enim quod aliquid sit persona, exigitur triplex determinatio: scilicet distinctio singularitatis que est in anima Socratis et in Socrate, que singulari sua existentia differt a qualibet re alia, qua etiam distinguitur ab universali. Et distinctio incommunicabilitatis, que est in Socrate ex eo quod non est communicabilis ut pars, quoniam non convenit ut pars in compositum cum alio; et talis distinctio non est in anima vel corpore; et ideo nec anima nec corpus persona est proprie, quia non est "per se unum" vel "per se sonans", sicut dicit Boetius in libro de duabus Naturis et una Persona Christi. Nichil enim horum est persona, ut ibi dicit. Tertia distinctio est distinctio dignitatis, que est in Socrate, ex eo quod eius humanitas non est commixta digniori forme in eo (...). Sed ultima distinctio non est in Ihesu secundum quod Ihesus, quoniam iesuitas coniungitur digniori forme in Filio Dei; et ita non distinguitur a digniori".

[159] Cf. *infra*, chap. 1.2.3.1.

[160] Cf. *infra*, chap. 1.2.3.3 and 1.2.3.4.

[161] Cf. Boeth., *c. Eut.*, c. 3, ed. Moreschini, pp. 217[235]-218[239], PL 64, 1344 D: "Quare autem de inrationabilibus animalibus Graecus ὑπόστασιν non dicat, sicut nos de eisdem nomen substantiae praedicamus, haec ratio est, quoniam nomen hoc melioribus applicatum est, ut aliqua id quod est excellentius".

[162] Cf. K. L. Lynch, "Some Fontes of the Commentary of Hugh de Saint Cher: William of Auxerre, Guy d'Orchelles, Alexander of Hales", *FS* 13 (1953), pp. 119-146; Landgraf, *Introduction*, p. 175; M. Bieniak, "The *Sentences* Commentary of Hugh of St.-Cher", in *Mediaeval Commentaries on the Sentences of Peter Lombard. Vol. 2*, ed. P. Rosemann, Leiden: Brill, 2010, pp. 130-131.

tences, copies verbatim the exposition elaborated by William of the three conditions that are necessary in order to speak of an individual substance.[163] Therefore, it is primarily under the influence of William's text that Hugh comes to define the soul as "communicable", hence as a substance which is not individual and lacks the character of a person.[164]

In the other work of Hugh at issue here – the question *De anima* – there also appears the term *aptitudo*, which is used in a very similar context in Stephen Langton's question *De persona*.[165] Indeed, whereas William of Auxerre does not consider the personal character of the separated soul, Hugh, like Langton, discusses extensively and in several contexts the problem whether the separated soul is a person. The discussion of the same problem and the presence of the same solution in the works of both theologians are accompanied by an analogous sentence structure and a similar lexicon. Indeed, Hugh and Stephen contrast the act of uniting with the suitability or aptitude for uniting with the body; moreover, in both treatments, the term 'aptitudo' plays a determining role:

---

[163] The soul-person doctrine in Hugh's Commentary on the *Sentences* has been studied by L.-B. Gillon, "La noción de persona en Hugo de San Caro", *Ciencia Tomista* 64 (1943), pp. 171-177, and by Principe, *Hugh of Saint-Cher's Theology*, pp. 47-48, pp. 84-88.

[164] Hugo de S. Caro, *in* I *Sent.* I, d. 25, ed. Breuning, pp. 384-385: "Item. Secundum hoc uidetur quod anima sit persona, quia anima est rationalis nature indiuidua substantia, ergo est persona. Contra: anima non est per se una, ergo non est persona. (...) Ad id quod obicitur, notandum quod triplex est distinctio, scilicet: singularitatis, que opponitur uniuersalitati; et distinctio incommunicabilitatis, que opponitur partialitati; et dignitatis, et hec opponitur inferioritati. Hec triplex distinctio exigitur ad esse persone. Primam non habent uniuersalia, et ideo nullum uniuersale persona est. Secundam non habet anima: anima enim creata est similiter communicabilis alii ad faciendum totum, et ideo anima non est persona. Terciam non habet Christus in quantum homo, quia humanitas Christi non obtinet dignitatem in Christo, set proprietas qua est filius dei, et illa facit eum esse personam; et ideo Christus in quantum homo non est persona. Primam distinctionem significat hoc nomen 'substantia' in diffinitione persone; secundam et terciam hoc nomen 'indiuidua', et ita patet quod non est ibi nugatio; per hoc idem patet quare anima non sit persona". A similar exposition appears in another work influenced by William of Auxerre, i.e. the *Summa* written by Roland of Cremona, III, 16. 18, ed. A. Cortesi, Bergamo: Edizioni Monumenta Bergomensia, 1962, pp. 52-53.

[165] Cf. *supra*, p. 54, n. 155. It should also be noted that William too uses a similar expression: "anima (...) apta est nata vivificare corpus"; cf. *supra*, p. 22. On the influence exerted by Stephen Langton on Hugh, see D. Van den Eynde, "Stephen Langton and Hugh of St. Cher on the causality of the Sacraments", *FS* 11 (1951), pp. 141-155; cf. R. Quinto, "Hugh of St.-Cher's Use of Stephen Langton", in *Medieval Analyses in Language and Cognition*, pp. 281-300.

HUGH OF ST-CHER	STEPHEN LANGTON
'regens' non dicit actum,	hoc nomen 'indiuidua' (...) non solum priuat actum componendi,
sed aptitudinem secundum quam anima apta est naturaliter regere corpus	set etiam aptitudinem, et ita cum anima extra corpus posita sit apta uenire in compositionem non est tunc substantia indiuidua

Hugh's thought reveals its proximity to Langton's question also with respect to another typical feature. Indeed, in the commentary on the second distinction of book III of the *Sentences*, Hugh adopts Langton's argumentation about the possibility that Christ had assumed the nature of soul.[166]

Hence, it is not excluded that Hugh had a direct knowledge of Stephen Langton's question *De persona* and was influenced by it.

* * *

The theory that the human soul is not a person is deeply rooted in twelfth-century theology: It seems to me that this is firmly demonstrated by the analysis presented above. From Gilbert of Poitiers onwards, theologians seem to be unanimous. However, the evolution that the position underwent does not only concern the terminology used in the texts. From Gilbert to Hugh, the change affects not only formulas but also some important aspects of the doctrine. The deeper transformation concerns the anthropological dimension of the problem, i.e., the conception of the ontological status of the human soul and of its relationship with the body. The following sections seek – first of all – to present the way in which this conception undergoes an evolution in the different texts and – secondly – to identify those factors that possibly influenced this transformation.

---

[166] Hugo de S. Caro, *in* III *Sent.*, d. 2, ed. Principe, p. 166[85-89]: "<Christus> potuit enim assumere naturam angeli, sed noluit. Sed naturam animae non potuit assumere sine carne: anima enim a principio suae creationis habet, ut sit pars, unde anima separata naturaliter appetit incorporari; inde est quod anima non est persona".

1.2.3 "THE SEPARATED SOUL IS NOT A PERSON". CONTROVERSIES AND MISUNDERSTANDINGS

1.2.3.1 From the question of universals to the individuality of the soul: Gilbert of Poitiers[167]

Fundamentally, the whole discussion about the soul-person centres on the concept of individuality. "Persona est nature rationalis indiuidua substantia":[168] an accurate definition of the concept of individuality is therefore necessary in order to determine the actual range of the notion of 'person'. Indeed, in his *Commentary* on Boethius' *Contra Eutychen et Nestorium*, Gilbert discusses extensively the meaning of the four notions contained in Boethius' definition; moreover, a passage is devoted in particular to nature and individuality. Let us ignore here the discussion about the first of these concepts. Rather, let us seek to determine the meaning Gilbert attributes to the second notion. First of all, it is therefore necessary to reflect briefly on Boethius' doctrine of individuality.

Boethius does not introduce the concept of individuality into his definition of 'person' in order to negate the personal character of souls. Indeed, in *Contra Eutychen et Nestorium*, he does not address the problem whether the human soul is a person: in his view, "individual" is chiefly opposed to "universal".[169] Hence, the need to point out that persons must be individual results above all from Boethius' conception of universals, namely, from a realist conception. The universal, i.e.

---

[167] I sincerely thank Luisa Valente for giving me very useful advice.

[168] Boeth., *c. Eut.*, c. 3, ed. Moreschini, p. 214[171-172], PL 64, 1343 C-D.

[169] Boeth., *c. Eut.*, c. 2, ed. Moreschini, p. 214[153], PL 64, 1343 B-C: "Rursus substantiarum aliae sunt universales, aliae particulares. Universales sunt quae de singulis praedicantur, ut homo, animal, lapis, lignum ceteraque huiusmodi quae vel genera vel species sunt; nam et homo de singulis hominibus et animal de singulis animalibus lapisque ac lignum de singulis lapidibus ac lignis dicuntur. Particularia vero sunt quae de aliis minime praedicantur, ut Cicero, Plato, lapis hic unde haec Achillis statua facta est, lignum hoc unde haec mensa composita est. Sed in his omnibus nusquam in universalibus persona dici potest, sed in singularibus tantum atque in individuis: animalis enim vel generalis hominis nulla persona est, sed vel Ciceronis vel Platonis vel singulorum individuorum personae singulae nuncupantur". In *Contra Eutychen et Nestorium*, the terms *individualis* and *singularis* are used interchangeably, even though some expressions suggest that individual realities constitute a subset of the singular ones. In none of his works does Boethius explicitly distinguish between these concepts; exclusively in his *Categories Commentary* does he introduce a difference between individuality and particularity: the first is defined as indivisibility into species or into other individuals, whereas the second means nonpredicability. Moreover, in Boethius' thought, the relationship between individuality and numerical difference remains unclear; cf. J. J. E. Gracia, *Introduction to the Problem of Individuation in the Early Middle Ages*, München – Wien: Philosophia Verlag - Catholic University of America Press, 1984, p. 100.

genus or species, is a substance. Let us here leave out the relationship between this universal substance and the individual substance: this complicated problem is unimportant for the question at hand.[170] As concerns the issue debated here, it should just be noted that an explicit exclusion of universals while dealing with the notion of the person would be meaningless in a nominalist framework. If no extra-mental reality corresponded to universal concepts, then it would be enough to define the person as a substance having a rational nature, without necessarily introducing the individuality notion.

Yet, bearing in mind the realist character of Boethius' position, it should be noted that the definition of the universal and the singular presented in *Contra Eutychen et Nestorium* concerns especially the logical, more than the metaphysical dimension of the two concepts. For universal notions are those notions which can be predicated of more than one singular reality, for example 'man', which can be predicated of Socrates, Plato, Cicero, etc. By contrast, particular terms, i.e. singular or individual terms, cannot be predicated of any other individual, because there are no individuals belonging to the species 'Plato' or 'Cicero'. As Jorge Gracia points out,[171] Boethius never in his entire work clearly discriminates between the epistemological and the metaphysical aspect of the individuality problem. In general, however, as revealed by his *De interpretatione Commentary*,[172] the distinction of nonpredicability is mainly related to the logical field, whereas the second concept, i.e. incommunicability, that Boethius uses more rarely, concerns the metaphysical aspect of the problem.

---

[170] In most cases, Boethius appears to hold that particular things share, in an integral and simultaneous way, one universal substance, which is individuated mainly by accidents; cf. Boeth., *In Isag.*, ed. Schepss - Brandt, CSEL 48, pp. 162²³-163³: "Genus uero secundum nullum horum modum commune esse speciebus potest; nam ita commune esse debet, ut et totum sit in singulis et uno tempore et eorum quorum commune est, constituere ualeat et formare substantiam"; *ibidem*, 200.5-7: "...quae enim unicuique indiuiduo forma est, ea non ex substantiali quadam forma species, sed ex accidentibus uenit", p. 241⁹⁻¹⁰, p. 271¹⁸⁻²⁰; Ch. Erismann, "Alain de Lille, la métaphysique érigénienne et la pluralité des formes", in *Alain de Lille, le Docteur Universel. Actes du XIeme Colloque intérnational de la Société Internationale pour l'Etude de la Philosophie Médiévale, Paris 23-25 octobre 2003*, ed. J.-L. Solère - A. Vasiliu - A. Galonnier, Turnhout: Brepols, 2005, pp. 25-26. Elsewhere, however, Boethius maintains that accidents are individual through the substance in which they are; cf. Boeth., *in Cat.*, I, c. 2 PL 64, pp. 169-172; Gracia, *Introduction to the Problem of Individuation*, pp. 63-107, in particular pp. 82-88, p. 100.

[171] *Introduction to the Problem of Individuation*, pp. 90-91, p. 110.

[172] Boeth., *in De int.*, PL 64, 319, pp. 462-464; cf. Gracia, *Introduction to the Problem of Individuation*, pp. 90-91.

In commenting on *Contra Eutychen et Nestorium*, Gilbert considerably modifies Boethius' definition of universals.[173] On the one hand, Gilbert still uses the concept of nonpredicability but, on the other, the fundamental opposition between the universal and the singular is replaced by the contrast between the singular and the individual. Gilbert states that universal notions are "plures secundum se", i.e., each universal is correlated to many singular substances. Indeed, a few lines later we read that: "Quidquid est, singulare est".[174] Gilbert's conception of universals is based on this assertion. For there cannot exist a unique substance shared by more than one individual thing, individuated by accidents alone. Universals do exist, but this does not mean that one and the same substance is present in many individuals; rather, it means that there are many single substantial forms that are similar to each other. It should be noted that this is no nominalist conception. According to Gilbert, universal concepts are correlated to actual realities, i.e. to single substantial forms. Now, the fact that these substantial forms can be called universals depends on their being similar to each other. Hence, the universal is based on the "substantialis forme similitudo", i.e. on similarity. How is this *similitudo* defined? Gilbert explains it through predicability:[175]

> Singularium nanque alia aliis sunt tota proprietate sua inter se similia. Que simul omnia conformitatis huius ratione dicuntur "unum diuiduum": ut diuersorum corporum diuerse qualitates tota sua specie equales. Alia uero ab aliis omnibus aliqua sue proprietatis parte dissimilia. (...)
>
> Omnis enim persona adeo est per se una quod cuiuslibet plena et ex omnibus, que illi conueniunt, collecta proprietas cum alterius persone similiter plena et ex omnibus collecta proprietate de uno uere indiuiduo predicari non potest: ut Platonis et Ciceronis personales proprietates de uno indiuiduo dici non possunt.
>
> Tota uero anime Platonis proprietas, id est quidquid de ipsa naturaliter affirmatur, de ipso Platone predicatur. (...)

---

[173] Gilb. Pict., *in C. Eut.*, ed. Häring, p. 269, PL 64, 1370 C-D: "Sed attende quod, cum superius subsistentes tantum et solis naturalibus, nunc et subsistentes et subsistentias rationalibus atque topicis differentiis diuidit et ait: RURSUS SUBSTANTIARUM ALIAE SUNT UNIVERSALES substantialis forme similitudine: ALIE sunt PARTICULARES, i. e. indiuidue plenarum proprietatum dissimilitudine. Que uero sunt universales queue particulares, descriptionibus et exemplis demonstrat, dicens: UNIVERSALES SUNT QUE plures secundum se totas inter se suis effectibus similes DE pluribus SINGULIS subsistentibus inter se uere similibus PREDICANTUR: UT HOMO ANIMAL LAPIS LIGNUM CETERAQUE HUIUSMODI QUE quantum ad subsistentias, que horum nominum sunt qualitates, UEL GENERA SUNT, ut animal lapis lignum UEL SPECIES ut homo".

[174] Gilb. Pict., *in C. Eut.*, ed. Häring, p. 270, PL 64, 1371 B.

[175] Gilb. Pict., *in C. Eut.*, ed. Häring, p. 270, p. 272, p. 274, PL 64, 1371 B, 1372 A-D.

Unde Platonis ex omnibus, que illi conueniunt, collecta proprietas nulli neque actu neque natura conformis est: nec Plato per illam. Albedo uero ipsius et quecumue pars proprietatis eius aut natura et actu aut saltem natura intelligitur esse conformis. Ideoque nulla pars proprietatis cuiuslibet creature naturaliter est indiuidua quamuis ratione singularitatis "indiuidua" sepe uocetur.

Illa uero cuiuslibet proprietas, que naturali dissimilitudine ab omnibus - que actu uel potestate fuerunt uel sunt uel futura sunt - differt, non modo "singularis" aut "particularis" sed etiam "indiuidua" uere et uocatur et est.

Nam "indiuidua" dicuntur huiusmodi quoniam unumquodque eorum ex talibus consistit proprietatibus quarum omnium cogitatione facta collectio nunquam in alio quolibet alterutrius numero particularium naturali conformitate eadem erit.

A universal concept is therefore a concept that signifies a property of a singular substance similar to the property of another singular substance. Further, the property of a substance is similar to another property if it can be entirely predicated of another substance. Likewise, the definition of the individual is based on the concept of predicability. For individual substances are those singular substances whose "tota proprietas" (i.e. the whole of the characteristics that can be predicated of a substance according to its nature) cannot be predicated of another substance. Now, the whole *proprietas* of a part of an individual can be predicated of the individual itself too; hence, no reality constituting a part of an individual can be individual.

Predicability is thus the connection between the universal and the soul. Yet, it remains certain that whereas the universal concept itself is predicated of a substance, the soul is not predicated as such, but it is its *tota proprietas* which is predicated. Indeed, according to Gilbert, a single soul is not the substantial form of man and is not a universal. For the soul *has* forms of its own and belongs to a genus and a species different from those to which the whole man belongs. But the soul has a characteristic that makes it similar to the universal: all its properties can be predicated of another singular substance, i.e. of man. Hence, the soul is not a person because "nulla persona pars potest esse personae".[176]

---

[176] Gilb. Pict., *in C. Eut.*, ed. Häring, p. 272, PL 64, 1372 A: "Persona est nature rationalis individva substantia. Secundum hanc diffinitionem humana anima uidetur esse persona. Non enim, sicut quidam dixerunt, est endilichia - hoc est forma - sed potius substantia i.e. subsistens habens in se formas et diuersorum generum accidentia. Et est nature rationalis. Intelligit enim atque discernit - et separata a corpore et in corpore posita - usque adeo quod homo, qui ex anima constat et corpore, sicut proprio corporis spatio distenditur ita propria anime potentia discernit. Est etiam cuiuslibet hominis anima - sub genere spiritus et anime specie - sua, qua ab omnibus que non sunt illa anima diuiditur, proprietate indiuidua. Sic igitur anima, que hominis est pars constitutiua, uidetur recte esse persona. Hoc

According to Gilbert, just as a universal concept designates a multiplicity of singular – but not individual – forms, so the soul possesses a form which is singular but not individual. It should be noted, however, that whereas a universal concept can be predicated of many because it denotes a *collectio* of forms which are similar to each other, the *tota proprietas* of the soul can be predicated of man not just by virtue of a similarity, but also by virtue of an identity: indeed, the rationality of Peter's soul is identical to Peter's rationality. In any event, it can be affirmed that, in Gilbert's *Commentary*, the 'predicability' concept, which is more properly reserved to universals, is utilized with respect to the soul too. (It is the concept of predicability that represents the key to understanding the fundamental difference between Gilbert's exposition and the argumentation developed by Alan of Lille in his *Summa "Quoniam homines"*).

What is in fact Gilbert's anthropological view? It might seem that he denies the personal character of the soul because he considers its nature as incomplete, intrinsically partial and always ready for union with the body. Yet, Gilbert's intention is in no manner to question the traditional dualist view of man. First of all, the reader is impressed by his manifest rejection of the Aristotelian theory. The soul is not *endilichia* or *forma*[177] but is truly a substance possessing its own forms and accidents. Indeed, it is through the generic form that the soul belongs to the genus "spirit", and it is through the specific form that it belongs to its species, i.e. the species "soul". Further, Gilbert does not even mention the soul's desire for union with the body. In addition, the soul is capable of knowing even after the separation from the body, as Gilbert explicitly states. It is therefore an independent substance. How can this view be reconciled with the negation of the personal character of the soul? If the nature of Plato's soul constitutes a part of the nature of Plato himself, should not we deduce that this nature is incomplete in itself?

Gilbert answers this question in an implicit manner:[178]

Tota uero anime Platonis proprietas – i. e. quicquid de ipsa naturaliter affirmatur - de ipso Platone predicatur. "Naturaliter" dicimus quoniam, quod non naturaliter de anima dicitur, non necesse est de Platone predicari: ut topica

---

tamen impossibile esse per hoc intelligitur quod nulla persona pars potest esse persone. Omnis enim persona adeo est per se una quod cuiuslibet plena et ex omnibus, que illi conueniunt, collecta proprietas cum alterius persone similiter plena et ex omnibus collecta proprietate de uno uere indiuiduo predicari non potest: ut Platonis et Ciceronis personales proprietates de uno indiuiduo dici non possunt. Tota uero anime Platonis proprietas, id est quidquid de ipsa naturaliter affirmatur, de ipso Platone predicatur".

[177] NB: Unlike some theologians of the first half of the thirteenth century, Gilbert does not distinguish between '*endilichia*' and '*forma*'. In this case, his interpretation of the Aristotelian definition seems to be more correct than the Avicennian one.

[178] Gilb. Pict., *in C. Eut.*, ed. Häring, p. 272, PL 64, 1372 A-B.

ratio, qua Platonis anima "pars" eius uocatur, de ipso Platone minime dicitur. Dicimus etiam "affirmatur" quia, quod ab anima Platonis negatur, non necesse est ab ipso negari: ut si dicatur anima esse incorporea, quo priuatorio nomine corporum subsistentia, que est corporalitas, remouetur ab ea, non ideo Plato incorporeus esse dicitur. Et sic quidem humana anima secundum predictam diffinitionem uidetur esse: secundum expositam uero rationem uidetur non esse persona.

Indeed, one might object: not all properties of the soul can be predicated of man, since we can affirm that Plato's soul constitutes a part of Plato but we cannot in the least affirm the same of Plato himself; consequently, the soul would have the distinction of 'nonpredicability' and would thus be a person. Gilbert answers that the argument is not valid because the only relevant characteristics are those which can be affirmed of the soul according to its nature. We may therefore conclude that, according to him, being a part of man does not belong to the nature of the soul. How can we justify this view?

In fact, the objection mentioned above rests on a fallacy. For Gilbert identifies "being a part" with having a nature totally enclosed by another nature. The statement that "being a part" belongs to the nature of the part is therefore contradictory. The same idea can be expressed in terms of "predicability" too: the thing A constitutes a part of the thing B, if all properties of thing A can be predicated of thing B as well. Hence, the statement that "being a part" constitutes a property of thing A means confusing language and its contents, i.e. meta-language and language.

Consequently, when Gilbert affirms that 'being a part' does not belong to the nature of the soul, he does so chiefly as a logician, not as a philosopher engaged in defining the relations between soul and body. His argumentation does not bear on the kind of ontological connection existing between soul and body: indeed, in this passage, his primary concern is the inner coherence of language.

As we have seen, Gilbert does not intend to postulate an intrinsic incompleteness within the nature of the soul. Hence, one might ask what is the reason why he decides to include in his exposition of Boethius' text a long and quite elaborate chapter in which he proves that the human soul cannot be called 'person', whereas Boethius does not deal with this problem. The reason for doing this probably lies in the debates that occurred among his contemporaries. Indeed, Gilbert seems to hint at a controversy among the theologians of his time: "Ut ergo pugnas uerborum sensuum conuenientia dirimat, dicendum est..." etc.[179] His commentary

---

[179] Gilb. Pict., *in C. Eut.*, ed. Häring, p. 272, PL 64, 1372 B. The expression *pugnas uerborum* also recalls Paul's First Letter to Timothy 6, 4.

might therefore represent his contribution to the solution of a problem which was perhaps common and hotly debated in his circles.

Finally, keeping in view the content of the debate on the soul-person in the following years, that is in the second half of the twelfth century, one might ask whether Gilbert's text considers the problem of the separated soul, i.e., more precisely, whether his *Commentary* contains an implicit answer to the question whether the soul is a person after the separation from the body. For it seems that the continuation of the chapter might be interpreted in this sense:[180]

Ut ergo pugnas uerborum sensuum conuenientia dirimat, dicendum est quod sicut diuiduum non modo actuali uerum etiam naturali similitudine: ita quoque indiuiduum non modo actuali, uerum etiam naturali dissimilitudine dicitur. Quicquid enim confert habitus, tollit priuatio.

Hoc autem clarius erit exemplis. Homo et sol a grammaticis "appellatiua nomina", a dialecticis uero "diuidua" uocantur. Plato uero et eius singularis albedo ab eisdem gramaticis "propria", a dialecticis uero "indiuidua". Sed horum homo tam actu quam natura appellatiuum uel diuiduum est, sol uero natura tantum non actu. Multi namque non modo natura uerum etiam actu et fuerunt et sunt et futuri sunt substantiali similitudine similiter homines. Multi quoque numquam actu sed semper natura similiter soles.

Sicut enim "homo" non a tota unius hominis sic neque "sol" a tota huius, quem uidemus, solis proprietate nomen est. Sed "homo" quidem ab aliquibus hominum subsistentiis tam actu quam natura, "sol" uero ab aliquibus non actu sed sola natura inter se inuicem tota substantia forme similibus nomina sunt.

Fuerunt enim qui iam non sunt: et erunt qui nondum sunt uel fuerunt: et nunc sunt tam actu quam natura homines infiniti. Ideoque ipsorum forme multe similiter natura et actu et fuerunt et erunt et sunt a quibus hoc ipsarum plena inter se conformitate uere diuiduum nomen hominibus ipsis inditum est.

Unus uero actu solus est sol preter quem nullus actu uel fuit uel est uel erit quamuis natura et fuerunt et sunt et futuri sunt infiniti: ideoque infinite sola natura subsistentie, inter se sola natura conformes a quibus hic uere diuiduum et uniuersale nomen est. Sicut enim ueri indiuidui plena proprietate nulla neque actu neque natura esse potest ita secundum plene proprietatis quamlibet partem naturalis saltem similitudo est.

Unde Platonis ex omnibus, que illi conueniunt, collecta proprietas nulli neque actu neque natura conformis est: nec Plato per illam. Albedo uero ipsius et quecumque pars proprietatis eius aut natura et actu aut saltem natura intelligitur esse conformis. Ideoque nulla pars proprietatis cuiuslibet creature naturaliter est indiuidua quamuis ratione singularitatis "indiuidua" sepe uocetur.

180 Gilb. Pict., *in C. Eut.*, ed. Häring, pp. 272-274, PL 64, 1372 B-1373 A.

Illa uero cuiuslibet proprietas, que naturali dissimilitudine ab omnibus - que actu uel potestate fuerunt uel sunt uel futura sunt- differt, non modo "singularis" aut "particularis" sed etiam "indiuidua" uere et uocatur et est.

Nam "indiuidua" dicuntur huiusmodi quoniam unumquodque eorum ex talibus consistit proprietatibus quarum omnium cogitatione facta collectio nunquam in alio quolibet alterutrius numero particularium naturali conformitate eadem erit.

Hac igitur ratione Platonis tota forma - nulli <actu> neque natura conformis- uere est indiuidua. Omnis uero pars eius singularis quidem est: non autem uere indiuidua quoniam multis est saltem natura conformis. Itaque anima eius, cuius tota forma pars est forme Platonis, non uero nomine dicitur "indiuidua". Ideoque quamuis ipsa sit rationalis nature substantia, nequaquam tamen potest esse persona.

Et generaliter, sicut dictum est, nulla cuiuslibet persone pars est persona quoniam partis eius ex omnibus, que ipsi conuenire intelliguntur, collecta proprietas naturaliter est diuidua. Ex his ergo intelligitur quia persona adeo est per se una quod eius tota proprietas nulli prorsus secundum se totam similitudine conferri potest: nulli ad constituendam personalem proprietatem coniungi.

The opposition between the concepts of '*natura et actu*' and '*non actu, sed saltem natura*' represents the central point of this long piece of argumentation. All individual concepts possess the distinction of "nonpredicability", i.e., they are dissimilar from any other concept. Likewise, "dividual" concepts designate those realities whose *tota proprietas* can be predicated of something else too, hence they designate those realities that are similar to each other. Yet, in order to speak of a "dividual" concept it is not necessary to have a *similitudo actualis*, i.e. an actual similarity: indeed, a mere "natural" similarity is sufficient. A similarity is merely "natural" when the nature of a thing is not shared in fact (*actu*) – since the similar thing does not exist – but can be shared by nature (*natura*), namely, there exists a hypothetical correlate in the similarity relation.[181] Gilbert explains the differ-

---

[181] Cf. Gracia, *Introduction to the Problem of Individuation*, pp. 158-159: "For example, the singular rationality whereby Plato is a rational being conforms to the singular rationality of Aristotle, by which he in turn is a rational being, since as far as rationality is concerned Plato and Aristotle are not dissimilar. This assumes that Plato and Aristotle exist. In such a case the conformity or likeness involved is a conformity in act. If one of the two did not exist but were only a possibility, then the conformity would be in nature, using Gilbert's terminology. In more standard language we could say, "in potency" or "in principle". This means, of course, that things like Plato's rationality, regardless of whether there are other entities that have them or not, have conformity by nature, that is they are potentially like others and therefore dividual. (...) The humanity, for example, which is composed of the rationality, animality, color, height, etc. of Plato, but not of his whiteness and five-foot-

ence between "being by nature and in act" and "being only by nature" using the example of man and sun. The name 'man' is actually shared by many individuals because there existed, exist and will exist many men. By contrast, there exists only one sun: there has never been and will never be any other sun except the one that we know. But the name 'sun' is not an individual name because we can hypothetically imagine an infinite number of suns illuminating the earth. Consequently, the name 'man' is dividual in fact and by nature, whereas the name 'sun' is dividual only by nature. Likewise, Socrates's soul is – at least by nature – not only similar but even identical to Socrates, since it is or can be a part of him, hence it is not a person.

Here again, let us point out that when Gilbert states that the soul – since it is a part of man –"naturaliter est dividua", he does not intend to postulate any incompleteness in the nature of the soul: in conformity with the first part of the exposition, the soul is not individual, because its whole *proprietas* (i.e., all that which is affirmed of it according to its nature) can hypothetically be ascribed to another reality. Hence, "to be dividual" does not belong at all to the nature of the soul: first of all, because "dividuality" properly refers to the concept of soul, not to the thing itself; secondly, because "to be dividual" means the relation between a part and the whole. The relation between soul and man, i.e. between a part and the whole, lies on a different plane with respect to the relation between the soul and its properties. Hence, the relation between soul and man cannot be placed inside the soul:

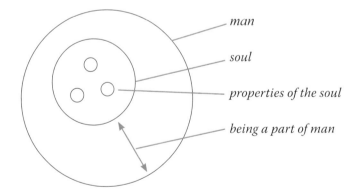

nine-inchedness, is dividual. It is dividual because all those features which Plato has in his humanity, or any other partial composite *id quo* which he has, conform to someone else's *id quo*, at least in potency. Even if there were no men other than Plato, Plato's humanity, just as we saw with his rationality, would be at least like others in potency and so would conform or be like others. This makes it a dividual".

Considering the subsequent debate on the soul-person, one might ask whether Gilbert introduces the opposition between "in act and by nature" and "only by nature" to demonstrate that the separated soul cannot be a person either. Actually, in all probability Gilbert already knew Hugh of St Victor's statements[182] according to which the separated soul is a person.[183] Yet, Gilbert's exposition makes no explicit mention of this problem. Further, keeping in mind some typical features of Gilbert's approach, the hypothesis that his text was aiming at a psychological problem looks improbable. Indeed, the example of man and sun concerns the field of language, not that of concrete reality. This is also revealed by the terminology used in the passage. Gilbert repeats several times terms such as 'dicitur', 'predicatur', 'affirmatur', 'uocatur', 'intelligitur' or 'nomina'. As is also the case in the passages we have examined earlier, the attention is focused on language. The name 'sun' is not individual because its whole property can hypothetically be predicated of many individuals: for the "tota proprietas" is that which is predicated. In my view, the *Commentary* lacks a reference to a determinate condition of the soul. Gilbert writes here as a logician, not as a theologian.

---

[182] This theory reappears in a spurious text probably coming from the school of St Victor; cf. Ps. Hugo de S. Vict., *sum. sent.* I, p. 15, PL 176, 70 D – 71 A: "Sed tamen potest opponi quod anima est rationalis substantia et individuae naturae (quae diffinitio est personae). Igitur si <Christus> assumpsit animam, etiam personam. Quod utique sequeretur si prius esset anima quam assumeretur. Est namque anima persona, sicut angelus. Quid enim est homo nisi anima habens corpus? Sed ideo non assumpsit personam; quia non erat persona quod assumpsit. Animam namque creando assumpsit; et assumendo creavit". Concerning the problem of the attribution of the *Summa sententiarum*, cf. E. Portalié, "Abélard", in *Dictionnaire de théologie catholique* I, edited by A. Vacant - E. Mangenot, Paris: Librairie Letouzey-Ane, 1903, pp. 53-54.

[183] Hugo de S. Vict., *sacr.* II, 1, c. 11, PL 176, 410 D-411 B: "Sed quid est quod vivere desinit, nisi quod moritur? Quid autem moritur, nisi solum corpus quod ab anima deseritur? Anima enim non moritur, nec vivere desinit, etiam quando vivificare desinit. Ergo solum corpus moritur. Sed homo, inquis, id est ipsa persona moritur. Quid est persona? Nonne individuum rationalis substantiae? Si ergo individuum rationalis substantiae persona est, rationalis utique spiritus, qui et simplicitate unus est, et natura rationis capax, proprie personam esse habet; ex se quidem in quantum spiritus rationalis est per se autem quando sine corpore est. Quando autem corpus illi unitum est in quantum cum corpore unitum est, una cum corpore persona est. Quando vero a corpore separatur, persona tamen esse non desinit; et ipsa eadem persona quae prius fuit, quoniam corpus a societate spiritus decedens, eidem spiritui personam esse non tollit, sicut prius quando jungebatur ipsi ut persona esset non dedit. Remanet itaque separata anima a carne, eadem persona spiritus rationalis, quae licet fortassis secundum usum loquendi homo jam dici non possit; quia id quod de terra sumptum erat, jam sibi unitum non habet, non tamen ideo minus persona est, et eadem persona quae prius fuit, quando et illud sibi unitum habuit; et propter ipsam unionem una cum illo persona fuit".

The reason why a reference to the separated soul seems improbable here is suggested by the example of man and sun:[184]

> Multi namque non modo natura uerum etiam actu et fuerunt et sunt et futuri sunt substantiali similitudine similiter homines. Multi quoque numquam actu sed semper natura similiter soles.

Indeed, according to Gilbert, the concept of man is dividual both in fact and by nature because present, future and past men are, will be or were similar "in fact" (*actu*); by contrast, the concept of sun is dividual by nature, although there never were and never will be other suns except the one that we know. Now, let us suppose that there is a soul which was never conjoined or which is in the state of separation and will never have its body again: nevertheless, the very hypothetical possibility of conjunction makes it dividual. For if the soul was never conjoined, it would never be dividual in fact (*actu*), but still it would be dividual by nature (*natura*), just like the sun, because the similarity or the natural conformity is based on the pure hypothetical possibility. Gilbert's reasoning certainly implies that the separated soul is not individual; but this does not depend on the actual condition of the soul – whether it be past or present or future – and not even on the features of the soul, but rather on our concept of soul, which involves a possibility of conjunction so as to form an individual. To my mind, here Gilbert does not refer to the separated souls because his argumentation concerns the concept of soul and not the soul existing in a particular state.

1.2.3.2 Simon of Tournai

The complexity of Gilbert's exposition is evident. This difficulty is primarily due to the epistemological approach adopted by the bishop of Poitiers. Actually, most theologians inspired by the *Commentary* on *Contra Eutychen et Nestorium* reasoned in metaphysical terms. This applies also to an author who copied verbatim long passages from Gilbert's writing, i.e. Simon of Tournai. Indeed, whereas Gilbert relates individuality to "nonpredicability", that is to a concept of a logical type, Simon adds to his text an interpretation of individuality conceived of as distinction in the physical space:[185] according to Simon, the soul is not individual because

---

[184] Gilb. Pict., *in C. Eut.*, ed. Häring, p. 273, PL 64, 1372 B.

[185] Sim. Torn., *sum.*, n. 2, ed. Schmaus, p. 61: "Item anima non solum non est individua individuali forma, sed etiam ratione locali. Non enim seorsum hinc positum est corpus, hinc autem anima. Sed toti corpori tota anima est infusa, ut nusquam possit dici corpus esse, ubi anima non sit, nusquam animam, ubi et corpus non constet esse. Unde et Johannes Scotus *Super hierarchiam Dionysii* ponit hoc paradigma: Sicut ignis infunditur toti carboni, ut nulla carbonis pars relinquatur inaccensa, sic anima infunditur toti corpori, ut

it is totally infused into the whole body, hence it cannot be distinguished in space by the place where it exists. Clearly, Simon's perspective is quite distant from Gilbert's. As we shall see below, even an author like Alan of Lille found it difficult to interpret the *Commentary* in an appropriate way.

1.2.3.3 From logic to psychology: Alan of Lille

Alan of Lille devotes a long chapter of his *Summa "Quoniam homines"* to the problem of the soul-person. The passage is in fact an interpretation of Gilbert's text. As was the case in the *Commentary* on *Contra Eutychen et Nestorium*, at the beginning of the chapter Alan[186] presents his theory of universals:[187]

> Forma similitudinis dicitur illa proprietas que informatione subiecti suum subiectum reddit consimile alii, ut albedo suum subiectum reddit simile aliis albis; similiter nigredo. Eadem dicitur communis, quasi suum subiectum cum alio uniens. Non enim dicitur communis aliqua proprietas quia comunicetur pluribus; nichil enim quod sit in uno est in alio; quicquid enim in singulari est, singulare est.

The universal, i.e. the *forma similitudinis*, makes several subjects similar to each other. In other words, the similarity principle may also be called *forma communis*: indeed, we say that similar things have something in common. Universals are therefore "communicable". As we have seen, the concept of "communicability"

---

nulla pars corporis relinquatur exanimis. Ergo nec de locali positione anima est individua, id est valde ab omni alia re divisa, cum dicto modo corpori sit infusa".

[186] On the problem of universals in Alan of Lille, see Erismann, "Alain de Lille, la métaphysique", pp. 27-41; A. de Libera, "Logique et théologie dans la *Summa "Quoniam hommes"* d'Alain de Lille", in *Gilbert de Poitiers et ses contemporains. Aux origines de la Logica Modernorum: Actes du 7ème Symposium européen de logique et de sémantique médiévales, Poitiers, Centre d'études supérieures de civilisation médiévale, 17-23 juin 1985*, ed. J. Jolivet - A. de Libera, Napoli: Bibliopolis, 1987, pp. 437-469; id., "Des accidents aux tropes", *Revue de Métaphysique et de Morale* 4 (2002), pp. 527-528 ; P.-N. Mayaud (ed.), *Le problème de l'individuation*, Paris: Vrin, 1991; J. Kohler, "Ut Plato est individuum. Die Theologischen Regeln des Alain de Lille über das Problem der Individualität", in *Individuum und Individualität im Mittelalter*, ed. J. A. Aertsen - A. Speer, Berlin-New York: Gruyter, 1996, pp. 22-36. Helpful discussion also in G. Angelini, *L'ortodossia e la grammatica. Analisi di struttura e deduzione storica della Teologia Trinitaria di Prepositino*, Roma: Università Gregoriana Editrice, 1972.

[187] Alan. de Ins., *sum. quon.* I, n. 34, ed. Glorieux, p. 172.

already appears in Boethius' works.[188] Paraphrasing Jorge Gracia's exposition,[189] we may say that a thing is "communicable" if it is able to become common to several subjects. Hence, within a traditional "realist" position, individuals participate in the universal, so that the latter becomes "communicable" to them. In Alan's view, however, a single *forma communis* cannot be shared simultaneously by many singular things. For this reason, Alan, like Gilbert, denies the existence of universal realities shared by several single essences: "quicquid enim in singulari est, singulare est". Alan's theory of universals, like Gilbert's, is based on similarity: for the *forma communis* is referred to many single forms united by *similitudo* but numerically distinct.

As in the case of Gilbert's *Commentary*, Alan introduces an analogy between universals and souls. Indeed, according to Alan, communicable realities are those realities which are a part of something else.[190] All realities which are a part of a substance are "communicable" because they have all of their properties in common with the substance they are a part of; in other words, the properties of a part are shared by the whole substance. Consequently, the concept of "communicabilitas" refers to the soul too, because the substance of the soul is a part of the substance

---

[188] Cf. *supra*, p. 59. *Incommunicabilitas* is one of the central notions in Richard of St Victor's treatise *De trinitate* as well, where it is mainly used about the divine essence. According to Richard, essence, i.e. the divine substance, is not "communicable" because there are not many individuals of the species "god" but there is only one God; cf. Rich. de S. Vict., *trin.* I, c. 17, ed. Ribailler, PL 196, 898 C-899 A. In order to define the Persons of the Trinity, Richard introduces a new definition, i.e., "persona divina sit divinae naturae incommunicabilis existentia" (*ibid.*, IV, c. 22, PL 196, 945 C): actually, according to the Victorine, Boethius' definition is inappropriate because it can be employed about the divine essence. Furthermore, Richard, like his master Hugh of St Victor, holds that the separated soul acquires the personal character; cf. *infra*, p. 83, n. 228.

[189] Gracia, *Introduction*, pp. 24-25: "Although there are several senses in which the term 'communicable' *(communicabile)* is used by philosophers and particularly by scholastics, the most central and pertinent to the present issue is the one in which the universal, for example, tree, is communicable to its instances, trees. To be communicable, therefore, means to be able to be made or become common to many. This relation is exactly the converse of the relation of participability. That which is capable of participation is simply what is able to take part in or be a part of something else which by that very fact of participation is made or becomes common to those things that participate in it. An individual, therefore, is said to be incommunicable because, unlike the universal, it cannot be made common to many or, as some followers of Plato prefer to put it, it cannot become 'participated by many'".

[190] Alan. de Ins., *sum. quon.* I, n. 34, ed. Glorieux, p. 172: "Illa res communicabilis actu vel natura, id est in alicuius rei compositione veniens, proprie non potest [non potest *scripsi* : potest *ed. Glorieux*] dici individuum, quia non est valde divisum ab omni re cum sit de aliquo, id est de substantia alicuius rei".

of man. For this reason, all the properties of Peter's soul are also Peter's properties; it is thus the rationality of Peter's soul which constitutes Peter's rationality.[191]

Alan's argumentation recalls that of Gilbert. Indeed, Alan too introduces a distinction between "in act" and "by nature". For individual substances cannot be "communicable" either in fact, or by nature. To explain the difference between the two concepts, Alan uses the example of the phoenix, which recalls Gilbert's digression about man and sun:[192]

> Hoc nomen phenix appellat unum solum. Ergo est nomen proprium. Non sequitur; quia appellat<iv>um nomen dicitur non quia aliquid appellet, sed quia plurium natura est appellativum. Similiter anima dicitur non esse individua quia quamvis actu divisa sit, natura tamen communicabilis est.

Nevertheless, there is a deep difference between the expositions elaborated by the two authors. First of all, it should be noted that where Gilbert spoke of a distinction of "nonpredicability", Alan uses the notion of "incommunicability". Both concepts have their origin in Boethius; but whereas the former belonged mainly to the logical field, the latter was used by Boethius rather to denote the metaphysical aspect of the problem. The same distinction remained commonly accepted in the twelfth century too. Indeed, the frame of reference in Gilbert's work is not the same as in Alan's. Whereas Gilbert argued especially with a view towards the inner coherence of language, Alan speaks as a theologian. This change of perspective has major consequences for the anthropological view related to the problem here at issue.

Indeed, Alan interprets *communicabilitas* as a property intrinsic to the soul's nature. When the theologian states that the soul is "actu vel natura communicabilis", it is not a question of predicability any more, but of "being a part in act or by nature". Therefore Alan places "being a part" inside the soul's nature,[193] and the

---

[191] Alan. de Ins., *sum. quon.* I, n. 34, ed. Glorieux, p. 173: "...natura partis est natura totius; quoniam sicut substantia anime cedit in substantiam hominis, ita omnis natura anime in natura totius. Unde Petrus est rationalis rationalitate sue anime, et sciens scientia sue anime".

[192] Alan. de Ins., *sum. quon.* I, n. 35, ed. Glorieux, p. 174.

[193] Alan. de Ins., *sum. quon.* I, n. 35, ed. Glorieux, p. 174: "Ergo cum proprius status anime sit etiam status hominis, eam non dividit ab omni re. Itaque nec ipse proprie potest dici individuum, nec anima proprie individua. Que quamvis post dissolutionem separetur a corpore, tamen natura communicabilis est; et ita non est individua; quamvis enim separetur actu, tamen eius natura exigit ut uniatur corpori; unde et naturaliter desiderat unionem corpori. (...) Item si anima modo est persona et prius non erat persona, accidentale est anime esse persona. Item in natura anime est ut non sit per se sed de alio; et ita anima natura non est individua; et ita natura non est persona. Ergo si est persona, contra naturam est persona".

nature he speaks of means the actual essence of the soul. Abandoning Gilbert's stringent logic, Alan affirms that "being a part" belongs to the very nature of the thing. This assertion gives rise to a number of important anthropological consequences which undermine the autonomous character of the soul. The soul, since it is a part of a composite, has its place in man. This incompleteness is engraved in the soul itself: for after a man's death the soul wishes to join with its body again. Being a person would thus be against its nature.

The *topos* of the natural desire that the separated soul feels for its body is not new in Christian theology. Actually, it already appears in Augustine's *De Genesi ad litteram*.[194] The condition of the soul after a man's death is also mentioned in the *Sentences* of Anselm of Laon († 1117), an author who, as is known, was intensely inspired by Augustine's thought:[195]

> Post dissolutionem anime et corporis manent quidam nexus qui faciunt ea unam personam. Nexus dicimus quod anima Petri plus respicit et expectat corpus Petri quam corpus Pauli.

Anselm adds this brief note while dealing with eschatological questions in his writings *De ultimo iudicio* and *De beatitudine*.[196] Indeed, Anselm speaks of the relations between soul and body to demonstrate that the individual human identity is not destroyed by death but is preserved until the resurrection of the body. Anselm does not consider the question whether the soul is a person and he surely

---

[194] Aug., *gen. ad litt.* XII, 35, 68, ed. Zycha, p. 432[15]: "Sed, si quem mouet, quid opus sit spiritibus defunctorum corpora sua in resurrectione recipere, si potest eis etiam sine corporibus summa illa beatitudo praeberi, difficilior quidem quaestio est, quam ut perfecte possit hoc sermone finiri; sed tamen minime dubitandum est et raptam hominis a carnis sensibus mentem et post mortem ipsa carne deposita transcensis etiam similitudinibus corporalium non sic uidere posse incommutabilem substantiam, ut sancti angeli uident, siue alia latentiore causa siue ideo, quia inest ei naturalis quidam adpetitus corpus administrandi: quo adpetitu retardatur quodammodo, ne tota intentione pergat in illud summum caelum, quamdiu non subest corpus, cuius administratione adpetitus ille conquiescat"; cf. *ibid.*, VII, 27. 38, ed. Zycha, p. 224[24], PL 34, 269: "Animam naturali appetitu ferri in corpus. Sed si ad hoc fit anima, ut mittatur in corpus, quaeri potest utrum, si noluerit, compellatur. Sed melius creditur hoc naturaliter velle, id est, in ea natura creari ut velit, sicut naturale nobis est velle vivere: male autem vivere jam non est naturae, sed perversae voluntatis, quam juste poena consequitur".

[195] Ans. Laud., *sent.*, 91, ed. Lottin, p. 78. Cf. R. Quinto, "Anselm von Laon", in *Grundriss der Geschichte der Philosophie (Begründet von Friedrich Ueberweg). Die Philosophie des Mittelalters, Band 2: 12. Jahrhundert*, ed. R. Imbach - T. Ricklin, Basel, forthcoming. I am sincerely grateful to Riccardo Quinto for allowing me to consult his work before publication.

[196] Cf. Ans. Laud., *sent.*, pp. 78-79, *Paris BnF* 12999, f. 26[vb]-28[ra].

does not mention any incompleteness of the soul. Yet, his statements are not very distant from Alan's exposition in the *Summa "Quoniam homines"*: actually, not only does Anselm maintain that the separated soul awaits its body, but he also maintains that soul and body form one person.

Therefore, on the one hand, the statement that "being a part" belongs to the nature of the soul quite probably derives from a misunderstanding due to the complexity of Gilbert's argumentation; but, on the other, Alan's anthropological considerations are related to certain doctrines already formulated in the previous decades. As we shall see below, other elements may have induced Alan to speak of the nature of the soul in this particular way.

Indeed, the *doctor universalis* addresses a problem that Gilbert, at least explicitly, does not deal with. The theologian examines the condition of the soul – according to Christian theology – after the separation from the body. Supposing that the union with the body deprives the soul of the personal character, can the soul become a person after the separation from the body? Alan rejects such a possibility: for it is not the union in act but the very nature of the soul that prevents it having a personality. The soul is not person even after the separation from the body, because it is "communicable" by nature.

The reason why Alan devotes a whole question to this problem is probably related to the fact that, during his schooling, some of the most eminent masters held the opposite opinion.[197] Alan relates a view according to which a separate soul is, indeed, a person, while a soul united to a body is not. Quite probably, Alan alludes to the position held by Peter Lombard in the fifth distinction of book III of the *Sentences*:[198]

> Persona enim est substantia rationalis individuae naturae, hoc autem est anima. Ergo si animam assumpsit <i. e. Filius>, et personam; quod ideo non sequitur quia anima non est persona quando alii rei unita est personaliter, sed quando per se est, absoluta enim a corpore persona est, sicuti angelus.

A similar opinion was commonly attributed to Hugh of St Victor as well.[199] Therefore, Alan's exposition is not purely speculative, but has also a polemical character.

---

[197] Alan. de Ins., *sum. quon.* I, n. 35, ed. Glorieux, p. 174: "Sunt tamen qui dicunt animam post dissolutionem esse personam. Quod sic probatur: anima post dissolutionem est res per se una, quia ulli unita. Ergo res individua. Ergo cum sit nature rationalis, est persona. (...) Item posito quod aliqua anima fuerit ante incarnationem Christi et illa post surmeretur a Verbo, iuxta hanc opinionem concedendum esset personam assumpsisse personam".

[198] Petr. Lomb, *sent.* III, 5, 3.2, ed. PP. Collegii S. Bonaventurae, pp. 481-485.

[199] Cf. *supra*, p. 67.

Another reason might have motivated Alan to deny the personal character of the soul in all its conditions. Alan of Lille was in fact one of the firmest opponents of the Cathar heresy.[200] Book I of his treatise *De fide catholica contra haereticos* gives us reason to believe that the struggle against the Cathars had some influence on the development of Alan's anthropology. Indeed, the dualism professed by the Albigensians had extremely heavy consequences for Christology too.[201] On the one hand, a theory according to which the human body is forged by the devil and is the source of moral evil threatened a fundamental truth of the Christian faith, i.e. the incarnation of Christ. On the other hand, opposing this theory, namely, asserting that the body is created by God and is thus good in itself, opened the way for a less dualist anthropology. For if infusion of souls into bodies is not the action of an evil spirit, then the human composite belongs to God's perfect plan. Consequently, if the union of soul and body is good and natural, then it had to be possible to explain it from a philosophical perspective. Quite probably, Alan of Lille, engaged in preaching against the Cathars, felt a compelling need to find this explanation.

1.2.3.4 Stephen Langton

(a) From communicabilitas *to* aptitudo

As previously observed, Stephen Langton, following in the path of Alan's teaching, takes up the concept of "incommunicability". According to both masters, the soul is not individual because it is "communicable" by nature, i.e., it constitutes just an element of an individual substance. Hence, "communicability" means a relation between a part and the whole. However, in his *Commentary* on Peter Lombard's *Sentences* as well as in the question *De persona*, Stephen Langton adds another

---

[200] On the history of Catharism, see, for example, M. Barber, *The Cathars. Dualist Heretics in Languedoc in the High Middle Ages*, London - New York: Longman, 2000; J. Duvernoy, *La religion des cathares*, Toulouse: Privat, 1976; M. Loos, *Dualist Heresy in the Middle Ages*, transl. I. Lewitová, Praha: Akademia, 1974; H. Fichtenau, *Heretics and Scholars in the High Middle Ages, 1000-1200*, transl. D. A. Kaiser, Pennsylvania: The Pennsylvania State University Press, 1998. I sincerely thank Valeria de Fraja for her valuable advice.

[201] Cf. Alan. de Ins., *fid. cath.* I, p. 12, p. 18, PL 210, 318 A, 321 B-C: "Item si veritas humanae naturae in hoc consistit, scilicet in corpore et spiritu maligno, Christus verus homo non fuit, quia nec spiritum malignum habuit, nec sibi univit; sed verus homo fuit ex eo quod corpus et animam habuit, ergo vel alii homines veri homines non sunt, vel corpus et animam habent. (...) Item si corpus est opus diaboli, homo bene facere non potest, quia arbor bona non potest facere fructum malum, nec arbor mala fructum bonum (Matth. VII). Item, si quodlibet corpus est opus diaboli, Filius Dei corpus non assumpsit, quia opus diaboli sibi non univit; et ita verum corpus non habuit, nec verus homo fuit. Quod quidam haeretici concedunt".

term stemming from Boethius that Alan does not use in this context. It is the term *'aptitudo'*. Apparently, it is a mere lexical change not affecting the doctrine: indeed, just as, according to Alan, "to be communicable" belongs to the nature of the soul, so, according to Langton, *aptitudo* constitutes a property intrinsic to the human soul:[202]

> ...hoc nomen 'indiuidua' in illa descriptione non solum priuat actum compo-
> nendi, set etiam aptitudinem, et ita cum anima extra corpus posita sit apta ue-
> nire in compositionem, non est tunc substantia indiuidua, quare nec persona,
> nec esse potest.

Yet, there is a difference between the two concepts. The term used by Alan still relates to the dispute about universals and besides, as we have seen, it expresses the relation between a part and the whole. By contrast, the term *'aptitudo'*[203] is al- ready far from the problem of universals. Indeed, this concept denotes a property or adequateness or suitability, or equally an ability or capability. Further, in Lang- ton's question *De persona*, the term *'aptitudo'* might refer, on the one hand, to the tendency of the soul to be a part of man; but, on the other hand, it should be noted that in the context of the problem of the separated soul, it is much more natural to think that Langton is here designating the ability of the soul to be united with the body. Hence, the attention shifts from the relation between a part and the whole

---

[202] Cf. Steph. Langt., *de pers.*, ed. Bieniak, pp. 100[172]-101[175].

[203] Cf. H. Merle, "Aptum natum esse. Aptitudo naturalis", in id., *Glossaire du latin philosophique médiéval*, Bruxelles: Union Académique Internationale, 1982, pp. 122-139; A. Blaise, *Dictionnaire latin-français des auteurs chrétiens*, Turnhout: Brepols, 1954, p. 92; J. F. Niermeyer, *Mediae latinitatis lexicon minus*, Leiden: Brill, 1976, p. 54. The nominal form 'aptitudo' does not exist in classical Latin and starts to be used only in the Middle Ages. Boethius employs this term as equivalent of 'nature'; cf. Boeth., *int. Anal.*, PL 64, 752 D: "Necessitas autem est duplex, haec quidem secundum naturam et aptitudinem, haec vero violenta et contra aptitudinem, sicut lapis ex necessitate et sursum et deorsum fertur, sed non propter eamdem necessitatem". Then, Alan of Lille speaks of an *aptitudo componendi* that characterizes properties because these are inclined to be united with a subject; cf. Alan. de Ins., *theol. reg.*, p. 5, PL 210, 625 A. In general, the term is used rather rarely before the Latin translation of Avicenna's works. The latter author, in his *Metaphysics*, uses the word *'aptitudo'* mainly to designate the ability of matter to receive form ("aptitudo recipere formam"); cf. Auic., *metaph.* VIII, 2, ed. Van Riet, pp. 388-390. In the treatise *De anima*, the same term usually refers to the potentiality of the body (I, 5, ed. Van Riet, p. 64[10-11]) or to the powers of the soul (I, 5, ed. Van Riet, pp. 95[23]-96[36]). For Thomas Aquinas, the meaning of the word *'aptitudo'* was similar to that of 'inclination' or 'tendency' ("aptitudo uel proportio appetitus"); cf. I[a]-II[ae], q. 25, a. 2, EL, p. 184b: "Manifestum est autem quod omne quod tendit ad finem aliquem, primo quidem habet aptitudinem seu proportionem ad finem".

to a different relation, i.e. that between the two parts of the composite. Actually, it seems that Hugh of St-Cher interprets Langton's argumentation in this sense:[204]

> Haec autem unibilitas inest animae naturaliter et substantialiter per quam differt ab angelo et haec est prima differentia animae et angeli. (...)
>
> Ad secundum, quod anima et angelus differunt accidente solo etc., dicendum quod "regens" non dicit actum, sed aptitudinem, secundum quam anima apta est naturaliter regere corpus illo triplici regimine quod diximus, et hanc aptitudinem habet anima etiam separata. Haec enim est illa unibilitas de qua supra diximus.

Hugh introduces a change analogous to the one introduced by Langton. Indeed, the latter replaces the distinction of *communicabilitas* with the concept of *aptitudo*, whereas Hugh identifies the adequateness to form a composite with *unibilitas*. Clearly, the first of the three concepts referred to the relation between soul and man; the second is ambiguous; finally, the third unmistakably concerns the relation between soul and body.

(b) The difference between soul and angel

Stephen Langton's question *De persona* is distinguished from the *Summa "Quoniam homines"* by a long digression about the incarnation of the Son of God and the difference between soul and angel. According to Langton, hypothetically, the Word might have assumed the angel's nature: just as He assumed the human nature by becoming man, so He might have become an angel by assuming the nature of angel. By contrast, the Word could not have assumed the nature of soul, because in becoming a soul He would no longer have been a person, which is inconceivable. Similarly, if the Word – just as He assumed a soul – had assumed an angel, then the unity of the second Person of the Trinity would have been lost, and He would have had not only two natures but also two persons.[205] Langton's argumentation

---

[204] Hugo de S. Caro, *q. de an.*, ed. Bieniak, pp. 169-170. Indeed, the same term was used in a very similar context by Thomas Aquinas: "Ad sextum dicendum quod secundum se convenit animae corpori uniri, sicut secundum se convenit corpori levi esse sursum. Et sicut corpus leve manet quidem leve cum a loco proprio fuerit separatum, cum aptitudine tamen et inclinatione ad proprium locum; ita anima humana manet in suo esse cum fuerit a corpore separata, habens aptitudinem et inclinationem naturalem ad corporis unionem"; cf. I[a], q. 76, a. 1, ad 6, ed. Gauthier, p. 210b.

[205] Steph. Langt., *de pers.*, ed. Bieniak, p. 100[155-169]: "Et ita cum anima ueniat in compositionem hominis, non est persona, quia non est substantia indiuidua, idest incommunicabilis compositione. Set angelus est persona, unde impossibile fuit et est filium dei assumpsisse angelum, quia si angelus assumeretur, ueniret in alicuius rei compositionem, quod fuit et est impossibile. Set possibile fuit eum assumpsisse angelicam naturam. Si

attests to a significant need, namely, a way to draw a sharp distinction between soul and angel. Indeed, this is the reason why, immediately after the excursus on the incarnation of the Word, Stephen Langton cites the doctrine expounded by Peter Lombard in book III of the *Sentences*:[206]

> Magister tamen in Sententiis dicit quod anima dum est in corpore non est persona, set dum est extra corpus est persona, quia tunc, ut dicit, est substantia indiuidua; quod non concedimus, quia hoc nomen 'indiuidua' in illa descriptione non solum priuat actum componendi, set etiam aptitudinem, et ita cum anima extra corpus posita sit apta uenire in compositionem, non est tunc substantia indiuidua, quare nec persona, nec esse potest.

Langton is probably referring here to the same passage in Lombard mentioned by Alan of Lille.[207] In a distinction devoted to the problems of the hypostatic union, Peter Lombard states that if the Word had assumed a soul preexisting its infusion into the body, He would have assumed a person. For, according to the Lombard, the separated soul is a person, just like the angel. This statement was commonly rejected by later theologians. Indeed, since the beginning of the thirteenth century, the text of the *Sentences* was often circulated together with a list of twenty-six opinions by Peter Lombard which were regarded as erroneous. And in fact, among the errors contained in book III, we find his doctrine relating to the personal character of the separated soul.[208]

---

enim assumpsisset angelum, non esset angelus, quia nunquam assumens est assumptum, et ita oporteret quod angelus ueniret in compositionem alicuius rei que esset filius dei. Set hoc impossibile. Set si assumeret angelicam naturam, esset angelus, quod possibile fuit eum esse; e contrario, possibile fuit filium dei assumere animam; set impossibile eum fuit assumere naturam anime, quia si assumeret naturam anime, esset anima, et ita ueniret in alicuius compositionem, et esset pars alicuius rei, et ita non esset substantia indiuidua, immo diuidua, et ita non esset persona, quod est impossibile. Pars enim alicuius rei non potest esse persona". Cf. id., "Quaestio de homine assumpto, et utrum Christus sit duo", 13, ed. L. O. Nielsen – S. Ebbesen, *CIMAGL* 66 (1996), p. 234[3-10]: "Item, Christus potuit assumere naturam angeli, sed non angelum. Angelus enim est persona, et sic haberemus quaternarium personarum. Econtra potuit assumere animam et assumpsit, sed non potuit assumere naturam animae, anima enim non est persona etiam extra corpus, quia est communicabilis. Si enim assumeret naturam animae, esset anima, et ita communicabilis, et ita posset esse pars alterius, quod est inconveniens".

[206] Steph. Langt., *de pers.*, ed. Bieniak, pp. 100[170]-101[175].

[207] Cf. *supra*.

[208] Cf. R. Quinto, "Stephen Langton", in *Mediaeval Commentaries on the Sentences of Peter Lombard. Vol. 2*, edited by P. Rosemann, Leiden: Brill, 2010, p. 72, n. 145. The list was reported by Bonaventure in his *Commentary* on the *Sentences*; cf. Bonav., *in II Sent.*, d. 44, ed. PP. Collegii S. Bonaventurae, II, 1016; see also "Prolegomena", in Petri Lombardi *Libri IV Sententiarum*, ed. PP. Collegii S. Bonaventurae, Ad Claras Aquas 1916, p. LXXIX.

One of the reasons why theologians like Alan of Lille or Stephen Langton declare themselves definitely against the Lombard's opinion might have been the dangerous similarity between soul and angel which was explicitly asserted by the author of the *Sentences*. It was a very imprudent statement in that particular historical context. Indeed, the second half of the twelfth century saw a vigorous expansion of the heresy *par excellence*:[209] the Cathar doctrine. A strong ontological dualism, expressed in more or less radical variants, formed the foundation of the doctrine professed by the Albigensians. Their ontological dualism had major anthropological consequences. Alan of Lille synthetically describes the Cathar doctrine with the following words:[210]

> Aiunt haeretici temporis nostri quod duo sunt principia rerum, et principium lucis, et principium tenebrarum.
>
> Principium lucis dicunt esse Deum, a quo sunt spiritualia, videlicet animae et angeli; principium tenebrarum, Luciferum, a quo sunt temporalia. (...)
>
> Praeterea dicunt, quod nullus alius est spiritus hominis, nisi angelus apostata, et quod in coelo non sunt spiritus, quia omnes spiritus qui in coelo erant, cum Lucifero ceciderunt.

According to the Cathars, man consists of two opposite realities. The body, created by Lucifer, bears an intrinsic evil and is the cause of moral evil. The material body constitutes a real prison for the spirit or the soul. Spiritual souls were created by God in heaven before falling down into bodies owing to the devil's action. Actually, these souls are nothing but fallen angels.[211]

In his treatise against heretics, Alan tries to refute these doctrines.[212] Surprisingly, however, in *Contra haereticos*, the reasons in favour of a distinction between

---

[209] Cf. Alan. de Ins., *fid. cath.*, Prol., PL 210, 308 B: "Hoc autem opus quatuor voluminum distinctionibus separatur (...); quorum primum contra haereticos; secundum, contra Waldenses; tertium, contra Judaeos; quartum, contra paganos editum esse cognoscitur". The first book is entirely dedicated to the Cathar doctrine.

[210] Cf. Alan. de Ins., *fid. cath.* I, 2; 9, PL 210, 308 C, 316 B.

[211] Cf. Fichtenau, *Heretics and Scholars*, p. 165.

[212] Cf. Alan. de Ins., *fid. cath.* I, 8; 10, PL 210, 315 A-B, 316 C-D: "Item, si diabolus creavit corpus hominis, Deus vero animam, quaeritur, qua auctoritate anima sit conjuncta corpori, et corpus animae? Si dicunt diabolum et Deum ad hoc convenisse, aliqua fuit conventio Christi ad Belial. Absit etiam ut dicamus Deum animam ad hoc creasse, ut uniret eam malae naturae, quia secundum hoc, posset anima causam peccati sui ad Deum retorquere. (...) Quibus rationibus et auctoritatibus probatur, quod anima est in corpore humano, et non daemones. Juxta hanc opinionem, cum Christus ejiciebat spiritum malignum a corpore humano, cum nullus alius spiritus esset in eo, corpus remanebat exanime. Item, si corpus hominis a diabolo, et spiritus hominis diabolus, homo totus quasi essentialiter malus est, et ita bonum agere non potest, nec mereri vitam aeternam. Item, variae cla-

the human soul and the angel are not so numerous. Moreover, almost all of them rest on the authority of the Scriptures, so that the problem is not approached from the philosophical point of view. Hence, one might ask why does Alan not insist on the specific difference between the two spiritual creatures, in this context. The reason might lie in a certain complexity of the Cathar theories on the human soul. Indeed, according to the Cathars, the spiritual soul, as identified with fallen angels, did not perform any corporeal function. In their view, the vital principle of the human body, as responsible for the senses and for motion, was mortal and inseparably related to blood.[213] This is probably one of the reasons why Alan devotes an extensive part of his treatise to the problem of the immortality of the soul,[214] rather than to the question of the difference between our soul and the angel.

Instead, it is the *Summa "Quoniam homines"* that contains a long passage devoted to the problem of the difference between soul and angel. At the beginning of book II of the *Summa*, in a section devoted to the theme of the creation of angels, Alan dwells on the problem of the bodies assumed by spiritual creatures.[215] After stating that angels do not assume bodies in a proper sense, but only assume corporeal forms, Alan poses an extremely interesting question, namely, whether the union of the spiritual creature with this corporeal form can give rise to a man or another animal.[216] The answer, definitely negative, is not based on the differ-

---

mant auctoritates, animam esse in homine, non angelum. Ait enim Christus: Nolite timere eos qui occidunt corpus, animam autem non possunt occidere; sed potius eum timete, qui potest corpus et animam mittere in gehennam (Matth. x). Et alibi ait: Quid prodest homini si lucretur universum mundum, animae vero suae detrimentum patiatur? (Matth. XVI; Marc. VIII.) Item idem ait: Qui odit animam suam in hoc mundo, in vitam aeternam custodit eam (Joan. XII)".

[213] Cf. Duvernoy, *La religion des cathares*, pp. 66-68.

[214] According to Ermenegildo Bertola, one of the reasons why Alan discusses the immortality of the soul at length might lie in the existence, during the twelfth century, of materialistic and pagan currents usually described as Epicureanism; cf. E. Bertola, "Alano di Lilla, Filippo il Cancelliere e una inedita *quaestio* sull'immortalità dell'anima umana", *Rivista di Filosofia neo-scolastica* 62 (1970), p. 249.

[215] Alan. de Ins., *sum. quon.* II, n. 134, ed. Glorieux, p. 273: "Set cum angeli boni assumant corpora aeria, queritur utrum dicendum sit quod illa corpora sunt humana corpora vel quod assumant humana corpora. Ad quod dicimus quod non. Assumunt enim similitudines humanorum corporum sed non humana corpora. Unde nec angeli qui apparuerunt Abrahe ad radicem Mambre dicendi sunt habuisse humana corpora set similitudines humanorum corporum".

[216] Alan. de Ins., *sum. quon.* II, n. 135, ed. Glorieux, pp. 273-274: "Set queritur utrum ex angelo et tali corpore factum sit unum et ita homo vel aliud animal. Si unum factum est, ex hiis potius homo videtur fuisse quam aliud animal; et cum homines fuerunt qui apparuerunt Abrahe, qui et dissoluti sunt post depositionem corporum, quod dicere nimis absurdum videtur esse. Et ideo dicimus quod duplex est assumptio corporis: alia per applicationem, alia per unionem. Per applicationem assumit iste sibi pallium vel tunicam; et

ence between the real human body and an imitation of it, but rather on the type of union and on the difference between the two spiritual substances, i.e., between soul and angel. Indeed, whereas the soul joined to the body becomes a man or, in other words, a human person, the identity of the angel does not change because of the union. The two types of union are therefore different: the human soul assumes its body and forms with it a new unity, i.e. man; by contrast, the angel assumes a body like clothing and does not thus become something different from itself.[217]

Alan's doctrine concerning the two types of union with a body maintains a perfect agreement with his theory of the soul-person. As we have seen, Stephen Langton too introduces in his question a link between the problem of the difference between soul and angel and the problem of the personal character of the soul. This correlation becomes even more evident in Hugh of St-Cher's question *De anima*.

1.2.3.5   William of Auxerre

The solution adopted by William of Auxerre regarding the problem whether the human soul is a person, brings nothing new, in substance, if compared with the works of his predecessors. William wishes to structure his exposition systematically; this implies, however, that the nuances enriching Gilbert's, Alan's and Stephen Langton's texts are lost. In this case, the negation of the personal character of the soul is based on the "distinction of incommunicability".[218] William states that 'communicable' things are all those things which are a part of something else. Hence, the soul is not a person because it is 'communicable', therefore it is not "per se una" or "per se sonans". Apparently, William does not address the question of the separated soul.

Nevertheless, the *Summa aurea* contains a chapter devoted to the problem of the difference between soul and angel.[219] The chapter reports a formula similar to

---

ideo ex assumente et assumpto non fuit unum. Est alia assumptio per unionem secundum quam anima assumit corpus; unde ex anima et corpore fit unum. Angelus autem non assumit corpus per unionem, set per applicationem; nec assumendo incipit esse quod non erat, nec deponendo desinit esse quod erat".

[217]   Massimiliano Lenzi suggests that the comparison drawn by Alan has its roots in Porphyry. Further, the term 'applicatio' appears to be present also in Calcidius' *comm. in Tim.* CCXXVII, ed. Jensen -Waszink, p. 221, p. 227; cf. Lenzi, *Forma e sostanza*, pp. 209-210.

[218]   Guill. Altissiod., *sum. aur.* III, 1, c. 3, q. 8, ed. Ribailler, pp. 36[53]-37[60]: "Et distinctio incommunicabilitatis, que est in Socrate ex eo quod non est communicabilis ut pars, quoniam non convenit ut pars in compositum cum alio; et talis distinctio non est in anima vel corpore; et ideo nec anima nec corpus persona est proprie, quia non est "per se unum" vel "per se sonans", sicut dicit Boetius in libro de duabus Naturis et una Persona Christi. Nichil enim horum est persona, ut ibi dicit".

[219]   Cf. Bieniak, "Una questione disputata", pp. 150-152.

those employed by William in the context of the discussion on the problem of the soul-person, i.e. the expression "per se stans":

> Et sunt alii qui dicunt quod angelus substantialiter differt ab anima in eo quod ipse per se est stans, corporis unitione aut amixtione non egens, quemadmodum anima.[220]

The question posed by William is the following: what is the foundation of the substantial – that is to say specific – difference between the two spiritual substances, i.e. between soul and angel? One of the possible answers considered by the theologian concerns the fact that the soul, unlike the angel, needs to be united with the body, thus it is not "per se stans". Interpreting this statement, may we conclude that, according to William, the inclination to be united with the body belongs to the nature of the soul? The answer is negative. Indeed, the subsequent lines of the text reject a similar hypothesis:[221]

> Et hoc non videtur verum esse. Nam quod dico "per se stans", in privatione sonat; quod patet si resolvas. Sed negatio sive privatio, cum nichil sit, quomodo dabit alii esse aut diversitatem secundum esse, quod proprium est substantialis differentie?

William solves the problem in a way similar to that adopted by Gilbert of Poitiers:[222]

> Tota uero anime Platonis proprietas – i. e. quicquid de ipsa naturaliter affirmatur- de ipso Platone predicatur. "Naturaliter" dicimus quoniam, quod non naturaliter de anima dicitur, non necesse est de Platone predicari: ut topica ratio, qua Platonis anima "pars" eius uocatur, de ipso Platone minime dicitur. Dicimus etiam "affirmatur" quia, quod ab anima Platonis negatur, non necesse est ab ipso negari: ut si dicatur anima esse incorporea, quo priuatorio nomine corporum subsistentia, que est corporalitas, remouetur ab ea, non ideo Plato incorporeus esse dicitur. Et sic quidem humana anima secundum predictam diffinitionem uidetur esse: secundum expositam uero rationem uidetur non esse persona.

According to Gilbert, "to be a part of a composite" does not belong to the nature of the part. Similarly, "not to be a part of a composite" does not affect in any way the nature of the thing that exists by itself because it is a mere privative relation. Evidently, William of Auxerre's reasoning is much closer to that elaborated by

---

[220] Guill. Altissiod., *sum. aur.* II, 1, c. 3, q. 4, ed. Ribailler, p. 262[23-25].
[221] Guill. Altissiod., *sum. aur.* II, 1, c. 3, q. 4, ed. Ribaillier, p. 262[26-29].
[222] Gilb. Pict., *in C. Eut.*, ed. Häring, p. 272, PL 64, 1372 A-B.

Gilbert of Poitiers than to the argumentation of Alan of Lille or Stephen Langton, who placed the fact of "being a part" inside the nature of the soul.

1.2.3.6 Hugh of St-Cher

As previously observed, Hugh, in his *Commentary* on the *Sentences*, addresses the issue of the personal character of the soul three times: once in the commentary on book I and twice in the commentary on book III. In the case of distinction 25 of book I, his exposition reflects that of William of Auxerre quite faithfully. Indeed, Hugh reports his threefold distinction, i.e. the *distinctio singularitatis, incommunicabilitatis* et *dignitatis*.[223] Like William, in this case Hugh does not address the problem of the separated soul. In contrast, in the commentary on the second and the fifth distinction of book III, the influence exerted by the *Summa aurea* is not decisive. And indeed, Hugh's exposition recalls that of Stephen Langton. First of all, Hugh states that Christ could not have assumed the nature of the soul because, in this way, he would have assumed the nature of a part;[224] secondly, Hugh takes up the criticism of Lombard's theory of the separated soul:[225]

Magister Hugo de sancto Victore: Anima, inquantum est spiritus rationabilis, ex se et per se habet esse personae, et quando ei corpus associatur, non. (...)

Sed magister Hugo et etiam Magister in littera videntur falsum dicere, quod anima separata sit persona. Anima enim creata est in corpore, non extra corpus per se. Et ita creata est non, ut ipsa pro se esset aliquid unum, sed ut unita corpori faceret aliquid per se unum. Et animae sanctorum naturaliter appetunt incorporari. Ergo anima separata non est persona.

It is worth observing that here Hugh does not explicitly state that being a part belongs to the nature of the soul. Rather, the Dominican master insists that the soul is joined to the body from the very first moment of its existence: hence, the soul was not created to subsist separately, but to form a composite. This, according to Hugh, results in the soul's natural desire to join with its body. Hence, finally, there might follow the natural ability to be united, that is *unibilitas*.

The theory that the soul is not a person because of its ability to be united with the body represented a view already commonly accepted in that period. This is confirmed by the analysis of two other texts dating from the first decades of the thirteenth century, i.e. the *Gloss* of Alexander of Hales and a disputed question by Philip the Chancellor.

---

[223] Cf. *supra*, pp. 54-55.
[224] Cf. *supra*, pp. 76-77.
[225] Hugo de S. Caro, *in* III *Sent.*, d. 5, ed. Breuning, pp. 351[353]-352[386]. The same criticism reappears in Alexander of Hales' *Glossa*, which is possibly another of Hugh's sources; cf. *infra*, p. 83.

1.2.3.7   Alexander of Hales

The *Glossa* of Alexander of Hales (†1245) on Peter Lombard's *Sententiae*, written not later than 1227,[226] shows an evident dependence on William of Auxerre's *Summa aurea*. Indeed, William's triad, namely, the characteristics of singularity, incommunicability and dignity, reappears in the *Gloss* on the fifth distinction of book III of the *Sentences*.[227] It is not without reason that the discussion of the problem of the soul-person is placed exactly at that point in the commentary. Actually, in the fifth distinction of book III, Peter Lombard had introduced his controversial opinion that the separated soul is a person. Since Alexander onwards, this became the typical context in which the problem of the personal character of the soul was dealt with: as we have seen, this is confirmed by the case of the *Sentences Commentary* of Hugh of St-Cher.

Alexander's exposition has another feature in common with the argumentation elaborated by Hugh: indeed, Alexander lays stress on the distinction between soul and angel. According to him, the author of the *Sentences* erroneously attributes the personal character to the soul, for he does not see the difference between the angel, who is a person, and the soul: the soul, unlike the angel, is always oriented toward the body and possesses faculties which need the presence of the body in order to be employed. Consequently, the soul will never be able to be a person.[228]

Alexander's argumentation too might have exerted an influence on Hugh's thought.

---

[226] "Prolegomena", in Alex. Halen., *gloss. in* III *Sent.*, ed. PP. Collegii S. Bonaventurae, p. 32*.

[227] Alex. Halen., *gloss. in* III *Sent.*, d. 5, n. 41, ed. PP. Collegii S. Bonaventurae, pp. 69³⁴-70⁴: "Persona igitur est naturae rationalis individua exsistentia, vel "persona est existens per se solum iuxta singularem quemdam existentiae rationalis modum". Est autem distinctio triplex: est distinctio singularitatis, et hanc habet anima; singularitatis et incommunicabilitatis, et hanc habet homo; singularitatis et incommunicabilitatis et dignitatis, et hanc habet Christus. Et ideo dicitur: 'secundum quemdam existentiae rationalis modum'".

[228] Alex. Halen., *gloss. in* III *Sent.*, d. 5, n. 42-43, ed. PP. Collegii S. Bonaventurae, p. 70⁵⁻¹⁹: "*Hic a quibusdam*₅₇₂,₃; et infra: *Quando per se, est anima persona*₅₇₂, ₇₋₈. Ergo anima separata a corpore est persona, et inde a resurrectione non erit persona. Quod falsum est. Unde dicendum quod Magister non dicit verum. Deceptus enim fuit per similitudinem angeli, qui est persona; sed non est simile, quia anima separata habet in se ordinem ad corpus, et ratione virium quae ... quaerit unionem corporis; sed angelus non sic. Item, Magister Richardus: «Quod humana persona in simplicitate substantie quandoque invenitur, non est de naturae ipsius conditione, sed de conditionis corruptione fore deprehenditur». 'In simplicitate substantie' ponitur ibi pro anima; ergo est persona. Solvitur per hoc quod sequitur: 'conditionis corruptione', quia conditio animae semper est ad corpus; et ita non est persona nisi extenso nomine personae. Unde in homine est multitudo substantiarum sub eadem personalitate"; cf. Rich. de S. Vict., *trin.* IV, c. 25, ed. Ribaillier, p. 190⁴⁻⁹, PL 196, 947 A-B.

1.2.3.8 Philip the Chancellor

The problem of the personal character of the separated soul also appears in a disputed question by Philip the Chancellor. The question is entitled *De incarnatione* and has come down to us in only one witness, i.e. the first volume of ms. Douai 434, just like Hugh of St-Cher's question *De anima*. Whereas Philip's *Summa de bono* evidently represents the main source of Hugh's questions, we do not know what the relation was between the questions written by the two masters: we have no external indications and, moreover, it is difficult to deduce this information from the contents of these texts.

As in the case of the commentaries by Alexander of Hales and Hugh, Philip introduces the problem of the separated soul while discussing the incarnation of Christ.[229] He presents the following argument: if the soul, separated from the body, acquired the personal character, then there would be two persons in Christ. How does Philip come to this conclusion? The problem probably concerns Christ's humanity in the *triduum*, i.e., the state in which the Word was united to the soul and the body, but the soul and the body of Christ were separated. In that condition, the past actual union of the soul with the body could no longer stand in the way of the personal character of the soul; hence, the Word would have been united to a person. It should be noted that a problem of this kind could be solved by means of the third distinction posited by William of Auxerre, i.e. the *distinctio dignitatis*.[230] Indeed, Philip too speaks of the "dignity of excellence";[231] however, even though the distinction of excellence in itself was sufficient to solve the question of the union of the Word with the soul in the *triduum*, Philip, like Alan of Lille and Stephen Langton, states that the soul is not a person when it is separated either, because its 'esse' depends on the body, to which the soul by nature wishes to be united:[232]

> Ad illud, scilicet quod anima exuta a corpore non acquirit, etc., respondeo quod ideo hoc contingit quia *ejus esse non est absolutum sed dependens a corpore*, cui naturaliter appetit uniri.

---

[229] Philipp., *qq. de incarn.*, q. 3 b, n. 26, ed. W. Principe, *Philip the Chancellor's Theology of the Hypostatic Union*, Toronto: The Pontifical Institute of Mediaeval Studies, 1975, p. 182[132-134]: "Item, anima ordinem habet: creatur in corpore. Item, separatur a corpore et, separata, non acquirit personalitatem. Sic nec, conjuncta divinae naturae humana anima [anima *scripsi: om. ms.*; natura *ed. Principe.*], personalitatem amittet".

[230] Cf. *supra*, pp. 54-55.

[231] Philipp., *qq. de incarn.*, q. 3 b, n. 34, ed. Principe, p. 183[165-169]: "Sed ubi unitur divina natura humanae, ejus esse, scilicet humanae naturae, non est per se unum et absolutum nec habens dignitatem excellentiae; ideoque non est persona, nec tamen tollitur ei aliquid, quoniam illud numquam habuit".

[232] Philipp., *qq. de incarn.*, ed. Principe, p. 183[163-165].

In order to understand the real weight of these words written by Philip, we just need to recall the solution of an article entitled *Utrum angelus et anima differant specie*, which is discussed in Thomas Aquinas's *Commentary* on book II of the *Sentences*:[233]

> Anima autem rationalis habet *esse absolutum, non dependens a materia;* quod est aliud a sua quidditate, sicut etiam de angelis dictum est: et ideo relinquitur quod sit in genere substantiae sicut species, et etiam sicut principium, inquantum est forma huius corporis: et inde venit ista distinctio, quod formarum quaedam sunt formae materiales, quae non sunt species substantiae; quaedam vero sunt formae et substantiae, sicut animae rationales.

It should be noted, however, that the doctrine expounded by Philip in the question *De incarnatione* appears to be in sharp contrast to that presented in his most famous work, i.e. the *Summa de bono.* Indeed, in a chapter of the *Summa* devoted to psychological questions, Philip claims that the rational soul is a substance *"ens per se"* and that its substance, as well as its operations, do not depend on the body. According to the Chancellor, the conjunction of soul and body represents the weakest union among those existing in nature. Moreover, this union is not immediate, but demands the presence of an intermediary.[234] The difference between Philip's two anthropological views is all the more remarkable because Philip, while discussing the soul in the *Summa*, cites the definition of the soul according to Aristotle (in the Avicennian version), "perfectio corporis naturalis organici",[235] and manifestly takes it into consideration, whereas the *Quaestio de incarnatione* makes no mention of this definition.

We are now led to ask why Philip, in two different contexts, adopts two positions that are so distant from each other. An hypothesis might be that, due to the influence of Parisian debates, Philip changed his position between the redaction of the *Summa* and the elaboration of the question, or *vice versa*. But one may specu-

---

[233] Thom. de Aquino, *in* II *Sent.*, d. 3, q. 1, a. 6 co., Edizioni Studio Domenicano, III, p. 190.

[234] Philipp., *sum. de bon.*, ed. Wicki, p. 284[103-107], p. 287[185-193]: "Quod etiam secundum quod substantia aliquo medio unitur patet, quia per se est substantia separabilis a corpore et etiam secundum operationes suas separabilis. Intelligere enim et reminisci sunt ipsius separate. Ergo nec est dependens a corpore secundum substantiam nec secundum operationes. Ergo secundum se non unitur corpori; quare indiget alio medio. Post hec queritur cuiusmodi unitas sit secundum unionem anime ad corpus. Et dicendum est quod est triplex unitas. (...) Tertia est in illis in quibus aliqua duo coniunguntur ita quod alterum separabile est ab altero, ut anima a corpore et corpus ab anima, et hec est minima. Et per hec deprehenditur quod minima unitas est in homine".

[235] Philipp., *sum. de bon.*, ed. Wicki, p. 231[24-25].

late whether the contrast between the two opinions was not due to the difference between the contexts in which they were affirmed. For both expositions perfectly harmonize with the theological tradition of the time. On the one hand, the insistence on the substantial character of the soul and on its lack of dependency on the body accords with Avicenna's influential view, which was adopted by several Latin authors in the first three decades of the thirteenth century; also the doctrine of intermediaries is not without precedent in the treatises devoted to the ontological condition of the soul.[236] On the other hand, outside a properly psychological context, the theory of the natural desire of the soul for the body reappears, with all its consequences, at first in Anselm of Laon's writings, then in the tradition started by Gilbert of Poitiers and marked by the interpretation offered by Alan of Lille. The writings of Philip the Chancellor attest to these two tendencies and clearly reveal the contrast between them.

1.2.3.9 From the *Summa Halesiana* to Thomas Aquinas's *Scriptum in Sententias*

In the 1240s and 1250s, the problem of the soul-person continued to be debated. On the one hand, from this point onwards the question remained related to the criticism of Lombard's theory; on the other hand, the solution presented by William of Auxerre in his *Summa aurea* became a permanent reference point. This produced some features common to all the treatments written around the middle of the century. To illustrate this, we will cite the examples of the following four works from that period:[237] the *Summa Halesiana*[238] and the *Sentences Commentaries* by Albert the Great,[239] Bonaventure[240] and Thomas Aquinas.[241]

All four of these authors explicitly address the problem whether the separated soul is a person. The *Summa Halesiana*, Albert and Bonaventure base their answers on the *distinctio incommunicabilitatis*. Clearly, this solution derives above all from William of Auxerre's *Summa*. In addition, in the *Summa Halesiana*, we find several allusions to the *De trinitate* by Richard of St Victor, in which the term '*incommunicabilis*' plays a very significant role.[242]

---

[236] Cf. *infra*, pp. 124-130.

[237] The question of the soul-person is also discussed in Odo Rigaud's *Commentary* on the *Sentences*, *Paris BnF, lat. 14910*, f. 367[ra-rb].

[238] Alex. Halen., *sum. theol.* I. 2, inq. 2, tr. 2.1, q. 1, c. 3, ed. PP. Collegii S. Bonaventurae, I, pp. 570-571; id., *sum. theol.* III, tr. 1, q. 4.1, c. 4, ed. PP. Collegii S. Bonaventurae, IV, p. 56.

[239] Alb. Magn., *in* III *Sent.*, d. 5, a. 15, ed. Borgnet, pp. 66-67.

[240] Bonav., *in* III *Sent.*, d. 5, a. 2, q. 3, ed. PP. Collegii S. Bonaventurae, III, pp. 135-137.

[241] Thom. de Aquino, *in* III *Sent.*, d. 5, q. 3, a. 2, Edizioni Studio Domenicano, V, pp. 336-340.

[242] References to Richard of St Victor's work are also evident in Alexander's *Glossa*; cf. *supra*, p. 83, n. 228.

Moreover, it should be noted that the four treatments make practically no mention of the problems relating to the hypostatic union, although all of them, except the one contained in the *Summa Halesiana*, are situated in that context. Rather, what is common is the connection with the topic of resurrection and the difference between soul and angel.

In all four texts, the conjunction of soul and body plays a very important role for the solution of the problem, although each author describes this connection in different terms. So, in the first half of the 1240s, the author of the *Summa Halesiana* speaks of "respectus ad corpus", thus recalling the expressions used by Anselm of Laon in his *Sentences*.[243]

In the face of an objection formulated in these terms,

Item, anima nostra est separabilis a corpore; ergo si separetur, uidetur quod remaneat individua, id est incommunicabilis, et ita persona.

the author of the *Summa* replies as follows:[244]

Ad aliud dicendum quod anima nostra persona non posset esse, quoniam non dicitur persona quia non communicatur, sed quia est incommunicabilis; et sic non est anima Petri, quoniam semper habet respectum ad corpus, cum quo unietur post resurrectionem.

Subsequently, Albert the Great solves the question of the soul-person by relying on the Aristotelian definition of the soul. On the basis of this doctrine, Albert concludes that the soul depends on the body in an essential way.[245]

The essential dependency on the body also appears in Bonaventure's *Commentary* on the fifth distinction of book III of the *Sentences*; in order to explain it, the Franciscan master avails himself of the concepts of *appetitus* and *aptitudo*.

---

[243] Cf. *supra*, p. 72.

[244] Alex. Halen., *sum. theol.* I. 2, inq. 2, tr. 2.1, q. 1, c. 3, ed. PP. Collegii S. Bonaventurae, I, pp. 570-571.

[245] Alb. Magn., *in* III *Sent.*, d. 5, a. 16, ed. Borgnet, p. 116: "Deinde quaeritur de hoc quod dicit: "Absoluta enim a corpore persona est sicut Angelus". Absoluta enim anima adhuc secundum suam diffinitiuam substantiam est endelechia corporis organici physici vitam habentis in potentia: ergo videtur quod essentialis sit dependentia ei ad corpus: igitur non potest esse incommunicabilis alteri incommunicabilitati: ergo anima non est persona: et hoc concedunt omnes. Si autem volumus sustinere Magistrum, tunc dicendum est, quod absoluta a corpore dicitur duobus modis, scilicet absoluta, id est, divisa a corpore: et sic non est verum. Vel, absoluta a corpore, id est, ab ordine ad corpus: et tunc loquitur Magister per hypothesim, scilicet si ponatur absolvi a dependentia quam habet ad corpus: quia tunc erit intelligentia quaedam de natura simili Angelorum".

Instead of using the term '*dependentia*', Bonaventure speaks of the *unibilitas essentialis*, which is also called *aptitudo uniendi cum corpore*.[246]

In the case of Thomas Aquinas's *Commentary* on the *Sentences*, the solution given to the problem of the soul-person is founded especially on the definition of the soul as a form; yet, Aquinas's exposition too contains the concepts of *unibilitas* and *aptitudo*. By contrast, in this context, Aquinas does not mention the notion of incommunicability and abandons the theme of the natural desire of the soul for its body: his exposition thus recalls Gilbert of Poitiers' *Commentary* on *Contra Eutychen et Nestorium*. According to Aquinas, the soul, as it is a form, does not constitute a nature as such, but is just a part of the human nature.[247] Hence, the

---

[246] Bonav., *in* III *Sent.*, d. 5, a. 2, q. 3, ed. PP. Collegii S. Bonaventurae, pp. 135-137: "Quamvis autem in anima separata sit reperire singularitatem et dignitatem, non est tamen reperire incommunicabilitatem, quia appetitum et aptitudinem habet, ut uniatur corpori ad constitutionem tertii. Et ideo necesse est, ipsam carere distinctione personalitatis; quoniam, si completior est anima, dum appetitus eius terminatur, quem habet respectu corporis resumendi, sicut vult Augustinus duodecimo super Genesim ad litteram, et tunc non habet in se intentionem personae; necessario sequitur, quod personalitate careat, cum est separata a corpore. Alioquin sequerentur praedicta inconvenientia, videlicet quod unio esset praeternaturalis, et separatio non esset poenalis; iterum, quod unio esset in animae praeiudicium, et separatio in praemium; quorum quodlibet falsum est. Et ideo non inmerito in hac opinione communiter non sustinent Magistrum, quamvis aliqui velint dicere, quod Magister intellexit de anima separata, circumscripta unibilitate ad corpus; et hoc est potius verbi palliatio quam expositio, sicut patet aspiciendo ad verba ipsius. Preterea, unibilitas sive aptitudo uniendi cum corpore non est animae accidentalis, sed est ipsi animae essentialis, et ita non potest ab ea separari vel circumscribi, salva ipsius natura".

[247] Thom. de Aquino, *in* III *Sent.*, d. 5, q. 3, a. 2, Edizioni Studio Domenicano, v, pp. 336-340: "Praeterea, angelus et anima separata non videntur differre nisi per hoc quod anima est unibilis. Sed unibilitas non impedit rationem personae. Ergo cum angelus sit persona, etiam anima separata erit persona. Probatio mediae. Id quod potest fieri per divinam virtutem, non immutat aliquid de ratione rei; sicut quod Deus possit assumere aliquem hominem, ut Petrum, non aufert Petro rationem personalitatis. Sed anima separata non potest uniri corpori nisi per resurrectionem, quae non erit naturalis, sed per divinam virtutem tantum. Ergo anima propter unibilitatem rationem personae non amittit. (...) Respondeo dicendum, quod de unione animae ad corpus apud antiquos duplex fuit opinio. Una quod anima unitur corpori sicut ens completum enti completo, ut esset in corpore sicut nauta in navi (...): et secundum hanc opinionem esset verum quod Magister dicit, quod anima est persona quando est separata. Sed haec opinio non potest stare: quia sic corpus animae accidentaliter adveniret: unde hoc nomen homo, de cuius intellectu est anima et corpus, non significaret unum per se, sed per accidens; et ita non esset in genere substantiae. Alia est opinio Aristotelis quam omnes moderni sequuntur, quod anima unitur corpori sicut forma materiae: unde anima est pars humanae naturae, et non natura quaedam per se: et quia ratio partis contrariatur rationi personae, ut dictum est, ideo anima separata non potest dici persona: quia quamvis separata non sit pars actu, tamen habet naturam ut sit pars. Ad primum ergo dicendum, quod anima separata, proprie loquendo, non est substantia ali-

question whether, for Aquinas, "to be a part" belongs to the nature of the soul, requires a negative answer: indeed, the soul is not a nature.

According to an unpublished study by Bernardo Carlos Bazán,[248] the argumentation advanced by Aquinas in his *Commentary* on the fifth distinction of book III of the *Sentences* constitutes the first witness to the evolution of his thought towards the positions held in his questions *De anima*. The thesis that the soul constitutes just a part of a nature is in fact not distant from the statement that the soul does not belong to a species. And, indeed, this was to become the doctrine Aquinas presented in the questions *De anima*.

***

The problem of whether the separated soul is a person began to be raised in the first half of the twelfth century and continued to be discussed after the death of Thomas Aquinas.[249] A factor contributing to the diffusion of this tradition was certainly the success enjoyed by a major school textbook, i.e. Peter Lombard's *Sentences*. Indeed, the *Sentences* handed down the doctrine, born at the school of St Victor, that the soul, after the body's death, is completely similar to an angel and thus becomes a person. Thanks to the widespread practice of commenting on this text, the Lombard's opinion, commonly considered as erroneous, occasioned a constantly renewed interest in our problem.

Yet, the typical features of the discussion mainly derived from another source: the peculiar shape of the debate was determined especially by Gilbert of Poitiers'

---

cujus naturae, sed est pars naturae. (...) Ad quartum dicendum, quod quamvis unio animae separatae ad carnem non possit fieri nisi per virtutem supernaturalem, tamen in ea est naturalis aptitudo ad hoc: et quod non potest unio compleri per virtutem naturalem, est ex defectu corporis, non ex defectu animae". On the problem of person in Aquinas, see for instance U. Degl'Innocenti, *Il problema della persona nel pensiero di S. Tommaso*, Roma: Libreria editrice della Pontificia Università Lateranense, 1967; R. Kalka, "Définition de la personne chez saint Thomas d'Aquin", *Journal Philosophique* 6 (1986), pp. 1-30.

[248] I am referring to the lecture given at the Université de Paris Sorbonne on 18th May 2006. I cordially thank Professor Bazán for his help and availability.

[249] See, for example, Duns Scotus, *quodl.* XIX, ed. Venice 1583, V, f. 115; Rich. de Mediav., *in* III *Sent.*, d. 5, a. 2, q. 1, ed. Venice 1509, p. 16rb: "Respondeo quod anima separata non est persona, nec etiam coniuncta, quia persona creata est "rationalis vel intellectualis naturae individua substantia" in se et per se complete existens, vel habens completum sue existentie modum. Anima autem separata non habet in se suum completum existentie modum, quia etsi non sit actu pars hominis, tamen apta nata est esse pars ex qua <cum> corpore unum per esssentiam constituitur quod verum non esset si ipsa in se et per se haberet suum completum existentie modum. Ex duobus enim complete existentibus in actu, vel altero eorum per se habente suum completum existentie modum, non potest unum per existentiam constitui, ut in secundo libro est ostensum. Anima etiam coniuncta non est persona; pars enim persone persona non est. Homo autem in se existens persona est, cuius pars est ipsa anima".

Commentary on Boethius' *Contra Eutychen et Nestorium*. Gilbert claims that a person cannot be a part of another person: this distinction contributes to explaining why neither a universal nor Christ as a man may be called person. In conformity with this principle, it cannot be stated that the human soul is a person, because this would oblige us to deny the personal character of the composite of soul and body, and hence of man himself. Gilbert's argumentation is closely related to the problem of universals: indeed, it is based on the concept of "nonpredicability", a term that denotes the epistemological approach adopted by the bishop of Poitiers. Later on, however, "nonpredicability" was replaced by another term stemming from Boethius, i.e. "incommunicability", a concept which was established in this context especially thanks to Alan of Lille's and Richard of St Victor's writings. Unlike Gilbert, Alan considers "to be a part" or "communicability" as a property intrinsic to the soul. In agreement with this interpretation, the theologian introduces a traditional Augustinian *tópos* into the debate on the soul-person, i.e. a *tópos* according to which the separated soul wishes to be conjoined with its body, having in view the resurrection. The vast majority of those thinkers who were later to address the problem of the personal character of the separated soul adopted the same approach as Alan. The argument founded on the future resurrection of bodies played an important role; there were other theological requirements, however, which spoke in support of the incompleteness or partialness of the soul's nature: on the one hand, the masters were seeking a definite and convincing explanation of the specific difference between the separated soul and the angel – and the more severe the conflict with the Cathar heresy became, the more pressing this need became; on the other hand, the problem of the personality of the soul was related to that of the unity of the human nature, especially because the latter had been assumed by the Son of God.

The analysis of the texts written in the second half of the twelfth century and the first half of the thirteenth seems to lead us to the conclusion that the three theological requirements mentioned above weighed more heavily in the debate on the soul-person than in the questions merely pertaining to the science of the soul: the example brought by the writings of Philip the Chancellor represents a particularly strong argument in favour of this hypothesis. The debate on the concept of person therefore appears to be a path towards the elaboration of a unitary image of man, independently of whether this image is thought of in terms of *unibilitas* or of form in an Aristotelian sense.

Part Two
Between Soul and Body:
the Powers of the Soul

INTRODUCTION

The problem of the union of the soul with the body in the thirteenth century cannot be easily confined within one thematic field. As already seen in the previous section, the problem of the unity of the human being is approached not only in the questions specifically relating to the conjunction of soul and body, but also in the chapters dealing with the definition of the human soul, in the questions concerning the difference between soul and angel, in an eschatological context and in the debates on the concept of person within a Trinitarian and Christological domain. Besides, there exists a range of contexts in which the unity issue, although not explicitly debated, is often involved. This happens in the case of the debate about the ontological status of the powers of the soul. The second section of this study is devoted to this problem.

For various reasons, the debate concerning the faculties of the human soul is of the utmost importance for us. First of all, the opinions relating to the ontological status of powers basically reveal the general anthropological view of an author, and especially his conception of the essence of the soul and the relation between soul and body. The adopted solutions thus represent a valuable indication that enables us to judge to what extent an author conceives man in terms of unity. It will be particularly interesting to establish what consequences the *unibilitas* theory may have on this type of debate. Secondly, some of the concepts appearing in the debate on the union of soul and body – for example the idea expressed by the adverb '*substantialiter*' – are equally present in the questions concerning the powers of the soul: their presence in a different context enables us to better understand the meaning of the key expressions employed to solve the basic problems. Further, the question of the powers intermediary between the rational soul and the body leads us again into the core of the problem of the psychophysical union, just like the debate on the immortality of the powers of the soul. Finally, it is mainly thanks to the complex debate on the faculty of memory that we can examine how the anthropological thinking in the first half of the thirteenth century is a combination of different traditions which are not always able to be reconciled with one another.

The structure of the following section is different from that of the preceding chapters. So far, we have examined the evolution of some doctrines which extend across a rather long lapse of time: from the early decades of the thirteenth century to Thomas Aquinas. Now we will concentrate exclusively on the third and fourth decades of the thirteenth century, leaving out entirely developments in the subsequent decades.

Our analysis will continue to be centred on Hugh of St-Cher's anthropology, except for the last chapter, in which we shall be guided by some of Hugh's contemporaries.

2.1

THE RATIONAL POWERS: THE SOUL AS IMAGE OF THE TRINITY

2.1.1   TWO TRADITIONS, TWO TYPES OF POWERS

Before addressing the problem of the ontological status of the faculties of the soul, and in order to understand the approach adopted by Hugh of St-Cher and other theologians of his time, we have to present some fundamental distinctions.

In the first years of the thirteenth century, John Blund delineates the *scientia de anima* using the following words:[1]

> Dicimus quod hoc nomen 'anima' est nomen concretum in concretione dans intelligere substantiam sub accidente quod copulatur per hoc verbum 'animo', 'animas'. Quantum autem ad illud accidens, dicimus quod dicit Aristoteles, animam esse perfectionem corporis organici habentis etc., et in hac comparatione anime ad corpus est anima perfectio ipsius, scilicet in quantum ipsa vivificat corpus, et sub hac comparatione subiacet anima physici speculationi; preter autem illud accidens considerata, subiacet speculationi metaphysici. (...)

> Forte dicet aliquis quod theologi est tractare de anima. Contra. Theologus habet inquirere qua via contingat animam mereri et demereri, et quid sit ad salutem, quid ad penam. Quid autem anima sit, et in quo predicamento sit, et qualiter infundatur corpori, non habet ipse inquirere.

John Blund, one of the first Latin intellectuals to be broadly influenced by Avicenna's and Aristotle's treatises on the soul, consigns psychology to the philosopher's – not the theologian's – competence. A few decades later, Hugh of St-Cher presents a totally opposite opinion. According to the Dominican master, the speculation pertaining to the essence of the soul or its powers forms part of theology.[2]

---

[1]   Ioh. Blund, *tract. de an.*, 2, 2, ed. Callus-Hunt, p. 7[1-18].

[2]   Hugo de S. Caro, *q. de an.*, 1, ed. Bieniak, p. 168[3-9]: "Quoniam multi errauerunt circa substantiam anime, ut dicit Augustinus De natura et origine anime ad Victorem, ideo utile est inquirere de anima, primo quid sit, quantum ad speculationem theologi pertinet; et sunt tria quesita: primo quid sit anima secundum diffinitionem et secundum essentiam et in quo differat ab angelo; secundo utrum unius et eiusdem sint anima rationalis et anima sensibilis et anima uegetabilis; tercio de principiis anime rationalis, utrum scilicet sit ex materia et forma".

This difference in orientation is significant. Indeed, both authors might have easily found strong arguments in support of their point of view. On the one hand, in the Latin West, there was a deep-rooted tradition of psychological speculation chiefly inspired by the Church fathers, among whom Augustine had the primacy.[3] On the other hand, by the reception of the texts of the new Aristotle, of Avicenna and, from the 1220s onwards, of Averroes, a specifically philosophical perspective began to emerge. To be sure, such a bipartition into psychological trends considerably simplifies the framework of the influences actually operating at the beginning of the century: among other things, we should not neglect the increasing weight of authors rather more difficult to be classified, such as Nemesius of Emesa and John Damascene. Yet, we will here make use of this simplified bipartite distinction because, in Hugh of St-Cher's thought, these two approaches – the philosophical one and the theological one – seem to introduce a division in the discourse about the soul. This division concerns the powers of the soul.

Before asking what Hugh and other authors of the first decades of the thirteenth century thought about the ontological status of the faculties of the soul, we should clarify which type of powers they were speaking of. For there are two types of powers which belong to two different contexts. On the one hand, we have the rational faculties, i.e. memory, reason and will. The discussion of this type of powers clearly belongs to the theological context and it is found especially in the commentaries on the third distinction of book I of Peter Lombard's *Sentences*. Besides the *Sentences* commentaries, in the 1220s and 1230s there appear a large number of disputed questions on the soul as image of the Trinity. Questions of this kind examine above all the three rational powers and very rarely the sensitive or vegetative powers. This limitation results from a tradition established by Philo of Alexandria, who held that only the higher part of the soul, i.e. the νοῦς or *mens*, was created in the image of God.[4] Philo's theory appears in Hilary of Poitiers's writings[5] and is assimilated by medieval authors mainly through Augustine.[6] Alexander of Hales expresses a similar idea in his *Gloss*. His opinion may be considered as characteristic of many theologians belonging to his generation: the vegetative soul and the sensitive soul are too closely linked with matter to be

---

[3] Cf. Tolomio, *L'anima dell'uomo, passim.*

[4] Phil. Alex., *quod deter.*, 83, 1, ed. Feuer, p. 70; cf. R. Javelet, *Image et ressemblance au douzième siècle. De Saint Anselme à Alain de Lille*, Strasbourg: Éditions Letouzey & Ané, 1967, I, pp. 21-22; II, p. 5.

[5] Javelet, *Image et ressemblance*, I, pp. 53-54; II, p. 27; cf. Hil. Pict., *tract. super Ps.* CXVIII, 10, 6-7, ed. Doignon, CCSL 61a, p. 92, PL 9, 566 A-C; M. J. Rondeau, "Remarques sur l'anthropologie de saint Hilaire", *Studia Patristica* 6 (1962), pp. 197-210.

[6] Aug., *trin.* IX, 11. 16, ed. Mountain, CCSL 50, p. 307, PL 42, 969; *ibid.*, XIV, 3. 6, ed. Mountain, CCSL 50A, pp. 427-428, PL 42, 1040; cf. Alc., *rat. an.*, 5, PL 101, 641 A; cf. Javelet, *Image et ressemblance*, I, pp. 58-60, II, p. 31.

considered as image of the divine Trinity, it follows that only the higher part of the soul, i.e. the rational soul, possesses this dignity.[7]

Thanks to Augustine, the West saw the diffusion of a practice leading the thinkers to compare memory, reason and will to the three divine Persons. At the beginning of the thirteenth century, this analogy was to become closely linked to another question, i.e. the question of the identity of the soul with its powers. According to the texts written by the theology masters, the ontological status of the rational faculties was determined by the solution given to this problem before the eruption of the debates relating to the status of the agent intellect.

On the other hand, we have the lower powers of the human soul, i.e. the sensitive and vegetative faculties. The problems related to these types of powers were not present in the early commentaries on Peter Lombard's *Sentences*, including Hugh of St-Cher's commentary; this applies also to the case of William of Auxerre's *Summa aurea*. Philip the Chancellor's *Summa de bono* was to be one of the first witnesses to the introduction of this debate into the Parisian Faculty of Theology. A chapter of the *Summa* entitled *Utrum potentia sensibilis et rationalis in eadem substantia fundentur*[8] greatly affected the later theological speculation about the ontological status of the lower powers of the soul.[9] The chapter is mainly inspired by Avicenna's *De anima*:[10] indeed, similar questions also appear in John Blund's *Tractatus*[11] and Dominicus Gundissalinus' *De anima*.[12] In this context, the problem of the identity of the soul with its powers is never touched. The formulation of Philip's question rather suggests that the rational and the sensitive powers might even belong to two or three different substances: the hypothesis of the identity of the rational soul with the sensitive and vegetative powers remains thus totally ignored.

In Hugh of St-Cher's reflection on the powers of the soul, the junction of these two trends – the theological one and the philosophical one – is limited. It is above

---

[7] Alex. Halen., *gloss. in* I *Sent.*, d. 3, n. 30, ed. PP. Collegii S. Bonaventurae, p. 52[5-12]: "Determinatum est de Trinitate per vestigium; nunc determinat de ea per trinitatem quae est in anima. Haec autem trinitas non sumitur secundum animam vegetabilem, quia ipsa non est separabilis a materia. Nec omnino secundum sensibilem, quia, licet sensus sit susceptivus sensibilium specierum praeter materiam, tamen ut sunt in materia et ideo non est conversiva ad Trinitatem increatam. Et ideo proprie trinitas creata est in superiori parte rationis"; cf. Ioh. Rup., *sum. de an.*, I, 33, ed. Bougerol, pp. 105[1]-107[70].

[8] Cf. Philipp., *sum. de bon.*, ed. Wicki, pp. 231[1]-237[195]; Lottin, *Psychologie et morale*, I, pp. 465-471.

[9] Cf. Zavalloni, *Richard de Mediavilla*, pp. 397-399.

[10] Auic., *de an.* V, 7, ed. Van Riet, pp. 154-174. About the importance of the Avicennian classification of the powers of the soul, see Hasse, *Avicenna's De anima*, p. 228, pp. 236-314, especially pp. 242-253.

[11] Ioh. Blund, *tract. de an.*, 4, ed. Callus-Hunt, pp. 10-13.

[12] Dom. Gund., *de an.*, 4, ed. Muckle, pp. 44-47.

all a simple coexistence, in which the two points of view are not seen in comparison with each other. For this reason, we will here deal with the ontological status of the rational powers and of the lower faculties separately. By contrast, the case of the concept of memory will avail to show some consequences of the junction of the theological tradition and Avicennianism.

2.1.2   THE IDENTITY OF THE SOUL WITH ITS POWERS

2.1.2.1   The Augustinian and Pseudo-Augustinian heritage

When Hugh of St-Cher, in his *Sentences Commentary*, addressed the theme of the soul as image of the Trinity, he had behind him a long series of works in which the same problem had already been discussed.[13] These texts have their primary source in Augustine of Hippo's *De Trinitate* and his interpretation of Genesis 1: 26 "Faciamus hominem ad imaginem et similitudinem nostram".[14] Trinity-God creates the human being in his own image: hence, man bears a created trinity in himself which reflects the uncreated Trinity of his Creator. This human trinity is principally identified with *mens*, *amor* and *notitia*, through which the soul knows God and itself.[15] It remains unclear whether the elements of this first triad may be defined as powers of the soul.[16] In any case, Augustine endows the soul with a second trinity too, which is composed of memory, reason and will, i.e. three rational powers.[17] Many later authors referred to this analogy, formulated by Augustine, in order to prove that the soul is identical with its powers. In effect, book

---

[13]   This reconstruction of the debate concerning the soul as image of the Trinity is principally based on P. Künzle's work *Das Verhältnis der Seele zu ihren Potenzen; problemgeschichtliche Untersuchungen von Augustin bis und mit Thomas von Aquin*, Freiburg: Universitätsverlag, 1956, *passim*; see also Javelet, *Image et ressemblance*, I, pp. 21-60.

[14]   Aug., *trin.* VII, 6. 12, ed. Mountain, CCSL 50, p. 266, PL 42, 945: "Et faciamus, et nostram, pluraliter dictum est, et nisi ex relativis accipi non oportet. Non enim ut facerent dii, aut ad imaginem et similitudinem deorum; sed ut facerent Pater et Filius et Spiritus sanctus, ad imaginem Patris et Filii et Spiritus sancti, ut subsisteret homo imago Dei. Deus autem Trinitas".

[15]   Cf. Aug., *trin.* IX, 1-12, ed. Mountain, CCSL 50, pp. 292-310, PL 42, 959-972.

[16]   Cf. Künzle, *Das Verhältnis*, pp. 7-18.

[17]   As regards the Augustinian theory of the soul as image of the Trinity, see also M. Schmaus, "Das Fortwirken der augustinischen Trinitätspsychologie bis zur Karolingischen Zeit", in *Vitae et Veritati. Festgabe für Karl Adam*, Düsserldorf: Patmos-Verlag, 1956, pp. 44-56; P. Hadot, "L'image de la Trinité dans l'âme chez Victorinus et chez saint Augustin", in *Studia Patristica*, VI, Berlin: Akademie-Verlag, 1962, pp. 409-442; G. O'Daly, *Augustine's Philosophy of Mind*, Berkeley: University of California Press, 1987; J. Brachtendorf, *Die Struktur des menschlichen Geistes nach Augustinus. Selbsreflexion und Erkenntnis Gottes in "De Trinitate"*, Felix Meiner, Hamburg, 2000; *Gott und sein Bild. Augustins De Trinitate im Spiegel gegenwärtiger Forschung*, edited by J. Brachtendorf, Schöningh, Paderborn, 2000.

x of *De Trinitate* contains several passages where the author appears to support the identity thesis. A considerable contribution to the success enjoyed by these passages was given by Peter Lombard, who inserted them in the third distinction of book I of the *Sentences*.[18] However, as Pius Künzle observes, the traditional opinion that the identity thesis was supported by Augustine may be subjected to doubt on the basis of *De Trinitate* itself. In fact, it seems that, in book xv, Augustine declares himself in favour of a real distinction between the soul and its powers.[19] This position is further clarified in the *Epistula* 169:[20]

> Primo ergo in hoc invenitur ista similitudo dissimilis, quod tria haec, memoria, intelligentia, voluntas, animae insunt, non eadem tria est anima; illa vero trinitas non inest, sed ipsa Deus est. Ideo ibi mirabilis simplicitas commendatur, quia non ibi aliud est esse aliud intelligere vel si quid aliud de Dei natura dicitur; anima vero quia est, etiam dum non intellegit, aliud est, quod est, aliud, quod intelligit.

Following Künzle's analysis, we may conclude that a faithful exegesis of the Augustinian theology did not necessarily lead to a general defence of the identity thesis. And yet we know that, before the thirteenth century, most Christian theologians maintained this doctrine and almost unanimously ascribed it to Augustine. By contrast, a true source of the theory of the identity of the soul with its powers is contained in the writings of Isidore of Seville, who was mainly inspired by Lactantius's thought.[21] Indeed, Isidore claims that the difference existing between memory, will and reason – just like between the other faculties of the soul – is a merely nominal difference, because these are simply different denominations of the same substance of the soul. Isidore clearly states that the soul constitutes the immediate principle of its own operations.[22] This is the most typical form of the identity thesis and will be taken up as frequently as the Augustinian texts.[23] One

---

[18] Petr. Lomb., *sent.* I, d. 3, c. 2, ed. PP. Collegii S. Bonaventurae, pp. 72-74; cf. Aug., *trin.* X, 11. pp. 17-18, ed. Mountain, CCSL 50, pp. 329-330, PL 42, 982-983: "Hic enim quaedam apparet trinitas memoriae, intelligentiae et amoris. "Haec igitur tria potissimum tractemus: memoriam, intelligentiam, voluntatem". Haec igitur tria, ut ait Augustinus in libro x De *Trinitate*, non sunt tres vitae, sed una vita; nec tres mentes, sed una mens, una essentia"; id., *trin.* IX, 5. 8, ed. Mountain, CCSL 50, p. 301, PL 42, 965: "Miro itaque modo tria ista inseparabilia sunt a seipsis; et tamen eorum singulum et simul omnia una essentia est, cum et relative dicantur ad invicem".

[19] Cf. Künzle, *Das Verhältnis*, p. 21; Aug., *trin.* XV, 17. 28, ed. Mountain, CCSL 50a, p. 503, PL 42, 1080.

[20] Aug., *ep.* CLXIX, 2. 6, ed. Goldbacher, CSEL 44, pp. 615^{23}-616^{1}, PL 33, 744; cf. Künzle, *Das Verhältnis*, p. 22.

[21] Cf. Künzle, *Das Verhältnis*, pp. 34-38.

[22] Cf. Isid. Hisp., *diff.* II, 29. 97, PL 83, 84 B-C.

[23] Künzle, *Das Verhältnis*, p. 38.

of the main reasons why this doctrine was later to become closely related to Augustinianism is that, in the following centuries, thinkers became acquainted with Isidore's thought principally through the influential Pseudo-Augustinian treatise entitled *De spiritu et anima*.[24] Among the outstanding authors who strongly supported the identity thesis by relying on Augustine's authority, Künzle mentions above all Bernard of Clairvaux,[25] Hugh of St Victor[26] and Peter Lombard. In particular, the author of the *Sentences* speaks of the identity of the soul with memory, reason and will by referring to some passages from *De Trinitate* which originally presented another Augustinian triad, i.e. *mens*, *amor* and *notitia*.[27] The thesis of the identity of the soul with its rational powers thus enters the third distinction of book I of Peter Lombard's *Sentences*. Henceforth, the problem of the ontological status of the rational faculties is mostly discussed by the authors commenting on this passage by Peter Lombard, and among them we shall find Hugh of St-Cher as well.

2.1.2.2   William of Auxerre

A substantial part of Hugh of St-Cher's *Sentences Commentary* consists in an almost verbatim reproduction of William of Auxerre's *Summa aurea*.[28] This does not apply to the commentary on the third distinction of book I. In order to understand the difference between the texts of the two authors, let us first concentrate on the doctrine of the soul as image of God which is presented in the *Summa aurea*.[29]

---

[24] Ps.-Aug., *spir. et an.*, 13, PL 40, 788-789: "Dicitur namque anima, dum vegetat; spiritus, dum contemplatur; sensus, dum sentit; animus, dum sapit; dum intelligit, mens; dum discernit, ratio; dum recordatur, memoria; dum consentit, voluntas. Ista tamen non differunt in substantia, quemadmodum in nominibus; quoniam omnia ista una anima est: proprietates quidem diversae, sed essentia una".

[25] Bern. Clar., *de conver.*, 2. 3, ed. Leclercq - Rochais, pp. 72-74, PL 182, 836 A-B; cf. Künzle, *Das Verhältnis*, pp. 59-63.

[26] Hugo de S. Vict., *didasc.* II, 5, ed. Buttimer, pp. 27²⁸-28¹⁰, PL 176, 754 A-B; cf. Künzle, *Das Verhältnis*, pp. 74-77.

[27] Petr. Lomb., *sent.* I, d. 3, c. 2, ed. PP. Collegii S. Bonaventurae, p. 74⁴⁻¹¹: "Sed iam videndum est quomodo haec tria dicantur una substantia: ideo scilicet quia in ipsa anima vel mente substantialiter existunt, non sicut accidentia in subiectis, quae possunt adesse vel abesse. Unde Augustinus in libro IX De Trinitate ait: «Admonemur, si utcumque videre possumus, haec in animo existere substantialiter, non tamquam in subjecto, ut color in corpore, quia etsi relative dicuntur ad invicem, singula tamen substantialiter sunt in sua substantia». Ecce ex quo sensu illa tria dicantur esse unum vel una substantia"; cf. Aug., *trin.* IX, 4. 5, ed. Mountain, CCSL 50, p. 297, PL 42, 963; cf. Künzle, *Das Verhältnis*, pp. 83-84.

[28] Cf. Landgraf, *Introduction*, p. 175; M. Bieniak, "The Sentences Commentary of Hugh of St.-Cher", in *Mediaeval Commentaries on the Sentences of Peter Lombard. Vol. 2*, edited by P. Rosemann, Leiden: Brill, 2010, pp. 129-131.

[29] Cf. Lottin, *Psychologie et morale*, vol. I, pp. 484-486; Künzle, *Das Verhältnis*, pp. 103-105.

William of Auxerre approaches the theme of the ontological status of the three
rational powers of the soul in book II of his *Summa*, when he speaks of the creation of man in the image of God. Like the other theologians of his time, William
relies principally on Augustine's *De Trinitate*. However, unlike the supporters of
the identity thesis, he does not ascribe the identity doctrine to Augustine, but cites
it as an opinion held by "some masters" (*quidam*).[30] Evidently, he is referring to the
doctrine transmitted by *De spiritu et anima* (although the title is not explicitly
mentioned): according to the *quidam*, the three rational powers are identical with
the soul itself and are distinguished from one another just by their acts.

William sharply criticizes this doctrine, accusing it of being not only against
God but also against all philosophy. First of all, only in God are being and having
power the same. If someone objects that in prime matter the power of receiving
a form coincides with the essence of prime matter itself, the answer is that the
power of prime matter is formless, hence it precedes any power or form.[31] Further,
the identity thesis is denied on Porphyry's authority: the philosopher clearly affirms that rationality constitutes a quality of the soul. Finally, William proposes
two further arguments based on his angelology. These arguments claim that, if the
soul were identical with its powers, then two absurd consequences would follow.
First, in order to retain the thesis that angel and soul are different as to species,
one should assert that they belong to two distinct genera as well. For this reason,
if the soul is identical with its powers, then the latter determine both its genus and
its species. Hence, if the generic and specific nature of the soul is determined by
its powers, then a specific difference with the angel is not possible unless admit-

---

[30] Guill. Altissiod., *sum. aur.* II, 9, c. 1, q. 6, ed. Ribailler, p. 243[69-75]: "Quidam tamen
dicunt quod hec tria sunt proprie unum, et intelligunt hoc de ipsa potentia. Dicunt enim
quod anima idem est quod sua potentia, sed dicuntur esse tres potentie propter diversos
actus, cum non sit nisi una anima et una potentia in essentia. Et hoc volunt habere verbis
beati Augustini, que dicunt quod hec tria sunt una vita, una anima, et per hoc quod ipse
dicit: «hec tria non sunt in anima ut in subiecto»; ergo non sunt qualitates anime, sed ipsa
anima".

[31] Cf. Guill. Altissiod., *sum. aur.* II, 9, c. 1, q. 6, ed. Ribailler, p. 243[83-93]: "Predicta vero
opinio est contra Deum. Ex illa enim opinione sequitur quod anime et angelo idem est et
esse et posse, quod soli Deo convenit propter sui extremam simplicitatem, licet in prima
materia videatur idem esse quod posse suscipere formam quamlibet. Talis enim potentia
non est aliqua potentia sed informitas potentie, precedens omnem potentiam et omnem
formam. Sic ergo nulla res habens esse non in aliam formam habet que non ipsa est, sed
materia que habet esse in alio, et ante perfectionem naturaliter habet nullam formam,
quamvis denominetur ab nominibus formarum per aliquam similitudinem; et ideo non
sequitur quod si materia est sua potentia, quod anima sua sit potentia, cum proprie non
dicatur materia habere aliquam potentiam vel aliquid posse".

ting the difference of genus too.[32] Second, the intellect of the soul and the intellect of the angel would be different as to species. Indeed, if the soul's species is totally determined by the cognitive power, i.e. by the intellect, then the intellect of the soul must be specifically different from that of the angel, because the two spiritual creatures belong to two different species.[33] Following Augustine and Peter Lombard, we should argue that powers complete the being of the soul but are not identical with it.[34]

William of Auxerre is not the first Latin author to reject the thesis of the identity of the soul with its powers: indeed, at the beginning of the twelfth century, William of Champeaux had maintained a similar position.[35] Furthermore, it should be noted that Avicenna too, in his *Liber de anima*, clearly states that the soul and its powers cannot be identified with one another.[36] Nevertheless, in spite of the accessibility of these sources and of the great authority exerted by the *Summa aurea*, William of Auxerre's direct successors immediately took up the identity thesis. The traditional Pseudo-Augustinian doctrine was to be defended with special force by Hugh of St-Cher.

2.1.2.3   Hugh of St-Cher

The arguments employed by William are cogent and coherent and certainly deserved to be considered by those who approached the problem of the trinity in the soul. Nevertheless, Hugh's *Sentences Commentary* clearly does not take into account the exposition elaborated by the secular master. This omission is astonishing chiefly because, in most cases, the Dominican commentator follows the *Summa aurea* very closely. By contrast, the commentary on the third distinction of book I seems to be more inspired by the Lombard's text than by the theological literature of Hugh's own time. The text is founded on the passages from Augus-

---

[32] Cf. Guill. Altissiod., *sum. aur.* II, 9, c. 1, q. 6, ed. Ribailler, p. 244[96-101]: "Preterea sequitur ex hac opinione quod anima et angelus non continentur in aliquo genere, quia non conveniunt in aliquo substantiali, quia nec anima nec angelus habet aliquod substantiale quod non sit ipsa; et ita cum anima et angelus sit diversarum specierum non communicant in aliquo substantiali; ergo non communicant in aliquo genere, quod manifeste falsum est".

[33] Cf. Guill. Altissiod., *sum. aur.* II, 9, c. 1, q. 6, ed. Ribailler, p. 244[102-104]: "Ex hoc etiam sequitur quod intellectus hominis et angeli sint diversarum specierum; et probatur quod hoc sit falsum, cum sint de eodem proprie et habeant eandem perfectionem".

[34] Cf. Guill. Altissiod., *sum. aur.* II, 9, c. 1, q. 6, ed. Ribailler, pp. 243[94]-244[109]; Künzle, *Das Verhältnis*, pp. 103-105.

[35] "Ponit iterum de anima et ratione. Sed iterum ratio, licet potentia sit animae, non tamen eiusdem cum anima substantiae sed eius inseparabilis forma. Nam quod in praedictis ratio et anima una est anima, convenienter est intelligendum, ut potius illa dicamus simul et inseparabiliter inhaerere et non idem etiam in substantia esse", ed. G. Lefèvre, in *Les variations de Guillaume de Champeaux et la question des Universaux: Étude suivie de documents originaux*, Lille 1898, p. 24; Künzle, *Das Verhältnis*, p. 50.

[36] Cf. Auic., *de an.* I, 5, ed. Van Riet, pp. 80[17]-81[5]; Künzle, *Das Verhältnis*, pp. 100-101.

tine's *De Trinitate* which are cited in the *Sentences*. Hugh entirely shares the interpretation of these texts given by Peter Lombard; yet, his commentary goes beyond a simple interpretation of Augustine. Indeed, it is interesting to draw a comparison between a passage of his writing and a passage excerpted from Augustine's correspondence:

AUGUSTINUS HIPPONENSIS[37]	HUGO DE SANCTO CARO[38]
Primo ergo in hoc invenitur ista similitudo dissimilis, quod tria haec, memoria, intellegentia, voluntas, animae insunt, non eadem tria est anima; illa vero trinitas non inest, sed ipsa Deus est.	...ideo subiungit triplicem dissimilitudinem: (...) tertia est inter trinitates: ille tres sunt unus deus, et non unius dei. Set ille tres sunt unius hominis, non unus homo.

A marked parallelism can be noticed between Augustine's and Hugh's statements. Hugh probably knows the epistle written by the bishop of Hippo quite well; however, whereas Augustine affirms that the rational powers are not identical with the soul, Hugh replaces 'soul' with 'man', thus distorting the meaning of the statements he finds in his source. Therefore, it seems that, in order to maintain the identity of the soul with its rational powers, Hugh was ready not only to contradict William of Auxerre, but also to conflict with the words of Augustine himself. Hence, it can be useful to observe how Hugh justifies the identity thesis in his text.

Hugh's commentary on the third distinction of book I consists of the *expositiones litterae* and five questions discussing various problems mentioned by Peter Lombard. The second and the fifth of these five questions concern the theme of the trinity of the soul. In both, Hugh declares himself definitely in favour of the identity of the soul with its powers, although he concentrates on two different aspects of this problem. In the second question, Hugh wonders whether the rational powers of the soul differ from one another. The central argument of the passage consists in the opposition between the fact of existing as accident and as essence. According to Hugh, the rational powers must exist in the soul in one of these ways: either as accidents or as essence of the soul. But memory, reason and will cannot exist in the soul as its accidents, because they are rational faculties and certainly the human soul is not conceivable without its own rationality. Indeed, if these faculties were simple accidents, we might think the human soul apart from its rationality. According to Hugh, this perspective is inadmissible; consequently, the rational faculties must exist in the soul in an essential way (*essentialiter*), i.e., they must be identical with the very essence of the soul.[39]

---

[37] Aug., *ep.* CLXIX, 2. 6, ed. Goldbacher, CSEL 44, p. 615[23-27], PL 33, 744; cf. *supra*, pp. 98-100.

[38] Hugo de S. Caro, *in* I *Sent.*, d. 3, *infra*, p. 194.

[39] Hugo de S. Caro, *in* I *Sent.*, d. 3, 2, *infra*, pp. 189-190: "Preterea. Memoria etc. aut sunt in anima accidentaliter, aut essentialiter. Si accidentaliter, ergo anima potest intelligi esse preter hec. Set idem est ratio quod intelligentia et uoluntas et memoria, ergo anima

This argument determines the solution of the problem. Even if the three rational powers can be distinguished as to their respective acts, they are basically identical with the essence of the soul, hence they are also identical with one another. Hugh then concludes that the soul is the immediate principle of its own intellectual operations.[40]

In the fifth question Hugh inserts in the commentary on the third distinction of book I of the *Sentences*,[41] he focuses his attention on another aspect of the problem of the trinity in the soul, i.e. the simplicity of the soul. Assuming that powers are present in the soul *essentialiter*, Hugh wonders how this mode of existence must be understood. Indeed, on the one hand, we might consider the powers of the soul as parts of its essence – "uel tanquam partes integrales in toto, uel tanquam partes essentiales"; but, in this case, we should admit that the soul is not simple – hence corruptible – because all composite realities are corruptible by nature. On the other hand, some hold the opinion that the three rational powers constitute the essential form or the perfection of the soul; consequently, according to this point of view, the soul is composed of matter and spiritual form. The second position too involves the admission of a composition in the soul, and this composition necessarily implies corruptibility. Yet, Hugh explains that the essential composition implies only one type of corruptibility. Indeed, a thing may become corrupt for two reasons: first, because it bears in itself the principle of corruption caused by the presence of opposite elements; second, because it does not bear the principle of conservation in itself. Composite things, as such, do not bear the principle of corruption in themselves but are corruptible because they do not possess the principle of conservation, so they naturally tend toward decomposition.

The idea that all that which is composite must be corruptible belongs to the Neoplatonic tradition and is present, for example, in the works of Calcidius,[42]

---

potest intelligi sine rationali, et hoc falsum. Si essentialiter, ergo sunt idem in essentia quod anima, ergo et idem erunt in essentia, non ergo diuersa"; cf. Lottin, *Psychologie et morale*, vol. I, pp. 486-487. Hugh's argument is not new: it appears, for example, in a treatise written by Ailred of Rielvaux († 1166); cf. Ailr. Riev., *dial. de an.* I, ed. Talbot, pp. 79¹-80¹⁴; cf. Künzle, *Das Verhältnis*, p. 73.

[40] Hugo de S. Caro, *in I Sent.*, d. 3, 2, *infra*, p. 190: "Solutio. Memoria quandoque dicitur pro actu memorandi, et ita de aliis duobus, et secundum hoc sunt diuersa; quandoque pro obiectis, idest pro memorato et uolito et intellecto, et secundum hoc idem possunt esse in essentia. Diuersa autem erunt in ratione quandoque pro potentia. Et sic eadem in essentia, diuersa accidente siue relatione. Et idem sunt in essentia quod anima. Hec enim est uera "anima est memoria", sensus enim est "anima habet potentiam memorandi", et ita de aliis duobus".

[41] Cf. Hugo de S. Caro, *in I Sent.*, d. 3, 5, *infra*, pp. 195-197.

[42] Calc., *comm. in Tim.* CCXXVII, ed. Jensen – Waszink, pp. 242-243; cf. Cass., *de an.*, 2, PL 70, 1285 C.

Claudianus Mamertus[43] and Nemesius of Emesa,[44] an author Hugh cites several times in the question on the soul. Finally, also Avicenna, in his *De anima*,[45] reiterates the same ideas: according to the muslim philosopher, the soul is totally simple, he therefore does not even admit in the soul a composition between the act of existing and the possibility of not being, as Verbeke explains in his introduction to Avicenna's psychology.[46] All that which is composite contains in itself the possibility of perishing, and this concerns in particular the composition of matter and form, because matter is conceived of in a Neoplatonic sense, i.e. as a non-being, a pure negativity.

In agreement with the Neoplatonic tradition, Hugh rejects all the positions denying the essential simplicity of the soul. This criticism becomes even more explicit in the third article of his disputed question *De anima*, where the theologian adopts a systematic approach to the problem of the various possible types of composition in spiritual substances. On that occasion, the Dominican master manifestly opposes the idea of spiritual form and matter and holds that the soul is composed of two different principles, i.e. *quo est* and *quod est*.[47] However, it should be noted that subsequently Hugh reiterated that this composition is only admissible "ratione siue comparatione", and not according to nature.[48] It follows that, in Hugh's mind, these principles can only be distinguished by a distinction of reason, by virtue of a purely theoretical abstraction, and do not constitute real parts of the soul.[49]

---

[43] Claud. Mam., *de stat. an.* II, 5, ed. Engelbrecht, CSEL 11, pp. 115-117.

[44] Nemes., *nat. hom.*, pp. 30^{71}-31^{90}; cf. Plato, *Phaedo*, 85e-86d, ed. Minio-Paluello, pp. 44^{22}-45^{17}.

[45] Auic., *de an.* V, 3, ed. Van Riet, p. 122^{71}: "Manifestum est igitur quod in eo quod est simplex non compositum aut radix compositi, non conveniunt effectus permanendi et potentia destruendi comparatione suae essentiae".

[46] G. Verbeke, "Le «De anima» d'Avicenne. Une conception spiritualiste de l'homme", in Auic., *de an.*, IV-V, ed. Van Riet, p. 35*.

[47] Hugo de S. Caro, *q. de an.*, 3, Solutio; ad 2, ed. Bieniak, pp. 180^{438}-181^{457}, p. 181^{463}-^{471}; cf. Bieniak, "Una questione disputata", pp. 142-147; id., "Filippo il Cancelliere ed Ugo di St.-Cher sull'anima umana" in *Ordine dei Predicatori e l'Università di Bologna. Atti del convegno (Bologna, 18-20 febbraio 2005)*, ed. G. Bertuzzi, Bologna: Edizioni Studio Domenicano, 2006, pp. 105-117; Philipp., *sum. de bon.*, ed. Wicki, I, pp. 65-70; Philipp., *q. de ymag.*, ed. Wicki, p. 176$^{243-247}$; cf. Lottin, "Un petit traité", pp. 469-475; id., *Psychologie et morale*, vol. I, pp. 430-442. On the meaning and the Boethian roots of the pair *quo est - quod est*, see especially C. Fabro, "La distinzione tra "quo est" e "quod est" nella "Summa de anima" di Giovanni De La Rochelle", *Divus Thomas* 41 (1938), pp. 508-522.

[48] Philip the Chancellor too denies that the soul is composed of parts; cf. Philip., *q. de ymag.*, ed. Wicki, p. 176$^{215-247}$.

[49] Hugh defines his position as "media via", i.e. a middle way between the total simplicity of the soul and its actual composition of two principles; cf. Hugo de S. Caro, *q. de*

The tendency to affirm the most complete possible simplicity of the soul is thus present both in Hugh's *Sentences Commentary* and in his disputed questions. This point of view probably derives from a conception expressed in the question *De anima*. Indeed, according to Hugh, the composition of parts, whatever they are, is proper to corporeal beings.[50]

What are then the causes which induce the Dominican theologian to affirm the identity of the soul with its rational powers? In the first place, Hugh intends to confirm the inseparability of reason from the concept of spiritual substance: the human soul is not conceivable except together with its rational faculties; hence, rationality cannot be an accident of the soul. Secondly, the essence of the soul cannot be "decomposable"; in other words, it is not possible to admit the presence of essential parts in the soul. For the same reason, the rational powers cannot be the substantial form of the soul, because the latter is not composed of spiritual matter and form. Finally, the composition of parts belongs solely to corporeal realities: affirming the simplicity of the soul thus coincides with defending its immateriality.

2.1.2.4   An anonymous question (ms. *Douai 434*, n. 115)

Probably in roughly the same period in which Hugh of St-Cher composed his questions, an anonymous master wrote a short disputed question on the problem of the ontological status of the powers of the soul. The question, entitled *Si anima est sue potentie*, is preserved in the first volume of the manuscript *Douai 434* and comes after another question, *De trinitate anime*, which is most probably to be ascribed to the same author.[51] The question concerning the identity of the soul with its powers represents a continuation of the preceding one, i.e. the question on the trinity in the soul. The relation between these two questions is significant: like his colleagues, our anonymous author relates the problem of the identity of the soul with its faculties to the theme of the soul as created in the image of the Trinity.

---

an., 3, Solutio, ed. Bieniak, p. 181[443]. Indeed, absolute simplicity was generally reserved only to God; cf. Petr. Lomb., *Sent.* I, d. 8, c. 4. 2, ed. PP. Collegii S. Bonaventurae, p. 99: "Hic de spirituali creatura ostendit quomodo sit multiplex et non simplex. "(...) Nichil enim simplex mutabile est; omnis autem creatura mutabilis est"; nulla ergo creatura vere simplex est"; Aug., *trin.*, VI, chap. 6, n. 8, ed. Mountain, CCSL 50, p. 237, PL 42, 929.

[50]   Hugo de S. Caro, *q. de an.*, 3, ad 11-12, ed. Bieniak, p. 183[534-539]: "Ad undecimum et duodecimum dico quod anima sua essentia numerabilis est, etiam separato omni accidente per quod distinguitur, licet intellectus et sensus non possit distinguere; et quod obicitur de puncto et unitate abstracta non est simile, quia illa non habent esse nisi in coniunctione pura intelliguntur abstracta; adhuc hoc non est illud, licet intellectus non possit distinguere. Item quod dicitur quod quae non habent materiam carent numero, intelligitur numero partium componentium esse eorum"; cf. Alan. de Ins., *fid. cath.* I, 30, PL 210, 333.

[51]   N. 114, according to Glorieux, "Les 572 Questions", p. 137.

Augustine's *De Trinitate* therefore continues to be present in the background. Nevertheless, it should be noted that, unlike Hugh of St-Cher, the anonymous author takes the Pseudo-Augustinian treatise *De spiritu et anima* as his starting point. Hence an important consequence: the thesis of the identity of the soul with its powers, which is held in our question, not only concerns the rational powers but also the vegetative and sensitive powers.[52] By contrast, it should be observed that in the two questions contained in Hugh of St-Cher's commentary, where *De spiritu et anima* is not cited, the identity of the soul with its powers concerns only the rational faculties, i.e. memory, reason and will.

The largest part of the question *Si anima est sue potentie* is a mosaic of Pseudo-Augustinian and Augustinian quotations; only the last lines of the text offer three arguments – one in favour and two against the identity thesis – inspired by Aristotle and John Damascene. Two of these arguments are reported by Philip the Chancellor and one by William of Auxerre: it follows that our author probably composed his question in a circle close to that in which the two theologians were active.

The solution presented in the text is short and unequivocal:[53] "Predictis rationibus concedi potest quod anima est sue potentie". The identity thesis is confirmed once again, against William of Auxerre and the new philosophical authorities.[54]

2.1.2.5 Philip the Chancellor and Alexander of Hales

Like Hugh's *Sentences Commentary*, Philip the Chancellor's *Summa de bono* was influenced by the *Summa aurea*. Nevertheless, in the question concerning the identity of the soul with its powers, Philip, just like Hugh, does not seem to take into account the solution proposed by William. Indeed, in the chapter of the *Summa* entitled *De bono nature*, Philip holds the identity thesis.[55] The solution

---

[52] An., *Questio si anima est sue potentie*, infra, p. 204: "Item. "Dicitur anima dum uegetat, spiritus dum contemplatur, sensus dum sentit, mens dum intelligit, ratio dum discurrit, memoria dum recordatur, uoluntas dum consentit. Ista tamen non differunt in substantia quemadmodum in nominibus, quoniam omnia ista una anima sunt". Item. "Tota anime substantia in hiis tribus plena et perfecta consistit: in rationabile, concupiscibile, irascibile, quasi quedam sua trinitate. Et tota quidem trinitas huiusmodi <est> quedam anime unitas et ipsa anima: deus omnia sua est, anima quedam sua. Potentie namque eius atque uires idem sunt quod ipsa; <ipsa> sue uirtutes uel accidentia non est"""; cf. Ps. Aug., *spir. et an.*, 13, PL 40, 788-789.

[53] Cf. an., *Questio si anima est sue potentie*, infra, p. 205.

[54] The same position (supported by similar arguments that are inspired by *De spiritu et anima*) is also maintained in William of Auvergne's *De anima*; cf. Guill. de Alv., *de an.*, 3, 6, ed. Le Feron, p. 92a-b; Künzle, *Das Verhältnis*, pp. 110-112.

[55] Philipp., *sum. de bon.*, ed. Wicki, I, pp. 252^{86}-253^{107}; cf. in particular p. 252$^{86-94}$: "Substantialiter autem dicuntur esse in anima, quia est potentia que accidens est in re cuius

offered by the theologian is particularly interesting. Philip distinguishes between three categories of powers: powers of the first type are accidental and can disappear without affecting the essence of their subject; powers of the second type, i.e. the natural powers, originate directly from the essence and constitute its properties; lastly, powers of the third type, i.e. the essential or substantial powers, are identical with the very essence of the subject, just as the power to receive a substantial form is identical with prime matter. The rational powers of the soul, says Philip, belong to the latter kind of powers. To support his position, the author of the *Summa de bono* quotes the passages in which Augustine maintains that the created trinity exists in the soul *substantialiter* or *essentialiter*.[56] We may thus conclude that, in the chapter *De bono nature*, Philip maintains the traditional identity thesis.[57] The same thesis – defended using similar arguments – is confirmed by Philip also in his disputed question entitled *De ymagine et similitudine nostra*.[58] It is possible to speak of different powers of the soul just referring to different actions accomplished by the soul itself: in fact, the rational powers are identical with the essence of the soul.

The identity doctrine in the version presented by Philip was later taken up by the anonymous author of the *Summa Duacensis*[59] and by Odo of Châteauroux († 1273) in his short disputed question entitled *"Faciamus hominem ad imaginem*

---

est potentia, et est potentia que consequitur essentiam sicut proprietas eius, et est potentia que est ipsa essentia adiciens quandam relationem ad actum. Verbi gratia potentia recipiendi similitudinem colorum est accidentalis pupille, deficit enim in ea per senium, potentia autem calefaciendi in igne est naturalis, potentia autem in materia recipiendi formam est ipsa substantia materie. Quanto magis potentia ipsius anime est ipsa, sed ad alium et ad alium actum relata. Et ideo dicitur quod anima est ipsa mens, ipsa intelligentia, ipsa voluntas, non quod hec accidentaliter sint in anima (...)".

[56] Aug., *trin.* XIII, chap. 4, PL 42, 963-964.

[57] Cf. Künzle, *Das Verhältnis*, pp. 108-109, pp. 228-229; Lottin, *Psychologie et morale*, I, pp. 488-489.

[58] Philipp., *q. de ymag.*, ed. Wicki, p. 176[227-239]: "Preterea, notandum quod triplex est potentia: accidentalis, ut potentia recipiendi colores; naturalis, ut potentia calefaciendi in igne; essentialis, ut potentia recipiendi formam substantialem, et hoc idem est essentiale cum eo cuius est potentia. Verbi gratia: prima materia est sua potentia, quia potens est recipere formam substantialem. Hoc ultimo modo dico sine preiudicio quod potentie anime sunt ipsa anima; sed inquantum ad alium et alium actum referuntur, diverse dicuntur potentie. Inquantum enim potens est memorari, dicitur potentia memorandi et sic de aliis potentiis. Ad hoc <quod> facit memorari, dicitur potentia memorandi, et sic de aliis potentiis. Ad hoc <quod> facit illud quod dicit Augustinus, De trinitate IX: "Admonemur hec in anima existere substantialiter, non tamquam in subiecto ut color in corpore" etc."; cf. Künzle, *Das Verhältnis*, p. 109.

[59] *Sum. Duac.*, ed. Glorieux, pp. 21-23; cf. Künzle, *Das Verhältnis*, pp. 106-107, pp. 225-226.

et similitudinem nostram".[60] Odo considerably abbreviates Philip's solution but preserves two important points, namely, (1) the analogy between the rational powers of the soul and the receptiveness of prime matter; (2) the quotation from book IX of Augustine's *De Trinitate.* Finally, John of La Rochelle too followed Philip's solution rather closely.[61]

What is most interesting, however, is the question of the relationship between the *Summa de bono* and Alexander of Hales' *Glossa* on Peter Lombard's *Sentences.*[62] There is a certain resemblance between the two texts; however, the solution presented by Philip in the chapter *De bono nature* is clearly different from that proposed in Alexander's *Glossa.* Philip proposes a tripartite classification of powers: (1) the accidental powers (2) the natural powers, i.e. properties; (3) the essential powers, i.e. those which are identical with the essence of the soul. This subdivision aims at demonstrating the identity of the soul with its rational powers, which belong to the third category. Alexander too inserts a tripartite subdivision in his exposition, but he does it for a different purpose: in fact, he aims at demonstrating the difference between the powers of the soul and the powers of God. Only the powers of God can be identified with the essence of the subject; on the other hand, the soul is a creature, and therefore it cannot be identical to its powers.

In order to clarify the difference between the powers of the soul and the powers of God, Alexander introduces a distinction between essence, substance and subject.[63] In general, it was rather unusual at the time to distinguish between essence and substance.[64] Yet, it should be noted that Alexander's distinction calls to mind the fundamental ontological distinction proposed by Gilbert of Poitiers. Indeed, the *Glossa* identifies the *essentia* with *quo est* or, using Gilbert's word, with *esse*,

---

[60] Cf. Kunzle, *Das Verhältnis*, p. 115, pp. 232-233; Lottin, *Psychologie et morale*, I, p. 489. Odo's question, just like the *Summa Duacensis*, is only preserved in ms. *Douai 434.*

[61] Cf. Ioh. Rup., *sum. de an.*, pp. 113[63]-114[94], pp. 182[1]-184[74]; cf. Kunzle, *Das Verhältnis*, pp. 122-123.

[62] Contradictory conclusions have been reached concerning the relative chronology of the two works: the editors of the *Glossa* maintain the temporal priority of Alexander's work, whereas Nicolaus Wicki argues for the priority of the *Summa de bono*. Cf. PP. Collegii S. Bonaventurae, "Prolegomena" in Alex. Halen., *Glossa in quatuor libros Sententiarum*, Firenze: Quaracchi, 1952, II, pp. 10*-18*; Wicki, "Introduction", in Philipp., *sum. de bon.*, I, pp. 64*-66*.

[63] Alex. Halen., *gloss. in* I *Sent.*, d. 3, ed. PP. Collegii S. Bonaventurae, p. 65[13-27]: "*Essentia* est illud, quo res est id, quod est, ut homo humanitate. *Substantia* vero, quo res est substans sive subsistit inseparabiliter. *Subiectum* est cui adveniunt aliqua et sine quorum aliquo vel quolibet res potest esse. Unde et definitur a Philosopho: «Subiectum est in se completum ens, occasio alterius existendi in ipso». (...) Subiectum dicitur anima respectu accidentium, substantia respectu proprietatum, essentia respectu essentialium".

[64] Cf., for example, Hugo de S. Caro, *in* I *Sent.*, d. 25, ed. Breuning, p. 386, n. 189: "Omnino idem est modo substantia et essentia".

i.e. the essential determination. The *substantia* is defined as the principle of sub-
sistence of a thing, namely, the principle by virtue of which a thing subsists and is
one. Finally, the *subiectum* means the subsisting thing, complete with all its essential determinations, which constitutes the subject for accidental determinations.

Alexander avails himself of this threefold distinction to determine the ontological status of the three rational powers of the soul. Memory, intelligence and will
– unlike the divine Persons – are not identical as to their essence, but rather form
the same substance. For the substance of the soul would be incomplete without its
powers.[65] Therefore, according to Alexander, the powers of the soul are different as
to essence, but identical as to substance.

In agreement with this view, Alexander proposes a division of powers different
from that proposed by Philip. Indeed, powers can be substantial (like the powers
of the soul), natural (like heat), accidental (like the power of seeing or the power of
running) or essential (like the powers of God).[66]

Philip's argumentations as we have presented it above and Alexander's treat-
ment certainly have at least one point in common. Both authors actually use the
distinction between accidents, properties and essence. But this is an Aristotelian
distinction, hence it is not necessary to assume a mutual dependence between
the two works on account of this similarity, also because Philip and Alexander
belonged to the same Parisian milieu during the same period. Nevertheless, as we
shall see later on, Philip in another passage seems to refer to the words formulated
by the Franciscan master.

The solution proposed by Alexander has some interesting consequences. First
of all, the essence of the soul can no longer be identified with memory, intellect
and will, because the essence of these three powers is not the same. Secondly, the
three rational powers can be defined as substantial powers of the soul – and not
as its accidents – because they form part of the substance of the soul. The solution

---

[65] Alex. Halen., *gloss. in* I *Sent.*, d. 3, ed. PP. Collegii S. Bonaventurae, p. 65[9-10, 19-21]: "Tres
enim personae conveniunt in essentia; memoria, intelligentia, voluntas in substantia, separantur autem in essentia. (...) Istae ergo tres potentiae distinguuntur secundum essentiam,
sed conveniunt in substantia, quia anima non est completa substantia sine suis potentiis.
Cum autem in eo quod dico 'substare' duo sunt: 'sub' et 'stare', anima uno modo supponitur
potentiis, alio modo e converso. Prout enim actus primo est ab anima, quae et operatur
per potentias, sic est super potentias; sed in quantum operatio est in anima mediantibus
potentiis, sic supponitur".
[66] Alex. Halen., *gloss. in* I *Sent.*, d. 3, ed. PP. Collegii S. Bonaventurae, p. 67[22-29]: "Potentia
dicitur multipliciter: tum substantialis, tum naturalis, tum accidentalis, tum essentialis.
Essentialis est sicut potentia Dei; substantialis sicut potentia animae; naturalis sicut potentia calidi in manu; accidentalis dupliciter: vel impressa, sicut potentia visibilis in pupilla;
vel contracta, sicut potentia currendi. Quando ergo dicimus quod tres sunt in anima, intelligitur substantialiter, non essentialiter".

here thus allows Alexander to block the attribution of the same absolute unity (which is proper only to God) to the soul, as well as to block the reduction of the rationality of the human soul to an accident. The reason why Alexander's position was adopted by contemporary as well as later theology masters becomes, then, absolutely clear. And among them there was – first of all – Philip the Chancellor.

As previously seen, in the chapter *De bono nature* contained in the *Summa de bono* and in the question *De ymagine*, Philip maintains the essential and substantial identity of the rational powers with the human soul and does not distinguish between the concept of essence and that of substance. However, this distinction does appear when Philip dwells on the problem of the identity of the soul with its powers for a third time. Actually, in the *Summa de bono*, about fifteen manuscript folios after the chapter *De bono nature*, there is a chapter entitled *De bono gratie*, where Philip inserts a digression on the relation between the soul and its powers. The passage quotes some points that are typical of Alexander's exposition.[67] First of all, this time Philip distinguishes between essence and substance and names also the third element of Alexander's division, i.e. the subject.[68] This distinction, however, is not affirmed in a systematic way and the meaning of the three notions is not clarified. Philip simply states that the powers of the soul are different as to essence but identical in respect to substance.[69]

It seems clear that Philip is inspired by Alexander, not conversely. And indeed, whereas the distinction between essence and substance is obviously introduced by Alexander in order to be able to avoid the complete identification of the soul with its powers, Philip, while adopting the same distinction, slips again into the identity thesis. According to Philip, essence and substance merely express two different points of view. Indeed, we speak of the substance of the soul if we consider it apart from all its functions. Similarly, we speak of rational powers in their substance if we consider them apart from their functions. Hence, if we consider the soul and its

---

[67] Cf. Künzle, *Das Verhältnis*, pp. 108-109.

[68] Philipp., *sum. de bon.*, ed. Wicki, I, p. 360[70-73]: "Et attende quod magis propria est hec: gratia est fides, caritas etc. quam hec: amnia est ratio, voluntas et huiusmodi; potius enim dicitur voluntativum et intellectivum. Et hec est causa quia anima dicit subiectum, non solum substantiam, gratia substantiam ita quod non subiectum".

[69] Philipp., *sum. de bon.*, ed. Wicki, I, pp. 359[58]-360[66]: "Considerare est igitur animam secundum substantiam, quasi non habito respectu ad aliquem actum, et est considerare eam secundum quod inclinatur ad actus, ut intelligendi et volendi et huiusmodi. Nec in hoc additur nova substantia, sed secundum quod attendimus eam intelligere dicimus eam intellectum vel magis proprie intellectivum, et secundum quod vult voluntatem vel vol-untativum. Una ergo substantia et plures vires secundum plures ad actus comparationes. Non differt ergo ratio a voluntate potentia in substantia, et tamen differt essentialiter, quia essentia potentie est in comparatione ad actum, substantia ipsa non alia est quam anime substantia".

powers in this way, then the substance of the soul and the substance of its powers are one and the same thing. By contrast, we speak of the essence of powers if we consider them in relation to their acts: for this reason, it is possible to affirm that powers differ as to their essence:[70]

> Una ergo substantia et plures vires secundum plures ad actus comparationes. Non differt ergo ratio a voluntate potentia in substantia, et tamen differt essentialiter, quia essentia potentie est in comparatione ad actum, substantia ipsa non alia est quam anime substantia

Fundamentally, Philip's argumentation does not go beyond the identity theory presented in *De spiritu et anima*:[71]

> Dicitur anima dum uegetat, spiritus dum contemplatur, sensus dum sentit, mens dum intelligit, ratio dum discurrit, memoria dum recordatur, uoluntas dum consentit. Ista tamen non differunt in substantia quemadmodum in nominibus, quoniam omnia ista una anima sunt.

Alexander of Hales' solution basically becomes ineffective in the *Summa de bono*.

Confirming the observations formulated by Pius Künzle,[72] we may conclude that Philip probably uses Alexander's exposition. Yet, it should be noted that, as it appears, Philip still does not know Alexander's solution when he writes the chapter *De bono nature*, because there he does not yet introduce the distinction between essence and substance. By contrast, Philip has recourse to this distinction in a chapter placed relatively close to *De bono nature*.[73] We might therefore suppose that the two works were composed at periods not very distant from each other.

2.1.2.6 Peter of Bar

In the early 1230s, that is after the composition of Philip the Chancellor's *Summa de bono* and Alexander of Hales' *Glossa*, in Paris, a young secular master – Peter of Bar[74] – composes a question entitled *De illo verbo: "Faciamus hominem ad im-*

---

[70] Philipp., *sum. de bon.*, ed. Wicki, I, p. 360[62-66].

[71] Ps. Aug., *spir. et an.*, 13, PL 40, 788-789. Cf. Künzle, *Das Verhältnis*, p. 109.

[72] Cf. Künzle, *Das Verhältnis*, pp. 109-110.

[73] I am referring in particular to the manuscripts *Padova, Biblioteca Antoniana 156* and *Città del Vaticano, Biblioteca Apostolica Vaticana, Vat. lat. 7669*; cf. Wicki, "Introduction", p. 32*, p. 37*.

[74] He is a scarcely known figure. His name derives from the French town Bar-sur-Aube, where he was active as a dean. Probably about 1230, Peter became master in theology at Paris. The few works ascribed to him – i.e. thirty-five, maybe thirty-six disputed questions and six sermons – quite probably date from this period. In 1244, Innocent IV named him cardinal together with two of his former colleagues from the Parisian Faculty of Theology,

aginem et similitudinem nostram.[75] The first part of this text, in which the theologian concentrates on the problem of the identity of the soul with its rational powers, reveals evident traces of the three texts discussed above, i.e., the *Summa aurea*, the *Glossa* of Alexander of Hales and the *Summa de bono* of Philip the Chancellor: the solution of the question consists in a mosaic of elements drawn from these three expositions.

First of all, Peter refers to William of Auxerre's criticism concerning the theory that the soul is identical with its powers just as prime matter is identical with its capacity to receive a substantial form. Just as William distinguished between *potentia* and *informitas potentiae*, attributing the former to the soul and the latter to prime matter, so Peter distinguishes between active power and passive power[76] and identifies the latter with the receptiveness of prime matter.[77] Following William, he states that only God can be identified with his active power; by contrast, the soul, since it is a creature, is identical with its passive power (just like prime

---

namely, Hugh of St-Cher and Odo of Châteauroux. It is known that Peter took part in the Council of Lyon and was papal legate in Spain; finally, in 1252, he became bishop of the Sabine region. He died at Perugia in the same year. About Peter of Bar's life and works, see F. Duchesne, *Histoire de tous les cardinaux francais*, Paris 1660, I, p. 225; A. Lecoy de la Marche, *La chaire française au moyen âge, spécialement au XIIIe siècle*, Paris 1886, p. 525; P. Glorieux, *Répertoire des maîtres en théologie de Paris au 13. Siècle*, Paris: Vrin, 1933, I, pp. 313-314; J. B. Schneyer, *Repertorium der lateinischen Sermones des Mittelalters für die Zeit von 1150-1350*, Münster: Aschendorff, 1972 (B. G. Ph. Th. M., 43), IV, p. 598.

[75] Like all the questions by Peter, this question too is uniquely preserved in ms. *Douai, Bibliothèque Municipale 434* and bears the number 514, according to the catalogue compiled by Glorieux, "Les 572 Questions", p. 242. The question has been edited and studied by Künzle, *Das Verhältnis*, pp. 114-115, pp. 229-231.

[76] The same distinction appears in the anonymous treatise *De potentiis animae et obiectis*, ed. D. A. Callus, in "The Powers of the Soul. An Early Unpublished Text", *RTAM* 19 (1952), p. 147[7-8]. The distinction probably comes from Aristotle; cf. Arist., *metaph.* V, 15, Translatio "media", ed. Vuillemin-Diem, p. 104[14-15]: "...activa vero et passiva secundum potentiam activam et passivam sunt et actiones potentiarum, ut calefactivum et calefactibile, quia potest, et iterum calefaciens ad calefactivum et secans ad sectum tamquam agentia".

[77] Petr. de Barro, *q. de illo verbo*, ed. Künzle, p. 230[23-43]: "Item in materia prima est potentia susceptiva cuiuslibet proprietatis. Aut idem est materia, quod illa potencia, aut non. Si non, vocetur illa potencia 'a' adhuc materia secundum se susceptiva cuiuslibet proprietatis. Ergo habet aliam potenciam quam 'a', vocetur 'b'. Aut materia est b aut non. Si non, tunc est processus in infinitum, si sic, ergo materia est sua potencia. Ergo similiter potest dici, quod anima est sua potencia. Contra. Nichil est sua potencia, nisi deus. Si enim creatura esset sua potencia, se ipsa potens esset. Quod cum nulla sit se ipsa potens, nulla creatura erit sua potencia. (...) Ad illud, quod obicit de materia prima, dicendum quod non est simile de potencia passiva, quam habet materia, et de potencia activa, nam quod creatura sit idem quod sua potencia passiva, non derogat creatori, sed quod creatura esset idem quod sua potencia activa, illud derogaret creatori, qui solus se ipso potens est".

matter), but somehow must be distinct from its active powers. For this reason, Hilary's passage ("anima est intelligentia") and Augustine's passage ("substantialiter sunt ipsa mens") should not be interpreted in a literal way. Actually, their affirmations denote a certain composition in the soul ("concretive intelligendum est illud"). For the human mind *is* not its powers, but *possesses* its powers.[78]

The inherence of the rational powers in the soul is explained by a distinction clearly adhering to the triad elaborated by Alexander of Hales, i.e. the distinction between essence, substance and the subject.[79] However, in some respects, his interpretation of the passage from the *Glossa* departs from the original text. In fact, Alexander defined essence as *quo est*, i.e. the essential determination of the soul, in the same sense as *humanitas* constitutes the essential determination of man. Peter affirms instead that *essentia* simply means the *res nuda*, i.e. the thing without its powers, whereas the concept of substance comprises also the powers of the thing: in plain words, essence means substance minus powers. According to Peter, the substance of the soul is not totally simple but composite, because it represents a *concretio*.[80] While considering the meaning attributed by Peter to the notion of *essentia* and *substantia*, we may conclude that, in the first part of his solution, the theologian follows in outline Alexander of Hales' argumentation and states that the rational powers of the human soul are identical as to substance, but different as to essence.[81]

---

[78] Petr. de Barro, *q. de illo verbo*, ed. Künzle, p. 230[32-38]: "Preterea: grave non est sua gravitas, neque leve sua levitas. Ergo neque anima sua potencia, videtur esse simile. *Solutio.* Dici potest, quod anima non est sua potencia et concretive intelligendum est illud, quod dicit Hilarius in sinodis, ut sit sensus: anima est intelligencia, i. e. intelligens, et sic de aliis. Ad illud Augustini similiter dicendum, quod oblique intelligendum est sub hoc sensu "substantialiter sunt ipsa mens", i. e. in ipsa mente".

[79] For instance, just like Alexander, Peter affirms that a substance is not complete without its powers; cf. Alex. Halen., *gloss. in* I *Sent.*, d. 3, ed. PP. Collegii S. Bonaventurae, p. 65[19]: "anima non est completa substantia sine suis potentiis"; Petr. de Barro, *q. de illo verbo*, ed. Künzle, p. 230[47]: "sine enim hiis non est anima substantia completa".

[80] In Hugh of St-Cher's question *De anima*, the same term is used to define the composition of the thing and of its accidents; cf. Hugo de S. Caro, *q. de an.*, 3, ed. Bieniak, p. 181[447-448].

[81] Petr. de Barro, *q. de illo verbo*, ed. Künzle, p. 230[44-49]: "Sine preiudicio tamen michi aliter videtur esse dicendum, ut distinguamus inter subiectum (!) et essenciam, dicentes, quod intelligencia, memoria, voluntas differunt secundum essenciam et conveniunt in substancia; sine enim hiis non est anima substantia completa et illa differunt. Differunt sic, quod essencia dicit rem nudam, substantia in concretione ad potencias naturales, subiectum in comparacione ad actus. Est ergo anima idem sua potencia, non in essencia, sed in substancia". The editor of the text follows the manuscript faithfully and, in this place, he reports the word '*subiectum*'. Note, however, that the context rather seems to require the term '*substantiam*'. Quite probably, this is a mistake made by the copyist: the shortened forms of '*subiectum*' (sb'm) and '*substantiam*' (sb'am) are actually very similar.

By contrast, in the second part of the solution, Peter adopts the first doctrine elaborated by Philip the Chancellor, which is explained in the chapter *De bono natura* and in the disputed question *De ymagine et similitudine nostra*,[82] but he does so through the *Summa Duacensis*, which in this case is his direct source.[83] Peter distinguishes between three types of powers: accidental faculties, the faculties deriving directly from the essence of the thing and, finally, the faculties identical with the thing as to substance. The powers of the soul belong to the third kind of faculties, namely, they are identical with the substance of the soul.[84]

Although the text is largely based on William of Auxerre's and Alexander of Hales' solutions, nevertheless Peter concludes his solution saying that the rational powers are identical with the soul ("est (...) indifferens a re cuius dicitur esse potencia"). To draw a conclusion, we can say that Peter of Bar's question has a strongly eclectic character.

* * *

At the beginning of the thirteenth century, the problem of the relationship between the soul and its rational powers is discussed by almost all the theologians who are active at Paris at the time. A majority of them remain clearly linked with the traditional identity doctrine, as we have observed in the works of Philip the Chancellor, Hugh of St-Cher, Odo of Châteauroux, Peter of Bar, John of La Rochelle, as well as in the *Summa Duacensis* and in the anonymous question *Si anima*

---

[82] Cf. *supra*, pp. 107-108.

[83] Cf. Künzle, *Das Verhältnis*, pp. 114-115.

[84] Petr. de Barro, *q. de illo verbo*, ed. Künzle, pp. 230[49]-231[59]: "Unde notandum quod triplex est potencia. Quedam est rei, cuius est, ut subiecti, et est accidentalis rei, et talis est potencia, qua pupilla oculi potens est recipere species rerum exteriores, que potencia comprobatur esse accidentalis, eo quod eam contingit in sene debilitari et quasi amitti. Est iterum alia potencia, que non est de rei essencia, sed de consequentibus essenciam, et hec semper esse rei comitatur et se tenet cum ipsa re. Talis potencia est caliditas, qua ignis dicitur posse ealefacere. Rursus est tercia potencia, que est idem in substancia et indifferens a re, cuius dicitur esse potencia. Talis est potencia anime"; cf. *sum. Duac.*, ed. Glorieux, p. 22: "Ad obiectionem vero solvendum de anima, qualiter scilicet anima sua voluntas et sua intelligentia cum nullum grave sit sua gravitas, distinguimus quoniam triplex est potencia: quedam enim est rei cuius est ut subiecti; et est ipsi rei accidentalis; et talis est potentia qua pupilla oculi potens est recipere rerum species exteriores; que potentia comprobatur esse sue accidentalis eo quod eam contingit in homine sene debilitari et quandoque amitti. Est iterum alia potentia que non est de rei essencia sed de consequentibus essentiam; et hec semper esse rei comitatur, et se tenet ipsa re; qualis est potentia qua ignis dicitur posse calefacere, scilicet caliditas. Rursum est tertium genus potentie que est in se substancia et indifferens a re cuius dicitur esse potentia; talis est illa qua dicitur prima materia susceptibilis cuiuslibet forme; que prima materia cum dicitur potentia dicitur prout est in relatione ad actum aliquem ordinata. Unde substantialiter ipsa materia primordialiter est sua potentia. Et si hoc est ibi, longe fortius est in anima quod ipsa est sua voluntas et sua intelligentia".

est sue potentie; a similar opinion is also expressed in William of Auvergne's treatise *De anima*.[85] By contrast, William of Auxerre's *Summa aurea* is the only work
of this period in which the identity thesis is definitely rejected. Yet another type of
view is formulated in Alexander of Hales' *Glossa*: in effect, the Franciscan master
tries to avoid both a simple identification of the soul with its powers and a position
according to which the rational powers are mere accidents of the soul. Later on,
Philip the Chancellor and Peter of Bar took up his solution, although they changed
it so as to make it compatible with the position maintaining, once again, the identity of the soul with its rational powers.[86]

One of the most interesting and complex aspects of this debate consists in the
problem of the meaning of the terms *'substantia'-'substantialiter'* and *'essentia'-*
'essentialiter'. At first, probably due to the influence of Augustine's *De Trinitate*,[87]
the terms *'substantia'* and *'essentia'* are used interchangeably, as we have observed
– for example – in Philip the Chancellor's first solution and in Hugh of St-Cher's
Sentences Commentary. According to these authors, powers are in the soul *sub-*
stantialiter or *essentialiter*, i.e., they are identical with the soul itself. Later on,
Alexander of Hales introduced a distinction between *essentia* and *substantia*. On
the basis of his solution, a group of masters affirmed that powers are in the soul
substantialiter but not *essentialiter*. However, this did not prevent some of these
scholars from maintaining that, even so, the soul *is* its powers: in fact, this affirmation appears in Peter of Bar's question *De illo verbo: "Faciamus hominem ad imag-*
inem et similitudinem nostram"[88] and in John of La Rochelle's *Summa de anima*.[89]

In my view, the most radical way to express the identity thesis appears in the
chapter *De bono nature* of the *Summa de bono* and in Philip the Chancellor's
question *De ymagine et similitudine nostra*. Indeed, Philip compares the rational

---

[85] Cf. *Quod potentiae animae non sunt distinctae ab ipsa anima*, in Guilelmus de Alvernia, *De anima*, ed. Le Feron, p. 91.

[86] John of La Rochelle too mentions Alexander's solution; cf. Ioh. Rup., *sum. de an.*, II,
60, ed. Bougerol, p. 184[67-74].

[87] Aug., *trin.* IX, 4. 5, ed. Mountain, CCSL 50, pp. 297[27]-298[31], PL 42, 963: "Simul etiam
admonemur si utcumque uidere possumus haec in anima exsistere et tamquam inuoluta
euolui ut sentiantur et dinumerentur substantialiter uel, ut ita dicam, essentialiter, non
tamquam in subiecto ut color aut figura in corpore aut ulla alia qualitas aut quantitas"; id.,
trin. IX, 5. 8, ed. Mountain, CCSL 50, p. 301, PL 42, 965: "Miro itaque modo tria ista inseparabilia sunt a seipsis; et tamen eorum singulum et simul omnia una essentia est, cum et relative dicantur ad invicem". See also the Pseudo-Augustinian *De spiritu et anima*, 13, PL 40,
788-789: "Ista tamen non differunt in substantia, quemadmodum in nominibus; quoniam
omnia ista una anima est: proprietates quidem diversae, sed essentia una".

[88] Petr. de Barro, *q. de illo verbo*, ed. Künzle, p. 231[59]: "...est idem in substantia et indifferens a re, cuius dicitur esse potencia".

[89] Cf. Ioh. Rup., *sum. de an.*, I, 35, ed. Bougerol, p. 113[64]: "...idem sunt secundum substan-
ciam quod ipsa mens que est suprema pars anime".

powers of the soul to prime matter's capacity to receive a substantial form. This comparison, sharply criticized by William of Auxerre and Alexander of Hales, describes the way in which a thing can be identical with its power efficaciously. For prime matter can only be defined through its capacity to receive form; in other words, the *esse* of prime matter is totally determined by this function.[90]

The way in which Philip the Chancellor, and maybe also Hugh of St-Cher, understands the identity of the soul with its rational powers may have important consequences for the problem of the conjunction of the human soul and body. On the one hand, this identity is described with the words '*essentialiter*' and '*substantialiter*'. These are the same terms used by Hugh to describe *unibilitas*, which is the soul's substantial difference in regard to the angel: "Haec autem unibilitas inest animae naturaliter et substantialiter per quam differt ab angelo".[91] Now, if in the question *De anima* the expression '*inest substantialiter*' describes the same type of relationship as the one existing between the soul and its rational powers, or between prime matter and its capacity to receive form,[92] then we should conclude not only that *unibilitas* fully defines the essence of the soul, but also that the soul *is* its own *unibilitas*.[93] This interpretation seems to find confirmation in an

---

[90] This comparison was assimilated by John of La Rochelle too; *sum. de an.* II, 1, ed. Bougerol, pp. 182[18]-183[30]: "Item, sicut materia prima habet potenciam ad susceptionem omnium formarum naturalium, sic anima habet potenciam ad susceptionem omnium specierum. Cum ergo materia prima sit ipsa potencia ad susceptionem formarum, igitur et multo forcius ipsa anima, que simplicior est et ymago Dei est, erit potencia ad susceptionem specierum omnium. Ergo potencia susceptiua specierum intelligibilium et sensibilium est ipsa anima. Ergo est sue potencie. Si negaretur scilicet quod ipsa materia prima non esset sua potencia, contra. In omnibus materialibus est potencia receptibilis per aliquid, et illud est materia prima; ergo ipsa materia prima est receptibilis formarum per seipsam; non ergo in ea differens id quod est ipsa, et ipsa potencia. Similiter ergo erit ex parte spiritualis substancie quod ipsa erit receptibilitatis specierum in seipsa". Let us observe, however, that one of the manuscripts of the *Summa de anima*, at the end of the chapter, cites William of Auxerre's objection as well; cf. *supra*, p. 101; Ioh. Rup., *sum. de an.* II, 1, ed. Bougerol, p. 185: "Nec ualet obiectio de prima materia: non uidetur idem esse et posse suscipere formam quamlibet; talis potentia non est aliqua potentia sed informitas (ed.: inferioritas) potentiae praecedens omnem potentiam et omnem formam. Unde non dicitur proprie materia habere aliquam potentiam, vel aliquid posse"; cf. Künzle, *Das Verhältnis*, p. 123.

[91] Hugo de S. Caro, *q. de an.*, 1, ed. Bieniak, p. 169[46].

[92] An element in favour of this hypothesis might be the fact that Hugh defines *unibilitas* as *aptitudo naturalis*: indeed, the term *aptitudo* was employed mainly in relation to the receptiveness of prime matter; cf. *supra*, p. 75, n. 203.

[93] Here, following Thomas Osborne, it may be worthwhile to recall what Étienne Gilson affirmed about the link between soul and body according to the theologians of the first half of the thirteenth century: "Some would call it 'unibility', others love or an inclination; still others preferred to say that the soul is, secondarily, the act and perfection of its body, but not one of them would hold the view that the very essence of this substance was

argument, proposed by John of La Rochelle in his *Summa de anima*, according to which the soul that is united with the body through its own *unibilitas*, is united with the body with its own essence: this type of union resembles very much the union between matter and Aristotelian form.[94]

Yet, on the other hand, the thesis of the identity of the soul with its rational powers seems incompatible with the *unibilitas substantialis* doctrine, conceived in this way. Indeed, at the time, the rational faculties were conceived of as powers independent from corporeal organs, since their main function consisted above all in the spiritual knowledge of God. Hence, the identification of the soul with its rational powers involves the definition of the soul through its contemplative functions, not through the capacity to vivify the body. In other words, if the essence of the soul is exhausted in the rational faculty, then the ability to be united with the body, i.e. *unibilitas*, can be nothing but an accident for the soul.

Finally, if we go back to Hugh of St-Cher's anthropology, we notice that the conclusions we can draw are quite limited. Indeed, whereas Hugh, in his *Commentary* on Peter Lombard's *Sentences*, supported the thesis of the identity of the soul with its rational powers, later on he embraced the *unibilitas* doctrine, i.e. in his disputed question *De anima*, where the identity thesis is no longer mentioned. Hence, on the one hand, we cannot exclude that Hugh, in that space of time, had given up the identification of the rational soul with its powers; but, on the other, it is not totally clear whether in the question *De anima* the meaning of the words '*essentialiter*' and '*substantialiter*' corresponds to that employed in the *Sentences Commentary*. Unfortunately, we do not have enough elements available to solve this problem.

---

to be the form of a body"; cf. E. Gilson, *History of Christian Philosophy in the Middle Ages*, New York: Random House, 1955, p. 361; Osborne, "Unibilitas", p. 228. Even though Hugh does not call the human soul a 'form', nevertheless, if this first conjecture were right, then the very essence of the soul would consist in the capability of uniting with a body, namely, in its *unibilitas*.

[94] Ioh. Rup., *sum. de an.* I, 37, ed. Bougerol, p. 115[4-5]: "Unitur anima corpori per suam unibilitatem: ergo unitur per suam essentiam; ergo sine medio".

2.2
THE SENSITIVE AND VEGETATIVE POWERS

2.2.1 THE UNION *PER MEDIUM*

2.2.1.1 Philip the Chancellor

As previously mentioned, in the thirteenth century, the debate concerning the sensitive and vegetative powers takes its particular shape thanks to the reception of sources inspired by Aristotle's thought. This type of speculation is introduced into the Parisian Faculty of Theology mainly as a result of Philip the Chancellor's activity. Among his most influential doctrines, let us note in particular the theory according to which there exist intermediary elements between the rational soul and the body. This doctrine is interesting for us in two respects: on the one hand, it directly concerns the problem of the conjunction of the human soul and the body; on the other, Philip's solution was to be almost entirely adopted by Hugh of St-Cher in his disputed questions. A closer analysis of the contents of Philip's exposition, as well as of his remote and direct sources, will therefore be helpful.

According to Philip the Chancellor, the rational soul is not united with the body immediately, but through what he calls "material dispositions" (*materiales dispositiones*). For the rational soul is not the prime form of matter: this function is carried out by a form called 'corporeity'. Then various intermediary forms intervene to prepare the body for the reception of its ultimate perfection. In the case of the human being, the form or ultimate perfection coincides with the rational soul.[95] The latter cannot be united with the body without the mediation of mate-

---

[95] Philipp., *sum. de bon.*, ed. Wicki, p. 284[89-102]: "Ad hoc respondeo quod anima secundum quid unitur per modum forme, secundum quid per modum substantie; utrique enim est proportionalis. Quod autem opponitur quod forma unitur se ipsa, quare anima se ipsa, secundum hoc dicendum est quod sunt quedam forme prime, quedam ultime, quedam medie. Prime forme cum prime sint, absque medio materie coniunguntur, ut est corporeitas. Ultime forme per medium coniunguntur, et quia ultime non sunt media neque dispositiones materiales ad aliarum coniunctionem. Ultima autem forma naturalium est anima. Medie autem et per medium coniunguntur quandoque et quandoque sunt media et quasi materiales dispositiones; verbi gratia potentia sensibilis per medium coniungitur suo subiecto, scilicet mediante ut dispositione materiali potentia vegetabili; et hoc quando est ultima perfectio. Quandoque autem ipsa eadem in nobiliori subiecto est medium et quasi dispositio materialis, scilicet comparatione anime intellective. Manifestum est igitur quod, licet sit ut forma, non tamen per se corpori necesse est coniungi".

rial dispositions. Philip calls the intermediary elements "material dispositions" because each of them carries out the function of form in regard to the body, after which it becomes like matter for the higher form. Philip distinguishes between two types of intermediary elements: on the one hand, the body – which is composed of prime matter and the *forma corporeitatis* – becomes conjoined with the soul through the "corporeal spirit" and the "elementary heat";[96] on the other hand, the rational soul needs the vegetative principle and the sensitive principle in order to carry out its function. Hence, according to Philip, there exist various intermediary elements which are, on the one hand, corporeal and, on the other, spiritual.

Further, it should be noted that Philip's exposition contains a puzzling ambiguity relating to the spiritual intermediary principles, i.e. – using Philip's words – the intermediary principles intervening on behalf of the soul. Indeed, in the chapter entitled *Utrum potentia sensibilis et rationalis in eadem substantia fundentur*, which deals with the problem of the ontological status of the sensitive and vegetative powers, Philip wonders whether, in the human being, the lower powers belong to the same substance as the rational faculty of man. In the first part of the chapter, the theologian defends the plurality of substances in the soul. According to this first opinion, the vegetative soul, the sensitive soul and the rational soul belong to three different substances, which does not mean that they constitute three souls: for the name 'soul' belongs only to the ultimate perfection of the living being. Only the rational substance, as it performs the function of the ultimate perfection, can thus be named the soul in man, whereas the other substances are subordinate to it. For this reason, we may properly speak of a vegetative soul only in plants and other vegetables, because the vegetative soul constitutes the highest perfection in them. Similarly, the sensitive principle may be called 'soul' only in animals, not in humans. Indeed, in humans, it is only the rational substance which should be called the soul, since the other substances are subordinate to it. Hence, the three substances, the rational, the sensitive and the vegetative, are united in such a way as to form only one soul, though consisting of three substances.[97]

Subsequently, Philip explains the coexistence of these three substances by comparing it to the union of the light of fire with the light of the sun: for the

---

[96] Cf. Philipp., *sum. de bon.*, ed. Wicki, pp. 286[170]-287[177].

[97] Philipp., *sum. de bon.*, ed. Wicki, pp. 233[79]-234[86]: "Sed licet sint tres substantie incorporee, non tamen sunt tres anime, eo quod anima nomen est perfectionis. Ideo non est anima vegetabilis nisi in plantis et consimilibus, quia earum est perfectio completa. Et non est anima sensibilis nisi in brutis, quia ibi similiter est perfectio. In homine autem sunt quasi materiales ad rationalem et rationalis est completio, et ipsa tantum est anima in homine, et ille tres uniuntur ita quod sint una anima. Et quod sint anima habent a completivo; et sic tres substantie incorporee et una anima".

weakest ray of light is united with the strongest ray of light, so that the two almost form one thing.[98] Further, Philip maintains that, in the human embryo, the vegetative soul precedes the sensitive soul and the sensitive soul appears before the rational soul.[99]

By contrast, in the second part of the question, Philip rejects the plurality of substances in the soul and defines the vegetative principle and the sensitive principle as simple powers belonging to the substance of the rational soul:[100]

> Si enim aliud est subjectum in quo est potentia sensibilis, aliud in quo est rationalis, quare actus huius impediret actum illius? Si autem occupatur per hanc potentiam circa sensibilia, impeditur negociari circa spiritualia per aliam potentiam. Apparet per hoc quoniam fundantur in una substantia, quod concedimus.

In view of the fact that the final part of the question contains this explicit adherence to the theory of the unity of substances in the soul, in the 1930s Odon Lottin[101] and, more recently, Nicolaus Wicki[102] have concluded that Philip positively declares himself in favour of this second doctrine. There are, however, some important reasons in favour of a different interpretation. First of all, Philip expounds the substance plurality doctrine very accurately, choosing convincing arguments and rejecting a number of objections. Moreover, it is remarkable that, in the section devoted to defending this solution, Philip uses expressions such as "si queratur a me", "dico quod" or "ego dico", which let us suppose a strong personal commitment to the presented position. Finally, the substance uniqueness thesis is con-

---

[98] Philipp., *sum. de bon.*, ed. Wicki, p. 234[88-93]: "Et unio earum potest ymaginari per radios. Sicut quandoque radius ignis et solis simul uniuntur et non sunt nisi quasi unus, et hoc proprter eorum spiritualitatem, et sicut contingit quod radius ignis corrumpitur et remanet solaris, sic est in animabus, quoniam due corrumpuntur cum corpore et tertia manet et separatur ab aliis et a corpore, sicut «perpetuum a corruptibili», sicut vult Aristoteles".

[99] Philipp., *sum. de bon.*, ed. Wicki, p. 234[94-95]: "Et si queratur a me, cum ita sint diverse, utrum sensibilis prius sit rationali, dico quod sic; sed prius istud est natura, sicut idem dicit. Et ergo dico quod non solum natura, sed etiam possibile est prius tempore".

[100] Philipp., *sum. de bon.*, ed. Wicki, p. 237[191-195].

[101] Lottin, *Psychologie et morale*, I, p. 467, pp. 478-479.

[102] Wicki, *Die Philosophie Philipps des Kanzlers*, p. 123. Furthermore, Wicki observes that the substantial unity thesis would seem to be consistent with the doctrine of the identity of the soul with its rational powers which is held by Philip (cf. *supra*, pp. 107-108). To my mind, however, the identity thesis runs contrary to there being a unique substance in the soul: indeed, if the rational soul is identical with memory, will and reason (which are basically only one power), then there is no room left for powers of a different type, such as the sensitive and vegetative ones.

tradicted mainly by the statements formulated by Philip a few pages below, with reference to the intermediary substances between the rational soul and the body. Indeed, in the chapter *De unione anime ad corpus*, where he expounds his doctrine of the union *per medium*, the plurality of substances in the soul is affirmed more than once. Philip's argumentation is the following: between the rational soul and the human body there exists a great ontological distance. For the rational soul is simple, incorporeal and incorruptible, whereas our body is composite, material and corruptible. A conjunction of two substances which are so different is thus inconceivable without the help of intermediary substances sharing in part the nature of the higher principle and in part the nature of the lower principle.[103] The spiritual intermediary elements Philip speaks of are nothing but the sensitive soul and the vegetative soul. For the sensitive soul is simple and incorporeal like the rational soul, but is corruptible like the body. Similarly, the vegetative soul is incorporeal but also corruptible and composite: its features make it therefore more similar to the body than to the rational soul. The two intermediary substances thus serve as material dispositions toward the ultimate perfection and connect the two opposite principles, i.e. the rational one and the corporeal one.[104]

It should be noted that in the chapter concerning the union *per medium*, Philip defines the sensitive principle and the vegetative principle as souls and substances. Considering the solution adopted in the chapter *Utrum potentia sensibilis et ra-*

---

[103] Philipp., *sum. de bon.*, ed. Wicki, pp. 285[139]-286[145]: "Ad quod intelligendum accipienda est distantia prime anime rationalis ad corpus. Et est multimoda distantia. Anima enim rationalis tres habet oppositiones ad corpus ipsum; est enim simplex, incorporea et incorruptibilis, corpus vero compositum, corporeum et corruptibile. Propter igitur nimiam sui distantiam a corpore non posset anima rationalis corpori coniungi, nisi advenirent dispositiones sive adaptationes alique, que essent media coniungendi hec ad invicem".

[104] Philipp., *sum. de bon.*, ed. Wicki, p. 286[145-164]: "Unde cum maior sit oppositio anime rationalis ad corpus quam anime sensibilis, et iterum anime sensibilis quam vegetabilis, plures exiguntur adaptationes seu dispositiones ad coniunctionem anime rationalis cum corpore quam anime sensibilis, et iterum anime sensibilis quam vegetabilis. Sunt ergo adaptationes per quas anima rationalis corpori coniungitur habentes convenientiam cum utroque, videlicet cum corpore et anima rationali. Ad quorum evidentiam sciendum quod est quedam substantia simplex, incorporea, corruptibilis, videlicet anima sensibilis. Hec enim est substantia simplex et incorporea. Quod sit simplex per hoc patet quod potest abstrahere species a materia per quas species fit ipsa cognoscitiva. Quod autem incorporea, patet. Hec ergo convenit cum corpore et anima rationali; cum anima in duabus dispositionibus, in eo videlicet quod simplex est et incorporea; cum corpore autem in una, videlicet in hoc quod est corruptibilis. Unde necesse est hanc esse mediam. Est iterum alia quedam substantia que est incorporea, sed est composita et corruptibilis, et hec precedit animam sensibilem, et est materialis dispositio ad recipiendum animam sensibilem in corpore, cuius est perfectio anima sensibilis. Hec autem non habet nisi unicam convenientiam cum anima rationali, videlicet incorporeitatem. Non est enim simplex cum non sit cognoscitiva, neque incorruptibilis cum non sit separabilis a corpore, sicut nec anima sensibilis. Exiguntur igitur ista coniungi corpori ad hoc ut ei coniungatur anima rationalis".

tionalis in eadem substantia fundentur, we must conclude that Philip employs a rather imprecise language: and indeed, in the *Summa de bono*, the thesis of the plurality of souls is decidedly rejected, whereas the rejection is not so definite with regard to the plurality of substances. How can we in fact conceive of a substance which is both simple and composite, corruptible and incorruptible at the same time? Therefore, the distinction of substances in the soul seems to form the foundation of the doctrine of intermediaries. It is for this reason that Roberto Zavalloni[105] concludes that, in fact, Philip maintains the theory of the plurality of substances in the soul. In my opinion too, this appears to be the most probable hypothesis, unless the secular master does not refer to a simultaneous existence of the three substances in the same individual, but only refers to the sequence of souls in the embryo. Indeed, one might suppose that, at the moment when the embryo is ready to receive the sensitive soul, the latter somehow absorbs the vegetative soul and, afterwards, the rational soul absorbs the sensitive soul, so that the two lower souls become powers of one single substance. Nevertheless, an explicit affirmation of this theory is lacking.

Whatever the correct answer to that problem is, it is certain that, according to Philip the Chancellor, the rational soul is not united to the body in an immediate way, but, in order to become united, needs the material dispositions acting as intermediaries. This doctrine accords excellently with the general conception of the unity of the human being professed by Philip. Indeed, the secular master states that the union of soul and body constitutes the most ephemeral composite among all kinds of hylomorphic compositions present in corporeal beings.[106]

The doctrine of intermediaries – in the form elaborated by Philip the Chancellor – was later taken up by many theologians: it reappears in the disputed questions by Hugh of St-Cher,[107] in an anonymous question studied by Ermenegildo Bertola,[108] in the *Summa Duacensis*[109] and in the *Summa de anima* by John of La

---

[105] Cf. Zavalloni, *Richard de Mediavilla*, pp. 397-398, pp. 407-409.

[106] Philipp., *sum. de bon.*, ed. Wicki, p. 287[185-196]: "Post hec queritur cuiusmodi unitas sit secundum unionem anime ad corpus. Et dicendum est quod est triplex unitas. Prima est que surgit ex duplici respectu forme ad materiam et materie ad formam, scilicet que sunt ad invicem inseparabiles, ut in corporibus supercelestibus, et hec est in corporibus maior unitas. Secunda est que surgit ex unico respectu in corporibus illis in quibus forma non separatur a materia ita ut maneat, sed materia separatur a forma, quod fit in omnibus corruptibilibus, et hec est minor. Tertia est in illis in quibus aliqua duo coniunguntur ita quod alterum separabile est ab altero, ut anima a corpore et corpus ab anima, et hec est minima. Et per hec deprehenditur quod minima unitas est in homine".

[107] Cf. *infra*, chap. 2.2.1.3.

[108] Cf. E. Bertola, "Alano di Lilla, Filippo il Cancelliere e una inedita "quaestio" sull'immortalità dell'anima umana", *Rivista di Filosofia neo-scolastica* 62 (1970), pp. 245-271.

[109] *Sum. Duac.*, 7, 2, ed. Glorieux, pp. 60-63.

Rochelle.[110] In addition, as Roberto Zavalloni maintains, Philip the Chancellor was the main forerunner of the doctrine of the plurality of forms in the individual which was developed towards the end of the thirteenth century.[111]

2.2.1.2   Sources of the doctrine of intermediaries

Since it is related to the speculation about the sensitive and vegetative powers of the soul, the debate concerning the presence of principles between the rational soul and the body is peculiar to the thirteenth century.[112] The roots of this debate, however, are very deep and cannot be confined to the Middle Ages. The doctrine of the intermediary principles must be viewed in the broader context of the Neo-platonic cosmology.[113] It is a system in which all ontological distance is filled with principles partly sharing the nature of the higher being and partly the nature of the lower being. In this conception, beings proceed uninterruptedly, moving from absolute simplicity to the utmost multiplicity and composition, from eternity to extreme changeability and precariousness and from the highest spirituality to the lowest corporeity. In this system, the constitution of man reflects the hierarchical structure of the universe.[114] For the human being is composed of two substances which are ontologically very distant from one another: in the first place, the soul, i.e. a spiritual substance, simple and immortal; secondly, the human body, a material substance, composite and corruptible, to which our soul is connected. The emphasis is laid on the independence of the soul: indeed, its survival is assured by its simplicity and incorporeity. Yet, at the same time, this dualist view makes it difficult to conceive the coexistence in one subject of two substances as different as soul and body. The introduction of the intermediary principles mainly derives from this problem.

The Christian thought of the Middle Ages regarded itself as an heir of Neo-platonic anthropology and shared its difficulties. The influence of Neoplatonism

---

[110]   Cf. Ioh. Rup., *sum. de an.* I, 37-40, ed. Bougerol, pp. 115-130. A similar doctrine also appears in Alexander of Hales' *Quaestiones disputatae 'antequam esset frater'*; cf. q. LXVI, 5, ed. PP. Collegii S. Bonaventurae, vol. III, p. 1323[20-30]; yet, it is difficult to judge whether the Franciscan master was inspired by Philip or availed himself of other sources.

[111]   Cf. Zavalloni, *Richard de Mediavilla*, p. 422; *infra*, p. 127, n. 133.

[112]   Cf. Zavalloni, *Richard de Mediavilla*, p. 422.

[113]   In fact, the mediation principle was already stressed by Plato; cf. Plato, *Tim.* 31 bc, ed. J. H. Waszink, Warburg Institute, London 1975 (Plato Latinus, 4), pp. 23-24; cf. A. Lovejoy, *The Great Chain of Being: A Study of the History of an Idea*, Cambridge: Harvard University Press, 1961, pp. 24-98; B. McGinn, *The Golden Chain. A Study in the Theological Anthropolgy of Isaac of Stella*, Washington D.C.: Cistercian Publications, 1972, pp. 51-102.

[114]   Cf. Bertola, "Alano di Lilla, Filippo il Cancelliere e una inedita "quaestio"", pp. 255-256; cf. T. Gregory, *Anima mundi. La filosofia di Guglielmo di Conches e la scuola di Chartres*, Firenze: Sansoni, 1955, pp. 123-174.

becomes evident, for example, in the treatises on the soul composed in the early Middle Ages.[115] Indeed, the two typical features of dualist anthropology are both present in one of the most influential writings of the time, i.e. the *De anima* of Cassiodorus († 580):[116] on the one hand, it insists on the independence of the soul;[117] on the other, it shows perplexity faced with the need to explain the way in which the soul is united with a body.[118] In order to describe the coexistence of the two substances of man, Cassiodorus, as well as other thinkers influenced by his treatise, avails himself of metaphors by which the body is compared to a fortress,[119] a temple[120] or a house[121] of the soul. The link between the two principles remains quite obscure: instead of proposing explanations of an ontological kind, early-medieval authors prefer to evoke an ineffable mystery of divine omnipotence.

Christian anthropology found a new source of inspiration in the writings of Pseudo-Dionysius the Areopagite. The highly authoritative writings of Pseudo-Dionysius provided a strong support for a view conceiving of the world as an uninterrupted sequence of descending ontological degrees. The influence exerted by Dionysius and the Neoplatonic cosmology manifested itself in twelfth-century anthropological texts: indeed, ontological hierarchy was to reflect itself clearly in the theory of man. Twelfth-century anthropology was strongly influenced not only by the *Corpus Dionysianum*, but also by the treatise *De differentia spiritus et animae* of Costa Ben Luca,[122] which was translated into Latin around 1130. In order to ex-

---

[115] A comprehensive survey of early-medieval anthropology is represented by the collection of texts edited by Ilario Tolomio, *L'anima dell'uomo: trattati sull'anima dal v al ix secolo*, Milano: Rusconi, 1979.

[116] On Cassiodorus' science of the soul, see also F. Zimmermann, "Cassiodors Schrift Über die Seele", *Jahrbuch für Philosophie und spekulative Theologie* 25 (1911), pp. 414-449; J. W. Halporn, "The Manuscripts of Cassiodorus' De Anima", *Traditio* 15 (1959), pp. 385-387; A. Crocco, "Il liber de anima di Cassiodoro", *Sapienza* 25 (1972), pp. 133-168; J. J. O'Donnell, *Cassiodorus*, Berkeley: University of California Press, 1979; L. Codispoti, *L'anima secondo Cassiodoro, illustre figlio di Squillace nel xiv centenario della sua morte 583-1983*, Catanzaro: Industria Grafica Silipo-Lucia, 1983; M. Di Marco, "Scelta e utilizzazione delle fonti nel De anima di Cassiodoro", *Studi e Materiali di Storia delle Religioni* 9 (1985), pp. 93-117.

[117] Cass., *de an.*, 1, PL 70, 1282 A-B: "Haec vero quoniam immortalis est, anima recte appellatur, quasi 'ἄναιμα, id est a sanguine longe discreta: quia et post mortem corporis perfectam ejus constat esse substantiam, sicut in subsequentibus suo loco declarabitur".

[118] Cass., *de an.*, 1, PL 70, 1284 C: "Mirum praeterea videtur rem incorpoream membris solidissimis colligatam, et sic distantes naturas in unam convenientiam fuisse perductas, ut nec anima se possit segregare cum velit, nec retinere, cum jussionem Creatoris agnoverit".

[119] Rab. Maur., *de an.*, 5, PL 110, 1114 C-D.

[120] Cf. Cass., *de an.*, VIII, PL 70, 1295 A; Rab. Maur., *de an.*, 5, PL 110, 1114 D.

[121] Alc., *rat. an.*, 12, PL 101, 645 A; Rab. Maur., *de an.*, 1, PL 110, 1110 B.

[122] Cf. R. C. Dales, *The Problem of the Rational Soul in the Thirteenth Century*, Leiden - New York: Brill, 1995, pp. 5-6, p. 74.

plain the conjunction of the human soul and the body, the author of the treatise
introduces intermediary elements between the two substances. His theory was
to leave a deep mark on twelfth- and thirteenth-century psychology. Among the
works later adopting the idea of the intermediary principles, let us mention, for
example, the treatises by Isaac of Stella († 1168),[123] Ailred of Rielvaux († 1167)[124] and
Alan of Lille.[125] According to Isaac of Stella, soul and body are united through the
phantasticum animae and the *sensualitas carnis*;[126] for Ailred, the intermediary
function is performed by the corporeal sense;[127] by contrast, Alan of Lille speaks of
"spirit".[128] All these elements play a double role: on the one hand, they fill the ontological gap between the two main components of man; on the other, they assure
communication between the soul and its instrument. For example, the spirit Alan
of Lille speaks of in his treatise *Contra haereticos*, is corporeal, but its subtlety and
agility makes it similar to an incorporeal substance.[129]

    Later on, the theory of the spirit as intermediary appeared also in *De motu
cordis*, composed by Alfred of Sareshel in 1210/1215.[130] According to the philoso-

---

[123] Cf. Isaac de Stella, *Epistola de anima*, PL 194, 1881. On Isaac and his anthropology,
see W. Meuser, *Die Erkenntnislehre des Isaak von Stella. Ein Beitrag zur Geschichte der
Philosophie des 12. Jahrhunderts*, Freiburg: Postberg, 1934; Künzle, *Das Verhältnis*, pp. 64-
67; McGinn, *The Golden Chain*; E. Dietz, "When Exile is Home: The Biography of Isaac
of Stella", *Cistercian Studies Quarterly* 41. 2 (2006), pp. 141-165; Bertola, "Alano di Lilla,
Filippo il Cancelliere e una inedita *quaestio*", pp. 256-258. A critical edition of Isaac's *Epistola* is being prepared by Caterina Tarlazzi and it will be published in *Medioevo* 36 (2011).
[124] Ailr. Riev., *dial. de an.*, ed. Talbot, p. 92; cf. Walter Daniel, "Vita Ailredi" in F. M.
Powicke (ed.), *Walter Daniel's Life of Ailred, Abbot of Rievaulx*, London: Thomas Nelson,
1950; C. H. Talbot, "Introduction", in Ailred of Rievaulx, *De anima*, London: The Warburg
Institute, 1952, pp. 1-57; A. Squire, *Aelred of Rievaulx. A Study*, London: Cistercian Publications, 1969; A. Hoste - C. H. Talbot, "Introduction", in Aelredus Rievallensis, *Opera omnia*,
ed. A. Hoste - C. H. Talbot, Turnhout: Brepols, 1971 (CCCM 1), pp. I-XII.
[125] Cf. *infra*, p. 127.
[126] Cf. Isaac de Stella, *Epistola de anima*, PL 194, 1881; Bertola, "Alano di Lilla, Filippo il
Cancelliere e una inedita *quaestio*", p. 257.
[127] Cf. Ailr. Riev., *dial. de an.*, ed. Talbot, p. 92; Bertola, "Alano di Lilla, Filippo il Cancelliere e una inedita *quaestio*", p. 257.
[128] On the doctrine of the spirit, see E. Bertola, "Le fonti medico-filosofiche della dottrina dello «spirito»", *Sophia* 26 (1958), pp. 48-61; id., "Alano di Lilla, Filippo il Cancelliere e
una inedita *quaestio*", pp. 259-264.
[129] Alan. de Ins., *fid. cath.*, 28, PL 210, 329 D: "Est namque in homine duplex spiritus,
spiritus rationalis et incorporeus, qui non perit cum corpore; et alius qui dicitur physicus
sive naturalis, quo mediante anima rationalis unitur corpori, et hic spiritus est subtilior
aere, et etiam igne, quo mediante fit sensus et imaginatio: et ille perit cum corpore".
[130] Cf. Ps. Arist., *motu cord.*, ed. Baeumker, pp. 37-38: "His habitis, intuendum diligen-
tius quod corpus, cuius hebes et solita naturaliter essentia est, et animam, quae quidem ob
subtilissimam incorporeae essentiae naturam vix cuiusquam providetur ingenio, medium
aliquid vincire oportuit, quod in neutris componentium termino, utriusque tamen naturae participatione aliqua, tam absone dissidentia in unius eiusdemque essentiae foedus

pher, soul and body are united by a "spirit" which is neither corporeal nor incorporeal, but whose structure is rather halfway between the two principles.[131]

The need to put an ontological hierarchy inside man was thus felt already in the twelfth century. However, the doctrine of intermediaries which was developed in the 1220s and 1230s is clearly distinguished from that elaborated in the preceding century. Its typical features derive mainly from the assimilation of Arabic and Jewish texts having an Aristotelian inspiration. Thanks to these new sources, the Latin thinkers shift their attention from intermediary elements of a corporeal kind, such as the "spirit", to intermediaries belonging to the soul. The latter perspective implies that the theme of mediation becomes closely related to the problems concerning the sensitive and vegetative powers of the soul. Thereby the idea of intermediary elements belonging to the body was not abandoned: indeed, even Thomas Aquinas still spoke of a mediation of a certain kind provided by a corporeal "spirit".[132] Nevertheless, in the thirteenth century, the Latin thinkers were to focus above all on the role played by the sensitive and vegetative powers in the conjunction of soul and body. The debate was oriented in this direction especially by Philip the Chancellor: the doctrine of the intermediary principles expounded in the *Summa de bono* was actually to become the main reference point for all thirteenth-century authors.

In his study on the doctrine of the plurality of forms in the individual, Roberto Zavalloni thoroughly examines the question of the main source of inspiration for Philip's theory of intermediaries.[133] According to Zavalloni, the traditional thesis[134]

---

uniret. Id igitur si omnimodam corporeae conditionis naturam effugeret, ab animae subtili essentia nihil disiungeret. Idem etiam, si totius corporeae condicioni leges admitteret, a primi corporis hebetudine non distaret. Nec plene igitur sensibile, nec omnino incorporeum esse oportuit".

[131] Alfred bases his theory of the spirit as intermediary on the authority of Aristotle, Costa Ben Luca, and Galen; cf. Ps. Arist., *motu cord.*, ed. Baeumker, pp. 40-41.

[132] Cf. Thom. de Aquino, *sum. c. gent.* II, 71, EL 13, 454a-b; cf. E. Bertola, "La dottrina dello «spirito» in S. Tommaso", *Sophia* 21 (1953), pp. 29-35.

[133] Zavalloni considers Philip as a forerunner of the doctrine of form plurality in the individual; I would rather speak of a "theory of intermediaries" or of "material dispositions", thus adopting the terms used by Philip himself ("Sequitur questio utrum per medium vel sine medio uniantur"; cf. Philipp., *sum. de bon.*, ed. Wicki, pp. 283-287). This terminological difference does not result from a new interpretation of Philip's thought, but rather from the context in which the thesis proposed by this theologian is situated. Indeed, the debate on form plurality is peculiar especially to the last decades of the thirteenth century; by contrast, our research focuses on the first decades of the century, when the problem was not yet structured in these terms. In fact, in this chapter, we deal with Philip's doctrine mainly because it can be interpreted as a corollary of Neoplatonic dualism, not viewing it as a particular application of Aristotelian hylomorphism. The terminology used by Zavalloni has been called in question also by Bazán, "Pluralisme de formes", *passim*.

[134] Cf. G. Théry, *L'augustinisme médiéval et l'unité de la forme substantielle*, in *Acta Hebdomadae Augustinianae-Thomisticae*, Roma: Marietti, 1931, p. 198; E. Gilson, "Pour-

that this doctrine is inspired by Avicebron's *Fons vitae*, is not correct: rather, the main source of our theory seems to be contained in Avicenna's *De anima*.[135] Zavalloni bases his conclusion mainly on three arguments: first, Philip the Chancellor, just like many later thinkers, picks up Avicenna's theory according to which the soul is not the immediate form of prime matter but rather represents the perfection of a body already prepared by the *forma corporeitatis*. Second, Avicenna's *De anima* contains the idea of some hierarchy inside the soul: for the vegetative and sensitive powers have a position which is subordinate to rationality.[136] Finally, as regards our problem, according to Zavalloni, the *Fons vitae* begins to be cited relatively late, i.e. not before the second half of the thirteenth century.[137] Avicenna's *De anima* should, then, be sufficient to explain the birth of Philip's doctrine.

Undoubtedly, Avicenna played an important role for the anthropology of the first half of the thirteenth century, including the theory of intermediaries. Indeed, in agreement with Zavalloni's statements, the idea that the soul is united with a body which is already prepared for the union is present in Philip's thought and certainly derives from Avicenna. Nevertheless, this does not mean that Avicebron's influence should be diminished. Actually, thanks to the complete edition of the *Summa de bono*, we can now recognize Avicebron's influence in this work. First of all, Philip probably knows the *Fons vitae* directly, but cites it using a different title, i.e. *Liber de materia et forma*.[138] Secondly, the Jewish philosopher exerts his influence on the *Summa de bono* also indirectly, that is through a short anonymous treatise entitled *De potentiis animae et obiectis*. According to the text's editor,[139] the treatise was employed by Philip in the *Summa*, and this opinion is confirmed by Nicolaus Wicki.[140] Undoubtedly, the anonymous author knew Avicebron's work very well: indeed, the latter is mentioned quite often, and always using the title *Liber de materia et forma*. The strong influence exerted by the Jewish philosopher is visible above all in the case of the theory of the intermediary elements. For, according to Avicebron, in man there exists a hierarchy of forms connecting intelligence and body. Just as in the *Summa de bono* lower forms play the role of material dispositions in regard to higher forms, so in the *Fons vitae* lower forms play the role of matter in regard to higher forms, which, in their turn, operate in lower forms.[141]

---

quoi saint Thomas a critiqué saint Augustin", *AHDLMA* 1 (1926), pp. 25-35.

[135] Zavalloni, *Richard de Mediavilla*, p. 420.

[136] Zavalloni, *Richard de Mediavilla*, pp. 423-428.

[137] Zavalloni, *Richard de Mediavilla*, pp. 421-422.

[138] Cf. Wicki, "Introduction", in Philipp., *sum. de bon.*, ed. Wicki, p. 47*.

[139] The treatise probably dates from 1220-1230; cf. D. A. Callus, "The Powers of the Soul. An Early Unpublished Text", *RTAM* 19 (1952), pp. 143-145.

[140] Cf. Wicki, "Introduction", in Philipp., *sum. de bon.*, ed. Wicki, p. 48*.

[141] Auicebr., *Fons vitae* V, 19, ed. Baeumker, 294[14-17]: "Oportet ut inferius sit hyle superiori, quia superius est agens in inferiori. Et ideo sapientes noluerunt appellare aliquam

Among Avicebron's intermediary forms, there are, on the one hand, the vegetative soul operating in the body and resembling the body thanks to its consistency (*crassitudo*), and, on the other, the sensitive soul operating in the vegetative soul and resembling the rational soul thanks to its subtlety.[142] The same hierarchy is adopted by the anonymous author of *De potentiis animae et obiectis*. The sensitive soul resembles the rational soul because it performs a cognitive function and is incorporeal, whereas the vegetative soul is incorporeal but performs no function of a cognitive kind. Besides the sensitive and vegetative powers, between soul and body there are also two corporeal intermediaries, i.e. the "spirit" and the *virtus elementaris*.[143]

---

substantiam formam certissime, nisi intelligentiam primam, quae uocatur ab eis intelligentia agens".

[142] Auicebr., *Fons vitae* III, 48, ed. Baeumker, pp. 185[27]-186[4]: "Iam ostendisti mihi actionem animae uegetabilis in natura; et patuit mihi quomodo earum actiones sunt sub uno genere. Ostende etiam actionem animae sensibilis in animam uegetabilem et quomodo actiones earum sunt sub uno genere", pp. 186[18]-187[7]: "Et etiam, quia anima animalis superat uegetabilem, ideo quod anima animalis coniungitur formis corporum, quae conueniunt ei in subtilitate, cominus et eminus, et extrahit eas a formis earum corporalibus, anima autem uegetabilis coniungitur essentiae corporum, quia conuenit eis in crassitudine, et hoc prope et continue tantum. (...) Ergo debet esse ut anima animalis sit agens in anima uegetabilem, ideo quia perfectior est ea et fortior. (...) Secundum hanc considerationem quam tibi ostendi in his tribus substantiis erit similiter dicendum de anima ratonali et intelligentia..."; cf. *ibid.*, v, 19-20, ed. Baeumker, p. 295[3-16]: "Causa in hoc est, quia forma prima quae coniuncta est materiae primae est spiritualis simplex, et forma ultima est corporalis composita; et inter haec extrema sunt media quae ligant illa et coniungunt illa; quia forma quae fuerit propinquior primae formae spirituali, illa erit subtilior et occultior; et e contrario, quia quae forma magis accesserit ad formam corporalem ultimam, erit spissior et manifestior. (...) Exemplum huius est quia forma intelligentiae est forma prima spiritualis quae coniuncta est materiae, et quae eam sequitur, est forma animae rationalis, deinde forma animae sensibilis, deinde forma animae uegetabilis, deinde forma naturae, deinde forma substantiae, deinde forma corporis, deinde forma figurae et coloris". It should be observed that Avicebron maintains the plurality of substances in the soul; cf. *ibid.*, III, 46, ed. Baeumker, pp. 181[20]-182[8]; *ibid.*, v, 22, ed. Baeumker, p. 299[6-13].

[143] *De pot. an. et ob.*, ed. Callus, pp. 149-150: "Comprehensionis enim natura sequitur esse. Est autem anima rationalis substantia incorporea separabilis a corpore, licet non separata. Anima vero sensibilis est substantia incorporea inseparabilis secundum quod sensibilis, licet eadem ipsa substantia sit separabilis secundum quod sit rationalis; utraque autem cognoscitiva et in hoc separantur ab anima vegetabili, sed convenit cum eis in eo quod est motiva. Sed differt in ratione movendi. (...) Cum autem anima sensibilis sit substantia incorporea corruptibilis, corpus autem cui coniungitur sit substantia corporea corruptibilis, et hec quidem sit simplex, illud vero (i. e. corpus) compositum ex corporibus, in duobus habet differentiam, in tertio vero habet convenientiam, scilicet, in eo quod est corruptibilis. Indiget ergo mediis duobus, quorum unum sit substantia simplex corruptibilis, sicut est elementum, et alio quod sit substantia simplex et incorruptibils, quemadmodum est corpus quod est de natura quinte essentie. (...) Et similiter est in compositione sensibilis cum corpore: habet unum substantiam incorpoream mediam, scilicet vegetabilem, et

Clearly, both the *Fons vitae* and *De potentiis animae et obiectis* are forerunners of the theory concerning the hierarchy of souls expounded in Philip the Chancellor's *Summa de bono*.

The importance of Avicebron's work for the development of the theory of intermediaries may be confirmed by drawing a comparison between Dominicus Gundissalinus' treatise *De anima* and the treatise by John Blund which bears the same title. Both authors avail themselves abundantly of Avicenna's *De anima*, but just one of them, i.e. Dominicus Gundissalinus, closely follows the *Fons vitae*. This is the reason why John Blund's *De anima* makes practically no mention of the doctrine of intermediaries, whereas Dominicus Gundissalinus quotes very faithfully the exposition appearing in the work written by the Jewish philosopher:[144]

> Fortior enim est actio animae rationalis quam animalis et animalis fortior quam vegetabilis. Anima enim vegetabilis movet partes corporis sine mutatione totius de loco ad locum; animalis vero movet totum corpus de loco ad locum totaliter et anima animalis coniungitur formis corporum convenientibus sibi in subtilitate cominus vel eminus, et abstrahit eas a formis rerum corporalibus. Anima vero vegetabilis coniungitur essentiae corporum quia convenit cum eis in spissitudine, et hoc proprie et continue tantum. Unde anima sensibilis agit in vegetabilem et vegetabilis in naturam, sed rationalis agit in sensibilem sicut intelligentia agit in rationalem. Oportet enim ut inferius sit quasi materia superiori eo quod superius agit in inferius; et ideo sapientes noluerunt appellare aliquam substantiarum formam simpliciter, nisi intelligentiam primam quae vocatur ab eis intelligentia agens.

Hence, it evidently appears that the theory of material dispositions derives mainly from Avicebron's *Fons vitae*, not from Avicenna's *De anima*. Consequently, even though Philip the Chancellor is inspired by the Arab philosopher when he speaks of the *forma corporeitatis* and of the body as predisposed to receive the rational soul, we have to conclude – in contrast to Zavalloni – that the main source of his theory of the intermediary elements is contained in the *Fons vitae*.

2.2.1.3   Hugh of St-Cher

As we have seen above, the theory of intermediaries presented in the *Summa de bono* presupposes a dualist conception of man. Indeed, in agreement with Avicenna's anthropology, Philip conceives of the union of soul and body as an accidental union of two complete substances, which resembles hylomorphic union only in

---

habet duo corpora, vel duo ex duplici natura corporali accepta pro mediis, scilicet spiritum et virtutem elementarem".

[144] Dom. Gund., *de an.*, ed. Muckle, pp. 46-47; cf. Auicebr., *Fons vitae* III, 48, ed. Baeumker, pp. 185[27]-186[4], pp. 186[18]-187[7].

some respects. The union *per medium* presents itself as a theory easily reconcil-able with such a view. The problem, however, becomes more complicated when an author accepts the doctrine of intermediaries and, at the same time, intends to affirm a less dualist anthropology, i.e. an anthropology in which the union be-tween the human soul and the body is no longer defined as accidental. This is the difficulty arising in the disputed questions written by Hugh of St-Cher.

The Dominican theologian adopts Philip the Chancellor's theory of interme-diaries very faithfully. Like Philip in the *Summa de bono*, Hugh in his questions deals with this problem on two occasions: first of all, in the second article of the question *Quomodo anima uniatur corpori* (corresponding to the chapter that Philip entitles *De unione anime ad corpus*),[145] where the problem of intermediaries represents the central theme of the question; secondly, in the second article of the question *De anima* (corresponding to the chapter *Utrum potentia sensibilis et rationalis in eadem substantia fundentur* of the *Summa de bono*),[146] where the problem plays a secondary role. In both cases, Hugh follows Philip faithfully and copies his texts verbatim. In any case, it may be useful to examine his expositions, especially in light of the doctrine of the *unibilitas substantialis* of the soul in re-gard to the body, which, as we have seen, was embraced by Hugh.[147]

The question *Quomodo anima uniatur corpori*[148] consists of two articles. The first is devoted to a traditional theme, which was addressed very frequently all through the Middle Ages, namely, *Utrum anima ita sit in toto corpore quod in qualibet eius parte*.[149] The first article relies to a great extent on the text of Philip the Chancellor's *Summa de bono*,[150] but contains also some original argumenta-tion. By contrast, the second article of the question, entitled *Quomodo anima uniatur corpori, sine medio uel per medium*, reports a passage from the *Summa de bono*[151] without substantial intervention by Hugh. We will first deal with this second article of the question.

This short text is composed of three arguments against and three arguments for mediation. The first paragraph abundantly resembles an argument appearing in Roland of Cremona's *Summa*.[152] 'Being' and 'being one' are identical for every

---

[145] Cf. *supra*, p. 122.

[146] Cf. *supra*, pp. 120-121.

[147] Cf. *supra*, chap. 1.1.2.2.

[148] The question is preserved in just one manuscript: like the other questions by Hugh, it forms part of the collection *Douai, Bibl. Mun. 434* and was classified by Glorieux with number 285; cf. Glorieux, "Les 572 Questions", p. 148.

[149] Cf. *infra*, pp. 183-185.

[150] Philipp., *sum. de bon.*, ed. Wicki, pp. 278[14]-292[58].

[151] Philipp., *sum. de bon.*, ed. Wicki, pp. 283[69]-286[164].

[152] Cf. Rol. Crem., *sum.*, in Hess, "Roland of Cremona's Place", p. 440: "Dicunt quod in homine est anima vegetabilis et anima sensibilis et anima rationalis. Sed hoc non potest stare, quia unius rei unica est perfectio prima, quia unius rei unicum est esse. Constat

existing thing; since being, in every composite of matter and form, is brought about by form, it is impossible that form is united with matter through something else; consequently, the soul too must be united directly with its body.

Secondly, the hypothesis of an intermediary raises a question concerning the ontological character of that intermediary: indeed, if that intermediary were an accident of the substance of the soul, then the union of soul and body would be merely accidental. It is evident that this solution would contradict the conclusions drawn by Hugh in his question *De anima*: as we have seen, according to the Dominican theologian, the soul is united with the body with its own essence, because *unibilitas* to the body constitutes an essential or substantial characteristic of the human soul. By contrast, if we admit an intermediary substance, then we do nothing but move the problem from one substance to the other, thus inevitably regressing *ad infinitum*. Moreover, in order for this substance to be united both with the soul and the body, it should have the nature of both of them. But this is impossible, because there is no substance which is at the same time incorporeal and corporeal.

The subsequent arguments are in favour of the presence of an intermediary. First of all, affirms Hugh, the presence of an intermediary would succeed in explaining that the soul is separable from the body both according to its substance and according to its operations. Moreover, the soul cannot represent the perfection of the body unless two powers are present, i.e. the sensitive power and the vegetative power, which prepare soul and body for their union. Indeed, this mediation is necessary because soul and body possess totally opposite characteristics: the soul is simple, incorporeal and incorruptible, whereas the body is composite, corporeal and corruptible. It is thus inevitable that two realities which are so distant on the ontological level are conjoined by the sensitive soul, which is simple and incorporeal but corruptible, and by the vegetative soul, which is incorporeal but composite and corruptible.

Hugh's exposition contains all the main arguments used by Philip the Chancellor to defend the presence of intermediaries in the union of soul and body. Unfortunately, we do not know whether Hugh, in his question, adopted a similar solution, because the only known manuscript handing down the question does not contain the solution of the article. Moreover, neither the structure of the text nor the reasons which are employed allow us to advance any hypothesis on this point.

---

autem quod anima est perfectio corporis organici potentia vitam habentis. Ergo haec anima vegetabilis est perfectio coporis organici potentia vitam habentis. Ergo haec anima vegetabilis est perfectio hujus corporis et haec anima sensibilis et haec anima rationalis. Ergo habet unicum corpus tres perfectiones primas, quod esse non potest. Iterum, si prima perficit, pro nihilo venit secunda et tertia"; cf. ms. *Paris, Bibliothèque Mazarine 795*, f. 34va; Lottin, *Psychologie et morale*, I, p. 465 .

However, in order to grasp the possible solution of the question here at hand, we can look for evidence in the second article of the question *De anima*, again by Hugh, which is entitled *Utrum anima rationalis et sensibilis et vegetabilis sint idem in eadem*. The article concerns chiefly the problem whether the soul is composed of many substances or is simple, but contains also several hints about the theme of the union *per medium*. Indeed, the first part of the argumentation in favour of the plurality of substances in the soul is based on the statement that the rational soul is united with the human body by means of two material dispositions, i.e. the sensitive soul and the vegetative soul. By quoting Philip the Chancellor word for word, Hugh maintains that the sensitive soul carries out a function of mediation between the rational soul and the body, and the vegetative soul carries out a similar function as regards the union of the sensitive soul with the body. Hence, the rational soul cannot be identical with the sensitive soul and the vegetative soul, because "nihil est perfectio alicuius et medium respectu eiusdem": the human soul consists therefore of three substances.[153] Subsequently, Hugh proposes an interesting question, which perfectly clarifies the meaning to be attributed to the notion of intermediaries in the union of soul and body. He raises a doubt: perhaps the mediation of the sensitive soul and the vegetative soul must be understood in the sense that the rational soul cannot operate in the body unless it is preceded by the action of the sensitive soul. In other words, the rational activity of man might depend upon the sensible data provided by the perception. And yet Hugh, just like Philip, rejects this hypothesis. The activity of the rational soul in the body is for the rational soul a second act, but the second act is not possible without the first act. In the case of the soul, the first act coincides with the fact of being perfection of the body. Now, according to Hugh, the rational soul cannot be perfection of the body without the mediation of the sensitive soul: for this reason, a man cannot be rational if he is not first animal. The sensitive soul and the vegetative soul are thus necessary in order for the rational soul to exist in man. It follows that their mediation does not concern operations but refers above all to being.[154]

---

[153] Hugo de S. Caro, *q. de an.*, 2, ed. Bieniak, pp. 171[124]-172[131]: "Primo quaeritur sic: nihil est perfectius alicuius et medium respectu eiusdem; sed anima sensibilis medium est inter corpus et animam rationalem perficientem ipsum, ergo anima sensibilis non est idem quod anima rationalis. Quod autem anima sensibilis sit medium quo anima rationalis insit corpori patet ex eo quod dicit Aristoteles in libro *De anima*, scilicet quod "vegetativum potest esse sine sensibili et non e converso et sensitivum sine rationali et non e converso". Sicut ergo vegetativum medium est inter sensitivum et corpus, ita sensitivum medium est inter corpus et rationale".

[154] Hugo de S. Caro, *q. de an.*, 2, ed. Bieniak, p. 172[144-156]: "Forte dicet quod anima sensibilis sive potentia sensitiva non est media sive dispositio ad hoc ut anima rationalis insit corpori, sed ad hoc quod operetur in corpore, eo quod intellectus non potest operari sine sensu. Contra: primus actus animae est quod est perfectio corporis organici, secundus actus eius est quod operatur in corpore et per corpus, sicut in ense primus actus est forma sive

In the solution of the article *Utrum anima rationalis et sensibilis et vegetabilis sint idem in eadem*, Hugh rejected – much more decisively than Philip the Chancellor had done – the theory of the plurality of substances in the soul. According to the Dominican theologian, the sensitive principle and the vegetative principle are powers belonging to the rational soul.[155] This does not mean that Hugh rejects the theory of intermediaries, but rather he affirms it again in that part of the article devoted to confuting the objections: the sensitive and vegetative powers are material dispositions in regard to the rational soul because they enable it to be united with the body, not because the intellect needs sensible data. For the human intellect can operate without the help of the sensitive faculty.[156]

In order to better understand what kind of mediation belongs to the sensitive and vegetative powers, we may compare the passage of the question with a more systematic exposition appearing in Hugh's commentary on the twenty-first dis-

---

figura eius, secundus secare, et patet quod secundus actus ensis non est nisi post primum et ex primo; ergo eodem modo secundus actus animae est post primum et ex primo; ergo ad hoc quod anima rationalis operetur in corpore, oportet quod perficiat corpus, sed hoc non potest esse nisi mediante sensibili; ergo ad primum actum animae rationalis praeexigitur sensibile; ergo sensibile medium est animae rationalis, non solum ut operetur in corpore, sed etiam ut sit in corpore. Preterea. Dato quod sensibile non praeexigitur ad hoc quod anima rationalis insit corpori, accidet quod erit homo sine animali, quod esse non potest, ergo oportet quod sensibile sit medium per quod anima inest corpori".

[155] Among the authors whose works have been examined here, only Avicebron clearly maintains the plurality of substances in the soul; cf. *supra*, pp. 128-129. All the other authors explicitly defend the unicity of substance in the soul; cf. Auic., *De anima* v, 7, ed. Van Riet, p. 159$^{12-13}$, p. 167$^{14-16}$; cf. Sebti, *Avicenne*, pp. 45-49; Dom. Gund., *de an.*, 4, ed. Muckle, p. 45$^{16-27}$: "Quamvis autem omnis anima sit substantia et hae tres simul sint in unoquoque homine quoniam in homine est anima vegetabilis et sensibilis et rationalis, non tamen tres substantiae sunt in homine; humana enim anima, cum sit una simplex substantia, habet vires animae vegetabilis et vires animae sensibilis et vires animae rationalis"; Ioh. Blund, *tract. de an.*, 4, ed. Callus-Hunt, p. 10$^{22-26}$: "Sed anima non dicetur in aliqua specie substantie quod in ea sint plures substantie, immo una sola substantia specificata per differentias. Pari ratione dicendum est quod in homine non sunt tres anime, immo una sola anima specificata per differentias tres, ut per vegetabile, sensibile, rationale"; *de pot. an. et ob.*, ed. Callus, p. 147$^{17-19}$: "Et sumatur obiectum communiter pro materia, cum ex parte essentie anime in se, cuius ex parte illa diversitas potentiarum, non inveniatur diversitas"; Rol. Crem., *sum.*, ms. *Paris, Bibliothèque Mazarine 795*, f. 34va; cf. Hess, "Roland of Cremona's Place", p. 440; Lottin, *Psychologie et morale*, I, p. 465: "Sensibilis et uegetabilis sunt uires anime rationalis in homine".

[156] Hugo de S. Caro, *q. de an.*, 2, ed. Bieniak, p. 175$^{246-250}$: "Ad primum quo dicitur quod nihil est medium et perfectio eiusdem respectu eiusdem, verum est secundum idem quod ante dicitur, quod sensibilis est materialis dispositio per quam inest anima rationalis corpori. Falsum est hoc, scilicet ideo dicitur medium, quia prius est operatio eius in quantum sensitiva quam operatio eiusdem in quantum est intellectiva et praeexigitur ut principium quia a sensu incipit opera intellectus".

tinction of book III of Peter Lombard's *Sentences*. When speaking about the union of the Divinity with the body of Christ through his soul, Hugh makes a list of the possible types of mediation. Only one of them, i.e. the *medium conjunctionis*, is indispensable for the union to exist in act. All the other types of intermediaries – i.e. (1) the participation intermediary (red colour between white and black), (2) the similarity intermediary (the soul between body and Divinity), (3) the proof intermediary (the middle term of a syllogism) and (4) the continuity intermediary (a point of a line) – are not indispensable for union; in other words, the conjunction is not dissolved if the intermediary principle disappears.[157] Inspired by the *Sentences*,[158] Hugh introduces this distinction to deal with the problem of the union of the Divinity with the body during the *triduum*, when the soul of Christ did not perform the mediation function between the Divinity and the body. This union was possible despite the lack of an intermediary principle because it was a similarity mediation, not a *mediatio conjunctionis*. According to Hugh, the similarity mediation serves just to make the union between two ontologically distant elements conceivable, but has no causal value. Indeed, the soul is an intermediary between the body and the Divinity because it is simpler than the body and, at the same time, less simple than God; and yet, the absence of the soul does not make the union of the Divinity with the body of Christ impossible.

If we apply the classification of the intermediary principles to the problem of the sensitive and vegetative powers, we may doubt whether the mediation performed by them in regard to soul and body corresponds to any of the different types of mediation Hugh enumerates in his *Sentences Commentary*. On the one hand, their mediation recalls the similarity mediation: indeed, the sensitive soul and the vegetative soul possess in part the characteristics of the rational soul and in part the characteristics of the body.[159] Yet, on the other hand, Hugh clearly states that man cannot be rational without being animal: one may easily deduce that the absence of the sensitive soul and the vegetative soul makes the union between the rational soul and the body impossible. The mediation of the sensitive and vegeta-

---

[157] Cf. Hugo de S. Caro, *in* III Sent., d. 21, ed. Principe, in *Hugh of Saint-Cher's Theology*, p. 231: "Per has auctoritates volunt probare quod divinitas in triduo fuit separata a carne. Cum tamen sancti dicant quod numquam fuit separata, ad primum dicendum est quod multiplex est medium, scilicet participationis, ut rubor inter albedinem et nigredinem; assimilationis: hoc enim similior divinitati quam caro, quia simplicior; item, similior est carni quam divinitas, quia minus simplex. Item, est medium probationis, ut in syllogismo; item, conjunctionis, ut cementum inter lapides et glutinum inter aliquas res conglutinatas, et amor inter amantes. De hoc medio verum est quod eo divisio, sequitur divisio extremorum, sed in aliis mediis non est sic; et sic patet solutio primi per distinctionem medii"; cf. Principe, in *Hugh of Saint-Cher's Theology*, p. 136.

[158] Cf. Petr. Lomb., *sent.* III, d. 21, c. 1, ed. PP. Collegii S. Bonaventurae, pp. 130-132.

[159] Cf. *infra*, p. 186.

tive powers must therefore be defined as *mediatio conjunctionis*, i.e. the strongest type of mediation among those enumerated in the *Sentences Commentary*.

As we have said, the doctrine of intermediaries can be easily fit into an anthropological view like that held by Avicenna or Philip the Chancellor, in which the ability to be united with the body is reduced to an accident and does not influence at all the essence of the soul. By contrast, the union *per medium* seems much more difficult to reconcile with a theory in which *unibilitas* to the body defines the substance of the soul and is considered as something essential. Hugh of St-Cher's anthropology confronts us with this problem.[160] Indeed, we have to consider the objection cited by Hugh in the question *Quomodo anima uniatur corpori*: the sensitive and vegetative powers – which constitute the intermediary elements necessary for the union between the rational soul and the body – are either substances or accidents. Clearly, Hugh rejects the first possibility: for the human soul is one substance. But if the sensitive and vegetative powers are but accidents of the soul, then the union between soul and body is accidental. We should therefore pose the following question: what is the ontological status of the lower powers of the soul?

We should affirm, first of all, that the sensitive and vegetative powers are not substances distinct from the rational soul. Secondly, on the basis of the arguments used by Hugh in his commentary on the third distinction of book I of the *Sentences*, i.e. in the discussion about the ontological status of the rational powers,[161] we may suppose two possible answers to our question. On the one hand, if the sensitive and vegetative powers are not necessary for the existence of the soul, they might be accidents of the soul. On the other hand, the lower powers might be identical with the essence of the soul, just as for Hugh memory, reason and will are identical with the essence or the substance of the rational soul.[162]

In order to understand which of these solutions is closer to Hugh's thought, we have to answer another question, namely, whether the lower powers are immortal as the rational soul is or, on the contrary, whether their existence is indissolubly connected to the mortal body. Therefore, the following section will be primarily devoted to determining the position held by Hugh concerning this problem. Subsequently, we will compare the perspective of the Dominican theologian with the thought elaborated by the other masters of his time.

---

[160] A similar problem appears also in the *Summa* of John of La Rochelle; cf. Ioh. Rup., *sum. de an.* I, 26, ed. Bougerol, pp. 85-89.

[161] Cf. *supra*, chap. 2.1.2, especially 2.1.2.3.

[162] It should be noted that Hugh does not distinguish between the concepts of essence and substance; cf. *supra*, p. 26, n. 80.

2.2.2   THE SURVIVAL OF THE SENSITIVE AND VEGETATIVE POWERS

2.2.2.1   Hugh of St-Cher

In Hugh of St-Cher's anthropology, the problem of the ontological status of the lower powers of the human soul is closely connected to the problem of the type of union existing between soul and body. Indeed, for Hugh, the rational soul can be conjoined with the body just by means of its vegetative and sensitive powers. This type of union seems difficult to reconcile with another theory supported by Hugh, according to which the ability to give perfection to the body belongs to the soul in an essential way: the recourse to the intermediary elements necessary for union evokes the suspicion that, in fact, it is an instrumental union which is exhausted in some determinate functions of the soul and does not involve its essence. Apart from the ontological status that, according to Hugh, the lower powers have inside the human soul, this suspicion is fully legitimate. Indeed, the reason why a theologian needs to posit the existence of intermediaries of an ontological kind is presumably that, from his point of view, the mere nature of the soul is not sufficient to explain the union between soul and body.

Yet, we may hypothetically consider a solution of this difficulty resting on the doctrine of the identity of the soul with its rational powers. We might suppose that the sensitive and vegetative powers have in the human soul the same ontological status as the rational powers. If the lower powers, which perform the function of intermediaries, were identical with the essence of the soul just like the rational faculties, then we might deduce that the mediation Hugh speaks of resolves into a purely logical distinction and therefore conclude that the human soul is united with the body through its own essence.

It clearly appears, however, that the identity of the soul with its powers does not concern the vegetative and sensitive faculties. This becomes evident above all in the fact that for Hugh the lower powers of the soul do not survive after a man's death: indeed, they are inseparable from the body. Hugh presents his opinion on the issue in the second article of the question *De anima*, entitled *Utrum anima rationalis et sensibilis et vegetabilis sint idem in eadem*. As we have seen above, this article faithfully reports a chapter of Philip the Chancellor's *Summa de bono*: actually, Hugh's opinion about the mortality of the lower faculties totally coincides with the opinion held by the secular master. The two theologians maintain that whereas the rational soul is immortal and can avail itself of its intellective faculties even when the body is absent, the vegetative and sensitive powers are closely connected to the body and cannot exist without it. This idea is expounded efficaciously in an objection appearing at the beginning of Hugh's article. One might suppose, he says, that the sensitive power remains in the soul after a man's death despite the absence of the body, hence in the absence of the instrument

which is indispensable to perform its functions. But such a situation is inconceivable because, according to Hugh, being and being able are not distinct in separate
substances – "in separatis idem est esse et posse"; hence, after the separation from
the body, only the powers which are identical with the substance of the soul can
remain. Now, the sensitive power is not identical with the substance of the soul because after the body's death the soul cannot perform in act any sensitive function.
Considering that a power does not exist if it cannot operate – "non est potentia
sine opere" – we must necessarily conclude that the lower faculties are not present
in the separated soul.[163]

According to Hugh, the sensitive and vegetative powers belong to the human
soul, but their being is indissolubly connected to the mortal body: these powers
can therefore be defined as accidents in regard to the soul. However, this does not
mean that the lower powers are accidents of man, i.e. of the soul-body composite:
indeed, Hugh repeatedly affirms that the subject of the powers coincides with the
substance of the rational soul, not with the human being as a whole.[164]

If combined, the theory of the union *per medium* and the doctrine which attributes an accidental status to the intermediary powers raise doubts about the
possibility of an essential union between soul and body. In the first article of the

---

[163] Cf. Hugo de S. Caro, *q. de an.*, 2, ed. Bieniak, p. 172[137-141]: "Forte dicet quod potentia
sensitiua remanet post separationem anime, licet non sentiat actu anima separata. Contra:
in separatis idem est esse et posse, neque est potentia sine opere, ergo si anima separata
haberet potentiam sensitiuam semper sentiret uel ad minus aliquando. Sed constat quod
nunquam sentit nec potest, ergo non habet potentiam sensitiuam"; cf. Aug., *Io. ev. tr.*, ed.
Willems, CCSL 36, p. 205, PL 35, 1558: "Filio enim hoc est esse quod posse. Homini non ita
est. Ex comparatione humanae infirmitatis, longe infra iacentis, utcumque corda sustollite;
et ne forte aliquis nostrum adtingat secretum, et quasi coruscatione magnae lucis horres-
cens, sapiat aliquid, ne insipiens remaneat: non tamen se totum sapere putet, ne superbiat,
et quod sapuit amittat. Homo aliud est quod est, aliud quod potest. Aliquando enim et est
homo, et non potest quod uult; aliquando autem sic est homo, ut possit quod uult; itaque
aliud est esse ipsius, aliud posse ipsius. Si enim hoc esset esse ipsius, quod est posse ipsius,
cum vellet posset. Deus autem cui non est alia substantia ut sit, et alia potestas ut possit,
sed consubstantiale illi est quidquid eius est, et quidquid est, quia Deus est, non alio modo
est, et alio modo potest; sed esse et posse simul habet, quia uelle et facere simul habet".

[164] Hugo de S. Caro, *q. de an.*, 2, ed. Bieniak, p. 176[284-288]: "Dico ad hoc quod re uera sensitiua potentia eiusdem speciei est in brutis et in hominibus, sed subiectum sensitiue potentie hinc et inde diuersum est. Hinc enim subiectum eius est anima rationalis, inde uero
anima sensibilis, et ideo cum subiectum eius in homine sit incorruptibile et ipsa secundum
substantiam quidem incorruptibilis, tamen secundum rationem corruptibilis". It should be
noted, however, that Hugh knew the Aristotelian principle according to which actions are
not proper to form, but to the hylomorphic composite operating through form; cf. Hugo
de S. Caro, *in* IV *Sent.*, d. 16, ed. Principe, p. 43: "Gratia enim, proprie loquendo, non agit in
forma aliqua proprie sed aliquid vel aliquis per formam, sicut ignis per igneitatem sive per
caliditatem, et Deus per gratiam".

question *De anima*, Hugh states that the ability to be united with the body determines the nature of the soul in an essential way; by contrast, on the basis of
the second article of the same question we must conclude that *unibilitas* actually depends on accidental aspects of the soul (i.e. on the vegetative and sensitive
powers) because, without them, it is not possible. Moreover, whereas in the first
article Hugh maintains that the *unibilitas substantialis* to the body remains in the
soul even after the separation from the body, in the second article the Dominican
author affirms that the separated soul does not possess the powers which are indispensable for the union in act to come about.

Is it possible, at least in part, to overcome these difficulties? In order to answer
this question, it may be helpful to use a rather imperfect and well-worn image,
which compares the soul-body relationship to the relationship between an operating system and the hardware of a computer. So, let us imagine that the operating system possesses a component which is necessary for the system both to be
installed and to operate in the computer. Let us suppose that this component is
then removed from the operating system itself. We might certainly conclude that,
in any case, a reference to the hardware remains in the essence of the operating
system, simply because the operating system as a whole was created to make the
computer work. Nevertheless, we cannot admit that such a mutilated system is
still capable of "giving life" to the hardware, because this capability depended on
a component which was removed. Hence, if we still want to define the essence of
this system as unitable, then we have to admit that we are dealing with an incomplete and curtailed essence. Now, the problem with Hugh's anthropology consists
in the fact that the "components"[165] of the soul which assure it the ability to be
united with the body are defined as accidents, not as essential aspects. Consequently, we can admit that some reference to the body remains – even after death
– in the soul which is united with the body by means of accidents; and yet we must
conclude that, in this type of union, the ability to become united is not essential,
but only accidental for the soul.

This incoherence we notice in Hugh's anthropology is related, at least to some
extent, to the fact that our theologian considers the lower powers of the soul as inseparable from the mortal body. We may doubt, therefore, if it was really necessary
to hold such an opinion, that is to say, if the theological context in which Hugh was
situated would have allowed a different solution of the problem concerning the
mortality of the sensitive and vegetative powers. Indeed, the anthropological texts
of the first half of the thirteenth century contain alternative solutions as well. In

---

[165] This term is improper here because Hugh repeatedly points out that the human soul
is not composed of parts; cf. Hugo de S. Caro, *q. de an.*, 3, ed. Bieniak, p. 181[452]: "Anima vero
et angelus prima compositione carent quae est ex partibus".

the following pages we will thus try to examine the various answers given by the
authors living in the first decades of the thirteenth century to the problem of the
survival of the lower powers of the human soul.

2.2.2.2 Avicenna and Dominicus Gundissalinus

The question concerning the fact that the sensitive and vegetative faculties remain
in the soul after the separation from the body becomes particularly relevant in
the Latin West at the moment of the reception of the Aristotelian psychology.
In Christian theology, this problem is necessarily related to the issue of the resurrection of the body. Indeed, even though, after the body's death, the soul exists without corporeal instruments, its ultimate destination consists in becoming
united to the glorious body: this view exerts some influence also on the way in
which the lower powers of the soul were conceived. By contrast, Aristotle's as well
as Avicenna's writings lack the perspective of resurrection; hence, also their conception of the lower powers of the human soul reveals at times very different com-
mitments from that held by the Christian theologians. Faced with the difficulties
arising from the convergence of two different traditions, the thinkers of the first
half of the thirteenth century look for new solutions allowing them to reconcile
these two psychological views. Dominicus Gundissalinus is one of the first authors in the Latin West to be confronted with these difficulties while addressing
the problem of the survival of the vegetative and sensitive powers.

Avicenna's *De anima* represents the main source for Dominicus Gundissalinus'
treatise on the soul. The doctrine elaborated by Avicenna is clear and unequivocal:
no vegetative or sensitive faculty can survive after the body's dissolution. Indeed,
all the powers operating by means of the body's limbs are accidents of the soul
and belong to it just by virtue of the conjunction with the body. Similarly, the
cognitive faculties which make use of corporeal images – like imagination, the *vis
aestimativa* or memory – cannot operate nor exist when the corporeal substratum
is lacking, because the latter is necessary for the reception and preservation of
images; hence, none of these faculties can survive after a man's death. Further,
since the body cannot be resurrected, the disappearance of the lower faculties of
the soul is definitive: indeed, these faculties will never be able to carry out their
functions again.[166]

---

[166] Auic., *de an.* v, 4, ed. Van Riet, pp. 59[49]-61[68]: "Dicemus nunc quod actiones istae
et accidentia ista sunt ex accidentibs quae accidunt animae sed dum est in corpore, quae
non accidunt ei nisi propter consortium corporis, et ideo trahunt secum complexiones
corporum. Accidunt etiam ipsa cum accidunt complexiones in corporibus: quasdam enim
complexiones sequitur aptitudo irascendi, et quasdam aptitudo concupiscendi, et quasdam
pavor et timor. (...) Imaginatio vero et concupiscentia et ira et huiusmodi sunt animae sed

In the largest part of his treatise on the soul, Dominicus Gundissalinus follows Avicenna's *Liber de anima* faithfully. In particular, the division and description of the powers of the soul reproduce the exposition by Avicenna almost verbatim. Indeed, Dominicus holds that imagination, memory and the lower part of the intellect – like all vegetative faculties – are for the soul accidents which depend on the body. This doctrine is clearly reiterated especially in the chapter *De interioribus virtutibus animalium*, where Dominicus firmly denies the immortality of these powers.[167] Nevertheless, some passages of the treatise suggest that Dominicus does not wish to preclude the lower powers of the human soul from having any kind of permanence. For this reason, again in the chapter *De interioribus virtutibus animalium*, the author makes mention of the permanence of these faculties "in potency":[168]

> Sciendum autem quod nullam virium vegetabilium, nullam sensibilium retinet anima exuta a corpore. Nihil enim est quod vegetando nutriat vel animando sensificet vel moveat. Has enim actiones non exercet anima nisi dum est in corpore. Vnde, sicut ex coniunctione corporis et animae fiunt, sic ex divisione utriusque pereunt, et vires earum non remanent in corpore vel anima, nisi in sola potentia.

This short reference, in no way justified or explained, conflicts with Avicenna's thought. The same applies to the final part of Dominicus' *De anima*: the last pages of the treatise are clearly distinguishable from the rest of the text both by their style and their content. While, in the preceding parts of the text, Dominicus was mainly basing himself on Avicenna's *De anima* and quoting large excerpts from it, here the supporting authorities are purely theological. Indeed, besides quotations from texts of the Fathers, several biblical references are mainly to be found here. This way of proceeding becomes transparent especially in the last paragraph of the work, where the author addresses the problem of the survival of some powers in the separated soul in relation to the moment of the resurrection. Actually, Do-

---

ex hoc quod est habens corpus, et sunt corporis ex hoc quod principaliter sunt animae ipsius corporis, quamvis sint animae ex hoc quod est habens corpus, non dico ex corpore".
[167] Cf. Dom. Gund., *de an.*, ed. Muckle, p. 83: "Imaginatio vero et concupiscentia et ira et alia huiusmodi sunt animae, sed ex hoc quod est habens corpus (...); sed ex hoc quod est habens corpus, non dico ex corpore. Similiter solicitudo, dolor, tristitia et memoria – nullum horum est accidens corpori ex hoc quod est corpus, sed sunt dispositiones rei coniunctae cum corpore, nec sunt nisi cum est coniunctio cum corpore"; *ibid.*, p. 96: "Ex his autem omnibus viribus animae rationalis, nulla virtus vegetabilis nulla sensibilis, nullus etiam intellectus activus, nec scientia ulla quae activo intellectui comparatur in anima exuta a corpore remanere cognoscitur".
[168] Dom. Gund., *de an.*, ed. Muckle, p. 83.

minicus distinguishes between three states of the human soul: (1) in the body, (2) outside the body and (3) after the resurrection, i.e. in the glorious body. The first state implies that the soul possesses and performs all its powers, unless some defect of the body prevents it from doing so. By contrast, the second state implies that no vegetative faculty is operating, but a sensitive power, i.e. memory, and a rational power, i.e. the contemplative intellect, still remain. Dominicus does not clarify whether the other faculties totally disappear or remain at least in potency, as he suggested in the chapter *De interioribus virtutibus animalium*. In any case, no vegetative power remains in the soul in the resurrection; as regards instead the sensitive and rational powers, Dominicus acknowledges his ignorance on account of the fact that philosophers do not address this subject. Indeed, Avicenna's *De anima* could provide no help on this issue because he did not admit the resurrection of bodies. In this way, Dominicus Gundissalinus' *De anima* offers only a partial answer concerning the survival of the lower powers.[169]

The most interesting aspect of Dominicus' exposition is undoubtedly the problem of memory. We will deal with this subject later on. For the moment, let us just observe that the Spanish thinker defends the immortality of memory – against Avicenna – on the basis of an "ex auctoritate" argument drawn from the Gospel, not on arguments of a philosophical character. This attitude reveals a clash which was in general to dominate the debate concerning the survival of the powers of the soul, namely, the conflict between needs of a dogmatic kind and needs of a philosophical kind.

---

[169] Cf. Dom. Gund., *de an.*, ed. Muckle, p. 103: "Postquam autem auxiliante Deo, iam sufficienter assignavimus quod rationalis anima omnes vires suas in corpore manens quantum in se est exerceat, et deinde quod exuta a corpore de vegetabilibus nullam, de sensibilibus vero unam scilicet memoriam, de intelligibilibus quoque unum scilicet contemplativum retineat, restabat ut ex omnibus viribus suis quas sit habitura recepto corpore monstraremus. Sed quia de hoc apud philosophos paene nihil invenimus, nos quasi ex nobis aliquid apponere non presumimus. Tres enim status habet anima; in corpore, deposito corpore, recepto corpore; primus est vivorum, secundus mortuorum, tertius resuscitatorum. In primo itaque ut praedictum est, omnes vires suas exercere cognoscitur nisi forte alicuius sui instrumenti vitio praepediatur. In secundo de vegetabilibus nullam, de sensibilibus vero unam scilicet memoriam retinet. Si enim dives damnatus apud inferos fratrum suorum memoriam non amisit dicens: habeo quinque fratres, quanto magis beatorum spiritus exuti a carne memoriam nostri non deserunt quos dum viverent in Christo dilexerunt (Luca XVI, 27), cum iam et angeli gaudeant pro conversione nostra. De intellectibus etiam unum scilicet contemplativum quo uno oculo beata anima videt Deum suum. Recepto vero corpore quod de vegetabilibus nullam sit habitura certi sumus. Sed de sensibilibus et intelligibilibus viribus quas sit habitura et quas non, nondum plene instructi sumus".

2.2.2.3 *Quaestiones antequam esset frater*

Between 1220 and 1236 Alexander of Hales wrote a question on the problem of the immortality of the powers of the soul. The arguments used in the text easily fall into two groups: the first group includes the philosophical arguments and recalls Avicenna's thought, whereas the second group gathers the theological arguments. As in the case of Dominicus Gundissalinus' *De anima*, the first group of arguments speaks against the survival of the vegetative and sensitive powers, whereas the second is evoked to support the thesis of the immortality of all the faculties of the soul.

On the one hand, Alexander observes that the powers which need the body to act are superfluous in the second state, i.e. when the soul subsists as separated. This concerns also those rational powers which need images to be able to operate. This is an argument clearly recalling Avicennian psychology.

On the other hand, since the soul gains merit or demerit by means of the vegetative and sensitive powers, it must be rewarded or punished by means of the same faculties. Moreover, the soul in heaven must be perfect; hence, it is not possible that it lacks some power. Further, if the lower powers are present in heaven, then one must conclude that they survive also while the soul is separated from the body, because otherwise one should admit that there will be a new creation.

Alexander thus concludes that all the powers of the human soul are immortal. For this reason, the lower powers of man should not be confused with the powers of animals and those of vegetables: whereas the former have the rational soul as their subject, the latter are indissolubly connected to the body. The sensitive and vegetative powers of man are immortal and, in addition, will perform some function in the afterlife: unfortunately, our theologian does not explain what kind of function it will be.[170]

The question written by Alexander makes clear that the thesis of the immortality of the lower powers did not give rise to any difficulty of a theological character: to the contrary, it was supported above all by the faith in the resurrection

---

[170] Cf. Alex. Halen., *q. ant.* XXXII, 3, ed. PP. Collegii S. Bonaventurae, p. 565[7-23]: "Postea quaeritur utrum sit immortalis secundum omnem vim. Quod non secundum omnem, videtur, quia quaedam vires non sunt agentes nisi per corpus; ergo, facta separatione a corpore, supervacuae essent; ergo deficiunt vegetabilis et sensibilis, et intellectualis apprehendens per phantasias. Contra: anima rationalis demeretur vel meretur in his, vel secundum ordinem ad has potentias; ergo, si demeretur vel meretur per se secundum has potentias, vel coniunctione ad has, erit praemiabilis in his vel punibilis. Item, anima non erit imperfecta in patria; non ergo deficient ibi hae potentiae; ergo separantur cum ea, cum non creabuntur ibi novae. Respondeo: Separantur cum ea potentiae ad sentiendum et ad vegetandum, quia ordinem habent in homine ad rationem; sed in brutis et in plantis ordinem habent ad corpus. Unde in iis corrumpuntur, sed in homine separantur nec supervacuae sunt".

of bodies. Such a perspective was shared also by John of La Rochelle's *Summa de anima*: indeed, the Franciscan master used Alexander's short question and he too declared himself in favour of the immortality of all the powers of the soul.[171]

2.2.2.4   Peter of Bar

Peter of Bar,[172] a colleague of Hugh of St-Cher at the Parisian Faculty of Theology, whom we have already met, devotes four questions to the theme of resurrection. In one of them, the master examines the future destiny of the powers of the human soul. The question is entitled *De hiis que ex parte anime manebunt* and, like all the other questions by this theologian, is preserved in manuscript 434 of the Bibliothèque Municipale of Douai and bears the catalogue number 157.[173] It can be found in the middle of the first volume, where it follows the question, again by Peter, concerning the characteristics of the resurrected body. The two questions may be considered as a whole: in the first, Peter wonders whether all parts of the human body will resurrect in their entirety and whether the characteristics of the mortal body, such as quantity, will be present in the blessed body. The question about the permanence of the faculties of the soul thus represents a continuation with respect to the preceding question. Moreover, both works make use of the same Augustinian passages in support of the defended solutions.

The question *De hiis que ex parte anime manebunt* is divided into three articles. The short introduction, in which Peter names three powers – i.e. the vegetative, sensitive and rational powers – suggests that each article corresponds with a type of faculty. Later on we will see that things are partly different. It should also be noted that, throughout the whole question, Peter adopts no systematic distinction between the three states of the soul, i.e. (1) in the mortal body, (2) separated and (3) in the resurrected body. His question therefore remains to some extent ambiguous: on the one hand, the title suggests that it concerns the survival of the powers of the soul; but, on the other, some passages seem to posit the disappearance of some faculties and their reappearance in the resurrection.[174] Peter does not solve this problem.

---

[171] Cf. Ioh. Rup., *sum. de an.* I, 45, ed. Bougerol, p. 142[35-40]: "Deficere uel interire non consequitur animam uegetabilem uel sensibilem eo quod anima est, sed eo quod totaliter ordinatur ad corpus. Vnde cum in brutis et in plantis totaliter ordinentur ad corpus, necesse est eas interire cum corpore. In homine uero non totaliter ordinantur ad corpus, immo ad racionem que immortalis est et ideo non intereunt cum corpore"; *ibid*, p. 143[56-66].

[172] On the figure of Peter of Bar see above, p. 112, n. 74.

[173] Cf. Glorieux, "Les 572 Questions", p. 140.

[174] Cf. Petr. de Barro, *Quaestio de hiis que ex parte anime manebunt* I, cf. *infra*, p. 206: "Integritas substantie corporis redibit seruata partium congruentia, ergo et integritas anime seruata partium potentialium congruentia, ergo et partes anime uegetabilis peribunt et redibunt, et nescio utra".

The first article of the question concerns the problem of the permanence of the vegetative faculties and is closely related to Peter's question on the resurrection of the body. Indeed, the provided solution reflects the conclusion reached by Peter in the question concerning the characteristics of the resurrected body (n. 156), i.e. the perfect integrity of the blessed body. In his view, if the body has to be complete and perfect in its dignity, then it is necessary that the generative and nutritive powers remain in it, although in the kingdom of heaven there will be no need to conceive children or eat food. The vegetative powers will have their function – certainly a different one from the earthly function – which will be carried out for the glory of God and in order to complete man's dignity. But Peter does not specify which acts will be proper to these powers, nor, more generally, does he make clear whether there will be acts assigned to these powers or not.

Peter also repeats that the presence of the two vegetative faculties is necessary by reason of the due remuneration they will have to receive: for these faculties have their own merits like the other faculties. In addition, the distinction between male and female stands for the mystical relation between Christ and the Church as bridegroom and bride: the distinction between sexes, hence the generative faculty too, must therefore persist in the afterworld.[175]

A further interesting characteristic of the first article consists in the fact that Peter mentions only two vegetative faculties, nutrition and reproduction, and omits the augmentative power, which in the Latin world was traditionally added to form a triad. This omission is not incidental, but derives from Avicenna's *Canon*: it cannot be excluded, in fact, that Peter knew the medical work of Avicenna.[176]

---

[175] Cf. Petr. de Barro, *Quaestio de hiis que ex parte anime manebunt* 1, cf. *infra*, p. 207: "Solutio. Dicit Augustinus: "Puto facile intelligi in conditione dignitatem fuisse prelatam. Transitura quippe est necessitas tempusque uenturam, quando inuicem sola pulcritudine sine ulla libidine perfruemur", ex quo patet quod actus necessitatis cessabunt, set actus pertinentes ad dignitatem manebunt, sicut patet in lingua et dentibus. Cessabit enim actus masticationis, manebit autem actus formationis uocis, quia primus actus necessitatis solius est, secundus autem dignitatis quantum ad laudem dei. Dicimus igitur quod licet actus generandi et nutriendi cessent, tamen generatiua et nutritiua manebunt quia meruerunt: corpus in quo sunt iuuit animam suo creatori, unde iustum est ut saltem in quietem premientur. Generatiua autem propter alias duas rationes manebit: una est quia per eam facta est multiplicatio filiorum dei et obseruata species que est dominium; alia est quia distinctio sexus in organis ipsius est indicium distinctionis Christi et ecclesie tanquam sponsi et sponse"; cf. Aug., *civ.*, 22, 24, ed. Dombard – Kalb, CCSL 48, pp. 850¹⁶⁵-851¹⁷⁰, PL 41, 791: "Puto facile intellegi in conditione corporis dignitatem necessitati fuisse praelatam. Transitura est quippe necessitas tempus que venturam, quando sola invicem pulchritudine sine ulla libidine perfruamur; quod maxime ad laudem referendum est Conditoris, cui dicitur in Psalmo: 'Confessionem et decorem induisti'".

[176] Among Peter's contemporaries, Roland of Cremona adopts the same bipartition. Indeed, Roland had medical knowledge; cf. Hasse, *Avicenna's De anima*, pp. 40-41; Hess, "Roland of Cremona's Place", p. 441.

The second article is devoted to the future destiny of three senses, i.e. taste, sense of smell and sight. Peter's arguments are analogous to those used in the first article of the question. The acts proper to the sensitive faculties in this life will not be the same in the heavenly land because there will be no corruptible world and our body will not be the same. However, the sensitive powers not only remain, but also remain active in some way. Their acts will be like our body, i.e. spiritual. In particular, our sight will no longer perceive sensible images, but will be able to see with the only help of divine light. Thanks to this light we will be able to perceive colours as well. Indeed, according to Peter, colour has a double cause: the first coincides with the elementary structure of the object which is illuminated; the second consists in light. For colour is nothing but the light introduced into matter. Now, the elementary cause will no longer be present in the afterlife, but our sight will be so perfect that we will be able to see thanks to light alone, by means of which we will also perceive the elementary cause which will no longer be present in the afterworld.[177]

As we have seen above, the number of articles in our question corresponds to the number of chief faculties in the soul. Hence, one would suppose that the third article would be devoted to the powers of the rational soul. Clearly, however, the listed powers are not those traditionally considered as the powers of the rational soul, i.e. reason, will and memory. Of these three powers, only memory is among those enumerated by Peter together with imagination and the possible intellect. These are the powers listed by Avicenna in his *De anima*. According to Avicenna, none of these three powers can survive the body's death, because their operations necessarily depend upon the presence of corporeal images. It is evident that Peter knows this Avicennian doctrine; indeed, in the third article of his question, the doubt no longer concerns the survival of the single powers, but rather their capability of operating through images. Peter's answer is clear: images do not survive the body's death, hence none of the faculties operating through them can continue

---

[177] Petr. de Barro, *Quaestio de hiis que ex parte anime manebunt* II, cf. *infra*, pp. 207-208: "Solutio. Re uera sensus omnes manebunt, set quia erunt corporis spiritualis habebunt spirituales actus, nec fiet gustus, aut odoratus, aut etiam uisus ut dicuntur sicut nunc. (...) Ad hoc quod opponitur de uisu dicimus quod non per sensus similitudines, set solius lucis beneficio [uel rerum quas uidebit] et Christi qui est ille agnus de quo in Apocalipsa: "Illuminabit eam agnus". Quod cum colorum habeat duas causas, unam ex parte elementorum, aliam ex parte luminis (color enim nichil aliud est quam lux profundata in materia), elementaris transibit cum sit transiens et illa que ex parte luminis manebit, unde fiet quasi lux; unde sufficiet uisui lux illa et ymagine non indigebit. Si autem queris quomodo distinctiones colorum percipiet, dicimus quod tante erit efficatie uisus, ut sub illa luce percipiet causam elementarem que transiit, unde et causas colorum, licet transierint, percipiet, quia habuit in illius causis distinctionem colorum que fuit. Non enim credimus quod nigrum uel fuscum uel liuidum sit in paradiso".

to operate in the absence of the corporeal means. Nor can images reemerge at the moment of resurrection, because, as Peter explains in the second article, corporeal instruments will not be the same as before, for our body will be spiritual and our senses will no longer be able to perceive sensible images. Nevertheless, the three faculties depending on our senses – imagination, memory and the possible intellect – will survive and be active: they will no longer operate through sensible images but in a spiritual way, thanks to the "interior light".[178]

Peter's question, and especially its final part, avails itself of Avicenna's psychology. Nevertheless, our theologian, like Alexander of Hales and John of La Rochelle, affirms that all the faculties of the human soul will be present in the afterlife. Peter's solution is not inspired by works of a philosophical kind, but mainly by texts of Augustine,[179] i.e. a theological authority. Indeed, the theory of the survival of the powers of the soul is clearly related to belief in the resurrection, because the activity of the lower powers will be possible thanks to the presence of the glorious body. A theological perspective, therefore, did not only support the immortality of the rational soul, but also the permanence in it – after the separation from the body – of all its sensitive and vegetative powers.

2.2.2.5 William of Auvergne

The thesis of the immortality of all the powers of the soul is held by another theologian living in the first half of the thirteenth century, William of Auvergne[180] († 1249). However, the theory formulated by William in his *De anima* is not proved by arguments of a theological kind, but has its foundation in his philosophical conception of the human soul. This attitude distinguishes William from the other masters of his time we have examined so far.

According to William of Auvergne, the rational soul is a complete and independent substance which makes use of the body as a musician uses an instrument.

---

[178] Petr. de Barro, *Quaestio de hiis que ex parte anime manebunt* III, cf. *infra*, p. 209.

[179] Cf. Aug., *civ.*, 22, 17, ed. Dombard - Kalb, CCSL 48, pp. 835[16]-836[25], PL 41, 778-779; Aug., *civ.*, 22, 24, ed. Dombard - Kalb, CCSL 48, pp. 850[165]-851[170], PL 41, 791.

[180] On William's anthropology and theological work, see for example A. Masnovo, *Da Guglielmo d'Auvergne a S. Tommaso d'Aquino*, Milano: Vita e pensiero, 1945; G. Jüssen, "Wilhelm von Auvergne und die Transformation der Scholastischen Philosophie im 13. Jahrhundert", in J. Beckmann - L. Honnefelder, *Philosophie im Mittelalter. Entwicklungslinien und Paradigmen*, Hamburg: Meiner, 1987, pp. 141-164; G. Jüssen, "Aristoteles-Rezeption und Aristoteles-Kritik in Wilhelm von Auvergne's *Tractatus De Anima*", in R. Työrinoja - S. Ebbesen - S. Knuuttila, *Knowledge and the Sciences in Medieval Philosophy. Proceedings of the VIII Internation Congress of Medieval Philosophy (S.I.E.P.M.)*, Luther-Agricola Society Series, Helsinki 1990, pp. 87-96; J.-B. Brenet, "Introduction", in Guillaume d'Auvergne, *De l'Âme (VII, 1-9)*, Paris: Vrin, 1998, pp. 7-83; F. Morenzoni - J.-Y. Tilliette (ed.), *Autour de Guillaume d'Auvergne († 1249)*, Turnhout: Brepols, 2005.

In the union of these two elements, the body has a totally passive role.[181] Indeed, it is the soul – not the psychophysical composite – which constitutes the only subject of all the human operations. Hence, the powers of the soul operate through the body but have their foundation only in the spiritual substance, i.e. the soul. It follows that the presence of corporeal organs is not necessary to the permanence of the powers of the soul. Actually, as William explains, the ability to play a lyre is present in a musician even if he has no instrument at his disposal. Likewise, if a person loses his eyes, he does not equally lose the ability to see, because if this person could have an artificial eye, he would be able to see just as he saw with his own eyes. Hence, if the human soul is the only subject of its own powers, then the immortality of the substance of the soul guarantees the survival of all its faculties too.[182]

---

[181] Cf. *supra*, chap. 1.1.2.4.

[182] Guill. de Alv., *de an.*, 3, 23, ed. B. Le Feron in *Guilelmi Alverni Episcopi Parisiensis Opera omnia*, vol. II, Paris 1674 (repr. Frankfurt-am-Main, 1963), *Supplementum*, pp. 149-150: "Quod si quid dixerit, quia quantum ad vires inferiores ex quibus sunt operationes hujusmodi necesse est animam humanam indigere corpore et membris corporalibus, verum utique dicit, si ista indigentia est solummodo quantum ad operationes hujusmodi peragendas: quemadmo dum cytharaedus indiget cythara quantum ad operationem cytharizandi exercendam, non autem quantum ad esse vel existere suum, et carpentarius eodem modo indiget dolabra, vel securi. Quod si dixerit quis quod vires illae non sunt separabiles a corpore, propter hoc quoniam operationes earum indigent ut non nisi in corpore, vel per corpus agi vel exerceri valeant; et propter hoc esse earum non potest salvari nisi in corpore et per corpus: facile est tibi videre levitatem et debilitatem ratiocinationis istius; et ad repellendum eam sufficere posset tibi exemplum de cytharaedo, et dolabra, et carpentario. Addam etiam tibi destructionem ratiocinationis istius aliam, et dico quoniam cujus est potentia, ejusdem est et actus, videre autem nullo modo oculi est, igitur nec potentia videndi, sive virtus visibilis. Nemo enim adhuc dixit, oculum videre, vel etiam videre posse. Amplius operatio nunquam est instrumenti, sed utentis illo, usus autem instrumenti non est nisi operatio quae per illud agitur: manifestum autem est, quod usus instrumenti nullo modorum est ipsius, nullum enim instrumentum utitur seipso. Jam autem patefactum est tibi quod anima humana per totum corpus aptata est ut ejusdem instrumentum, et quia totum corpus secundum omnia membra organica, vel officialia instrumentum ipsius est, virtus vero operandi per instrumentum in quantum instrumentum animae est. Manifestum est igitur tibi per hoc quod virtus videndi sive potentia apud animam est, et in ipsa. Quapropter non est possibile ipsam esse in oculo; quod etiam exemplo Aristotelis manifestum est quia si ervatur alicui oculus et alius aptetur, et in locum illius, sicut saepe factum est, homo ille videbit aeque ut prius, et hoc non nova virtute vel nova porentia visibili, cum nec novus novam potentiam videndi secum attulerit, nec prioris oculi virtus in illum se transfuderit, virtute igitur quae remansit post eruitio nem oculi illius videlicet hujusmodi hominis. Quapropter remansit in illa, et hoc est quod intendebam, ipsi etiam omnes philosophi qui de anima rationali aliquid dignum memoria locuti sunt vel scripserunt, vires omnes hujusmodi vires animarum dixerunt esse, non autem corporum vel

The doctrine of the immortality of the lower powers of the soul presented by William of Auvergne is clearly derived from a strong anthropological dualism. The role and the status that our theologian assigns to the human body are not substantially different from those of a dress or an artificial instrument: the human subject is identified above all with the soul, whereas the body plays a totally secondary role. The immortality of all the powers of the soul thoroughly confirms this conception of man, a conception distant not only from that of Aristotle but also of Avicenna.

* * *

A view of the anthropological texts from the first half of the thirteenth century makes it clear that the theory – professed by Philip the Chancellor and embraced by Hugh of St-Cher – according to which the sensitive and vegetative powers are inseparable from the body and die at the moment of a man's death was not shared by everyone. The survival of the lower powers of the human soul are chiefly supported by the faith in the resurrection. Indeed, the glorious body will be perfect and complete with all its functions. Moreover, man gains merit or demerit by means of the lower powers; they will thus have to share the due reward or the punishment. These theological arguments play an influential role in the questions by Alexander of Hales and Peter of Bar. Further, supposing that at the end of time there will be no new creation, we have to conclude that powers remain in the soul even when it becomes separated: this opinion is clearly expressed by Alexander. Finally, William of Auvergne defends the immortality of all the powers of the soul by means of philosophical arguments, describing the soul as the only foundation of human activities.

In a sense, the thesis of the survival of the lower powers makes the resurrection easier to conceive: in this way, the separated soul will have all the powers necessary to give life to the resurrected body. A similar view would turn out to be quite useful, especially for theologians such as Philip the Chancellor and Hugh of St-Cher, who considered these powers as intermediary elements necessary for the union between soul and body. Nevertheless, the two theologians state that the lower powers of the soul are mortal: so it seems that the resurrection of the body is not only superfluous for the separated soul, but also totally inexplicable from a philosophical point of view.

However, if we consider the problem of the survival of the powers of the soul from the perspective of Aristotelian philosophy, the position held by Philip and Hugh (deriving from Avicenna's *De anima*) seems closer, in some respects, to the philosophy of the Greek thinker than that defended by most masters living in the

---

membrorum. (...) Quapropter sicut pereunte oculo, non perit virtus visiva, sic pereunte toto corpore, non perit anima humana vel in parte, vel in toto"; cf. 4, 9, ed. Le Feron, p. 165.

first half of the thirteenth century. Indeed, according to Aristotle, the human soul can only survive if it has a faculty which can be performed without the body. Similarly, all the powers operating by means of the body must disappear due to the separation from corporeal organs, because only the psychophysical composite can be considered as the true subject of powers and of human actions.[183] Consequently, if a faculty cannot exert its functions due to the lack of an organ, then it cannot be affirmed that the soul has this faculty in itself.

It is certain that Aristotle did not see the disappearance of the lower powers of the soul as a source of worry. Indeed, the Greek philosopher, like Avicenna, did not await the resurrection of bodies. In any case, it should be noted that this problem would never have been significant in the context of the anthropology presented in the *Peri psyches*. Indeed, according to Aristotle, the psychophysical union does not originate thanks to the mediation of sensitive and vegetative powers, but is a consequence of the very nature of the soul. In other words, this conjunction is not based on the functions performed by the soul in its body, but is founded on the reciprocal ontological dependence of the two principles which are conceived of as matter and form.[184] It follows that the soul, as long as it exists, can never lose its ability to give life to the body, because this ability does not depend on its particular powers: to the contrary, the faculties of the soul arise from the very nature of the soul-form.

Like his contemporaries, Hugh of St-Cher does not accept all the ramifications of Aristotle's psychology. This becomes evident mainly on the basis of his exposition concerning the vegetative and sensitive powers of the soul. First of all, Hugh states that the rational soul is not united to the body in an immediate way but through its lower faculties. Secondly, according to the Dominican theologian, the subject of the powers of the soul coincides with the rational soul only, and not with man, i.e. with the psychophysical composite.

Yet, the difficulty implied by Hugh's thought does not concern his disagreement with Aristotle's thought, but the inner incoherence of his doctrine. The analysis of the anthropological doctrine of the Parisian master, and in particular of his teaching concerning the union between soul and body, induces us to conclude that Hugh contradicts his own statements about the essential and immortal *unibilitas* of the human soul in regard to the body. It seems that the *unibilitas substantialis* doctrine is not sufficiently integrated into the other aspects of his anthropology, particularly into his teaching concerning the powers of the soul.

---

[183] Cf. Arist., *de an.* II, 1 (Bekker 413 a).
[184] Cf. Arist., *de an.* II, 1 (Bekker 412 b-413 a).

2.3
THE PROBLEM OF MEMORY

2.3.1 TWO TRADITIONS, TWO TYPES OF MEMORY

At the beginning of the second part of the present book, I introduced a distinction between two types of literary sources employed in the psychological speculation at the beginning of the thirteenth century, i.e. the theological sources and the philosophical sources. This distinction, rather simplified and imperfect, nevertheless helps to explain why Hugh of St-Cher and most of his contemporaries deal with the rational powers and the lower powers in two distinct contexts, posing different questions and using arguments of different types. The same distinction might be useful also in examining the discussion developed by the same authors about the concept of memory.

Indeed, we may divide memory into two different kinds of powers according to the sources we refer to. On the one hand, we may define memory as a rational faculty which is identical with the essence of the soul and – like the soul – immortal. But, on the other hand, we may consider it as a sensitive or animal faculty, which depends on sensible images and therefore perishes with the body. These two points of view meet in the psychological speculation flourishing in the first decades of the thirteenth century, and this confrontation gives rise to a debate engendering various solutions. Before approaching this debate, let us consider its main sources, i.e. Augustine's and Avicenna's thought.[185]

Augustine of Hippo dwells on the problem of memory several times in his writings: this is in fact one of the central elements of his psychology. Hence, his view of memory goes through a number of transformations and it would thus be difficult to outline an adequate and complete picture of his thought in this regard.[186] We

---

[185] Actually, the sources of the thirteenth-century debate on memory are much more abundant; in particular, in the first half of the thirteenth century, authors were frequently inspired by the division of the powers of the soul introduced by John Damascene; cf. Philipp., *sum. de bon.*, ed. Wicki, pp. 158-164; Ioh. Rup., *sum. de an.* II, 3, 68-81, ed. Bougerol, pp. 197-220; Lottin, "La psychologie de l'acte humain chez saint Jean Damascène et les théologiens du XIIIe siècle occidental", in *Psychologie et morale*, I, pp. 400-409.

[186] Among the several works about this problem, we should mention especially J. A. Mourant, *Saint Augustine on Memory*, Villanova: Villanova University Press, 1980; A. Solignac, "'Memoria' dans la tradition augustinienne", in *Dictionnaire de spiritualité. Ascé-*

know, however, that early thirteenth-century theologians draw inspiration mainly from *De Trinitate*, which situates memory in the mind as image of Trinity-God. The importance of this view held by Augustine is increased by the fact that Peter Lombard included it in his *Sentences*.[187] It follows that the description of memory expounded in *De Trinitate* occupies a prominent position in the theological writings of the first half of the thirteenth century.

Augustine's *De Trinitate* sees in the highest part of the soul, i.e. in *mens*, the image of the triune God.[188] First of all, the mysterious unity of the three divine Persons is represented by the essential unity of memory, intellect and will. It is through these three elements that the mind can know itself and, above all, can know God ("anima capax Dei"): for the soul is image of the Trinity principally when it directs its inner eye to the prime and eternal truth ("anima particeps Dei").[189] The analogy between mind and God goes through the immortality of the soul as well. Indeed, whereas God is eternal, the soul, as image of Him, is immortal. Hence, if the created trinity (memory, intellect, will) is immortal, then the human memory shares the blessed life as it is an essential part of the soul conceived of as image of God.[190]

However, the conception of memory as one of the sensitive faculties is not foreign to Augustine's thought. In his earlier works, memory is described as a power which makes use of sensible images and is shared by man and animals.[191] The theologians of the first half of the thirteenth century, however, mainly assimilate the Augustinian view presented in *De Trinitate*, where memory is identified with *mens* and thus constitutes an intellective principle. The proper object of this spiritual memory is not reduced to the sensible world, but is mainly identified with the immutable Principle of all things, that is to say with God. According to this

---

tique et mystique, doctrine et histoire, vol. x, Paris: Beauchesne, 1980, pp. 994 b-1002 b; O'Daly, *Augustine's Philosophy of Mind*, pp. 131-148; N. Cipriani, "Memory", in A. Fitzgerald (ed.), *Augustine Through the Ages: An Encyclopedia*, Grand Rapids, Michigan: Eerdmans Publishing Company, 1999, pp. 563-564; B. Cillerai, "Agostino: La memoria al centro dell'*actio animae*" in *Tracce nella mente. Teorie della memoria da Platone ai moderni*, ed. M. Sassi, Pisa: Edizioni Scuola Normale, 2007, pp. 99-117; B. Cillerai, *La memoria come* capacitas Dei *secondo S. Agostino: unità e complessità*, Pisa: ETS, 2008.

[187] Cf. *supra*, p. 99.

[188] Cf. Aug., *trin*. x, ed. Mountain, CCSL 50, pp. 310-332, PL 42, 971-984; XIV, ed. Mountain, CCSL 50a, pp. 421-459, PL 42, 1035-1058.

[189] Cf. Solignac, "*Memoria* dans la tradition augustinienne", p. 998 b; Cipriani, "Memory", p. 564.

[190] Cf. Aug., *trin*. XIV, 3-6, ed. Mountain, CCSL 50a, pp. 426-433, PL 42, 1038-1042; cf. Javelet, *Image et ressemblance*, I, p. 356; Cipriani, "Memory", p. 564.

[191] Aug., *ord*., 2, 2, 6-7, ed. Green, CCSL 29, pp. 109-111, PL 32, 996-997; id., *an. quant*., 33, 71-72, ed. Hörmann, 1986, CSEL 89, pp. 218-220, PL 32, 1074-1075; cf. Cipriani, "Memory", p. 564.

view, which was assimilated by medieval theology,[192] memory thus represents the highest part of man and the cornerstone of the soul's immortality.[193]

From the beginning of the thirteenth century, the Latin West becomes acquainted with a deeply different conception of memory, i.e. the conception inspired by Aristotle's thought.[194] The strongest influence is exerted by Avicenna's *De anima*:[195] indeed, from the very beginning of the thirteenth century, his description of the powers of the soul deeply influences the Latin psychology.[196] According to Avicenna, memory is a part of the sensitive faculties shared by man and animals.[197] Its position in the hierarchy of the powers of the soul is among the inner senses, after the *vis aestimativa*. According to Avicenna, the *vis aestimativa* acquires the *intentiones* which take form on the basis of sensible images but lie on a higher level compared to the latter.[198] The task of memory consists in gathering and preserving the *intentiones* offered by the *vis aestimativa*, just as imagination gathers sensible images.

According to Avicenna, memory is directed toward the corruptible world and its activity fundamentally depends on sensible images, hence on the body. Imagination and memory need a material substrate. Indeed, the forms gathered by these faculties must be impressed on the corporeal "spirit": without this support, the existence of memory is no longer justified.[199] Consequently, memory, like all the other sensitive faculties of man, cannot survive the separation of the soul from the

---

[192] Cf. Solignac, "*Memoria* dans la tradition augustinienne", pp. 999 a-1002 b; Javelet, *Image et ressemblance*, I, p. 110.

[193] Cf. Javelet, *Image et ressemblance*, I, p. 356; II, p. 90.

[194] Aristotle conceives of memory as a primary sensitive faculty, which belongs to the intellective faculty "just by accident"; cf. Arist., *mem.*, 1, Bekker 450 a, 451 a; Arist., *an. post.* II, 19, Bekker 100 a.

[195] The division of the powers of the soul presented by Avicenna derives not only from Aristotle's thought, but also from Al-Farabi; cf. Verbeke, "Le «De anima» d'Avicenne", pp. 48*-49*.

[196] Cf. Hasse, *Avicenna's De anima*, p. 228, pp. 236-314.

[197] It should be noted, however, that Avicenna distinguishes between memory and reminiscence (*recordatio*): whereas the former is also present in animals, the latter is only proper to man; cf. Auic., *de an.* IV, 3, ed. Van Riet, p. 40[61-63]: "Memoria autem est etiam in aliis animalibus. Sed recordatio quae est ingenium revocandi quod oblitum est, non invenitur, ut puto, nisi solo in homine"; cf. Verbeke, "Le «De anima» d'Avicenne", pp. 55*-56*.

[198] Avicenna describes the nature of the *intentiones* by means of the example of lamb and wolf. The *intentio* then coincides with the judgement the lamb associates with the figure of the predator. This judgement lies in the memory of the lamb even when the sensible image is not present, and it enables the animal to flee as soon as the shape of the wolf is perceived; cf. Auic., *de an.* I, 5, ed. Van Riet, p. 86[93-006]; Verbeke, "Le «De anima» d'Avicenne", p. 51*.

[199] Cf. Verbeke, "Le «De anima» d'Avicenne", pp. 69*-70*.

body,[200] because the disappearance of sensible images implies the loss of all the powers which make use of them.[201]

Sensitive memory is, according to Avicenna, the only possible type of memory. Indeed, intelligible forms cannot be preserved by the soul, because only sensible forms are impressed on the material substrate.[202] Further, intellective knowledge does not originate from sensitive knowledge, but derives from a different source, i.e. the agent intellect.[203] Intelligible forms can be received by the human intellect, but cannot be preserved.

We may thus conclude that, for Avicenna, the soul separated from the body does not possess any type of memory. Indeed, on the one hand, the soul loses the sensitive memory, because it lacks the material substrate necessary to preserve sensible forms; on the other hand, it does not possess intellective memory, because this is totally impossible. What is possible, for the separated soul, is therefore knowledge, not remembrance.

As previously seen, the description of the powers of the soul presented in Avicenna's *Liber* is picked up – quite often in a verbatim way – by Dominicus Gundissalinus. Following Avicenna, Dominicus describes memory as a sensitive and not an intellective faculty, which depends on sensible images and is possessed both by men and animals.[204] As a sensitive power, memory should disappear after death: and, indeed, this is the opinion often repeated in Dominicus' treatise *De anima*.[205] Theological reasons, however, motivated the Spanish philosopher, in the last lines of his work, to retract this position. For, if the separated soul does not possess any memory of its earthly life, then how could the rich man who, in the Gospel

---

[200] Cf. Auic., *de an.* IV, 4, ed. Van Riet, pp. 66[65]-67[69]: "Dicemus autem quod, postquam ostendimus omnes virtutes sensibiles non habere actionem nisi propter corpus, et esse virtutum est eas sic esse ut operentur, tunc virtutes sensibiles non sunt sic ut operentur nisi dum sunt corporales; ergo esse earum est esse corporales; igitur non remanent post corpus".

[201] The problem of the absence of the sensitive faculties in the afterlife has been studied in depth by J. R. Michot, *La destinée de l'homme selon Avicenne. Le retour à Dieu (maʿad) et l'imagination*, Leuven: Peeters, 1986, *passim*.

[202] Cf. Auic., *de an.* V, 6, ed. Van Riet, p. 148[35-40]; Verbeke, "Le «De anima» d'Avicenne", pp. 69*-70*.

[203] Cf. Auic., *de an.* V, 5, ed. Van Riet, p. 128[51-64]; Verbeke, "Le «De anima» d'Avicenne", p. 66*; P.-M. de Contenson, "Avicennisme latin et vision de Dieu au début du XIIIe siècle", *AHDLMA* 26 (1959), pp. 55-67.

[204] Dom. Gund., *de an.*, 10, ed. Muckle, pp. 96[16]-97[11].

[205] Dom. Gund., *de an.*, 10, ed. Muckle, p. 97[12-14]: "Ex his autem omnibus viribus animae rationalis, nulla virtus vegetabilis nulla sensibilis, nullus etiam intellectus activus, nec scientia ulla quae activo intellectui comparatur in anima exuta a corpore remanere cognoscitur"; 9, ed. Muckle, p. 83[12]; cf. *supra*, p. 141.

according to Luke, is condemned to torment in hell,[206] be able to remember his living brothers? Moreover, how is it possible to explain the joy of angels for our conversion, if angels could not recall the time when we sin? Finally, is it possible that the souls of the blessed do not remember that they loved Christ all through their lives? It follows that the separated soul must preserve memory, even though it is a sensitive faculty.[207]

In Dominicus Gundissalinus' treatise *De anima*, the Avicennian doctrine of memory thus conflicts with a theological perspective. The same contrast was to arise at the Parisian Faculty of Theology when Avicenna's psychology was compared with the Augustinian doctrine. The debate concerning the problem of memory, which took place in the 1220s and 1230s, was partly fueled by the tension developing between these two different conceptions.

2.3.2   PHILIP THE CHANCELLOR

Philip the Chancellor deals with the problem of memory twice, in the *Summa de bono* and in the disputed question *De ymagine et similitudine nostra*. In both works, the theme of memory is placed within a theological frame, since it forms part of the debate on the soul as image of God. This context largely determines Philip's approach as well as the meaning attributed to memory. Indeed, the main authority is Augustine. In his *Summa de bono*, Philip has the goal of comparing two different descriptions of memory, which are both ascribed to the Church father. In the first description, which is expounded in the pseudo-Augustinian treatise *De spiritu et anima*, the author compares memory to the Holy Spirit: indeed,

---

[206] Cf. Luke 16:27.

[207] Dom. Gund., *de an.*, 10, ed. Muckle, p. 103[16-25]: "Tres enim status habet anima; in corpore, deposito corpore, recepto corpore; primus est vivorum, secundus mortuorum, tertius resuscitatorum. In primo itaque ut praedictum est omnes vires suas exercere cognoscitur nisi forte alicuius sui instrumenti vitio praepediatur. In secundo de vegetabilibus nullam, de sensibilibus vero unam scilicet memoriam retinet. Si enim dives damnatus apud inferos fratrum suorum memoriam non amisit dicens: habeo quinque fratres, quanto magis beatorum spiritus exuti a carne memoriam nostri non deserunt quos dum viverent in Christo dilexerunt, cum iam et angeli gaudeant pro conversione nostra". Philip the Chancellor's *Summa de bono* contains a similar passage. Even though memory is enumerated among the sensitive powers, i.e. together with sense, sensuality and fantasy, the Holy Scripture suggests that it is an immortal faculty. For this reason, Philip mentions the same passage from Luke's Gospel which appears in Dominicus Gundissalinus' *Trattato de anima*; cf. Philipp., *sum. de bon.*, ed. Wicki, p. 158[2-5]: "Sequitur questio secunda qua queritur de potentiis anime secundum quas venit in speculationem theologi et dicuntur sensus et sensualitas, phantasia et memoria. De memoria enim habetur de divite epulone in Luc. xvi, qui erat in inferno et recordatus est fratrum suorum".

just as the Spirit proceeds from the Father and the Son, so memory completes the work of knowledge and love, while preserving the truth known to us and what is beloved.[208] By contrast, in *De Trinitate*, Augustine presents a different position, according to which memory is the source of knowledge and love because it preserves in itself the image of God that was put in each soul. Within this view, memory corresponds to God the Father, who originates the intellect (the Son) and the will or love (the Holy Spirit).[209]

The second type of memory described by Augustine in *De Trinitate* corresponds to spiritual memory. Inspired by Augustine, Philip defines it as "ductio in naturaliter intelligendum et diligendum quod est summa bonitas et veritas" or "ductus anime in naturaliter intellectum et dilectum",[210] i.e., that which leads the soul to know God and itself. This type of memory is not directed toward past things, but towards that which can always be known as a present reality: for the soul can always know itself and know its own Creator, of whom it is the image.[211]

Hence, how can we define the memory described in *De spiritu et anima*? It seems that Philip identifies this type of memory with the "memoria per phantasmata". It is a faculty that preserves what is acquired by the knowledge which is directed toward the sensible reality: "cogitatio autem est cum per similitudinem aliquo modo ex phantasmatibus acceptam suo conspectui obicitur, post quam intellectus possibilis per similitudines rerum intellectas fit in actu".[212] This type

---

[208] Philipp., *sum. de bon.*, ed. Wicki, p. 250[30-40]: "Et dicendum est quod aliter accipitur memoria ab Augustino in Sermone de Ymagine quam in libro De Trinitate. Unde dicit: "Ex hiis quasi excellentioribus anime dignitatibus iubemur Deum diligere ut quantum intelligatur tantum diligatur et in quantum diligitur semper in memoria habeatur. Nec solus sufficit intellectus, nisi fiat voluntas in amore eius; nec hec duo sufficiunt nisi memoria addatur, qua semper in mente intelligentis et diligentis maneat Deus". Ecce hic dicitur ab Augustino memoria continuatio amoris et notitie in virtute cognitiva et motiva, que continuatio quia ex utraque procedit Spiritui Sancto comparatur qui est ex Patre Filioque procedens. Secundum ergo quod memoria ponitur ultimum post notitiam et amorem sumitur pro conservatione veritatis note et bonitatis dilecte; prius enim est nosse, secundum diligere, ultimum conservare".

[209] Philipp., *sum. de bon.*, ed. Wicki, pp. 250[41]-251[47]: "Aliter autem accipitur memoria in libro De Trinitate, ut patet in XIIII. Dicitur enim memoria conservatio naturaliter intelligendorum et diligendorum sive habitus ducens in naturaliter intelligenda et diligenda, memoria secundum quod precedit notitiam et amorem. Et ponitur primum actus conservandi in se similitudinem Dei et secundum illam ductio in naturaliter intelligendum et diligendum quod est summa bonitas et veritas in libro De Trinitate: "Meminerim te, noverim te, amaverim te"".

[210] Philipp., *sum. de bon.*, ed. Wicki, p. 251[56-57].

[211] Cf. Philipp., *sum. de bon.*, ed. Wicki, p. 251[66-67]: "Est autem hec memoria presentium, memoria vero supradicta est preteritorum".

[212] Philipp., *sum. de bon.*, ed. Wicki, p. 251[59-61].

of memory is subordinate to knowledge because it depends on the acquisition of images; indeed, its proper object are past things. Hence, unlike the memory described in *De Trinitate*, the *memoria per phantasmata* is mortal, because the images on which it necessarily depends are transient as well.[213]

As we have seen above, in the *Summa de bono*, Philip distinguishes between two types of memory: the immortal one, which can be compared to the first Person of the Trinity, i.e. the Father, and the mortal one, i.e. the *memoria per phantasmata*. Is it possible to compare the mortal memory to the third Person of the Trinity, i.e. the Holy Spirit? If the answer is positive, we might conclude that, according to Philip, a lower faculty – which is defined as an animal or a sensitive power by the new philosophical sources – can be considered as an element of the created trinity, namely, as an element of the image of God. Philip's exposition is not totally clear in this regard, but the text suggests this solution.[214]

Also Philip's disputed question *De ymagine et similitudine nostra* contains a distinction between two types of memory. Philip formulates the following doubt: assuming that there exist two memories – one destined for knowledge (*cognitiva sive comprehensiva*), the other responsible for the preservation of that which is known (*retentiva*), namely, one preceding and the other following knowledge – which of these two memories forms part of the image of God?[215] Philip answers that these are in fact two different faculties but they can both be considered as a part of the image of God. The first faculty, namely the one that precedes knowledge, is called *memoria naturalis*: this is the memory described in Augustine's *De Trinitate*, it occupies the higher part of the soul and can be identified with *mens*. "Natural memory" constitutes the source of the knowledge of the mind itself and of God; it precedes intelligence and love and thus represents the Father. The second memory too, which is defined as *thesaurus specierum*, can be compared to God the Father. This type of memory preserves the forms that are needed by the intellect to operate: in this regard, Philip mentions Nicholas of Amiens's *Ars catholicae fidei*, according to which the intellect is a power that comprehends things by using forms ("intellectus est potentia animae adminiculo formae rem

---

[213] Philipp., *sum. de bon.*, ed. Wicki, p. 251[47-51]: "Et differt hec memoria a memoria eorum quorum cognitio habetur per sensum aut quorum amor consequens est cognitionem, quia hec memoria non est per phantasmata, sed per se ipsam aut per aliquod lumen a principio ipsi anime datum. Et hec memoria est permanens, reliqua vero que est per sensum est per phantasmata et transibilis per phantasmatum deletionem".

[214] Cf. *supra*, p. 156, n. 208-209.

[215] Philipp., *q. de ymag.*, ed. Wicki, p. 177[248-250]: "Duplex est memoria, cognitiva sive comprehensiva et retentiva. De qua dicitur quod memoria, intellectus et voluntas sunt ymago dei? De cognitiva non, quia hec non differt ab intellectiva. Sed retentivam precedit intellectiva".

comprehendens")[216]. Hence, on the one hand, the memory called *thesaurus specierum* precedes the intellect, but, on the other, the same memory can be viewed as subordinate to intellect and will, because it preserves what is known and loved. These are, in fact, two aspects of the same faculty; consequently, according to which aspect is considered, this memory represents either God the Father or the Holy Spirit. It follows that also the *memoria-thesaurus specierum* forms part of the image of Trinity-God.[217]

Now, if the *memoria naturalis* corresponds to spiritual memory, is it possible to identify the *memoria-thesaurus specierum* with the *memoria per phantasmata*? It is not easy to answer because Philip, in the question *De ymagine et similitudine nostra*, does not mention at all the Avicennian division of powers. Moreover, it is not clear in which way memory and intellect acquire the forms of things, although quite probably Philip refers here to sensible knowledge. Lastly, we do not know whether the *memoria-thesaurus specierum* is mortal or remains in the separated soul.

Despite several unclear points, these two texts by Philip enable us to formulate a few interesting observations. First of all, according to Philip, the human soul does not contain just one type of memory, but at least two different classes of memory: one is proper to intellectual knowledge, the other to sensible knowledge. Secondly, sensitive memory, that is to say the *memoria per phantasmata*, is not immortal, but disappears with the separation from the body.[218] Finally, it seems that Philip does not exclude the possibility of considering sensitive memory as an element of the created trinity, i.e. as an element of the image of God.

---

[216] Nich. Amb., *ars cath.*, ed. Dreyer, p. 78[21-22].

[217] Cf. Philipp., *q. de ymag.*, ed. Wicki, p. 177[262-276]: "Solutio. Duplex est memoria. Naturalis, que est partis superioris. Hec dei meminit et sui et est idem quod mens et hec parens est intellectus. Alia est memoria que est thesaurus specierum, et hec similiter uno modo parens est intellectus, alio modo non. Sicut enim ex visibili procedit visus actus, sic ex memoria intellectus actus. Unde in libro De articulis fidei: intellectus est potentia anime res adminiculo forme comprehendens, que forma prius est in memoria. (...) Tertio modo potest dici memoria continuatio amoris in vi cognitiva et motiva. Aliquando etiam dicitur conservatio intelligendorum et diligendorum ducens in illa. Ex hiis patet quod uno modo precedit, alio modo sequitur, et ita nulla est contrarietas preassignata".

[218] Unsolved remains, however, the problem of the quotation from Luke's Gospels cited by Philip at the beginning of the chapter *De potentiis anime*, where the author refers to the survival of sensible memory in the afterworld; cf. *supra*, p. 155, n. 207.

2.3.3   THE *SUMMA DUACENSIS*

The chapter of the *Summa de bono* in which Philip speaks of two types of memory provided the main source for a similar exposition contained in the anonymous *Summa Duacensis*;[219] further, it seems that the anonymous author also knew the question *De ymagine et similitudine nostra*.[220] His exposition, which is clearer and more simple than Philip's texts, raises again the problem of the difference between two kinds of memory, mentioning the same authorities and using arguments very similar to those we have found in the *Summa de bono*. However, the anonymous author considerably modifies Philip's solution.

First of all, in the *Summa Duacensis*, 'memory' has three meanings. According to the anonymous author, the first two derive from the Holy Scripture. The first meaning of 'memory' is described in *De spiritu et anima* and in a biblical commentary by Rabanus Maurus: it is the memory that follows the intellect and will and corresponds to the Holy Spirit.[221] The second meaning of 'memory' coincides instead with that described by Augustine in *De Trinitate*, i. e. memory as the source of knowledge and of the love for God and for oneself ("ductio in id quod naturaliter est intelligendum et naturaliter diligendum"). Memory, understood in this sense, is the first element of the created trinity and corresponds to God the Father.[222]

---

[219]   *Sum. Duac.*, 4. 3, ed. Glorieux, pp. 20-22.

[220]   Indeed, the *Summa* mentions the *memoria-thesaurus specierum*; cf. *sum. Duac.*, 4. 3, ed. Glorieux, p. 21.

[221]   *Sum. Duac.*, 4. 3, ed. Glorieux, pp. 20-21: "Ad horum omnium que obiecta sunt solutionem notandum quod memoria tripliciter sumitur. In sacra enim pagina dupliciter accipitur ut iam patebit, et modo alio et diverso in physicis. Ut ergo planius et melius possimus venari diffinitiones memorie, sumamus auctoritatem Augustini in libro *de sermone ymaginis* que consors est et eadem auctoritas Rabani *in xvi Ecclesiastici*; in quorum sermone uterque adproprians ternarium dignitatum anime ad trinitatem personarum in hunc modum prosequitur dicens: "sicut ex Padre Filius et ex utroque Spiritus Sanctus, ita et ex intellectu voluntas et ex utroque memoria". (...) Ex hac auctoritate conici potest et extrahi quod memoria prout hic accipitur est continuatio intelligentis cum diligente. Unde etiam dici potest copula gnerantis et geniti. Per modum ergo istum accepta memoria Spiritui Sancto attribuenda est; et ad alias duas proprietates se habet comparata per modum posterioris eo quod ab eisdam causata est. Secundum autem hunc modum loquentes, Rabanus et Augustinus ponunt memoriam tertio loco et sic a posteriori".

[222]   *Sum. Duac.*, 4. 3, ed. Glorieux, p. 21: "Alio autem modo et diverso loquitur Augustinus attribuens memoriam vel mentem Patri. Unde secundum hanc viam loquentes, describere possumus memoriam sic dicendo: memoria est conservatio similitudinis Dei in ipsa anima per quam ipsa anima naturaliter ducitur in id quod naturaliter est intelligendum et naturaliter diligendum, hoc est in primum verum et primum et summe bonum. Et illorum duorum actuum primus referendus est ad cognitionem, reliquus ad affectum. Unde patere potest quod memoria nihil aliud est quam ipsa ductio in duo predicta. Id autem quod ducit per modum per quem ducens est vel quoad hoc quod ducit prius est

It appears that, according to the anonymous author, these two meanings do not correspond to two distinct faculties, but only describe two different aspects of one reality which can be image both of the Father and of the Holy Spirit.[223] On the other hand, it is clear that the first two meanings of memory are radically different from the third one, i.e. from the *memoria-thesaurus specierum*. This type of memory belongs properly to physical or philosophical speculation and, unlike the memory representing God the Father or the Holy Spirit, it preserves in itself images, i.e. the species of sensible things. The two memories can in no way be confused with each other, because the memory representing a divine Person belongs to man in a natural way and is immortal; by contrast, the memory that preserves sensible images is nothing but an accident for man and can easily be erased.[224]

On the basis of the exposition presented in the *Summa Duacensis*, we can easily understand that, according to our anonymous author, sensitive memory cannot be considered as a component of the image of the divine Trinity. This dignity only belongs to the memory which remains in the soul even in the eternal life.

2.3.4   THE DISPUTED QUESTIONS OF PETER OF BAR

Peter of Bar touches on the problem of memory in two disputed questions.[225] The first, entitled *Quaestio de illo verbo: "Faciamus hominem ad imaginem et simili-tudinem nostram"*, recalls the expositions – concerning the Augustinian theme of the soul as image of the Trinity – written by Philip the Chancellor, by the anonymous author of the *Summa Duacensis* and by Alexander of Hales:[226] it clearly transpires that Peter knows and employs all these texts, while closely following

---

et principatum debet optinere. Quare memoria per hunc modum accepta prior est; et ita merito Patri attribuenda".

[223] *Sum. Duac.*, 4. 3, ed. Glorieux, p. 21: "Et ita plane patet quod memoria secundum unam sui acceptionem Patri habet proprie tribui; secundum autem aliam Spiritui Sancto; et ita loquuntur varie actores et sancti expositores de illa".

[224] *Sum. Duac.*, 4. 3, ed. Glorieux, p. 21: "Tertio autem modo accipitur memoria secundum phisice vel philosophice loquentes hoc modo: memoria est thesaurus in quo recipiuntur ymagines rerum vel species per extrinsicas similitudines accepte. Hoc autem nichil attinet memorie supra dupliciter diffinite; immo differt multipliciter a memoria secundum quod Patris est. Et primum per hoc quod memoria secundum quod est in homine et Patri attributa, inest homini naturaliter et indelebiliter <indelibiliter *ed.*> et in opere prior naturaliter. Sed modo tertio accepta est hominis accidentaliter et delebiliter et ultimo loco operativa".

[225] Both questions are preserved only in ms. *Douai, Bibl. Mun. 434*, cf. *supra*, pp. 112-113.

[226] On Alexander, cf. *infra*, chap. 2.3.5.

especially the *Summa Duacensis*.[227] Peter's second question, entitled *De hiis que ex parte anime manebunt*, dwells instead upon a different problem, i.e. the survival of the powers of the soul after a man's death.[228]

The two questions address the theme of memory from two completely different points of view. Indeed, the question about the soul-image relies chiefly on Augustine's *De Trinitate* and the main problem it deals with concerns the position of memory within the image of God ("does memory correspond to the Father or to the Holy Spirit?").[229] The emphasis is laid on the immortal memory which, together with will and reason, constitutes the mind, i.e. the higher and immortal part of the soul.[230] By contrast, in the question *De hiis que ex parte anime manebunt*, Peter considers exclusively the sensitive memory, which operates through sensible images, hence it does not belong to the highest part of the soul. When Peter describes the *memoria per phantasmata*, he is mainly inspired by Avicenna, not by theological sources. Nevertheless, the Parisian master attributes to this type of memory a *post mortem* survival and some activity. Indeed, Peter states that sensitive memory can operate in the afterworld thanks to the interior light, although sensible images and every operation occurring through the latter disappear with death.[231]

If the sensitive memory is immortal, then can we consider it as an element of the divine Trinity? In his question *De illo verbo: "Faciamus hominem ad imaginem et similitudinem nostram"*, Peter seems to reject this possibility. Indeed, he draws a distinction between two types of memory. On the one hand, he postulates natural memory and divides it, in its turn, into two different species: (1) the memory that represents God the Father and precedes intelligence and will, and (2) the memory that preserves what is known naturally and loved and corresponds to

---

[227] Cf. Künzle, *Das Verhältnis*, p. 115, pp. 229-231.

[228] Cf. *supra*, chap. 2.2.2.4.

[229] Petr. de Barro, *q. de illo verbo*, ed. Künzle, p. 231[60-64]: "Secundo queritur sic: hec tria tribus personis appropriantur, memoria Patri, intelligencia Filio, voluntas Spiritui sancto, et sicut ex Patre Filius et ex utroque Spiritus sanctus, sic ex memoria intelligencia et ex utraque voluntas. Huic ordini Augustinus contrarius est in libro de sermone imaginis, ubi dicit, quod ex intellectu et voluntate nascitur memoria".

[230] Aug, *trin.*, XV, 7, 11, ed. Mountain, CCSL 50A, p. 457[12-13], PL 42, 1065: "Non igitur anima, sed quod excellit in anima, mens vocatur".

[231] Petr. de Barro, *Quaestio de hiis que ex parte anime manebunt* III, cf. *infra*, p. 209: "Preterea. Ymaginatio, memoria non sunt sine organo, restat ergo quod in dissolutione corporis deficiente organo et ymagines et fantasmata rerum defecerunt, ergo quod in restitutione corporis aut non fiet ymaginatio aut memoria per ymagines aut fantasmata, aut omnium que per ymaginem et memoriam apprehenduntur ymagines et fanthasmata redibunt, quod tamen non sit possibile, ut uidetur. Relinquitur quod non fiet ymaginatio aut memoria aut intellectus per similitudines rerum, quod concedi potest. Sicut enim in luce et per eam uidebit oculus que decent uidere ipsum, sic in luce interiori et per lucem interiorem ymaginabuntur et memorabuntur et intelligemus ea que decent nos ymaginari etc".

the Holy Spirit.[232] On the other hand, Peter posits acquired memory. The memory of this type does not belong to the soul in a natural way because it is somehow acquired by the soul: Peter probably refers here to the acquisition of images by means of sensible knowledge. Hence, the second type of memory does not belong to the image of God, because the image of God is in the soul in a natural way.[233]

The distinction between natural memory and acquired memory is based especially on the relevant object of knowledge. The memory of the first type is called 'natural' because its object coincides with what can be known and loved in a natural way, i.e. God and the mind itself ("ductus naturalis in id quod naturaliter cognoscendum et diligendum est" – "conservatio naturalis eorum, que naturaliter amantur et intelliguntur"). The second type of memory is distinguished from the first because its object is not accessible to the soul in a "natural" way, but must be acquired: its object probably coincides with the images of the sensible world. We can thus suppose some analogy between the acquired memory Peter speaks of in his question *De illo verbo...* and the *memoria per phantasmata* described in the question *De hiis que ex parte anime manebunt*.

Like his main source, i.e. the *Summa Duacensis*, Peter of Bar introduces a very clear distinction between intellective memory (primary or natural) and sensitive memory (acquired or *per phantasmata*). For sensitive memory, even if it is immortal, cannot be considered as an element of the created Trinity conceived by Augustine. This dignity belongs uniquely to spiritual memory, which has God and the soul itself as its object.

---

[232] Petr. de Barro, *q. de illo verbo*, ed. Künzle, p. 230[72-90]: "Respondetur: memoria duplex; uno modo memoria quasi ductus naturalis in id, quod naturaliter cognoscendum et diligendum est, vel quod idem est, memoria est conservatio similitudinis dei in ipsa anima, per quam ipsa anima naturaliter ducitur in id, quod naturalitat est cognoscendum et diligendum, hoc est in primum verum et summum bonum. Memoria ergo nichil aliud est quam ipsa ductio in duo predicta. Id autem, quod ducit per modum, per quem ducens vel quo ad hoc quod ducit, prius est et principatum debet obtinere, et sic memoria per hunc modum accepta prior est et ita merito Patri appropriatur. - Aliter quandoque memoria accipitur prout est conservatio naturalis eorum, que naturaliter amantur et intelliguntur; sic memoria prior non est, set ultima, et ita nulla est contrarietas si obiciatur sic secundum ultimum ordinem, secundum quem memoria est ultima intelligencia. (...) Ultimum ergo est memoria secundum quod est conservatio naturalis cogniti et amati. Naturalis enim est ordo, ut conservemus cognita et amata, et sic duplex est memoria naturalis".

[233] Petr. de Barro, *q. de illo verbo*, ed. Künzle, p. 231[64-68]: "Respondebat, quod uno modo sumitur memoria ut naturalis, alio modo ut acquisita. Sed nichil est, quia memoria secundum quod est unum de tribus predictis non est acquisita, sic enim secundum illa tria non esset naturaliter homo imago trinitatis".

2.3.5   THE *GLOSS* OF ALEXANDER OF HALES

Philip the Chancellor treats the question of memory in the same chapter of the *Summa de bono* in which he considers the problem of the identity of the soul with its powers.[234] In a similar way, Alexander of Hales too deals with memory in the *Gloss* on the third distinction of book I of the *Sentences*, just before examining the question of the ontological status of the powers of the soul.[235] The problem of memory is therefore integrated into what we have defined as the "theological context".

Alexander poses two questions. First, just like Philip and the anonymous author of the *Summa Duacensis*, the theologian wonders how to reconcile the contrasting authorities as regards the role of memory in the created image of the Trinity. Indeed, Augustine, in book IX of *De Trinitate*,[236] as well as Anselm[237] affirm that memory (i.e. the mind) occupies the first place in the trinity of the soul and therefore corresponds to the Father. By contrast, in the book *De imagine* (i.e. in *De spiritu et anima*),[238] it is maintained that memory represents the Holy Spirit. Hence, which position is correct?

Alexander answers that there exists a twofold memory. The first kind of memory preserves the objects of the intellect and will and therefore occupies the last position in the trinity of the soul. By contrast, the memory of the second kind preserves in itself the resemblance of good and truth, toward which the soul can be directed in a natural way. This memory gives rise to intelligence and will and therefore corresponds to God the Father.[239] In this passage, which is devoted to

---

[234] Cf. *infra*, chap. 2.1.2.5.

[235] Cf. *infra*, chap. 2.1.2.5.

[236] Cf. Aug., *trin.* IX, 12, 17-18, ed. Mountain, CCSL 50, pp. 308-309, PL 42, 970; Alex. Halen., *gloss. in* I *Sent.*, d. 3, n. 37 b, ed. PP. Collegii S. Bonaventurae, p. 57[11-12].

[237] Cf. Ans. Cant., *monol.*, 48, ed. Schmitt, pp. 1-87, PL 158, 199; cf. Alex. Halen., *gloss. in* I *Sent.*, d. 3, n. 37 a, ed. PP. Collegii S. Bonaventurae, pp. 56[27]-57[7].

[238] Cf. Ps.-Aug., *spir. et an.*, c. 35, PL 40, 805; cf. Alex. Halen., *gloss. in* I *Sent.*, d. 3, n. 37 a, ed. PP. Collegii S. Bonaventurae, p. 57[8-15].

[239] Alex. Halen., *gloss. in* I *Sent.*, d. 3, n. 37 a, ed. PP. Collegii S. Bonaventurae, pp. 57[20]-58[5]: "Respondeo: duplex est memoria. Quaedam est de rebus intellectis et de rebus volitis, ut permaneant et conserventur in intellectu et affectu; et ista consequitur ad intelligentiam et voluntatem. Et sic intelligitur auctoritas Augustini super 17 Eccli. et in libro *De imagine*. Est alia quae praecedit, quae extendit se ad omne tempus; et haec est retentio sive conservatio essentialis similitudinis veri et boni. Quando enim anima creata est, habet potentiam convertendi se supra se ipsam secundum verum et bonum quae ipsa est, vel secundum verum et bonum quae Deus est; et sic intelligentia et voluntas procedunt a memoria. Per hanc enim similitudinem, quae in hac memoria conservatur, potest se intelligere, et per consequens velle sibi bonum".

the position of memory in the image of the Trinity, Alexander does not take into account the *memoria per phantasmata*.

Sensitive memory appears in the second question posed by Alexander. In this case, the question concerns the way in which we must classify memory. Indeed, following some authorities, memory of past things is a rational faculty and therefore is not a part of the sensitive soul. Confronted with this problem, Alexander answers that memory operates in two ways. First of all, it preserves forms: sensitive memory thus gathers sensible forms. Similarly, intelligible memory preserves the forms of intelligible things; but this second faculty – i.e. intelligible memory – performs another activity as well: through intelligible forms, it is directed toward that which has been known previously. This second activity is proper to the memory described by Augustine in *De Trinitate*, which coincides with eternal memory that precedes intelligence and will and corresponds to God the Father.[240]

On the basis of Alexander's complex and rather confused exposition, we may observe that, in his view, sensitive memory represents a faculty which is clearly distinct from intelligible memory. This distinction is chiefly based on the difference between the objects of these two faculties: for sensible forms are the object of sensitive memory, whereas intelligible forms are the object of intellective memory. The memory of the second kind is directed toward the soul itself and God, and is a part of the image of the Trinity. By contrast, sensitive memory does not lie in the noblest part of the soul and therefore is not considered as an element of the created trinity described in Augustine's *De Trinitate*. However, as we have observed while examining a disputed question by Alexander, this does not mean that sensitive memory is mortal: it survives in the separated soul together with the other sensitive faculties.[241]

---

[240] Alex. Halen., *gloss. in* I *Sent.*, d. 3, n. 37 a, ed. PP. Collegii S. Bonaventurae, p. 60[18-30]: "Respondeo: memoria duplicem habet actum: uno modo ut retinet formas sensibiles, et sic est animae sensibilis; memoria autem intelligibilis est formarum intelligibilium vis retentiva secundum unum eius actum. Alius est actus in quantum per formam intelligibilem retentam fit conversio supra rem prius intellectam; et sic est tantum animae intelligibilis et extendit se ad omne tempus et praecedit intelligere, quia intelligere fit per similitudinem. Unde Augustinus, x *De Trinitate*: "Cognoscat semetipsam anima nec quasi absentem quaerat, sed intentionem voluntatis, qua per alia vagabatur, statuat in se ipsam et se cogitet; ita videbit quod nunquam sui non meminerit, nunquam se non amaverit, nunquam nescierit, sed aliud secum amando, cum eo se confudit et concrevit quodam modo"".

[241] Cf. *supra*, chap. 2.2.2.3.

2.3.6   JOHN OF LA ROCHELLE

John of La Rochelle, in the chapter *Qualiter anima est representatiua Trinitatis* of his *Summa de anima*, dwells briefly on the problem of memory. His exposition contains elements which might suggest its closeness to all the treatments on the soul as image of the Trinity we have examined above. Like the other theologians, John wonders whether memory represents the first Person of the Trinity, i.e. God the Father, or corresponds to the third Person, i.e. the Holy Spirit.[242] His solution particularly recalls the question *De illo verbo* of Peter of Bar,[243] because John uses the terms "*memoria innata*" and "*memoria acquisita*". However, the meaning of these expressions does not totally coincide with that of the pair introduced by Peter (*memoria naturalis - memoria acquisita*). Indeed, for Peter, acquired memory is radically different from natural memory and therefore is not a part of the image of the Trinity.[244] By contrast, John maintains that acquired memory corresponds to the Holy Spirit if it is considered *quantum ad fieri*, and corresponds to God the Father if it is considered *quantum ad esse*. Acquired memory thus represents an element of the image of God in the soul, just like natural memory.

John's interpretation is definitely different from the position held by Peter of Bar. This divergence probably derives from the fact that, according to John, acquired memory, just like natural memory, has the ultimate truth, i.e. God, as its proper object.[245] By contrast, as previously seen, according to Peter's interpreta-

---

[242] Ioh. Rup., *sum. de an.* I, 35, ed. Bougerol, p. 111[1-17]: "Consequenter queritur qualiter est representatiua Trinitatis ipsa anima. Dubitabit autem aliquis quomodo secundum predicta, scilicet memoriam, intelligenciam, uoluntatem, fiat coaptacio ad Trinitatem personarum, quoniam dicit Augustinus: memoria Patri, intelligencia Filio, uoluntas Spiritui sancto. Et racio huius est quia ex memoria prime ueritatis generatur intelligencia eius; ex utroque uero procedit amor prime ueritatis; memoria ergo Patri, intelligencia Filio, uoluntas Spiritui sancto. - Contra. Ecclesiastici 17 (1): *Secundum ymaginem suam fecit illum*; Glossa: sicut ex Patre Filius et ex utroque Spiritus sanctus, ita ex intellectu uoluntas, et ex utroque memoria; ergo intelligencia Patri, uoluntas Filio, memoria Spiritui sancto. - Item, Augustinus in *Sermone de ymagine*: (12-16) "Ex his quasi ex excellencioribus anime dignitatibus, iubemur Deum diligere, ut quantum intelligatur, tantum in memoria semper habeatur; nec solus sufficit intellectus, nisi sit uoluntas in amore eius; nec hec duo sufficiunt nisi memoria addatur qua semper in mente intelligentis et diligentis maneat Deus"; memoria ergo procedit ex intelligencia et uoluntate; non ergo aptabitur Patri".

[243] Cf. *supra*, pp. 160-162.

[244] Cf. *supra*, pp. 161-162.

[245] Cf. Ioh. Rup., *sum. de an.* I, 35, ed. Bougerol, p. 111[18]-112[30]: "Respondeo. Est memoria duplex, scilicet innata et acquisita ; memoria ueritatis innata est principium intelligencie et uoluntatis; est enim sicut dictum est, uis conseruatiua similitudinis prime ueritatis impresse a creacione. Et secundum hoc memoria Patri, intelligencia Filio, uoluntas Spiritui sancto. Memoria uero acquisita prime ueritatis potest considerari duobus modis, quia

tion, acquired memory quite probably corresponds to the *memoria per phantas-mata*, i.e. the memory directed toward the sensible world.[246]

In the chapter devoted to the image of the Trinity in the soul, John does not touch on the theme of sensitive memory; rather, this problem is treated in the part of the *Summa* devoted to the exposition of the philosophical theories concerning the powers of the soul. John faithfully describes both the doctrine of memory elaborated by John Damascene[247] and that elaborated by Avicenna,[248] but he does not relate them to Augustine's thought. Hence, as regards the theme of memory, the *Summa de anima* remains a simple review of opinions, not claiming to provide a synthesis nor offering a unitary view of the problem of memory.

* * *

The analysis of the texts composed at the Parisian Faculty of Theology in the early thirteenth century shows an extremely complex picture, where many and varied positions are present. It is certain that the reception of Avicenna's psychology plays a part in fueling the debate about human memory; still, this does not mean that the thought produced by the Parisian theologians was radically transformed. First of all, let us observe that the idea of spiritual memory is not questioned at all. Although Avicenna decidedly rejected any kind of preservation of intelligible forms, the Latin theologians unanimously affirm the existence of a spiritual memory belonging to the highest part of the soul, i.e. to the mind. This type of memory, corresponding to that described in Augustine's *De Trinitate*, operates in a relation of close interdependence with intellect and will, and, together with these two powers, forms the image of the divine Trinity. This memory is called natural (Philip the Chancellor, the *Summa Duacensis*, Peter of Bar) or innate (John of La Rochelle) for two reasons: first, its object coincides with what can be known and loved in a natural way, i.e. God and the mind itself; second, this type of memory is a part of the soul in a primary way and is inseparable from it. Intelligible memory is thus called 'natural' because: (1) it is directed toward that which is naturally accessible and (2) is immortal.

The agreement about the role and character of "natural memory" is a stable point of this debate. It is equally clear that all the theologians whose texts we have

---

quantum ad fieri aut quantum ad esse. Quantum ad fieri, naturaliter procedit acquisita memoria ex intellectu et uoluntate; et secundum hoc intellectus qui est generans uoluntatem attribuitur Patri, uoluntas que est genita Filio, memoria ex utroque procedens Spiritui sancto. - Quantum uero ad esse, memoria prime ueritatis acquisita potest esse principium intelligencie, uoluntatis et ipsius ueritatis; et secundum hoc fiet assignacio sicut prius: memoria Patri, etc".

[246] Cf. *supra*, p. 162.

[247] Cf. Ioh. Rup., *sum. de an.* II, 71, ed. Bougerol, pp. 201-202.

[248] Cf. Ioh. Rup., *sum. de an.* II, 102, ed. Bougerol, pp. 249-251; cf. Ioh. Rup., *tract. de div.* II, 10, ed. Michaud-Quantin, pp. 76-78.

examined draw a sharp distinction between natural memory and the *memoria per phantasmata*. Natural memory forms part of the mind, i.e. of the highest part of man and, as such, it cannot be confused with a sensitive faculty. For this reason, most thinkers do not consider sensitive memory as an element of the natural trinity in the soul. Only Philip the Chancellor seems to admit the possibility of identifying this memory with the image of the Holy Spirit; nevertheless, his texts are not clear in this regard.

Finally, the Parisian masters offer different solutions to the question of the immortality of sensitive memory. Philip the Chancellor and the anonymous *Summa Duacensis* consider the *memoria per phantasmata* to be a mortal faculty, which disappears at the moment the soul becomes separated from the body. By contrast, Peter of Bar openly states that sensitive memory remains in the separated soul, although in the afterworld it changes its manner of operating. As we have seen in the preceding chapter, such a position is held also by Alexander of Hales in one of his questions *Antequam esset frater*.[249]

2.3.7   WILLIAM OF AUVERGNE'S *DE ANIMA*: MEMORY, THE IMMORTALITY OF THE SOUL AND THE RESURRECTION

The question of the immortality of human memory is approached in an original way by the bishop of Paris, William of Auvergne. William mentions this theme in a context radically different from that in which it is approached by the authors we have considered so far. Indeed, he relates the problem of memory to the demonstration of the immortality of the soul.

After presenting several arguments in favour of the immortality of the human soul, William integrates into his treatise *De anima* a chapter registered with the following words: "Ostendit immortalitatem animae ex resuscitatione mortuorum".[250] Indeed, resting on testimonies made by persons who were raised from the dead, William intends to prove that the soul does not perish together with the body.[251] The theologian thus mentions several examples drawn from classical myths, Hebraic beliefs or tales about the early Christians, in which men who were miraculously resuscitated recalled what their souls had known in the afterworld. In particular, William points out the case of a little Hebrew boy brought

---

[249]   Cf. *supra*, chap. 2.2.2.3.

[250]   Guill. de Alv., *de an.*, 4, 30, ed. Le Feron, pp. 189 b-190 b.

[251]   Cf. Guill. de Alv., *de an.*, 4, 30, ed. Le Feron, p. 189 b: "Ad resurrectiones vero mortuorum quae in gente christianorum pene innumerabiles factae sunt veniam, quoniam nullum dubitationis relinquunt vestigium de vita animarum post mortem corporum".

back to life by one of the prophets.[252] The argumentation elaborated by the theologian is clear and simple: if the boy's soul had not survived death, how could it be brought back into the body it had abandoned? It is impossible that it was created again: indeed, the boy remembered having gone back into his body and, moreover, he had retained the memory of his life before death. It clearly follows that his soul had never ceased to live.[253]

The story reported by William serves to demonstrate the immortality of the soul, but it also coincides with an affirmation of the existence of a memory of a sensitive type in the separated soul. According to William, the fact that the resuscitated boy had retained the memories of his life before death constitutes an unfailing proof of the existence of one and the same soul in the resuscitated person and in that person before death.[254]

William's demonstration involves several interesting implications. According to him, if the resurrection coincided with the creation of a new soul, then a resurrected person could retain no memory of his or her past life. This implies that memory could not persist if there were no continuity of being. Quite probably, this conviction held by William concerns not only the faculty of memory, but extends to the very identity of the human person. For it seems that the persistence of the same soul after death and at the moment of resurrection ensures not only the protection of particular memories, but also one's self-consciousness. In William's perspective, personal identity thus remains closely connected to the continuity of the existence of man in his spiritual dimension.

Lastly, let us observe that William of Auvergne, probably like many other theologians of his time, considers the problem of the immortality of the soul as inseparable from that of the resurrection. Indeed, the bishop of Paris maintains that immortality can be proved by means of the resurrection of man; consequently, he assumes that the resurrection is not possible without the immortality of the soul. This conviction, which is rarely manifested in medieval anthropological writings, appears though to be implicitly shared by many thinkers of that age. In fact, such

---

[252] Probably William refers to a miracle made by the prophet Elisha; cf. 1 Kings 17:22: "Exaudivit Dominus vocem Heliae et reversa est anima pueri intra eum et revixit".

[253] Cf. Guill. de Alv., *de an.*, 4, 30, ed. Le Feron, p. 189 b: "In gente vero Hebraeorum puer unus per unum ex prophetis gentis illius suscitatus narratur, et restituta anima illius corpori suo, quae nisi vixisset post mortem corporis, nec restituta videretur; novam vero animam illi corpori creatam et datam nullo modorum possibile est, cum ipsa anima pueri illius certissime recordarerur se redijsse atque reminisceretur multorum ex his quae ante mortem corporis sui gesserat in illo".

[254] The importance William attributes to the memory of a sensitive type in relation to the future life clearly conflicts with the role attributed to this type of faculty by Avicenna; cf. pp. 153-154.

an approach helps us to understand the extreme importance attributed to the immortality of the soul in medieval theology.[255]

---

[255] It is worth observing that the conviction that the resurrection is necessarily connected to the immortality of the soul is sometimes abandoned by today's theologians, especially among Protestants; see, for example, O. Cullmann, *Immortality of the Soul or Resurrection of the Dead? The Witness of the New Testament*, London: Epworth Press, 1958; M. J. Harris, *Raised Immortal: Resurrection and Immortality in the New Testament*, Grand Rapids: Eerdmans, 1985. For a more complete bibliography on this subject, see R. Heinzmann, "Das Verhältnis von Leib und Seele in Verständnis der Frühscholastik", *Theologie und Philosophie* 49 (1974), p. 544; cf. id., *Die Unsterblichkeit der Seele und die Auferstehung des Leibes*, p. 1; V. Froese, "Body and Soul: A Selected Annotated Bibliography", *Direction* 37. 2 (2008), pp. 243–247.

CONCLUSION

The analysis of Hugh of St-Cher's anthropological writings represents the starting point and the chief purpose of this book. The conclusion we formulate here, therefore, concerns primarily the thought of this Dominican master. Nevertheless, any understanding of Hugh's works would be impossible without a comparison with the doctrines of his contemporaries and a consideration of the positions held in the twelfth century. This comparison has revealed a number of more general tendencies which appear both in twelfth-century and thirteenth-century authors. The following paragraphs will attempt to summarize them briefly.

The debate on the problem of the union of soul and body which took place in the twelfth and thirteenth centuries was mainly a result of the tension between two opposite needs, namely, the need to protect both the unity of man and the immortality of the soul. Although, at first glance, it may seem that the theological literature of that age considered the latter to be more urgent than the former, we cannot conclude that one is more important than the other. Indeed, on the one hand, all – or almost all – medieval treatises on the human soul contain an extensive section devoted to the defence of the immortality of the soul and, therefore, of its independence with regard to the body. But on the other hand, the word 'man' itself – as well as the two most important words in the medieval anthropological language, 'human nature' and 'person' – involves a view of the human being which must be, at least to some extent, unitary. Furthermore, this view is reinforced by two dogmas that are central for the Christian religion: the incarnation of the Word of God and the resurrection of the flesh.

Our analysis of the texts devoted to the *scientia de anima* has revealed above all the centrality of the concept of person in medieval anthropology. Indeed, it is an extremely important notion for dogmatic theology as a whole, since it is indispensable both to express the mystery of the Trinity and to form a conception of the unity of Christ. The enquiry aimed at clarifying the meaning of the term *'persona'* was mainly guided by Boethius' thought: the definition given by Boethius – "rationalis naturae individua substantia" – remained a reference point throughout the Middle Ages. This definition cannot be ignored because the entire theological edifice rests on its correct and coherent interpretation. Now, the same concept of person induced thinkers in the twelfth and thirteenth centuries to affirm the ontological unity of the human being. A fundamental step on this path was represented by Gilbert of Poitiers, who maintained that the human soul is not a person because it is not individual. Indeed, by definition the soul cannot be individual because everything that can be said of it can also be predicated of man as a whole. Therefore, according to Gilbert, the concept of soul as such excludes individuality. Gilbert's theory was taken up by Alan of Lille and several later authors. Alan – who was inspired by Gilbert's text but opposed Peter Lombard's *Sentences* (where the separated soul is considered as a person, similar to an angel) – states that the separated soul is not a person because it is communicable by nature or, in other words, because the fact of being a part of man belongs to the very nature of the soul. We must note that this justification is fundamentally foreign to Gilbert's thought because Gilbert conceived of the relation between soul and man primarily as a relationship between concepts, which is not intrinsic to the nature of the soul. By contrast, in order to justify the lack of the character of person in the separated soul, Alan of Lille and many later authors, including Hugh of St-Cher, use the idea of a certain incompleteness involved in the nature of the soul itself and bring into play the natural desire that the soul feels for its body (in reality an idea already asserted by Augustine).

The soul is never a person, is never individual, and always remains a part of man: these statements become a fixed point for theology from the early thirteenth century onwards. They clearly contrast with the traditional doctrine of the substantial self-sufficiency and independence of the human soul with regard to the body, and they contribute to weakening the anthropological dualism that had prevailed in the Latin West during the previous centuries. The move towards a less dualist view of man found a new expression in the *unibilitas substantialis* doctrine. It would seem that this theory was first affirmed in the second redaction of William of Auxerre's *Summa aurea*, a work which exerted a great influence on the theology elaborated during the following decades. William, who had deep knowledge of the doctrine according to which the human soul is not a person (as clearly stated by Stephen Langton), availed himself of the *unibilitas substantialis* theory in order to explain what the foundation of the specific difference between the human soul and the angel is. For William, the two spiritual substances, namely the rational soul and the angel, belong to two different species, because the soul possesses by nature the ability to be united with the body, whereas the angel is independent of any connection with corporeal realities. The essential innovation of this doctrine consists in the fact that William lets the specific or substantial difference of the soul depend upon the connection with the body. Indeed, as William affirms elsewhere, this type of difference cannot be caused by an accidental characteristic. Hence, the ability to be united with the body must represent for the soul something more than an accident. The doctrine elaborated in the *Summa aurea* is particularly important because it places itself in sharp contrast with Avicenna's anthropology, which strongly influenced Latin thinkers in the early decades of the thirteenth century. In his *De anima*, Avicenna holds that the inclination toward the body represents a mere accident of the soul and does not contribute to defining its essence. According to Avicenna, the essence of the soul can be grasped if we consider the soul as abstracted from its conjunction with the body. By contrast, William's doctrine lets the specific difference of the soul depend upon the psycho-physical union.

The theory of the substantial inclination of the soul to its conjunction with the body was developed in the period in which Aristotle's *De anima* began to exert an influence on the Parisian masters, and it is quite probable that this influence contributed to the birth of this doctrine. In any case, whereas the *Summa aurea* does not mention the definition of the soul as form, Hugh of St-Cher, in his disputed question on the soul, takes up William's doctrine and also mentions Aristotle's *De anima*. Moreover, Hugh introduces the neologism '*unibilitas*' into the aforementioned doctrine and, while repeating that the separated soul is not a person, states that the substantial ability to be united with the body (*unibilitas substantialis*) remains in the separated soul. In this way, the *unibilitas substantialis* doctrine acquires its typical formulation, a formulation which was to be adopted later by John of La Rochelle and Bonaventure. Furthermore, the term '*unibilitas*' was still to play an important role in the psychological language of the last decades of the thirteenth century.

A reading of the anthropological texts of the thirteenth century would seem to lead us to conclude that the doctrine of the essential 'unibility' of the soul was easier to accept than the Aristotelian thesis of the soul-form, for the concept of form had a clear materialistic connotation and carried the idea of inseparability from matter. By comparison, the doctrine of *unibilitas substantialis* offered the advantage of emphasizing the unity of the human being and the strong connection between soul and body, while not endangering the immortality of the rational soul.

Furthermore, it seems that the role of this doctrine was no less influential than that of Avicennian anthropology: indeed, faced with the growing need to powerfully express the unity of man, Avicenna's *De anima* provided no help. Indeed Avicennian anthropology reduces the connection between soul and body to a mere accident and, moreover, denies the faith in the resurrection of the body. In these respects, therefore, Avicenna's thought was no closer to medieval Christian theology than was Aristotle's. It might thus be appropriate to re-evaluate the influence exerted by Avicenna's psychology on the acceptance of Aristotelian anthropology by the Latin West. The idea that Avicenna's mediation was necessary to bring about the assimilation of the Aristotelian conception of the soul in the Latin West is present in a number of works, even recent ones,[1] devoted to the study of medieval psychology. This idea seems to be related to the implicit conviction

---

[1] Cf. Lenzi, *Forma e sostanza*, pp. 121-122, p. 130, p. 156, p. 167.

that, before the arrival of Aristotle's "new" works, Latin authors had no need to support and justify the unity of the human being by means of philosophical arguments. Nevertheless, our analysis of the anthropological texts from the twelfth and thirteenth centuries clearly shows that, at the moment of the reception of Aristotle's *De anima*, the Latin world already manifested a tendency to seek effective explanations of the connection between soul and body and of those aspects which – just like those aspects regarding the *persona* – appeared to result from a fundamental unity of man. The need to explain the unity of man cannot therefore be reduced to a product of the reception of the new philosophical works, Aristotle's *De anima* in particular; rather, it was already present in the Latin world before the diffusion of the Aristotelian translations. Now, Aristotle's thought offered an attractive answer to the question of the unity of the human being; by contrast, according to Avicenna's interpretation of Aristotelian anthropology, the soul is not the form but just a perfection of the body, and its substantial definition does not depend upon its being a perfection in this way, but is formulated apart from the psychophysical relation. Avicenna's interpretation thus makes the Aristotelian solution basically ineffective, and hence his philosophy was not able to provide an adequate answer to the questions posed by the Latin theologians.

Because of its weakness, the Avicennian solution was instrumental in the birth and success of the *unibilitas substantialis* doctrine, although this cannot be regarded as the only reason for the spread of the doctrine. Indeed, the doctrine was mainly rooted in the demands of medieval Christian theology, notably the interpretation of the concept of person, the need to justify the specific distinction between the human soul and the angel, the unity of human nature, and the prospect of the resurrection of the body. Finally, the birth of this doctrine was also fostered by the reception of Aristotle's *De anima*.

We should acknowledge, however, that the *unibilitas substantialis* theory remains rather obscure and its ontological foundations were not adequately clarified by Hugh of St-Cher, nor by any other author. In the face of this obscurity, it becomes very important to identify the consequences of this doctrine on different aspects of the anthropology maintained by those authors who embraced it. The study of the writings of Hugh of St-Cher as well as those of John of La Rochelle and other contemporary authors reveal an extremely complex picture, marked by inconsistencies often linked to the persistence in their thought of elements of a dualist psychology.

On the one hand, Hugh and his contemporaries attributed a radical meaning to the terms 'essentialiter' and 'substantialiter'. Indeed, these expressions were used to assert that the rational powers belong to the human soul in an essential way, in other words, to express the doctrine of the identity of the soul with its powers. Consequently, it appears that in affirming that *unibilitas* belongs to the soul *es-*

sentialiter or *substantialiter*, Hugh maintains the identification of the very essence of the soul with its *unibilitas* to the body.

But, on the other hand, Hugh, like most of his contemporaries (except for William of Auxerre and, to some extent, Alexander of Hales), maintained the doctrine according to which the human soul is identical with its rational powers, i.e. memory, reason and will. This theory actually reduces the essence of the human soul to rationality alone (which is basically independent of the conjunction with the body), thus leading us back to the traditional Neoplatonically-oriented dualism. Moreover, Hugh states that the union of soul and body is not direct, but needs ontological mediation through the sensitive and the vegetative power. Now, in the texts written by the Dominican theologian, the vegetative and sensitive powers are not considered to be faculties identical with the essence of the soul, but as mere accidents of it. Hence, in the end, a doctrine considering the ontological mediation of the lower powers as necessary to the conjunction of soul and body reduces the psychophysical union to an accidental union and therefore contradicts the *unibilitas substantialis* theory. This incongruity can be noticed both in Hugh of St-Cher's anthropology and in the anthropology elaborated by John of La Rochelle in his *Summa de anima*.

Hugh's texts present a further incongruity. In agreement with the contents of the first article of the question *De anima*, the ability to be united with the body should remain in the soul even after separation from it. However, in the second article of the same question, Hugh states that the vegetative and sensitive powers, which perform the function of intermediaries needed to fulfil the union, are mortal and do not remain in the human soul after separation from the body. This statement is clearly difficult to reconcile with the idea of the immortality of the *unibilitas* to the body.

The problem of the permanence of the lower powers in the separated soul was given contrasting solutions by the Parisian masters in the first half of the thirteenth century. The overall framework of the debate was complicated by the fact that, at the time, different classifications of the powers of the soul were available. In particular, the answer to the question concerning the survival of human memory involved great difficulties, in particular because the thinkers aimed at protecting both the Augustinian concept of intellective memory (which was expounded in *De Trinitate*) and the influential Avicennian doctrine of the powers of the soul. Indeed, Avicenna not only denied the existence of intellective memory, but also considered sensitive memory to be a mortal faculty. The problem of sensitive memory was not unimportant because, according to one of the major theologians of the time, William of Auvergne, the fact that resuscitated persons had memories of their mortal lives was a truth attested by the Scriptures (as observed also by Dominicus Gundissalinus and Philip the Chancellor) and, in addition, was an irrefutable proof of the immortality of the soul. In William's view, memory thus became the cornerstone of human identity and assured the continuity of a person's being.

In the face of the pressing need to protect the immortality of sensible memory, a need deriving directly from the commonly adopted exegesis of the Bible, it became very difficult to allow the Avicennian doctrine of memory into medieval Christian thinking. The position held on the immortality of memory and other sensitive faculties represents a clear difference between Avicenna's thought and the thought elaborated by the theologians of the first half of the thirteenth century. This difference should not be underestimated, especially with an eye toward re-evaluating the affinity of Avicennian psychology to the *scientia de anima* elaborated in the Latin West.

The reception of the new philosophical sources, especially Aristotle's *De anima*, is often regarded as a revolutionary event for medieval anthropology, an event which overturned the dualist conception and pushed the Latin masters in a new direction, namely towards a unitary view of man. It is beyond question that Aristotelian psychology was of the utmost importance for the development of the *scientia de anima*; and yet, in the light of the texts we have examined here, the orientation of the Latin West towards a unitary anthropology must be regarded as an evolution rather than as a sudden change of direction. Certainly, this does not mean that Aristotle's doctrine was somehow implicit in the works of Latin authors before the *De anima* was known, or that it could be easily accepted in circles in which the immortality of the soul was without doubt a non-negotiable value and where anthropological dualism was firmly established. The turn towards Aristotle's doctrine was neither necessary nor inevitable; however it was made possible thanks to a movement which took place within medieval Christian thought and which tried to acknowledge a greater unity of man. It was this tendency which brought about a slow but unmistakable evolution in anthropology, in conformity with the complex dynamics we have been able to observe in the material presented here.

Appendix
Text Editions

INTRODUCTION

(A) THE DISPUTED QUESTIONS (*DOUAI 434*)

This appendix contains the first edition of five disputed questions preserved in the MS *Douai 434*:[1]

> (1) a question by Hugh of St-Cher, *Quomodo anima uniatur corpori*;[2] (2) a question by Peter of Bar, *De hiis que ex parte anime manebunt*[3] and three anonymous questions, (3) *De trinitate anime*,[4] (4) *Si anima est sue potentie*[5] and (5) *De humana natura*.[6]

Owing to the presence of a note placed at the beginning of the question, the first of these texts has been attributed to Hugh of St-Cher. The note reads *frater h.*: according to Odon Lottin, there is no doubt that it refers to Hugh of St-Cher.[7] So far, no argument has been advanced against this attribution.

The question *De hiis que ex parte anime manebunt* contains no explicit attribution. However, this writing clearly represents a continuation in regard to the question that precedes it in the manuscript, i.e. question n. 156, which is devoted to discussing the characteristics of the resurrected body. Now, the manuscript explicitly attributes question n. 156 to *magister* Petrus de Barro. Hence, quite probably question n. 157 was also written by the same author.[8]

Like the two questions by Peter of Bar, the two anonymous questions n. 114 and 115 are also closely related to each other. We can thus suppose that they were both composed by the same anonymous author.

---

[1] Cf. *supra*, p. 1.

[2] Ms. *Douai 434*, I, f. 119vb; q. n. 285 according to the catalogue by Glorieux, "Les 572 Questions", p. 148.

[3] Ms. *Douai 434*, I, f. 86^{rb-va}; q. n. 157, cf. Glorieux, "Les 572 Questions", p. 140.

[4] Ms. *Douai 434*, I, f. 70rb; q. n. 114, cf. Glorieux, "Les 572 Questions", p. 137.

[5] Ms. *Douai 434*, I, f. 70rb; q. n. 115, cf. Glorieux, "Les 572 Questions", p. 137.

[6] Ms. *Douai 434*, II, f. 189^{ra-va}; q. n. 550, cf. Glorieux, "Les 572 Questions", p. 245. From question n. 482 onwards, Glorieux ceases to number the leaves and starts to number the pages. Consequently, according to the catalogue, the question n. 550 appears on *folia* 379^a-380^a.

[7] Cf. Lottin, "Un petit traité", pp. 468-475; id., "Quelques 'Questiones'", pp. 79-81; Bieniak, "Una questione disputata", pp. 131-133.

[8] Cf. Glorieux, "Les 572 Questions", p. 258.

Up to the present, except for the ms. *Douai 434*, no other witness of the five aforementioned questions has been found; hence, the present edition is based on only one manuscript. Inevitably, an edition of this kind is subject to several limitations: indeed, it is probable that some distortions caused by the transmission of the text have not been identified.

The lack of a second witness is particularly noticeable in the case of Hugh of St-Cher's question *Quomodo anima uniatur corpori*: indeed, the Douai manuscript does not transmit the solution of the two articles the question consists of. Our edition therefore presents an incomplete text. Nevertheless, it should be noted that the reconstruction of the text we have at our disposal has been helped by the fact that Hugh, in his question, follows a chapter of Philip the Chancellor's *Summa de bono* quite closely.

By contrast, in the case of Peter of Bar's question *De hiis que ex parte anime manebunt* the text transmitted by the Douai manuscript is complete; however, a passage of the question seems corrupt and therefore remains incomprehensible.[9]

Finally, the three anonymous questions do not present major textual problems.

(B) HUGH OF ST-CHER'S *SENTENCES COMMENTARY* (I, 3)

The text has been established on the basis of the following manuscripts:

B   *Basel, Universitätsbibliothek, B II 20* (XIV sec.), f. 4va-6ra;[10]
P   *Padova, Biblioteca Universitaria, 853* (XIII s.), f. 4vb-6vb;[11]

The two witnesses represent only a small part of the text tradition[12], so a comparison between them does not allow any hypothesis about their position in the *stemma*. Nevertheless, it seems that neither of the two witnesses served as an exemplar for the other.[13]

---

[9] Cf. *infra*, p. 209.

[10] G. Meyer - M. Burckhardt, *Die mittelalterliche Handschriften der Universitätsbibliothek Basel. Beschreibendes Verzeichnis. Abteilung B: Theologische Pergamenthandschriften*, Basel: Verlag der Universitätsbibliothek, 1960, I, pp. 179-185.

[11] A.I. Lehtinen, "The Apopeciae of the Manuscripts of Hugh of St. Cher's works", *Medioevo* 25 (1999-2000), pp. 33-34.

[12] The first book of the *Commentary* is transmitted in at least twenty manuscripts, cf. B. Faes de Mottoni, "Les manuscrits du commentaire des Sentences d'Hugues de St. Cher" in *Hugues de St-Cher, Bibliste et Théologien*, ed. L.-J. Bataillon, G. Dahan and P.-M. Gy, Turnhout: Brepols, 2004, pp. 279-280.

[13] While preparing the edition of Hugh's *Commentary* on the distinctions 23-25 of book I of the *Sentences*, I could examine the characteristics of the two manuscripts more

Manuscript B is mainly characterized by numerous interventions made by a second hand in the margin or in the space between the lines. Many of these corrections suggest that B was compared with another witness, whereas some others seem to be insertions added in order to enrich the text and do not necessarily involve the existence of a second manuscript. The present edition rejects almost all isolated readings introduced into B *secunda manu*, for example:

p. 187, l. 10 - relatiuis P*p*B: correlatiuis *s*B

p. 188, l. 30 - facit *p*B: facies P facit hoc *s*B

p. 191, l. 115 - quia P*p*B: anima *s*B

In only one case, a correction of *s*B is accepted against the agreement of *p*B and P because it renders the text more comprehensible:

p. 187, l. 19 - illa sunt *s*B: *om.* P*p*B

In a significant number of cases, the agreement of P and *s*B is preferable to the reading of *p*B, for example:

p. 188, l. 42 - creature P*s*B: creatore *p*B

p. 191, l. 102 - minor P*s*B: minus *p*B

p. 194, l. 199 - exsistunt P*s*B: exsistentia *p*B

Where there are no corrections by a second hand, P at times presents better readings than B but at other times the opposite is true. In general, P seems to offer a less corrupt text.

Considering that the edition relies on only two manuscripts, all variants have been mentioned in the philological *apparatus*.

The lemmas and quotations from Peter Lombard's *Sentences* are followed by page and line numbers from the *Sentences*' edition from 1981.

---

closely. On that occasion, I collated seven manuscripts: besides B and P, I examined microfilms of *Assisi, Bibl. Com., Fondo Antico 130* and *131; Città del Vaticano, Bibl. Ap. Vat., Vat. lat. 1098; Venezia, Bibl. Naz. Marciana, III.174 (2785)* and saw the original of *Firenze, Bibl. Naz., Conventi soppressi I.6.32*. In the case of distinctions 23-25, B corrects a considerable omission of P and conversely: therefore, these two manuscripts seem to be independent of each other. Indeed, when compared with the remaining witnesses examined, there are no particular similarities between P and B. By contrast, it clearly appears that P shares a large number of readings with the Florence manuscript. The latter is an interesting manuscript because, unlike the other witnesses examined, it offers Hugh's *Commentary* in the margin of the text of Peter Lombard's *Sentences*; cf. Lehtinen, *The Apopeciae*, p. 30. Moreover, the Florence MS seems to present a particularly good text; cf. Principe, *Hugh of Saint-Cher's Theology*, pp. 155, 159. Unfortunately, it was impossible for me to use it for this edition.

(C) ABBREVIATIONS

add. – addidit
inf. – inferior
iter. – iteravit
ms. – codex manu scriptus
mss. – codices manu scripti
om. – omisit
p (ante sigla alicuius codicis) – forma pristina textus
s (ante sigla alicuius codicis) – secundus status textus

HUGO DE SANCTO CARO

\<QVOMODO ANIMA VNIATVR CORPORI\>

\<i\>

Quesitum est utrum anima ita sit in toto corpore quod in qualibet eius parte. Videtur quod sic.   5

\<1\> Seneca ad Lucilium: "Quem locum optinet deus in mundo, hec locum optinet anima in corpore". Sed deus ita est in toto mundo quod in qualibet eius parte, ergo et sic anima in corpore.

\<2\> Ad idem. Angelus excellentior est in suis corporibus quam anima, ut dicit Augustinus quod nulla est excellentior creatura quam angelus. Sed dicit Damasce-   10
nus quod "angelus non operatur nisi ubi est", ergo anima non operatur nisi ubi est. Sed in qualibet parte corporis operatur, ergo ibi est. Dicit enim Damascenus quod omnis spiritualis creatura habet suum locum spiritualem siue intellectualem in quo est et operatur.

\<3\> Item. Augustinus: "Anima est in toto corpore simul tota", siue in singulis   15
partibus corporis simul tota, ergo ipsa est tota in qualibet parte aut totalitate essentie, aut uirtutis, aut potentiarum. Non totalitate uirtutis: ex hoc enim sequeretur quod rationcinaretur in pede et audiret in oculo; nec totalitate potentiarum: hoc constat. Restat ergo quod totalitate essentie, et ita essentia anime est in qualibet parte corporis. Hoc idem probatur sic: uirtus anime est in qualibet parte corporis.   20

\<4\> Item. Anima essentialiter est perfectio totius corporis, ergo essentialiter est in toto, ergo et in qualibet eius parte.

Hoc concesso, contra:

---

2 *Douai, Bibliothèque Municipale 434*, I, f. 119vb; q. n. 285, cf. Glorieux, "Les 572 Questions", p. 148.   20 hoc idem probatur... parte corporis] uacat *add. interl. et marg. ms.*

---

6 Seneca ad Lucilium : Sen., *epist.* 65, 24, ed. Hense, p. 209: "Quem in hoc mundo locum deus obtinet, hunc in homine animus".   10 Augustinus : Cf. Aug., *serm.*, 293D, 3, ed. Morin, p. 512¹⁷: "Et illud uerum est, quantumlibet magnus sit homo, minus eum esse quam est angelus minor". 10–11 Damascenus : cf. Ioh. Dam., *fid. orth.* I, 13, ed. Buytaert, p. 58³⁵⁻⁴⁰, PG 94, 853: "Angelus autem corporaliter quidem in loco non continetur, ut typum accipiat, et formetur. Verum tamen dicitur esse in loco, quia adest intelligibiliter et operatur secundum suam naturam; et non est alibi, sed illic intelligibiliter circumscribitur ubi et operatur. Non enim potest secundum idem in diuersis locis operari".   12 Damascenus : cf. Ioh. Dam., *fid. orth.* I, 13, ed. Buytaert, p. 58³⁵⁻³⁹, PG 94, 853; cf. Phil. Canc., *sum. de bon.*, ed. Wicki, p. 292⁵⁶⁻⁵⁸: "Unde Damascenus: "Angelus dicitur esse in loco, quia intelligibiliter circumscribitur ubi operatur"".   15 Augustinus : cf. Aug., *imm. an.*, c. 16, 25, PL 32, 1034: "Anima uero non modo uniuersae moli corporis sui, sed etiam unicuique particulae illius tota simul adest"; cf. id., *ep.*, 131, 4, PL 22, 1126; cf. Phil. Canc., *sum. de bon.*, ed. Wicki, p. 278¹⁴⁻¹⁶. 20 Item augustinus... parte corporis : Cf. Phil. Canc., *sum. de bon.*, ed. Wicki, pp. 279⁴⁹-280⁷⁰.

Anima simplicior est puncto, quia punctus situalis est, anima non. Sed idem
25   punctus numero non est in qualibet parte linee, ergo nec eadem anima numero est
in qualibet parte corporis.

    Quesitum est etiam ubi sedem habet anima. Dicunt quidam quod in corde, alii
quod in cerebro. Set Ieronimus siue Beda super illud Mc vii$_{21}$ "ab intus enim de
corde hominum male cogitationes procedunt" etc. dicit: "Anime locus principalis
30   non iuxta Platonem in cerebro, sed iuxta Christum in corde est".

    Sed contra dicit Augustinus sic: "Et si anima sit in toto corpore, intensius enim
est in corde et cerebro". Ex quo arguitur sic: primi actus anime sunt uiuificare et sen-
sificare, ergo cum anima sit intensius in cerebro quam in aliis membris, cerebrum
magis est uiuificatum et sensificatum quam cetera membra. Sed dicunt philoso-
35   phi contrarium, et Cassiodorus in libro De anima dicit quod "nullus sensus est in
cerebro".

    <1> Ad oppositum sic. Anima tota est in manu, tota in pede. Sed pes et manus
simul cum semel sint in diuersis locis, ergo eadem anima simul est in diuersis locis.

    <2> Item. Anima liberior est extra corpus quam in corpore, ergo si in corpore
40   manens est in toto corpore simul, multo fortius extra corpus ponetur simul esse in
diuersis locis.

    <3> Item. Anima est perfectio corporis, ergo animam esse in aliquo est perficere
illud in quo est. Sed anima rationalis non est perfectio cuiuslibet partis corporis,
ergo non est in qualibet parte corporis.

45   <4> Item. Gregorius Theologus dicit quod "deus primo creauit res spirituales,
secundo corporales, tertio compositas ex hiis", et potuit facere sic, ergo ita quod
primo fecerit unum hominem et nihil aliud fecerit in toto mundo, anima ista est
tota ubique per essentiam, per presentiam, per potentiam, ergo est deus.

    <5> Item. Anima commensuratur corpori, sed eque uiuificat magnum corpus ut
50   paruum. Contingat ergo unum corpus attingere usque ad celum enpireum, anima

---

24 anima *scripsi*] linea *ms.*

---

24 anima simplicior... anima non : cf. Auic., *met.*, 3, 1, ed. Van Riet, p. 106^{58}: "Punctum uero
est unitas situalis et linea dualitas situalis et superficies ternarietas situalis et corpus quaternarietas
situalis".   26 anima simplicior... parte corporis : Cf. Phil. Canc., *sum. de bon.*, ed. Wicki, p. 278$^{29-33}$.
28 Ieronimus siue Beda : recte *gl. ord.* in Mc 7, 21 (marg.), ed. Brepols, t. IV, p. 107, col. b; Hieron.,
in Math., II, ed. Hurst – Adriaen, CCSL 77, pp. 131^{1525}-132^{1527}, PL 26, 112.   31 Augustinus : recte
Ps. Aug., *spir. et an.*, 18, PL 40, 794: "Sicut enim Deus ubique est totus in toto mundo, et in omni
creatura sua: sic anima ubique tota in toto corpore suo, tanquam in quodam mundo suo, intensius
tamen in corde et in cerebro, quemadmodum Deus praecipue dicitur esse in coelo".   35 Cassiodorus
in libro De anima : cf. Cass., *an.* X, ed. Halporn, CCSL 96, p. 555, PL 70, 1294B: "Denique oculos
nostros defigimus omnino cogitantes, aurium sensus obstruitur, gustus cessat, nares ab odoratibus
vacant, lingua non habet vocem, et multis modis per talia signa cognoscitur anima in suis quodammodo cubiculis occupata".   41 anima liberior... locis : Phil. Canc., *sum. de bon.*, ed. Wicki,
p. 288$^{204-205}$.   44 anima est perfectio... parte corporis : cf. Phil. Canc., *sum. de bon.*, ed. Wicki,
p. 287$^{198-200}$.   45 Gregorius Theologus : cf. Greg. Naz., *in Theoph.*, 10-11, ed. Engelbrecht, CSEL
46.1, pp. 96-98, SC 358, pp. 122-126.   50 anima commensuratur... paruum : cf. Phil. Canc., *sum.
de bon.*, ed. Wicki, p. 280$^{71-72}$

tota est in qualibet parte corporis, ergo simul tota est in terra et in celo.

<6> Item. Si anima tota totum repleret corpus, quomodo potest diabolus, qui est spiritus, esse in corpore humano? Secundum hoc erunt duo spiritus in eodem.

<ii>

Secundo quesitum est quomodo anima unitur corpori, sine medio uel per medium. 55

<1> Videtur quod sine medio, quia ens et unum idem sunt, ergo idem est quo res est ens, et quo unum. Sed omne compositum ex materia et forma est ens per formam, ergo est unum per formam, ergo forma per se est unita materie. Sed anima est forma corporis, ergo per se est unita corpori, ergo sine medio.

<2> Preterea. Si est unita per medium, queritur de illo medio, utrum sit sub- 60 stantia uel accidens. Si accidens, ergo unio anime et corporis est ab accidenti, ergo ipsum compositum est accidentale. Si substantia, aut corporalis, aut spiritualis. Si spiritualis, eadem questio que prius, utrum scilicet uniatur corpori per medium aut sine medio. Si corporalis, redit eadem questio.

<3> Item. Necesse est quod omne medium uniens aliqua duo extrema habeat 65 naturam extremorum, quia si non conuenit plus cum extremis quam extrema inter se, eque possunt illa extrema sine illo et cum illo. Sed non est possibile aliquod tale medium esse inter animam et corpus, quod partim sit corporeum, partim incorporeum, ergo impossibile est corpus et animam uniri per medium.

Contra. 70

<1> Secundum substantiam suam anima separabilis est a corpore, et secundum operationes diuersas que sunt eius, ut intelligere, reminisci et huiusmodi. Ergo anima nec secundum substantiam, nec secundum proprias operationes dependet a corpore, ergo secundum se non coniungitur corpori.

<2> Item. Non perficitur corpus per animam nisi quod est uegetatiuum et sen- 75 sitiuum. Hec aut sunt dispositiones necessarie adaptantes, aut non. Si non, ergo sine hiis potest anima coniungi indifferenter, quod falsum est. Si necessarie, ergo sunt medium uniens uel media unientia.

<3> Item. Ea que maxime differunt non coniunguntur nisi per medium conueniens. Set anima rationalis maxime distat a corpore, quia simplex est, incor- 80

---

52 corpus] totum *iter. ms.*

---

58 uidetur... unita materie : Phil. Canc., *sum. de bon.*, ed. Wicki, p. 283[69-74]. 64 preterea... eadem questio : Phil. Canc., *sum. de bon.*, ed. Wicki, pp. 283[81]-284[88]. 69 necesse... per medium : Phil. Canc., *sum. de bon.*, ed. Wicki, p. 283[82-86]; cf. Ps.-Dionys., *cael. hier.*, c. 13, 3, ed. Chevallier, II, pp. 947-948 (PG 3, 301 A). 74 secundum substantiam... corpori : Phil. Canc., *sum. de bon.*, ed. Wicki, p. 284[103-107]. 78 Non perficitur... unientia : Phil. Canc., *sum. de bon.*, ed. Wicki, p. 284[108-111].

porea, incorruptibilis; corpus uero compositum, corporeum et corruptibile; ergo coniunguntur per medium conueniens.

Queritur quid est illud. Videtur quod anima sensibilis et uegetabilis. Anima enim sensibilis simplex et incorporea, set corruptibilis, et ita conuenit cum anima rationabili in duobus, cum corpore uero in uno; uegetabilis uero incorporea, sed composita et corruptibilis, et ita conuenit cum anima rationabili in uno, cum corpore uero in duobus. Ergo hec sunt medium siue media unientia.

<***>

---

88 *solutio quaestionis abest*

---

82 ea que... conueniens : Phil. Canc., *sum. de bon.*, ed. Wicki, p. 285[140-145].   87 queritur quid... unientia : Phil. Canc., *sum. de bon.*, ed. Wicki, p. 286[151-164].

HUGO DE SANCTO CARO

In I Sententiarum

Distinctio tertia

*Apostolus namque ait*₆₈, ₂₁₋₂₂ etc. In precedenti posuit auctoritates ueteri et noui testamenti ad ostendendum fidem de unitate essentie et trinitate personarum. Set quia superbi et garuli potius querunt rationes quam auctoritates, ideo idem nunc probat per rationes.

Primo ergo hic probat quod unus deus est, et per quatuor argumenta.

P 5ra Primum est: creatura est, ergo creator est (locus | ab effectu, si sumas id quod est creatura et creator, uel a relatiuis, si sumas ea quantum talia). Si enim creatura est, ab alio est; illud aliud aut est ab alio aut a nullo; et ita procedatur in infinitum, aut dabitur quod aliquid est a nullo, et est creator siue deus.

Secundum argumentum est: aliquid est mutabile, ergo aliquid est inmutabile, quia si aliquid est mutabile ab aliquo est mutabile, et iterum de illo queritur aut est mutabile aut non, et proceditur in infinitum, uel peruenitur ad aliquid quod est immutabile, et illud est deus.

Tertium: est bonum, et aliquid melius est eo, et sunt ab alio, ergo illud est optimum.

Quartum: est aliquid pulcrum, et aliquid est pulcrius eo, et illa sunt a tertio, ergo illud est pulcherrimum.

Postea ostendit quomodo uestigium trinitatis appareat in creaturis, et dicit quod unumquodque quod est habet unitatem, speciem et ordinem; item, in quolibet est origo, pulcritudo et delectatio; item, aliquid a quo sit, et per quem sit, et in quo. Per unitatem intellegitur pater, quia sicut unitas a nullo set omnia ab illa, ita et pater. Per speciem filius, quia sicut species notificat et honorificat id cuius est species, ita filius patrem. Per ordinem spiritus sanctus, quia sicut ordo est connexio ordinatorum, sic spiritus sanctus patris et filii, quia sicut bonitas dei facit quod res sunt, ita etiam

---

3 Distinctio tertia *marg.* BP   4 precedenti] capitulo *add. interl.* B   4 posuit] magister *add. interl.* B   6–7 nunc probat B] probat nunc P   8 primo *iter. marg.* B   10 et P] uel B   10 relatiuis P*p*B] correlatiuis *s*B   12 aut P] uel B   13–14 ergo aliquid est inmutabile, quia si aliquid est mutabile ab aliquo est mutabile B] *om.* P   15 aut non] est *add.* B   16 illud P] id B   17 tertium] est *add. interl.* B   17 melius est eo B] est melius P   17 sunt B] non P   19 aliquid] est *add. interl.* B   19 et illa sunt *s*B] *om.* P*p*B   21 et dicit P*s*B] et dicitur *p*B   24 pater *marg.* B   24 ita P] *om.* B   24 ita et pater P*p*B] sic omnia a patre et ipse a nullo *s*B   25 sicut P] *om.* B   27 quia] uel *praem. sed del.* B

---

21 dicit : cf. Petr. Lomb., *sent.* I, d. 3, 1. 6, ed. PP. Collegii S. Bonaventurae, p. 70²³⁻²⁴.

facit ordinem in rebus, et ita per ordinem bonitas intellegitur, et ita spiritus sanctus
similiter. Per alia trinitas intellegitur.

30   Tertio ostendit quomodo in anima sit ymago trinitatis, et facit per memoriam,
intelligentiam et uoluntatem.

<i>

Set obicitur de quarto argumento sic: tertium argumentum bonum est, quia
bonitas ordinat et refert causam ad effectum, et ita bonitas cause ponit aliquid
in effectu bonitatis. Set non sic pulcritudo: non enim refert causam ad effectum
35   (pulcritudo enim fabri nihil ponit in eius effectu), et ita non ualet argumentum. | B 4ᵛᵗ

Solutio. Duplex est pulcritudo, scilicet nature, quam sic notificat Augustinus:
"Pulcritudo est uiuidus color et elegans dispositio membrorum". Et est pulcritudo,
scilicet competens ordinatio exemplaris in mente artificis. Talis pulcritudo ordinat
causam ad effectum, et talis pulcritudo ex parte cause ponit aliquid pulcritudinis in
40   effectu, et ideo bene ualet argumentum.

Postea obicitur quod hic dicitur, quod philosophi cognouerunt trinitatem, uel
cognoscere potuerunt per creaturas. Creature enim non referuntur ad deum in
quantum pater uel filius uel spiritus sanctus, set in quantum diuina essentia, quia
creature sunt a deo non in quantum pater, set in quantum essentia, ergo per
45   creaturas non potest intelligi trinitas, set tantum unitas essentie.

Item. Cognitio trinitatis solum est per fidem. Set philosophi non habuerunt
fidem, ergo non cognouerunt trinitatem per creaturas neque per rationes.

Item. In Exo iii quod magi defecerunt in tertio, et glose dicunt "idest in cognitione spiritus sancti", ergo non cognouerunt spiritum sanctum, ergo pari ratione nec
50   patrem, neque filium; uel dicas quare potius hoc dicatur de spiritu sancto quam de
patre et filio.

---

30 quomodo P] quod B   30 facit *p*B] facies P facit hoc *s*B   32 argumentum B] *om.* P   33 refert]
quod *add.* B   35 ita P] ideo B   35 argumentum] uel species quali uel quanto qualiscumque species
communis ad quanti et quali qualemcumque, set pulcritudo creatur a quali et quanto decenti, ut patet
in eius notificatione, unde species communis quam pulcritudo, et ita differunt et species et causa illud
creatum, pulcritudo enim creatur a quali et quanto decenti *add.* B.   36 sic P] *om.* B   37 uiuidus
B] inuidus P   42 creature P*s*B] creatore *p*B   44 pater] etc. *add.* B   44 in quantum *marg.* B
46 set tantum unitas essentie. Item cognitio trinitatis *marg.* B   48 Exo iii] legitur *add. et iter.*
marg. B   48 in tertio] singno (!) *add.* B   48 glose dicunt P] glossa dicit B   49 nec P] neque B

---

32 argumento : cf. *supra*, l. 19-20.   32 tertium argumentum : cf. *supra*, l. 17.   36 Augustinus :
cf. Aug., *civ.* XXII, 19, ed. Dombart - Kalb, CCSL 48, p. 838, PL 41, 781: "Omnis enim corporis pul-
chritudo est partium congruentia cum quadam coloris suauitate".   41 hic dicitur : cf. Petr. Lomb.,
sent. I, d. 3, 1. 7, ed. PP. Collegii S. Bonauenturae, p. 71²⁰⁻²⁶.   48 Exo iii : recte Ex 8, 14.   48 glose
dicunt : cf. Pseudo-Petrus Pictaviensis, *Glossa in* I Sententiarum, d. 3, 1, ms. *Napoli, Bibl. Naz. VII*
C 14, f. 5ʳᵇ: "Set ad notitiam tertie persone pertingere non potuerunt, quod signatum est in eo quod
magi Pharaonis in tertio signo defecerunt. Nam cum mutasset Moyses uirgam in serpentem, aquas
in sanguinem, hoc magi fecerunt; set sciniphes de puluere facere non potuerunt".

Solutio. Philosophi uno modo habuerunt cognitionem de trinitate non proprie,
set confuse, idest indistincte, idest non in quantum persone sunt distincte quomodo fideles christiani nouerunt, set quia nouerunt potentiam dei per magnitudinem
P 5rb rerum, sapientiam per pulcritudinem, | bonitatem per gubernationem et conser-   55
uationem. Ob hoc dicitur quod cognitionem trinitatis habuerunt, et quia per illa
trinitas cognosci poterat.

Quare autem dicantur in cognitione spiritus sancti defecisse, hoc ideo est quia
bonitas spiritui sancto tribuitur, et ipsi defecerunt in potissimo effectum bonitatis,
scilicet incarnatione filii quam non nouerunt, unde Augustinus: "Inueni in philoso-   60
phis scriptum "in principio erat uerbum et uerbum erat apud deum", set numquam
inueni "uerbum caro factum est"".

Item. Obicitur contra iamdicta quod philosophus Mercurius intellexit trinitatem proprie et distincte. Dicit enim ipse Mercurius: "Monas monadem genuit, et
in se suum reflectit ardorem", quod Augustinus exponit ita: "Pater filium genuit";   65
reliquum quod sequitur de processione spiritus sancti intellegitur.

Solutio. Potest dici quod hoc sciuit per inspirationem, non per creaturas, uel
potest dici quod dixit, set non intellexit uirtutem dicti, sicut de Caypha dicitur.

<ii>

Item. Obicitur quod in littera dicitur, quod memoria, intelligentia et uoluntas
idem sunt in essentia. Potentie cognoscuntur et diuersificantur per suos actus, set   70
actus memorandi et aliorum duorum sunt diuersi in specie, ergo potentie diuerse.

Ad hoc soluunt quidam et dicunt quod sunt diuerse, set dicuntur et sunt eiusdem essentie, quia insunt eidem essentie, scilicet anime. Set contra. Pari ratione
passiones et habitus et potentie dicentur eiusdem essentie cum sint in anima, et
hoc falsum.   75

Preterea. Memoria etc. aut sunt in anima accidentaliter, aut essentialiter. Si
accidentaliter, ergo anima potest intelligi esse preter hec. Set idem est ratio quod
intelligentia et uoluntas et memoria, ergo anima potest intelligi sine rationali, et hoc

---

53 idest P] scilicet B   53 non P] om. B   56 habuerunt P] hueruerunt B   59 tribuitur P]
attribuitur B   61 et uerbum erat apud deum marg. P   65 exponit ita P] ita exponit B   69 quod
in littera dicitur PpB] de hoc quod dicitur in littera sB   73 insunt iter. marg. B

---

60 Augustinus : cf. Aug., civ. X, 29, ed. Dombart - Kalb, CCSL 47, pp. 306-307, PL 41, 309.   61 in
principio... : Io 1, 1.   62 uerbum caro factum est : Io 1, 14.   64 Mercurius : cf. Ps.-Herm., vig.
quat. phil. II, 1, ed. Hudry, CCCM 143 a, p. 35; Alan. de Ins., theol. reg., 3, PL 210, 624 C.
65 Augustinus : cf. Vigil. Taps., de unit. Trin., c. 11, PL 42, 1165.   68 de Caypha dicitur : cf. Ioh
11, 49-52; Aug., c. Faust. XVI, 23, ed. Zycha, CSEL 25. 6, pp. 466-467, PL 42, 331.   70 Potentie...
suos actus : cf. Arist., somn. et vig., 1, ed. Siwek, p. 173[9] (Bekker: 454a): "Cuius est potentia, eius
quoque est actus"; de pot. an. et ob., ed. Callus, p. 148[3-5]; Philipp., sum. de bon., ed. Wicki,
p. 1046[207-210]: "...in naturalibus cognoscitur potentia secundum actus et per potentias essentia"; cf.
infra, anonymus, Si anima est sue potentie, p. 205, l. 34.   72 quidam : cf. Guill. Altissiod., sum.
aur. II, t. 9, 1. 6, ed. Ribaillier, I, p. 243[76-81].

falsum. Si essentialiter, ergo sunt idem in essentia quod anima, ergo et idem erunt
in essentia, non ergo diuersa.

Preterea. Secundum hunc modum aut sunt unita anime, aut non. Si non, ergo
faciunt unum et sunt idem | in essentia quod anima, ergo anima est plura, siue tria.   B 5ʳᵃ
Si unita, illud aut est anima, aut aliud. Si anima, ergo idem sunt cum anima, et ita
inter se idem in essentia. Set illud non est anima, ergo hoc est contra id quod postea
dicitur in littera, quod ipsa sunt essentialiter in anima. Et preterea sequeretur quod
essent eadem in essentia cum illo quicquid illud esset, et ita etiam ipsa essent idem
in essentia, non ergo diuersa.

Solutio. Memoria quandoque dicitur pro actu memorandi, et ita de aliis duobus, et secundum hoc sunt diuersa; quandoque pro obiectis, idest pro memorato et
uolito et intellecto, et secundum hoc idem possunt esse in essentia. Diuersa autem
erunt in ratione quandoque pro potentia. Et sic eadem in essentia, diuersa accidente siue relatione. Et idem sunt in essentia quod anima. Hec enim est uera "anima
est memoria": sensus enim est "anima habet potentiam memorandi", et ita de aliis
duobus.

*Apostolus namque ait*₆₈, ₂₁₋₂₂, Ro i. Illud 'namque' refertur ad proximum quod
precessit; *inuisibilia dei*₆₈, ₂₂, idest pater, ut patet Ad Hebreos i₃ "Qui cum splen-
dor" etc., "uerba uirtutis sue portansque omnia"; *uirtus*, idest filius, *diuinitas*, idest
spiritus sanctus.

<iii>

*Qua excellit inter alias creaturas*₆₉, ₂₋₃: et hoc uidetur quia optimus homo melior optimo angelo, ergo simpliciter homo angelo. Contra. In Mat 11₁₁: "Inter natos
mulierum non surrexit maior Iohanne Baptista. | Qui autem", scilicet angelus, "mi-   P 5ᵛᵃ
nor est in regno celorum, maior est illo". Ergo minor angelus melior est optimo
homine.

Item. "Minuisti eum paulo minus ab angelis"; si ergo Christus minor est angelis,
ergo quilibet alius homo. Set huic est contrarium Ad He i₄: "Tanto melior angelis
effectus quanto <differentius> pre illis nomen hereditavit".

---

79 ergo et inter se ipsa hec tria, scilicet *add. marg.* B   79 idem erunt P] erunt idem B   82 est
interl. B   84 ergo P] *om.* B   85 in littera *iter. marg.* B   88 dicitur P] sumitur B   95 Ro i]
ait B   95 refertur P] *om.* B   96 precessit] continuatur *add. marg.* B   97 uerba B] uerbali P
97 portansque *scripsi cum Vulg.*] quia BP   99 et P] ex B   99 et hoc uidetur quia optimus homo
melior est optimo angelo *iter. marg.* B   100 homo] homo melior est *add. marg.* B   100 angelo]
simpliciter *add.* P   101–102 scilicet angelus minor B] minor scilicet angelus P   102 est B] *om.* P
102 maior est] uel *add. sed del.* B   102 illo B] eo P   102 minor PsB] minus *p*B   103 homine
duplex opinio est... tantum hac utuntur ratione *hic posuit* B   104 Minuisti eum paulo minus P]
palo minus minuisti eum B   104 est *interl.* B

---

104 Minuisti eum... : He 2, 7.

Solutio. Patet quod homo excellit non tantum omnes, nec dicit in littera 'omnes', set indefinite 'inter alias'; uel potest dici quod homo secundum quid, idest secundum animam, est dignior omnibus creaturis, nec omnis anima, set alique. Et hoc non secundum sui naturam, set per gratiam, ut in matre domini, uel per unionem 110 deitatis, ut in Christo. Nec sequitur "optimus homo" etc., "ergo simpliciter"; regula Aristotelis sic intelligitur: "si optimus in quantum talis", etc.

Duplex opinio est.

Dicit una quod angelus simpliciter dignior omni anima quantum ad naturam anime, quia aliqua dignior omni angelo, hoc est ab alio, non per naturam anime. 115

Alia opinio dicit quod anima simpliciter dignior omni angelo, quia aliqua anima <est dignior omni angelo>.

Set notandum quod anima potest considerari secundum statum, idest secundum quod corpori est alligata, et sic non est dignior; uel secundum naturam, et sic dignior. Ex eo enim quod aliqua anima plus de gratia accipit a domino quam aliquis 120 angelus, probabile est quod meliora et subtiliora naturalia habuit. Set non est necessarium: sicut etiam in uas indignius posset plus mitti de oleo quam in nobilius. Tamen hac utuntur ratione.

***

Scilicet a natura$_{69,\,6}$, idest a ratione; *ut per certum*$_{69,\,15}$ sensui si deus uel trinitas.

Ex perpetuitate creaturarum$_{70,\,13\text{-}14}$, quia ex eo quod creature principium ha- 125 buerunt intelligitur creator esse sine principio. Et hoc probari potest: constat quod creature ab aliquo fuerunt. Illud autem habuit principium, aut non, et sic usque in infinitum, uel uenitur ad id quod est sine principio.

Dum fecit opera$_{69,\,8}$, per rerum magnitudinem potentia, per pulcritudinem sapientia, per conseruationem bonitas relucet, et ita habes uestigium trinitatis. *Vt* 130 *deus omnium*$_{69,\,11\text{-}13}$: hic elicitur primum argumentum. *Alio etiam modo*$_{69,\,21\text{-}22}$:

---

107 tantum B] tamen P   107 creaturas excellit, nec hoc dicit in littera quod *marg.* B   108 aliquas B] alias P   110 non secundum sui naturam P*p*B] non sui natura *s*B   112 Aristotelis] *marg.* B; enim illa *add.* B   113 duplex] super hoc *add. marg.* B   114 dicit una P] una dicit B   114 quantum] est de natura sui *add. marg.* B   114 ad *del.* B   115 anime] quod autem *add.* B   115 quia P*p*B] anima *s*B   115 ab alio] scilicet per gratia uel per unitione diuinitatis, ut anima Christi *add. marg.* B   118 notandum P] notatur B   120 domino P] deo B   121 quod B] quia P   121 naturalia habuit] secundum illud Mat$_{25,\,15}$: "Dedit unicuique propriam ui<rtutem>", sicut dicitur etiam de angelis *add. marg.* B   121 naturalia *marg.* P   121 habuit P*p*B] habeat *s*B   123 tamen P] tantum B   124 per certum *scripsi cum Petr. Lomb.*] preceptum PB   124 sensui] increatum sensui *add.* B   124 trinitas] istud quantum dicat linea d ad insignum intrat *add. marg.* B   125 quod B] *om.* P   126–127 quod creature ab aliquo fuerunt illud autem B] *om.* P   128 uenitur P*s*B] inuenitur *p*B   129 rerum B] rei P

hic elicitur secundum argumentum. Et procedit hic Augustinus ut Pitagoras, qui in aurea cathena inferius ponit inanimata, secundo uegetata, tertio bruta, quarto rationalia, et per istorum omnium remotionem intelligit deum esse.

135   *Considerauerunt etiam quicquid est in substantiis*$_{69, 31\text{-}32}$ etc. Set accidentia sunt in substantiis, ergo sunt corpus uel spiritus. | Solutio. In substantiis, idest in numero substantiarum siue de numero. Et hic ponitur tertium argumentum.   B 5rb

Intellexerunt etiam corporis speciem$_{70, 1\text{-}2}$, idest pulcritudinem. Hic sumitur iiii argumentum.

140   *Ideo que incorporalis*cf. $_{70, 8}$, idest incorruptibilis: nunc restat querere utrum per ea que secundum (distinctio iii), *arte diuina*$_{70, 23}$, idest sapientia patris que est filius; *et speciem*$_{70, 24}$, idest formam; *et ordinem*$_{70, 24}$, idest statum; *nature corporum*$_{70, 25\text{-}26}$, hoc legitur intransitiue; *que uisu*$_{70, 3}$ etc.: per hoc duos sensus omnes alii intelliguntur; *ordinem aliquem petit*$_{70, 27\text{-}28}$, idest proprium locum, cum est extra

145   proprium; *aut tenet*$_{70, 28}$, cum est in proprio loco; *sicut sunt pondera*$_{70, 28}$, pondus est impetus rei tendentis ad proprium locum, unde hoc pertinet ad hoc quod dicit 'petit'; *uel locationes*$_{70, 28}$: hoc pertinet ad 'tenet'$_{70, 28}$; *amores*$_{70, 29}$: hoc pertinet ad 'petit'. Anima enim ex amore petit iungi deo; *uel delectationes*$_{70, 29}$, hoc ad 'tenet'. | Cum enim delectatur in deo anima, tunc ei coniuncta est, et ibi tenet pro-   P 5vb

150   primum locum. *Filius*$_{71, 1}$ scilicet *ueritas*$_{71, 2}$ patris, quia loquitur ipsum uere ut est, et equalis est illi sicut sermo uerus, quia ita est in re, ut dicit et ueritas «adequatio mentis cum re». *Quam cum ipso*$_{71, 2}$, ut alium aput alium ut diuerse persone; *et in ipso patre*$_{71, 2\text{-}3}$, ut eiusdem essentie; *que forma est*$_{71, 3}$, idest exemplar; *ab uno facta*$_{71, 3}$, idest a patre; *ad unum referuntur*$_{71, 3\text{-}4}$, naturaliter.

155   *Neque suis finibus salua essent*$_{71, 4\text{-}5}$, idest intra terminos sue existentie stabi-

---

132 alio etiam modo hic elicitur secundum argumentum B] om. P   132 hic Augustinus P] Augustinus hic B   133 uegetata P*p*B] uegetabilia *s*B   134 istorum omnium P] omnium istorum B   137 ponitur P] ponit B   143 legitur P] lege B   143 duos sensus P] sensus duos B   145 proprium] locum *add.* B   147 pertinet ad] hoc quod dicit *add.* B   147 hoc P] om. B   147–148 ad hoc quod dicit tenet; amores pertinet ad *marg.* B   152 alium] et *add.* B

---

132 Augustinus : cf. Aug., *civ.* VIII, 6, ed. Dombart - Kalb, CCSL 47, p. 222, PL 41, 231. 132 Pitagoras : cf. Macr., *in somn. Scip.* I, 14, 15, ed. Willis, p. 58^{11}; Pseudo-Petrus Pictaviensis, *Glossa in* I Sententiarum, d. 3, 1, ms. *Napoli, Bibl. Naz. VII C 14*, f. 4vb: "Sic per consideratione creaturarum peruenerunt philosophi ad cognitionem creatoris considerantes quemlibet corpus esse uel spiritum et neutrum horum esse deum. Hec fuit aurea catena Pytagore, quam constituit ex iiii machinis: primo ponit inanimata, secundo animata bruta, tertio rationalia, quarto per remotionem singulorum perpendebat deum esse"; Guill. de Conch., *gl. super Plat.*, 74, ed. Jeauneau, CCCM 203, p. 129$^{7\text{-}9}$; cf. A. Lovejoy, *The Great Chain of Being: A Study of the History of an Idea*, Harvard University Press, Cambridge 1961, pp. 24-98; B. McGinn, *The Golden Chain. A Study in the Theological Anthropolgy of Isaac of Stella*, Cistercian Publications, Washington D.C. 1972 (Cistercian Studies Series, 15), pp. 70-102.   151–152 adequatio mentis cum re : cf. Auic., *metaph.* I, 4, ed. Van Riet, p. 55$^{58\text{-}60}$; Guill. Altissiod., *sum. aur.* I, 12, 3, ed. Ribaillier, p. 228$^{40\text{-}41}$; cf. J. T. Muckle, "Isaac Israeli's Definition of Truth", *AHDLMA* 1 (1933), pp. 5-8; G. Schulz, *Veritas est adequatio intellectus et rei. Untersuchungen zur Wahrheitsbegriff*, Leiden: Brill, 1993, *passim*; J. Woleński, "Izaak Israeli i Tomasz z Akwinu o prawdzie", *Studia Judaica* 8 (2005), pp. 5-13.

lita non remanerent, nisi deus sua bonitate ea seruaret in esse. Termini cuiuslibet creature sunt nichil, et nichil quia omnis creatura de nichilo facta est et in nichil rediret, nisi deus eam inter terminos, idest in esse.

*Inuidit et dedit*cf. 71, 6-7 etc. *Alia quantum uellet*71, 6-7, quoad rationalia hoc dicit. Homo enim manet in bono quantum, idest quamdiu, uult, quia nemo aufert sibi gratiam quamdiu uult, et ita 'quantum' est temporale; uel aliter, ut sit quantitatiuum.

*Quantum uellet*71, 6-7, uoluntate coniuncta actui et dilectioni, idest quantum actu diligunt uel operantur, aliter esset falsum, quod ibi dicitur. Multi enim uolunt esse ualde boni uoluntate remota ab actu, nec tamen sunt.

*Alia quantum posset*71, 7, hoc quoad irrationalia, que secundum naturam manent quantum possunt, idest donec deus subtrahit conseruationem ab eis; *donum*71, 8, non datum, set donabilis. Non enim spiritus sanctus datus est ab eterno. *A quo sumus*71, 12: 'a quo' significat auctoritatem, et connotat esse a nullo, quod soli patri conuenit per operationem, et conuenit esse ab alio, et hoc filio in conseruationem, et conuenit esse ab aliis, et hoc spiritui sancto.

*Tertio*71, 25, Exo iiii; *signo*71, 25, quod fuit signum et plaga; *in mente*71, 29, idest in sinderesi; *sit particeps*72, 4, per gratiam; *eius ymago*72, 4-5, reperitur, scilicet in naturalibus. *Iam ergo in ea*72, 7, scilicet mente; *et quicquid aliud ad se*72, 20-21, etc., idest quicquid dicitur absolute, et singulariter et essentialiter de qualibet per se, et simul de omnibus singulariter.

*Memoria*72, 30 etc. Non sunt proprie relatiua, set dicuntur relatiua, quia memoria est uoliti et econtrario, et sic de aliis. Et notatur quod hic memoria sumitur communiter prout est de presentibus, preteritis et futuris. *Quod enim memorie mee non memini*72, 31, idest cuius memoria mea non meminit; uel sic: id memorie mee quod, idest cuius, non memini. *Illud non est*72, 31-32 etc. *Quam ipsa memoria*72, 32, idest ipsa memorata, quia ipsa memorata per se sunt in memoria, uolita uero per accidens.

*Quicquid per intelligibilium*cf. 73, 5-6 etc. Hic fit distributio pro bonis tantum, aliter esset instantia ut in peccato, et hoc patet per uerba in littera que dicit: *Voluntas etiam nostra totam intelligentiam meam, totamque memoriam meam capit, dum utor toto eo quod intelligo et memini*73, 8-10. Ecce dicit 'utor', set utimur tantum bonis, aliorum enim abusio est.

***

158 in esse conseruaret *add. marg.* B   160 nemo B] *om.* P   162 uoluntate B] quantitate P   164 tamen P] tantum B   166 possunt idest *marg.* B   167 donabilis B] donans P   168 connotat *iter.* B   169 conuenit PpB] connotat sB   171 in] idest *praem.* BP   171 idest in *om.* P   178 est *marg.* B   180 memini] memoria......presentibus, preteritis et futuris *hic posuit* P   181 ipsa PsB] ipsea pB   183 tantum P] *om.* B   184 ut *del.* B   184 in littera *iter. marg.* B   185 nostra B] mea P

184 dicit : cf. Aug., *trin.* X, 11. 18, ed. Mountain, CCSL 50, p. 330, PL 42, 984.

*Hic attendendum*₇₃, ₂₂ etc. Ostendit magister autem trinitatem increatam per creatam, scilicet per memoriam, intellectum et uoluntatem.

190 Et hoc triplici similitudine: <1> prima | fuit quia | sicut ista una essentia, una uita, et tantum ad se referuntur, ita pater et filius et spiritus sanctus. Et sicut ista equalia, quia sicut memoria intelligentia et uoluntate, ita econtrario, et de singulis sic est, sic et ibi est. <2> Item. Hic nichil maius aut minus, quia memoria capit totum intellectum et econtrario, et ita de singulis, scilicet memorata in aliis, intellecta et

195 uolita. <3> *Et quicquid est in memoria*cf. 72, 33-73, 1 est in aliis et econtrario, et sic etiam ibi nichil maius uel minus.

Set quia dixerat quod memoria etc. sunt una essentia et una uita, et quia hoc dubium est, ideo consequenter determinat qualiter sunt unum in essentia. Et dicit quod ideo quia substantialiter exsistunt in anima. Et ideo, ne propter predicta

200 crederetur omnino similitudo trinitatis increate et create, ideo subiungit triplicem dissimilitudinem: <1> prima est quod tres persone sunt in deo ita quod etiam sint deus; set predicta tria sunt, scilicet memoria etc., ita quod non sunt homo. <2> Secunda differentia est trinitatis increate ad continens trinitatem creantem, non ad trinitatem creatam: et est talis deus trinitas, non est una persona; set continens tri-

205 nitatem creatam est unus homo. <3> Tertia est inter trinitates: ille tres sunt unus deus, et non unius dei; set ille tres sunt unius hominis, non unus homo.

<iv>

Set queritur quare tres persone non dicantur unius dei? Hec est uera 'sunt unius essentie' quia sunt una essentia, ita uidetur uerum esse 'sunt unius dei', quia sunt unus deus.

210 Quidam soluunt addentes hanc dictionem 'tantum', ut fit sensus 'non unius dei tantum, set quia etiam sunt deus'. Alii dicunt: quamuis uerum sit dicere quod sint unius dei, tamen propter errorem qui posset ibi elici non conceditur, et hoc propter diuersam constructionem aliquando nominis concretiui et abstractiui in genitiuo casu. Cum enim dicitur 'tres persone sunt unius essentie', constructio fit in

215 indemptitate essentie, idest sunt una essentia. Set cum dicitur 'deus Habraham', in habitudine cause efficientis, idest est creator ipsius Habrahe. Ita aliqui uellent intel-

---

188 autem B] ante P   191 ista P] ita B; sunt *add. marg.* B   192 memoria] in *add. interl.*
B   192 intelligentia] est *add.* B   192 et] in *add.* B   193 sic B] set P   195 est in B] et in P
199 exsistunt PsB] exsistentia *p*B   199 ideo P] *om.* B   201 dissimilitudinem] magister *add.* B
202 ita] sunt in homine *add. marg.* B   204 creatam] sicut prius *add.* B   205 unus homo] et
una persona *add. marg.* B   205 est inter P] *om.* P   207 queritur P] obicitur B   207 hec est uera
P] hoc est uerum B   208 una P] una *om.* B   208 quia sunt unus P] quia unus B   211 quamuis
PsB] quam *p*B   212 tamen P] tantum B   213 aliquando *del.* B   215 in] constructio fit *praem.*
B   216 est *marg.* B   216 ita P] sic B

---

211 alii : cf. Steph. Langt., *in* I *Sent.*, 34, ed. Landgraf, p. 46; cf. Quinto, "Stephen Langton", pp.
62-64.

ligere 'tres persone unius dei', idest create et increate ab uno deo. Set si constructio intelligatur intransitiue, uera est ut hec: 'creatura salis'.

***

Postea per aliam trinitatem creatam ostendit trinitatem increatam, nec est su-perflua propter primam, quia per aliam similitudinem quam prius idem ostendit: ista trinitas est mens, notitia sui ipsius et amor.

<1> Prima similitudo huius trinitatis ad aliam est quia, sicut nascitur de mente notitia – ut si mens reflectatur super se ipsam, sciet quid: quia ymago dei est, a quo est et ad quem finem est –, et amor sui ipsius procedit ex illis – scilicet mente et notitia sui ipsius –, ita et filius a patre et spiritus sanctus ab utroque. <2> Secunda similitudo quia sicut equalitas etc. <3> Tertia est quia sicut ista mutuo sunt in se ipsis, ita et ille tres persone.

<v>

Set obicitur quod dicit quod memoria, intelligentia et uoluntas substantialiter siue essentialiter sunt in anima, ergo uel sicut superius in inferiori (et patet quod hoc falsum); uel tanquam partes integrales in toto; uel tanquam partes essentiales, ut forme essentiales insunt. Si primo modo, ille | partes aut sunt unite in anima, aut non. Si non, ergo anima est plura. Si sic, ergo anima est totum integrale, ergo composita naturaliter, ergo corruptibilis. Si secundo modo, iterum quero: aut sunt unita, aut non. Si non, ergo anima est plura; et uidetur quod non possunt uniri, quia tres perfectiones in uno numero uniri non possunt. Si dicat quod illa tria sunt unum in essentia, adhuc quero: aut est unitum, aut non. Si non, ergo ut prius. Si sic, aut anime, aut alii. Si alii, non ergo substantialiter sunt in anima. Si anime, ergo sunt forma perfectiua anime, ergo anima composita est ex materia et forma, ergo corruptibilis, quia omne compositum corruptibile.

Quod autem dicuntur tria, hoc est secundum quod referuntur ad se inuicem uel secundum quod comparantur ad tres actus suos diuersos.

P 6rb

---

217 increate P] causate B   218 uera P] uerum B   219 trinitatem increatam] *marg.* B   219 nec] trini etc. *praem. sed del.* B   220 per] aliquam *add. p*B ; quamdam *add. s*B   222 huius trinitatis ad aliam est *iter. marg.* B   223 quid *del.* B   224 et] ita *add. interl.* B   224 scilicet mente P] mente scilicet B   226 quia sicut equalitas etc.] quia sicut inter personas increatas est equalitas, ita inter ista tria *marg.* B   226 mutuo P*s*B] muto *p*B   228 intelligentia P] et intellectus B   231 unite P*s*B] unitate *p*B   232 aut P*s*B] ut *p*B   232 totum integrale P] integrale totum B   233 composita P] conponitur B   236 quero aut] id *add.* P   237 si alii *marg.* B   240 quod] ad hoc dicunt quidam *add. marg.* B   240 autem P] hec B   240 tria B] *om.* P

Set obicitur: ex quo sunt idem in essentia cum anima, quomodo ergo sunt ipsa in anima? Respondent quod sunt per modum ydemptitatis, uel per modum forme, ut trinitas est in unitate.

245   Solutio. Hic est triplex opinio.

Vna dicit ista tria idem sunt in essentia quod anima, et hii negant animam compositam esse, scilicet ex forma substantiali et materia. Set dicunt ibi esse compositionem concretionis, scilicet accidentis cum subiecto.

Alia dicit quod illa tria forma essentialis et perfectiua anime per quam agit id
250   quod agit, sicut ignis per igneitatem diuersa facit. Et ita ponunt animam compositam ex materia et forma spiritualibus. Quod autem obicitur "omne com | positum   B 5^{vt}
est corruptibile", distingunt hanc, quia potest esse sensus "est corruptibile", idest "habet in se principium corruptionis", scilicet contrarietatem, et sic falsa: supercelestia enim, que non sunt composita ex contrariis elementis, non sic sunt corrupti-
255   bilia; uel potest esse sensus "est corruptibile", idest "non habet principium conseruationis sui in esse", et sic uera est, quia omne quod est, quantum in se, tendit ad non esse.

Tertia dicit quod iste tres potentie insunt per modum accidentis ipsi anime. Et dicunt quod potest esse ipsius anime perfectiuum deus inmediate: indidit ei quan-
260   dam uirtutem per quam potest diuersa, nec illa uirtus est anima, nec ille potentie, immo anima, ut spiritus quidam, siue ut substantia spiritualis, potest intelligi preter illa. Simile est in saphiro uel adamante, cui insita est uirtus per quam potest diuersa. Et ipsi ponunt animam simplicem, quia non est facta ex preiacenti materia.

Set istis obicitur: hoc quod hic dicitur "quia substantialiter insunt anime" sic
265   exponunt, idest "naturaliter" uel "inseparabiliter per modum substantialis", quia immediate post creationem anime insunt ei potentie, et sunt naturales anime.

**

Iuxta proprietatem sermonis$_{73,\ 25}$, idest iuxta significatum horum nominum, 'memoria', 'intellectiua' et 'uoluntas' que diuersa sunt, et per hoc uidentur esse diuersa. Et hoc est contra primam opinionem. *Et hec tria etiam ad se ipsa referun-*

---

242 obicitur] eis *add.* B   242–243 ipsa in P] in ipsa B   243 quod] non *add. sed del.* P   243 sunt P] insunt B   243 insunt per modum idemptitatis *add. marg.* B   246 dicit] quod *add. marg.* B 249 tria] sunt *add. marg.* B   250 id quod agit P] *om.* B   253 et *del.* B   253 sic] est *add. interl.* B   254 contrariis elementis P] elementis contrariis B   254 sic *del.* B   254–255 corruptibilia *iter. marg.* B   255 non habet] in se *add.* B   256 uera P] uerum B   256 quod est] quia de nihilo *add. marg.* B   258 per modum P*s*B] per medium *p*B   259 potest esse P*p*B] potissimum *s*B 259 perfectiuum P*s*B] perfectiuus *p*B   259 deus] est *praem.* B   259 inmediate] qui *add.* B 260 potentie P*s*B] potest *p*B   262 saphiro uel P] *om.* B   262 adamante P*s*B] adampnante *p*B 263 ipsi P] isti B   264 anime P*s*B] anima *p*B   266 potentie et sunt P] et sunt potentie B

---

264 hic dicitur : cf. Petr. Lomb., *sent.* I, d. 3, 1. 6, ed. PP. Collegii S. Bonaventurae, p. 74$^{5-8}$; Aug., *trin.* IX, 4. 5, ed. Mountain, CCSL 50, p. 297, PL 42, 963.

tur$_{73, 29-30}$: ista relatio est inseparabilitas. Non enim sunt relatiua que substantialia   270
sunt, set quia unum non potest esse sine alio, quod est consequens relatiuorum siue
ad relatiua, unde ponitur hic antecedens pro consequenti.

    Nisi etiam nouerit se$_{73, 31-32}$: Augustinus super Io xii "ut credo" dicit: "Nunc
uisos possumus diligere, ignotos uero non". *Cum et*$_{74, 2}$, idest quamuis; *quia si rela-*

P 6va *tiue*$_{74, 9}$, dicitur enim memoria | intellectorum uel uolitorum, quia non in quantum   275
intellecta uel uolita, set in quantum memorata, et ita de aliis: Sortes dicitur pater
Platonis non in quantum Plato, set in quantum filius.

    Naturaliter diuinitus in mente instituta$_{74, 13}$, idest ad ymaginem dei condita,
et ideo potest inuestigare diuina. *Recoli*$_{74, 15}$, per memoriam; *conspici*$_{74, 15}$, per
intelligentiam; *concupisci*$_{74, 15}$, per uolunatatem.   280

    Aliud est itaque trinitas$_{74, 28}$, scilicet increata; *in re alia*$_{74, 28-75, 1}$, quam sit ipsa,
scilicet in homine.

    Non propter ea $_{75, 18}$, scilicet tantum; *ac diligit se*$_{75, 19}$, quia ratione duce agno-
scit a quo sit et quid sit et ad quid sit, et ideo diligit se. Hic innuitur quod trinitas
creata, que est in mente, dicitur ymago increate non ideo tantum quia una substan-   285
tia sunt et quia equalia sibi sunt et quia anima per illa se intelligit, diligit, meminit,
set etiam ideo quia per illam trinitatem creatam mens ipsa potest intelligere deum
et meminisse et diligere. Simile enim simili intelligitiur, et simile sibi simile amat et
appetit. Memoria etiam non fit nisi in precedenti apprehensione, apprehensio autem per asimilationem. Et hoc supra tactum est in illis uerbis Augustini "quisquis   290
uiuaciter perspicit" etc. Hoc enim magnum est quod anima habet in se quo potest
intelligere deum et diligere et memorare et appetere.

    Amat se, manet trinitas$_{75, 27-28}$, creata que est ymago increate; *substantialiter
exsistunt*$_{75, 31-32}$, idest naturaliter quia anima naturaliter se diligit et cognoscit.

    Cum se cognoscit$_{76, 3}$, idest intuetur: consequens pro antecedente, aliter ibi esset   295

B 6ra nugatio; *et est sola parens*$_{cf. 76, 3}$, sicut solus pater genuit | filium; *qui de ipsa*$_{76, 4}$,
istud 'de' equiuoce ponitur hic. Aliter enim amor procedit de mente, et aliter de
notitia: primum 'de' notat <causam materialem>, secundum causam efficientem.

---

270 que P*p*B] quia *s*B   275 intellectorum *iter. marg.* B   275 uolitorum] memoria set tantum
per accidens *add.* B   275 non *interl.* B   276 aliis] sicut *add. marg.* B   278 in mente *om.*
P   280 intelligentiam B] intellectum P   281 aliud P*s*B] et *p*B; ad *add.* P   283 quam sit ipsa
scilicet in homine non propter ea B] *om.* P   284 et quid sit P] *om.* B   286 diligit B] *om.* P
289 etiam B] et P   289 in P*p*B] cum *s*B   291 uiuaciter P*s*B] uiuant *p*B   291 magnum est P]
magnum B   292 memorare P*p*B] memorari *s*B   293 creata] potest etiam alio modo *add. marg.*
B   293 que est P] est que B   295 esset] ymago *add. sed del.* P   297 enim] esset *add. sed del.*
P   298 secundum P] *om.* B   298 efficientem] 'de mente' enim procedit ut de subiecto in quo est
quasi de causa materiali; 'de notitia' quasi de causa efficienti *add. marg.* B

---

273 Augustinus : Aug., *trin.* XIII, 20, ed. Mountain, CCSL 50 A, p. 419, PL 42, 1036: "Inventum
neminem diligere quod penitus ignorat".   290 Augustini : Aug., *trin.* XV, 20. 39, ed. Mountain,
CCSL 50 A, p. 517, PL 42, 1088; cf. Petr. Lomb., *sent.* I, d. 3, 2, ed. PP. Collegii S. Bonauenturae, p.
74^{13}.

*Nec minor est amor parente*76, 9-10 etc. Contra. Aliquis diligit se magis quam sit diligendus, ergo non equalis amor parenti. Solutio. Loquitur de bene disposito et non peruerso, et talis tantum se diligit quantum debet; uel aliter: duplex est dilectio terrenorum, una quoad corpus, et alia quoad celestia et ad deum; et de hac ultima hic intelligit.

Dum tantam$_{76,\,9}$, sine scilicet elatione; *quanta est*$_{76,\,9}$, ut sit sine pusillanimitate; *quanta est*$_{76,\,9}$, ergo anima habet quantitatem. Solutio. Hoc non est dictum quoad ipsam animam, set quoad ea que circa eam sunt. Anima enim cognoscit se tantam quanta est quando cognoscit a quo est, quia a deo, et quid est, quia est spiritus rationalis capax dei, et ad quid, quia ad fruendum deo. Item. Anima se tantum diligit quantum se nouit et quanta est quando propter deum et ad eterna se diligit, non ad temporalia. Cum enim tendit ad quod creata est (ut sit particeps bonitatis dei), tunc cognoscit totam dignitatem suam et diligit se totam, et ita sunt equalia mens, notitia et amor, quia mens tota cognoscitur, tota diligitur.

Amans in amore$_{76,\,13}$, mens amans in amore, ut formatum in forma secundum quod sunt habitus; uel ut agens in actione secundum fit actus; *et amor in notitia*$_{76,\,13}$, ut effectus in causa; *notitia in mente*$_{76,\,14}$ ut forma in subiecto, uel tanquam in origine secundum quod mens est synderesis.

Tri | nitatem in unitate$_{76,\,19}$: trinitas est in unitate ad modum forme uel per   P 6ᵛ
modum ydemptitatis, uerbi gratia homo consideratus ut similitudo substantialis indiuiduorum inest illis per modum forme, uel si consideretur secundum quod uniuersale eorum, tunc inest illis per modum ydemptitatis. Idem enim uniuersale et particulare, et ita inde(?) notat uel habitudinem quasi formalem, uel habitudinem ydemptitatis in hac "trinitas est in unitate", econtrario est in hac, "unitas est in trinitate".

Quapropter$_{76,\,29}$, quasi diceret quia autoribus et rationibus congruis et similitudinibus ostensa est unitas in trinitate et econtrario.

Qua propter$_{76,\,29}$ etc. *Et rectorem*$_{77,\,2}$, ergo rector est demonium in operibus eorum peruersis. Solutio. Est rector, idest potens cohercere eos a malo, unde Ysa xxvii: "Ponam circulum in naribus tuis". *Set trinitatem*$_{77,\,3}$, scilicet credamus; *una*

---

299 minor est] *aliquid add. interl.* B   300 ergo non] est *add.* P   302 una P] et B   304 quanta est] elatio *add. sed del.* B   306 eam P*p*B] ipsam *s*B   306 sunt] animam *praem.* B   308 est spiritus rationalis *scripsi*] spiritus rationalis est P spiritus rationabilis B   310 enim] anima *add.* B   310 tendit P] attendit B   310 ad quod] quod ad P hoc *add.* B   311 dignitatem suam P] suam dignitatem B   312 quia mens] cum *add. interl.* B   316 synderesis] Extendit se ad contemplationem$_{76,\,18}$, tanquam per ymaginem ad exemplar *add. marg.* B   318 similitudo P*p*B] simulitudino *p*B   320 idem] est *add.* B   328 naribus P*s*B] narribus *p*B

---

308 spiritus rationalis est capax dei : cf. Aug., *trin.* XIV, 8, 11, ed. Mountain, CCSL 50 A, p. 436, PL 42, 1044; Petr. Lomb., *sent.* I, d. 3, 2, ed. PP. Collegii S. Bonaventurae, p. 72$^{6-8}$.   327–328 Ysa xxvii : *recte* Isa 19, 28.

est natura$_{77, 4\text{-}5}$, contrarium hoc; *non una persona*$_{77, 5}$, contra Sabellium; *ueraciter*$_{77, 7}$ etc., quia non esset ibi ternarius essentiarum uel personarum; *rursus*$_{77, 7}$ 330 etc., scilicet si esset alia substantia patris, alia filii, alia spiritus sancti; *hoc autem totum non potest*$_{77, 15}$: contra hoc dixit Sabellius dicens unam personam modo esse patrem, quando uult, modo filium, modo spiritum sanctum.

    <Explicit distinctio tertia>

---

329 contrarium *scripsi*] contrarrium BP   329 hoc] est *add. marg.* B   329 non] hoc *praem.* B   329 contra] hoc est *praem. marg.* B   330 esset PsB] esse *p*B   330 rursus PsB] russus *p*B 331 substantia P] substantialia B   332 Sabellius PsB] Scabellius *p*B

---

329   contra Sabellium : cf. Aug., *civ.* X, 24, ed. Dombart - Kalb, CCSL 47, p. 297, PL 41, 301.

Quesitum est de trinitate anime secundum quam ipsa est imago trinitatis 70rb increate.

<1>

5

Primo utrum illa tria, scilicet memoria, intelligentia et uoluntas, prout sunt imaginis increate, sunt potentie vel actus; uel aliquod eorum actus, reliqua potentia; uel unum actus, cetera potentie.

Si dicat quod sint potentie, contra:

10 <1> potentia id quod est non est ex potentia, ergo potentia id quod est non est proles potentie. Set ista sunt ut ymago trinitatis: intelligentia est proles memorie, ergo saltem intelligentia non est potentia; eadem ratione nec uoluntas, quia ipsa procedit ex utraque.

<2> Item ad idem. Augustinus in libro De trinitate dicit: "Ingenium, doctrina,
15 ususque sunt memoria, intelligentia et uoluntas". Set doctrina uel usus non sunt potentie, ergo nec illa predicta.

<3> Item. Trinitas increata distinguitur uel accipitur secundum actum, cum dicitur "deus meminit se, intelligit se", ergo trinitas creata, si uere est ymago, similiter sumenda est penes actus, et ita redit primum.

20 Si dicat quod sunt actus, contra:

<4> ex actu memorandi non nascitur actus intelligendi, set actus ex sua potentia, ergo <actus intelligendi> non est proles memorie.

<5> Ad idem Augustinus, De spiritu et anima: "Mens habet ymaginem in potentia cognoscendi deum, et similitudinem in potentia diligendi".

---

2 *Douai, Bibliothèque municipale 434*, vol. I, f. 70rb, q. n. 114, Glorieux, "Les 572 Questions", p. 137.   8 unum actus *scripsi*] unum potentia *ms.*   17 actum *scripsi*] actus *ms.*   21 set actus *scripsi*] set potentia *ms.*

---

14 Augustinus in libro De trinitate : X, 11, 17, ed. Mountain, CCSL 50, p. 329, PL 42, 982: "Cum ergo dicuntur haec tria, ingenium, doctrina, usus, primum horum consideratur in illis tribus, quid possit quisque memoria, intelligentia, et voluntate"; cf. Petr. Lomb., *sent.* I, d. 3, 2, ed. PP. Collegii S. Bonaventurae, p. 72¹³⁻¹⁴, PL 192, 531.   18 dicitur : cf. Aug., *trin.* XIV, 8. 11, ed. Mountain, CCSL 50 A, p. 436, PL 42, 1044: "Ecce enim mens meminit sui, intelligit se, diligit se; hoc si cernimus, cernimus Trinitatem, nondum quidem Deum, sed imaginem Dei"; cf. Petr. Lomb., *sent.* I, d. 3, 2, ed. PP. Collegii S. Bonaventurae, p. 72¹⁰⁻¹², PL 192, 531.   23 Augustinus, De spiritu et anima : cf. Ps. Aug., *spir. et an.*, 7, PL 40, 784: "Facta siquidem a Deo mens rationalis, sicut ejus imaginem suscepit, ita cognitionem et amorem".

<6> Item ad idem. Augustinus: "Hec tria naturaliter diuinitus in mente hominis sunt constituta", ergo non sunt actus.

<7> Item. Secundum Augustinum hec trinitas est in puero, quia coeua est nature, ergo non est actuum, set potentiarum. Si uero dicat quod unum est potentia, reliqua uero actus, eadem est obiectio de puero.

<8> Item. Si in equalitate est ibi complexus, non erit alterum actus, alterum potentia, set uel omnia actus, uel omnia potentie.

<9> Item de numero. Si illa tria sunt unum in essentia, ergo non sunt tres potentie.

<10> Item de ordine. Si in trinitate increata nihil prius aut posterius, ergo in creata, que est eius ymago, nihil debet esse prius uel posterius. Item, mutuo referuntur ad se, ergo ibi non est prius uel posterius, ergo neque ordo.

<11> Item. In trinitate increata nulla memoria, quia ibi nulla recordatio preteritorum, ergo in creata, si uere est eius ymago, superfluum est ponere memoriam.

<12> Item. Memoria est intelligentia preteritorum, ergo comprehenditur sub intelligentia sicut species sub genere, ergo non facit numerum cum illa, neque est illi connumerabilis, et ita ibi erit potius binitas quam trinitas.

<13> Item. Dicit Augustinus: "Mens gignit notitiam suam cum se nouit, set non gignit amorem suum cum se amat". Queritur unde hoc. Si dicat quod notitia est proles, quia primo exit a mente, contra dicit Augustinus: "Quidam appetitus precedit partum mentis". Set ille appetitus est amor uel uoluntas, ergo magis debet dici parens mentis amor quam notitia.

<14> Item. Augustinus: "Non dicitur proles quecumque notitia, set notitia cum amore", ergo magis amor proles quam notitia.

<15> Item. Vnus pater plures potest habere filios, cum plures de ipso procedant; quare non similiter mens habebit diuersas proles, scilicet sui notitiam et amorem, cum utrumque de illa procedat?

Solutio. Ponit Augustinus simile de hac generatione et uisione corporali sic: antequam uideam coloratum, color est in subiecto sicut manens. Cum autem dirigo aciem oculi super coloratum, color agit et immutat organum uidendi offerendo se potentie uidendi, et similiter potentia uidendi agit ut sit uisio actus, et sic ex con-

---

46 parens *interl. ms.*

---

25 Augustinus : Aug., *trin.* XV, 20. 39, ed. Mountain, CCSL 50 A, p. 517, PL 42, 1088: "Quae tria in sua mente naturaliter diuinitus instituta quisquis uiuaciter perspicit".   27 secundum Augustinum : cf. Aug., *trin.* X, 11. 17, ed. Mountain, CCSL 50, pp. 329-330, PL 42, 982.   42 Augustinus : cf. Aug., *trin.* IX, 12. 17, ed. Mountain, CCSL 50, p. 308, PL 42, 970: "Cur enim mens notitiam suam gignit cum se nouit, et amorem suum non gignit cum se amat?".   44 Augustinus : Aug., *trin.* IX, 12. 18, ed. Mountain, CCSL 50, p. 310, PL 42, 972: "Partum ergo mentis antecedit appetitus quidam quo id quod nosse uolumus quaerendo et inueniendo nascitur proles ipsa notitia".   47 Augustinus : cf. Aug., *trin.* IX, 12. 18, ed. Mountain, CCSL 50, p. 310, PL 42, 972.   52 Augustinus : cf. Aug., *trin.* VII, 1. 2, ed. Mountain, CCSL 50, pp. 248-249, PL 42, 935-936.

cursu rei uisibilis cum uidente nascitur uisio quasi proles. Et prima est ibi quedam
uoluntas cernendi uel dirigendi aciem oculi cum uisibili uel super uisibile, et sic est
ibi quedam trinitas. Eodem modo est in anima, quia memoria offert se intellectui ex
quo generatur sui notitia, et ex utroque procedit amor sui. Vnde meminisse sui est
60   tenere similitudinem sui apud se, et offerre intellectui ad cognoscendum: sic meminisse dei est tenere similitudinem dei apud se. Necesse uero est in illa similitudine
rem uidere, cogitare, uero eandem rem notam ab aliis notis discernere.

Quod queritur utrum illa tria sint actus uel potentie, responderi potest quod
sunt potentie comparate ad suos actos, uel actus ut sunt in suis potentiis, non dico
65   actu, set prout in suis principiis. Et sic semper ibi sunt, sicut adamas dicitur semper
trahere ferrum, et sic non est obiectio de puero.

<ad 1 et 4> Et bene concedendum est quod potentia non nascitur ex potentia,
set actus bene nascitur ex duobus, scilicet ex sua potentia, sicut uisus ex potentia uidendi, uel ex illo cui assimilatur, sicut uisus ex colore; et hoc secundo modo
70   mens dicitur parens notitie, uel memoria intellectus. Vnde ipsum cognitum ut est
se offerens sic est in memoria, et ex concursu eius oblati cum potentia intelligendi
nascitur intellectus. Vnde si intellectus supra se ipsum reflectatur ad hoc, erit ibi
eadem trinitas, quia intellectus in quantum habet rationem offerentis, quia se sibi
offert, habet rationem memorie; in quantum autem se uidet est intellectus, ex qua
75   <ratione> nascitur intellectus actus.

<ad 10> Quod obicitur "mutuo ad se referuntur, ergo ibi non est ordo", dicimus
quod non ualet, quia et si non sit ibi ordo secundum actus, tamen ibi est ordo secundum modum essendi, sicut in trinitate increata, et si non sit ordo secundum actus, est tamen ordo secundum modum habendi essentiam, quia filius a patre habet
80   essentiam et spiritus sanctus ab utroque.

<ad 9> Quod obicitur de numero, dicendum quod non sequitur "sunt una
essentia, non ergo tres potentie". Instantia: "sunt una essentia, non ergo tres
persone".

<ad 11> Quod autem obicitur "in trinitate increata non est memoria" falsum
85   est, quia ratio memorie, ut hic accipitur, est offerre se, que et si conuenit cuilibet
persone, tamen appropriatur patri, quia ex illa oblatione nascitur intellectus.

<ad 12> Quod obicitur "memoria est solum preteritorum", dicendum quod
ibi memoria accipitur secundum quod est pars prudentie; hic autem aliam habet
rationem, ut dictum est.

90   <ad 13> Item. Ab utroque notitia paritur a cognoscente et cognito. Itaque mens,
cum se ipsam cognoscit, sola parens est notitie sue; cognitor enim et cognitum ipsa

---

62 discernere] Augustinus, De anima et spiritu: "Oculos anime mens, mentis aspectus ratio, intellectus uisio" *marg. ms. et resp. Ps. Aug., spir. et an.* 10 (*PL* 40, 785)   89 ut dictum est] Augustinus
de trinitate ix... quam nouit *hic posuit ms.*

---

66 quod queritur... de puero : cf. p. 201, l. 27.

est (Augustinus, De trinitate ix, capitulo xi): "Omnis secundum speciem notitia similis est ei rei quam nouit".

<ad 14 et 15> Ad aliud dicendum quod notitia <est> proles mentis, non amoris, licet utrumque procedat ex mente, quia cum generatio sit generis sui datio, mens autem et intellectus sint in anima secundum intellectum: patet quod sunt eiusdem generis. Amor tunc est in anima secundum affectum, et ita non exit a mente per modum generationis. Voluntas enim, unumcumque procedat, copulatrix est parentis et prolis, et ideo nec parens, nec proles dici potest; nec est mirum ab eodem esse duo, alterum per modum generationis, reliquum uero alio modo, ut caliditas est in luto a sole per modum generationis et assimilationis, durities autem est in luto a sole non per modum generationis.

95

100

<II>

Postea queritur utrum in anima sit ymago illa trinitatis increate, prout anima actus suos, scilicet memorari et intelligere etc., reflectitur in se, uel prout conuertit eos in deum.

<1> Et secundum quod conuertit se in deum uidetur, quia dicit Augustinus in libro De trinitate xiiii: "Anima non est ymago nisi eius cuius est capax", ergo est ymago secundum quod meminit uel intelligit deum.

<2> Set contra. Illa tria in trinitate increata sunt ibi inuicem equalia, prout in se conuertuntur, ergo similiter et in anima, prout in se conuertuntur eius actus, non prout in deum.

<3> Ad idem. Si uelles fideliter depingere ymaginem Achilli respicientis pedes suos, non depingeres ymaginem Achilli respicientem ad pedes, set magis respicientem ad pedes sui ipsius. A simili si in trinitate increata actus conuertuntur in seipsam, similiter et in trinitate creata conuerti debent in seipsam, ut maior sit adequatio ymaginis et ymaginati.

Solutio. Vt uult Augustinus, anima est proprie ymago in quantum est capax dei, scilicet in quantum meminit, nouit et intelligit summum bonum. Similiter in trinitate increata illa tria sunt secundum conuersionem ad summum bonum, unde deus summe beatus, non quia nouit se uel meminit se etc., set quia meminit et nouit summum bonum. Similiter anima est uere ymago dum meminit, nouit et diligit summum bonum.

Ex hoc facilis est responsio ad obiecta.

105

110

115

120

---

114 Achilli respicientem *ex* respicientem Achilli *corr. ms.*

---

92 Augustinus, De trinitate ix, capitulo xi : IX, 11, 16, ed. Mountain, CCSL 50, p. 308, PL 42, 970. 107–108 Augustinus in libro De trinitate xiiii : XIV, 8, 11, ed. Mountain, CCSL 50, p. 436, PL 42, 1044: "Eo quippe ipso imago eius est quo eius capax est eiusque particeps esse potest, quod tam magnum bonum nisi per hoc quod imago eius est non potest". 118 Augustinus : cf. p. 203, l. 108.

ANONIMI

SI ANIMA EST SUE POTENTIE

Queritur si anima est sue potentie, quod uidetur. In libro De spiritu et anima
dicitur: "Sensus, ymaginatio, ratio, intellectus, intelligentia et huiusmodi omnia in
anima nihil aliud sunt quam ipsa. Alie et alie proprietates propter uaria exercitia,
set una anima; proprietates quidem diuerse, set una essentia; secundum exercitium
multa sunt, secundum essentiam uero unum sunt in anima et quod ipsa".

Item. "Dicitur anima dum uegetat, spiritus dum contemplatur, sensus dum
sentit, mens dum intelligit, ratio dum discurrit, memoria dum recordatur, uoluntas dum consentit. Ista tamen non differunt in substantia quemadmodum in
nominibus, quoniam omnia ista una anima sunt".

Item. "Tota anime substantia in hiis tribus plena et perfecta consistit: in rationabile, concupiscibile, irascibile, quasi quadam sua trinitate. Et tota quidem trinitas
huiusmodi <est> quedam anime unitas et ipsa anima. Deus omnia sua est, anima
quedam sua. Potentie namque eius atque uires idem sunt quod ipsa; <ipsa> sue
uirtutes uel accidentia non est".

Item. Augustinus, ix De trinitate, capitulum iiii: "Admonemur si possumus uidere, hec tria in anima existere substantialiter, uel, ut ita dicam, essentialiter, non
tanquam in subiecto ut color, nec sunt sicut tres partes, nec se habent sicut uinum,
aqua et mel ex quibus fit una potio; non enim sunt unius substantie quamuis ex eis
fiat una substantia. Idem, quomodo ista non sint unius essentie non uideo". Idem
dicit xii capitulo; ix libro, capitulo xi. Item, v capitulo: "Miro itaque modo circa ista

---

3 *Douai, Bibliothèque municipale 434*, vol. I, f. 70rb; q. n. 115, Glorieux, "Les 572 Questions", p.
137.   19 essentialiter *cum Aug. scripsi*] substantialiter *ms.*

---

4 De spiritu et anima : Ps. Aug., *spir. et an.*, 4, PL 40, 782.   9 Dicitur anima... quod ipsa : Ps. Aug.,
spir. et an., 13, PL 40, 788-789.   13 Tota anime... accidentia non est : cf. Ps. Aug., *spir. et an.*, 13,
PL 40, 789.   18 Augustinus, ix De trinitate, capitulum iiii : cf. Aug., *trin.* IX, 4. 5, ed. Mountain,
CCSL 50, pp. 297-298, PL 42, 963: "Simul etiam admonemur si utcumque uidere possumus haec
in anima exsistere et tamquam inuoluta euolui ut sentiantur et dinumerentur substantialiter uel, ut
ita dicam, essentialiter, non tamquam in subiecto ut color aut figura in corpore aut ulla alia qualitas
aut quantitas"; Aug., *trin.* IX, 4. 7, ed. Mountain, CCSL 50, p. 299, PL 42, 964: "Sed non unius
substantiae sunt, aqua, uinum, et mel, quamuis ex eorum commixtione fiat una substantia potionis.
Quomodo autem illa tria non sint eiusdem essentiae non uideo".   23 xii capitulo : cf. Aug., *trin.* IX,
12. 18, ed. Mountain, CCSL 50, p. 309, PL 42, 970-971: "Quod ergo cognoscit se parem sibi notitiam
sui gignit quia non minus se nouit quam est nec alterius essentiae est notitia eius, non solum quia
ipsa nouit, sed etiam quia se ipsam sicut supra diximus".   23 ix libro, capitulo xi : cf. Aug., *trin.*
IX, 11. 16, ed. Mountain, CCSL 50, pp. 307-308, PL 42, 970: "Ex quo colligitur quia cum se mens
ipsa nouit atque approbat sic est eadem notitia uerbum eius ut ei sit par omnino et aequale atque
identidem quia neque inferioris essentiae notitia est sicut corporis neque superioris sicut dei".   23 v
capitulo : cf. Aug., *trin.* IX, 5. 8, ed. Mountain, CCSL 50, p. 301, PL 42, 965: "Miro itaque modo tria
ista inseparabilia sunt a semetipsis, et tamen eorum singulum quidque substantia est et simul omnia
una substantia uel essentia cum et relatiue dicantur ad iuicem".

in se inseparabilia sunt a semetipsis, et tamen eorum singulorum quidem essentia, et similia omnia una essentia uel substantia".

25

Item. Genesis xvii, "secundum ymaginem suam fecit illum", Glossa: "Sicut deus pater, deus filius, deus spiritus sanctus, non tres dii set unus tres habens personas, ita et anima intellectus, anima memoria, anima uoluntas; non tamen tres anime set una anima tres habens dignitates, in quibus mirabiliter ymaginem dei gerit".

Item. Gramatica et musica non dicuntur deus quia in eadem substantia, ergo nec illa tria.

30

Item. Materia est potentia recipiendi formam; pari ratione anima est sua potentia.

Set contra. "Potentie cognoscuntur per actus", ergo ubi diuersi actus secundum essentiam et speciem, et diuerse potentie. Et sicut actus a potentiis, ita diuersitates actuum a diuersitate potentiarum, et non econtrario.

35

Item. Damascenus: "Quorum substantia eadem, eorum et opera eadem; quorum autem nature differentes, horum et operationes differentes".

Solutio. Predictis rationibus concedi potest quod anima est sue potentie.

---

32 materia *scripsi*] memoria *ms.*

---

26 Genesis xvii : recte Sir 17, 1.   26 Glossa : *gl. ord.* in Eccl 17, 1 (marg.), ed. Brepols, t. II, 760, col. b; cf. Ps. Aug., *spir. et an.*, 35, PL 40, 806: "Et sicut Deus Pater, Deus Filius, Deus Spiritus sanctus; non tamen tres dii, sed unus Deus et tres personae: ita anima intellectus, anima voluntas, anima memoria; non tamen tres animae in uno copore, sed anima una et tres vires. Atque in his tribus divinam imaginem gerit mirabiliter in sua natura noster interior homo, et ex his quasi excellentioribus animae viribus jubemur diligere Conditorem, ut in quantum intelligitur, diligatur; et in quantum diligitur, semper in memoria habeatur".   32 materia est potentia recipiendi formam : cf. Philipp., *Q. de ymag.*, ed. Wicki, p. 176²³¹⁻²³²: "Prima materia est sua potentia, quia potens est recipere formam substantialem"; Guill. Altissiod., *sum. aur.* II, 9, c. 1, q. 6, ed. Ribaillier, p. 243⁸⁴⁻⁸⁵: "…in prima materia videatur idem esse quod posse suscipere formam quamlibet".   34 Potentie cognoscuntur per actus : cf. Arist., *somn. et vig.*, 1, ed. Siwek, p. 173⁹ (Bekker: 454a): "Cuius est potentia, eius quoque est actus"; anonymus, *de pot. an. et ob.*, ed. Callus, p. 148³⁻⁵; Philipp., *sum. de bon.* II, ed. Wicki, p. 1046²⁰⁷⁻²¹⁰: "…in naturalibus cognoscitur potentia secundum actus et per potentias essentia"; Hugo de S. Caro, *In I sent.*, d. 3, *supra*, p. 189, l. 70.   37 Damascenus : Ioh. Dam., *fid. orth., tr. Burgundionis* II, 37, ed. Buytaert, p. 142⁷⁻⁹.

PETRUS DE BARRO

DE HIIS QUE EX PARTE ANIME MANEBUNT

<i>

⁵ Sequitur de hiis que ex parte anime manebunt. Vnde, cum anima habeat tres potentias, scilicet uegetabilem, sensibilem et rationalem, primo queritur de uegetabili; que cum habeat duas partes siue uires, nutritiuam et generatiuam, queritur utrum ille maneant.

¹⁰ <1> Videtur quod non, quia dicit Augustinus: "Cum perfecta erunt regimina, non erit generatio", ergo nec uis generatiua. Ad quid enim esset? Ex quo penitus cessabit actus eius, idest nutritiua cessabit, quia resurget corpus spirituale, idest non egens alimentis, ergo cessabit nutritiua.

Set contra.

¹⁵ <1> Integritas substantie corporis redibit seruata partium congruentia, ergo et integritas anime seruata partium potentialium congruentia, ergo et partes anime uegetabilis peribunt et redibunt, et nescio utra.

<2> Item. Dicit Augustinus quod non potestas, set egestas comedendi et bibendi corporibus glorificatis detrahetur, ergo pari ratione non potestas generandi uel ²⁰ nutriendi set egestas detrahetur; manebunt igitur ille uires.

<3> Item. Oculus seruabitur quia fuit organum anime in seruitio dei, ergo pari ratione organum generatiue et nutritiue, set non est organum sine uirtute, ergo manebit uirtus.

<4> Item. In eodem susceptibili erit premium suo modo, sicut fuit et meri- ²⁵ tum. Set meritum fuit in generatiua uel abstinendo, uel agendo, ergo et in ea erit premium, ergo manebit; similiter et nutritiua.

<5> Item. Scientie manebunt ad decorem, non ad usum, ergo pari ratione uires anime.

---

3 *Douai, Bibliothèque municipale 434*, vol. I, f. 86rb; q. n. 157, Glorieux, "Les 572 Questions", p. 140.   11 ad quid] ergo *add. sed. del. ms.*   11 enim *interl. ms.*   21 seruabitur *scripsi* : priuabitur *ms.*

---

8 duas partes : cf. Auic., *can.* I, 1, 6. 2; cf. Rol. Crem., *sum.*, ms. *Paris, Bibl. Mazar. 795*, f. 34va; cf. Hasse, *Avicenna's De anima*, 40-41.   10 Augustinus : cf. Aug., *en. Ps.*, 70, 2, 4, ed. Dekkers – Fraipont, CCSL 39, p. 963$^{47-49}$, PL 36, 894: "Si ergo omni generationi superventurae, usque ad finem saeculi: finito enim saeculo, iam nulla superveniet generatio".   12 resurget corpus spirituale : cf. 1 Cor 15, 44.   15 integritas... congruentia : cf. Petr. de Barro, *Questio circa ea que ad corpus pertinent*, ms. *Douai, Bibliothèque Municipale 434*, vol. I, f. 86^{ra-rb}; Cf. Aug., *civ.* XXII, 18, ed. Dombard – Kalb, CCSL 48, p. 837$^{32-34}$, PL 41, 780: "Sicut ergo est mensura uniuscuiusque partis, ita totius corporis, quod omnibus suis partibus constat, est utique mensura plenitudinis, de qua dictum est: in mensuram aetatis plenitudinis christi"; Eph 4, 10-16.   18 Augustinus : cf. Aug., *serm.* 242 A, ed. Morin, p. 329$^{28-30}$: "Resurgent ergo corpora, quia resurrexit Christus; sed non habebunt aliquam indigentiam, quia et Christus, cum resurrexit, potestate manducauit, non egestate"

Solutio. Dicit Augustinus: "Puto facile intelligi in conditione dignitatem fuisse prelatam. Transitura quippe est necessitas tempusque uenturam, quando inuicem sola pulcritudine sine ulla libidine perfruemur", ex quo patet quod actus necessitatis cessabunt, set actus pertinentes ad dignitatem manebunt, sicut patet in lingua et dentibus. Cessabit enim actus masticationis, manebit autem actus formationis uocis, quia primus actus necessitatis solius est, secundus autem dignitatis quantum ad laudem dei. Dicimus igitur quod licet actus generandi et nutriendi cessent, tamen generatiua et nutritiua manebunt quia meruerunt: corpus in quo sunt iuuit anima<m> suo creatori, unde iustum est ut saltem in quietem premientur. Generatiua autem propter alias duas rationes manebit: una est quia per eam facta est multiplicatio filiorum dei et conseruata species que est dominium; alia est quia distinctio sexus in organis ipsius est indicium distinctionis Christi et ecclesie tanquam sponsi et sponse.

<ii>

Secundo queritur de potentiis anime sensibilis, et maxime de gustu et odoratu et uisu.

<1> Nam ad quid manebit gustus, cum nichil possit gustare (fit enim gustus per duorum corporum coniunctionem)? Item, odorari, quia odoratus non fit sine resolutione (ibi autem nec resolutio, nec commixtio corporum erit).

<2> Item. De uisu queritur utrum fiat per receptionem similitudinum sicut modo, aut non. Si sic, quomodo ergo clausis oculis uidebimus oculo corporali, sicut uult Augustinus? Si non, quomodo ergo distinguet oculus colorum | differentias?

<3> Item. Dicit Augustinus quod sensus transibit in rationem et ratio in intellectum, quod impossibile uidetur: quoniam licet corpus resurget spirituale, non tamen erit spiritus, unde nec sensus erit potentia spiritus. Set ratio est potentia spiritus, ergo non poterit transire sensus in rationem.

Solutio. Re uera sensus omnes manebunt, set quia erunt corporis spiritualis habebunt spirituales actus, nec fiet gustus, aut odoratus, aut etiam uisus ut dicuntur

---

39 conseruata *scripsi*] obseruata *ms.*

---

29 Augustinus : Aug., *civ.* XXII, 24, ed. Dombard – Kalb, CCSL 48, pp. 850^{165}-851^{170}, PL 41, 791: "Puto facile intelligi in conditione corporis dignitatem necessitati fuisse praelatam. Transitura est quippe necessitas tempusque venturam, quando sola invicem pulchritudine sine ulla libidine perfruamur; quod maxime ad laudem referendum est Conditoris, cui dicitur in Psalmo: "Confessionem et decorem induisti"". 41 generatiua... sponse : cf. Aug., *civ.* XXII, 17, ed. Dombard – Kalb, CCSL 48, p. 835^{16}-836^{25}, PL 41, 778-779. 51 Augustinus : cf. Aug., *gen. ad litt.* XII, 20, 43, ed. Zycha, CSEL 28.1, p. 410^{24}, PL 34, 471: "Hinc enim erat, quod me dormiens in somniis uidere sciebam nec tamen illas corporalium rerum, similitudines, quas uidebam, sic ab ipsis corporalibus discernebam, quemadmodum eas cogitantes etiam clausis oculis uel in tenebris constituti discernere solemus". 52 Augustinus : recte ps.-Aug., *spir. et an.*, 12, PL 40, 787: "Discernemus mente, discernemus et corpore, cum sensus nostri corporei uertentur in rationem, ratio in intellectum, intellectus in intelligentiam, intelligentia in Deum mutabitur".

sicut nunc.

<ad 1> Item. De gustu et odoratu dixit Augustinus in libro Confessionis: "Cum
amo deum meum, amo lucem, uocem, odorem, cibum et complexum interioris hominis, ibi fulget quod non capit locus, ibi sonat quod non capit corpus, ibi reddet
quod non sparget flatus, ibi satiat quod non diminuit edacitas, ibi heret quod non
diuellit satietas".

<ad 2> Ad hoc quod opponitur de uisu dicimus quod non per sensus similitudi-
nes, set solius lucis beneficio uel rerum quas uidebit et Christi qui est ille agnus de
quo in Apocalipsa: "Illuminabit eam agnus". Quod cum colorum habeat duas causas, unam ex parte elementorum, aliam ex parte luminis (color enim nichil aliud est
quam lux profundata in materia), elementaris transibit cum sit transiens et illa que
ex parte luminis manebit, unde fiet quasi lux; unde sufficiet uisui lux illa et ymagine
non indigebit. Si autem queris quomodo distinctiones colorum percipiet, dicimus
quod tante erit efficacie uisus, ut sub illa luce percipiet causam elementarem que
transiit, unde et causas colorum licet transierint percipiet, quia habuit in illius causis distinctionem colorum que fuit. Non enim credimus quod nigrum uel fuscum
uel liuidum sit in paradiso.

<ad 3> Ad ultimum dicimus quod sensus dicitur transire in rationem non quod
fiat sensus ratio, set propter efficaciam sue uirtutis, uel quia eo quod ordinatus sit ad
rationem premiabitur non secundum quod decet ipsum in se, set secundum quod
decebit eum in suo ordine.

<iii>

Item. Vltimo queritur de ymagine, memoria et intellectu possibili, utrum maneant secundum suos actus.

<1> Videtur quod sic, ut sicut se habet sensibile ad sensum, sic ymaginabile
ad ymaginem, memoriale ad memoriam, intelligibile ad intelligentiam; ergo sicut
sensus perficiatur in perceptione sui obiecti, sic et illa.

<2> Preterea. Quomodo posset ymaginari uel memorare uel intelligere aliquis
homo glorificatus, nisi per ymaginem aut fanatasma rei cognite, cum res non ueniat
in essentia sua?

---

60 complexum] et *add. ms.*

---

59 Augustinus in libro Confessionis : Aug., *conf.* X, 6, ed. Verheijen, CCSL 27, p. 159[12-18], PL 32,
782-783: "Et tamen amo quandam lucem et quandam vocem et quandam odorem et quendam cibum
et quendam amplexum, cum amo Deum meum, lucem, vocem, odorem, cibum, amplexum interioris
hominis mei, ubi fulget animae meae, quod non capit locus, et ubi sonat, quod non rapit tempus,
et ubi det, quod non spargit flatus, et ubi sapit, quood non minuit edacitas, et ubi haeret, quod non
divellit satietas".   66 Apocalipsa : cf. Ap 21, 23: "Et civitas non eget sole neque luna ut luceant in
ea nam claritas Dei inluminavit eam et lucerna eius est agnus".

Si hoc concedatur, contra.

<1> † Ymagines absentium <...> ibi autem nihil alius <...> enim tempus amplius   90
non est. †

<2> Item. Neque intellectus erit ad receptionem fantasmatum, quia dicit beatus
Dyonisius quod angeli uident sensibilia uirtute animi deiformis, scilicet nos autem
erimus sicut angeli dei, unde sicut angeli sine receptione ymaginum a rebus res
cognoscent, ita et nos.   95

<3> Pretera. Ymaginatio, memoria non sunt sine organo; restat ergo quod in
dissolutione corporis deficiente organo et ymagines et fantasmata rerum defecerunt; ergo quod in restitutione corporis aut non fiet ymaginatio aut memoria per
ymagines aut fantasmata, aut omnium que per ymaginem et memoriam apprehenduntur ymagines et fanthasmata redibunt, quod tamen non fit possibile, ut uidetur.   100
Relinquitur quod non fiet ymaginatio aut memoria aut intellectus per similitudines
rerum.

Quod concedi potest. Sicut enim in luce et per eam uidebit oculus que decent
uidere ipsum, sic in luce interiori et per lucem interiorem ymaginabuntur et memorabuntur et intelligemus ea que decent nos ymaginari etc. Vnde fiet quod, sicut   105
nunc deum non nisi in creatura intelligimus, ita et tunc creaturam non nisi in creatore recognoscemus. Habens enim anima deum apud se, lucem ueram uidebit ipsam, et in ipsa que decuit animam uidere et quocumque modo, unde Beda: "Quod
semel recipitur, semper habetur sine mutatione".

---

91 ymagines... non est] *textum corruptum esse puto*   93 deiformis *scripsi*] deformis *ms.*   98 aut
memoria] aut intellectus per similitudines rerum *add. sed del. ms.*

---

91 ymagines... non est : cf. Ap 10, 5-6: "Et angelum quem vidi stantem supra mare et supra terram
levavit manum suam ad caelum, et iuravit per viventem in saecula saeculorum qui creavit caelum
et ea quae in illo sunt et terram et ea quae in ea sunt et mare et quae in eo sunt quia tempus amplius non erit".   93 Dyonisius : cf. Ps.-Dionys. *div. nom.*, c. 7, 2. 3 (PG 3, 869 C), ed. Suchla,
p. 197$^{14-16}$; Chevallier, p. 401, col. 4: "Etenim et angelos scire dicunt sermones quae sunt terrae,
non secundum sensus cognoscentes sensibilia existentia, sed secundum propriam deiuisae mentis
uirtutem et naturam".   96 ymaginatio... organo : cf. Auic., *de an.* IV, 4, ed. Van Riet, pp. 66^{65}-67^{69}:
"Dicemus autem quod, postquam ostendimus omnes virtutes sensibiles non habere actionem nisi
propter corpus, et esse virtutum est eas sic esse ut operentur, tunc virtutes sensibiles non sunt sic
ut operentur nisi dum sunt corporales; ergo esse earum est esse corporale; igitur non remanent post
corpus"; cf. Dom. Gund., *de an.*, ed. Muckle, pp. 82-83.   97-98 in dissolutione... defecerunt : cf.
Dom. Gund., *de an.*, ed. Muckle, pp. 97-98.   108 habens... quocumque modo : cf. Dom. Gund.,
de an., ed. Muckle, pp. 99-101.   108 Beda : recte *gl. ord.* in Ro 11, 29 (marg.), ed. Brepols, t. IV,
p. 298, col. b: "Secundum electionem et propter patres sunt saluandi: quia dona, idest promissiones
et uocatio, idest electio ab eterno sunt sine penitentia, idest sine immutatione consilii dei"; cf. Aug.,
praed. sanct. XVI, 33, PL 44, 985: "Sine poenitentia sunt dona et vocatio Dei: id est, sine mutatione
stabiliter fixa sunt".

ANONIMI

\<DE HUMANA NATURA \>

Questionis de humana natura quatuor sunt partes: prima quid \<sit\> ueritas humane nature; secunda quid sit de ueritate humane nature, scilicet an totus homo,
an aliquid de homine; tertia an ueritas mutabilis sit, an permanens; quarto an multe
ueritates sint, an una.

\<i\>

Antequam autem opponatur, supponatur pro principio, una existente substantia et uno corpore et una carne, quod duplex est potentia in carne una, scilicet una
corruptionis, altera incorruptionis, et hoc propter animam et propter corpus. Supponatur etiam quod nulla creatura in se duas habet substantias nisi homo, unde
angelus unicam habet substantiam. Supponatur etiam quod est potentia ante actum et est potentia cum actu, unde in carne humana est potentia incorruptionis
ante actum et potentia corruptionis cum actu, et iste sunt una potentia in genere et
multe in comparatione ad actum.

\<1\> Considerandum etiam quid dicitur secundum rectum et quid secundum
obliquum, quoniam non sunt multe ueritates humane in Adam, est tamen potentia multarum ueritatum in eo. Sciendum etiam quod in Sententiis dicitur humana
natura quinque modis, unde queratur quo illorum modorum sumatur hic 'humana
natura'. Dicendum utique quod differt ipostasis et essentia, quoniam modus ipostasis est ab inferiori, modus autem essentie a superiori. Vnde sic differunt ueritas et
natura, unde natura dicitur corpus et anima simul coniuncta habens poten | tiam
susceptiuam ueritatis. Vnde Anselmus in libro De ueritate: "Veritas est rectitudo
sola mente perceptibilis", et talis est ueritas humane nature, que dici debet recte necessitas esse hominis perpetui, et hec est sua ratio; res autem huius ueritatis est anima cum suis potentiis essentialibus et corpus cum suis potentiis essentialibus. Set
duplex est potentia, scilicet materialis et immaterialis; que autem materialis est potentia ad corruptionem, et immaterialis ad incorruptionem; et hec ultima potentia
est de ueritate humane nature.

18

---

3 *Douai, Bibliothèque municipale, 434*, vol. II, f. 189ra, q. n. 550, Glorieux, "Les 572 Questions", p.
245.   4 quid *del. ms.*   10 principio *scripsi*] principio quod *ms.*   24 unde] di *add. sed del. ms.*
25 Ansel *ex* Anselli *corr. ms.*

---

25 Anselmus in libro De ueritate : Ans. Cant., *de uer.* 11, ed. Schmitt, p. 191^19^: "Possumus, igitur,
nisi fallor, definire quia ueritas est rectitudo mente sola perceptibilis".

<2> Vnde caro secundum speciem augetur? Caro uero secundum materiam non augetur, quapropter duplex est potentia in carne. Opponatur ergo in hunc modum: "Omne quod intrat in os et in uentrem cadit, in secessum emittitur", ergo nichil alimenti in corpore remanet. Ad hoc Beda: "Quamuis tenuissimus humor, cum digeritur, in secessum uadit", et ita nichil remanet. Adhuc Augustinus: "Quatuor sunt genera humorum, quorum quidam accipiuntur ut mutent et mutentur, ut cibus amittens speciem suam in corpus uertitur", et ita secundum Augustinum aliquid remanet. Istud etiam probari posset per Aristotelem, si opus esset adhuc. In Sententiis dicitur quod si "puer statim post ortum moriatur, tamen in illo statu resurget quem haberet si esset triginta annorum". Et ita uidetur quod hic sit augmentatio sine omni intrinseco adueniente. 35 40

<ad 2> Ad primum dicendum, sicut dicit magister in Sententiis, quod non inficimur quin ibi traseant in carnem singularem, set non in carnem quam receperant a primis parentibus. 45

<ad 1> Ad aliud dicendum quod caro duplicem habet potentiam, ut predictum est, unde nichil transit de carne secundum quod ipsa habet potentiam inmaterialem ad incorruptionem, set secundum quod habet potentiam materialem ad corruptionem.

Ad alia dicendum quod duplex est caro, una scilicet qua deponetur, et alia que resurget, et uniuntur iste due carnes in humana natura. Melius tamen dicitur duplex caro, ut patet in auro inpuro. Si enim depuretur aurum inpurum, partes inpure eiciuntur, partes uero pure <non>, unde caro inpura deponetur, set pura remanebit, et hec puritas et inpuritas causatur ex eo quod magis uel minus conuertit se ad inferiora uel ad superiora. Vnde dicendum quod deponetur caro cum una potentia, et remanet cum alia. 50 55

<ii>

<1> Adhuc queritur utrum costa Ade ex qua fiebat Eua sit de ueritate humane nature. Quod non uidetur, quia cum diminuatur secundum costam, et diminuretur

---

55 inferiora *ex* inferiorum *corr. ms.* 55 quod *scripsi*] quod non *ms.*

---

34 Omne ...emittitur : Mt 15, 17: "Non intellegitis quia omne quod in os intrat in uentrem uadit et in secessum emittitur". 35 Beda : cf. *gl. ord.* in Mc 7, 19 (marg.), ed. Brepols, t. IV, p. 107, col. b: "Sed quamuis tenuissimus humor et liquens esca, cum in uenis et artubo cocta fuerit et digesta, per occultos meatus (quos Greci poros uocant) ad inferiora dilabitur, et in secessum uadit". 36 Augustinus : cf. *gl. ord.* in Mc 7, 19 (marg.), ed. Brepols, t. IV, 107, col. b: "Quedam sic accedunt, ut etiam mutent et mutentur, sicut et ipse cibo amittens speciem suam in corpus nostrum uertitur et nos refecti in robur mutamur"; id., *De diuersis quaestionibus*, 73, 1, ed. Mutzenbecher, CCSL 44 A, p. 210$^{24-28}$, PL 40, 84. 39–40 In Sententiis : cf. Petr. Lomb., *sent.* II, d. 30, 15, ed. PP. Collegii S. Bonaventurae, pp. 504^{29}-505^3: "Ratio. Quod etiam ratione ostendi potest hoc modo: Puer qui statim post ortum moritur, in illa statura resurget, quam habiturus erat si uiueret usque ad aetatem triginta annorum, nullo uitio corporis impeditus".

humana natura. Et si non, queratur ergo que menbra sint de ueritate humane nature
60   et que non.

<2> Adhuc, sunt potentie dignitatis in corpore humano, scilicet loqui et con-
similia, secundum que homo dicitur dignissima creaturarum; et sunt alie potentie
necessitatis, sine quibus nullo modo potest esse. Et prime sunt potentie sine quibus
non potest bene esse. Queratur utrum tam ille quam iste sint de ueritate humane
65   nature.

<3> Adhuc, Caym habebat ueritatem humane nature: aut ergo tantum ab Adam,
aut ab Eua tantum, aut ab utrisque. Constat quod non ab altero tantum, quoniam
tunc non exigitur nisi secundum unius ad eius generationem. Si ab utrisque, ergo
cum una sit ueritas humane nature in Adam et alia in Eua, uidetur quod in Caym
70   multe sint ueritates humane nature. | 189

<4> Adhuc, queratur utrum in asino sit huiusmodi duplex caro, una scilicet
que sumitur ex primis parentibus, et alia que tota die fluit et refluit; quod uidetur, quoniam sumit secundum a suo generante et similiter per nutrimentum sumit
carnem.

75   <5> Adhuc, queratur utrum capilli decisi sint de ueritate humane nature.

<6> Adhuc, queratur qualiter caro nostra differt a carne Christi.

<ad 1> Ad primum dicendum quod aliud est dicere "quid est de ueritate humane
nature", et aliud "quid est totius humane nature". Dicendum ergo quod de ueritate
humane nature sunt corpus et anima, de ueritate totius humane nature sunt po-
80   tentie singulorum menbrorum, de ueritate totius humane nature corruptibilis sunt
potentie minimarum partium singulorum menbrorum. Dicendum ergo quod cum
ex costa Ade fit Eua, de proprietate materialis corporis aliquid deperditur, set de
ueritate potentie ad incorruptionem nichil diminuitur, unde Augustinus in libro
Contra Adamantium: "Corpora saluandorum tunc erunt spiritualia et non spiritus,
85   sine contrarietate et rebellione", set sic non erit de dampnatis.

<ad 2> Ad aliud dicendum quod omnes potentie, siue fuerint dignitatis siue
necessitatis, dummodo fuerint potentie inmateriales ad incorruptionem, sunt de
ueritate humane nature.

<ad 3> Ad aliud dicendum quod Caym ab utrisque recepit ueritatem humane
90   nature, set tamen unitis, unde per illam unionem fit una ueritas humane nature in
Caym. Vnde dicendum quod sicut potentias regis in ipso rege est singularis, respectu tamen subditorum ipsa est uniuersalis; sic dicendum quod si conparetur poten-

---

61 potentie *ex* potentiei *corr. ms.*   82 Eua *scripsi*] Eua quod *ms.*   86 omnes *scripsi*] oms *ms.*

83–84 Augustinus in libro Contra Adamantium : cf. Aug., *c. Adim.* 12, 4, ed. Zycha, CSEL 25. 1,
p. 142, PL 42, 145: "Unde et supra dixerat aliam esse caelestium corporum gloriam et aliam terre-
strium. Quod autem spirituale corpus in resurrectione futurum dicit, non propterea putandum est,
quod non corpus, sed spiritus erit, sed spiritale corpus omnimodis spiritui subditum dicit sine aliqua
corruptione uel morte".

tia ad animam Ade, sic una est, si autem conparetur ad nos, uniuersalis est, unde in Adam fuit una ueritas humane nature, set tamen in eo fuit potentia multarum ueritatum. 95

<ad 4> Ad aliud dicendum quod in asino non est huiusmodi duplex potentia, quoniam in eo nulla est potentia ad incorruptionem, et hoc quoniam in eo nulla est respectu sui actus, cum suus actus sine incorruptibilitate existat.

<ad 5> Ad aliud dicendum, sicut dicit Augustinus, quod capilli sunt de ueritate humane nature quoad decorem, unde Augustinus: siue sint quoad necessitatem, 100 siue quoad decorem, semper sunt de ueritate humane nature, unde in Euangelio: "Vnus capillus non remanet".

<ad 6> Ad ultimum dicendum quod in semine duo sunt, sicut dicit Augustinus, substantia scilicet corpulenta et ratio inuisibilis, et secundum utramque fuimus in lumbis Ade post peccatum. Set Christus non erat ibi nisi secundum corpulentam 105 substantiam (?), quoniam ab illa ratione inuisibili est fomes peccati et concupiscentia, unde cum in Christo neutrum erat, nec illa ratio. Similiter secundum substantiam aut corpulentiam habens (?) carnem; et hoc dupliciter, scilicet secundum potentiam materialem ad corruptionem <et> secundum materialem incorruptionem: erat utique in Christo potentia passibilitatis et potentia ad incorruptionem. 110

---

102 remanet *ex* marenet *corr. ms.*   107 in *interl. ms.*

---

99 Augustinus : cf. Aug., *en. Ps.* LI, 9, ed. Dekkers – Fraipont, CCSL 39, p. 629, PL 36, 605: "Qui quidem capilli non superflue facti sunt a deo in corpore hominum, sed ad aliquod ornamentum; tamen quia sine sensu praeciduntur, illi qui haerent corde in domino, sic habent ista terrena tamquam capillos".   101 in Euangelio : cf. *gl. ord.* in Mt 10, 30 (interl.) et in Lc 12, 7 (interl.), ed. Brepols, t. IV, p. 40, col. a; p. 185, col. a: "Omnem curam in eum proicite, apud quem capillus non peribit". 103 Augustinus : Aug., *gen. ad litt.* X, 20, ed. Zycha, CSEL 28.1, p. 323, PL 34, 423: "Cum enim sit in semine et uisibilis corpulentia et inuisibilis ratio, utrumque cucurrit ex Abraham uel etiam ex ipso Adam usque ad corpus Marie, quia et ipsum eo modo conceptum et exortum est".

Bibliography

BIBLIOGRAPHY

(A) JOURNALS AND SERIES

AHDLMA	*Archives d'Histoire Doctrinale et Littéraire du Moyen-Âge*
AL	Aristoteles Latinus, Union Academique Internationale (Corpus philosophorum medii Aevi Academiarum consociatarum auspiciis et consilio editum), 1961 ff.
B. G. Ph. (Th). M. (N. F.)	Beiträge zur Geschichte der Philosophie (und Theologie) des Mittelalters (Neue Folge), 1891 ff.
CCSL	Corpus Christianorum, series latina
CCCM	Corpus Christianorum, continuatio mediaevalis
CIMAGL	*Cahiers de l'Institut du Moyen-Âge grec et latin*
CSEL	Corpus Scriptorum Ecclesiasticorum Latinorum
EL	Sancti Thomae de Aquino Opera omnia iussu Leonis XIII P. M. Edita (Editio Leonina)
EP	Sancti Thomae Aquinatis Doctoris angelici ordinis praedicatorum Opera omnia ad fidem optimarum editionum accurate recognita, 25 voll., Parmae: Typis Petri Fiaccadori, 1852-1873; Reprint: New York: Usurgia, 1948-1950
FS	*Franciscan Studies*
GCS	Die griechischen christlichen Schriftsteller der ersten drei Jahrhunderte
PG	J.-P. Migne, Patrologiae Cursus Completus, series graeca
PL	J.-P. Migne, Patrologiae Cursus Completus, series latina
RTAM	*Recherches de théologie ancienne et médiévale*
SC	Sources Chrétiennes

(B) MANUSCRIPTS

Anonymus, *Questio de humana natura* (ed. in this vol., pp. 211-214)
   Douai, Bibliothèque municipale, 434, vol. II

Anonymus, *Questio de trinitate animae* (ed. in this vol., pp. 200-203)
   Douai, Bibliothèque municipale, 434, vol. I

Anonymus, *Questio si anima est sue potentie* (ed. in this vol., pp. 204-205)
   Douai, Bibliothèque municipale, 434, vol. I

Anselmus Laudunensis, *Sententiae seu flores sententiarum*
  Paris BnF 12999

Hugo de Santo Caro, *In Sententias* (I, 3; ed. in this vol., pp. 187-199)
  Basel, Univ. Bibl., B II 20
  Padova, Bibl. Univ., 853

Hugo de Sancto Caro, *Questio quomodo anima uniatur corpori* (ed. in this vol.,
  pp. 183-186)
  Douai, Bibliothèque municipale, 434, vol. I

Odo Rigaldus, *In Sententias*
  Paris BnF, lat. 14910

Petrus de Barro, *De hiis que ex parte anime manebunt* (ed. in this vol., pp. 206-
  210)
  Douai, Bibliothèque municipale, 434, vol. I

Petrus de Barro, *Questio circa ea que ad corpus pertinent*
  Douai, Bibliothèque municipale, 434, vol. I

Ps.-Petrus Pictaviensis, *Glossa* in I *Sententiarum*
  J. N. Garvin, *Papers*, University of Notre Dame Archives, CGRV 4/6
  Paris, Bibl. Nat. lat. 14423

Rolandus Cremonensis, *Summa*
  Paris, Bibliothèque Mazarine 795

Ps.-Stephanus Langton, *Summa "Breves dies hominis"*
  Bamberg, Staatsbibliothek, Patr. 136
  Oxford, Bodleian Library, Laud. Misc. 80

(C) EDITED SOURCES

Ailr. Riev.   Ailredus Rievallensis
  dial. de an. *Dialogus de anima*, ed. C. H. Talbot, London: The Warburg
              Institute, 1952.

Alan. de Ins.   Alanus de Insulis
  fid. cath. *De fide catholica contra haereticos sui temporis, praesertim
              Albigenses*, PL 210, 305 A-430 A.
  sum. quon. *Summa "Quoniam homines"*, in P. Glorieux, *"La somme
              Quoniam homines d'Alain de Lille"*, AHDLMA 20 (1953), pp.
              113 -364.
  theol. reg. *Theologicae regulae*, PL 210, 618 B-684 C.

Alb. Magn.   Albertus Magnus

de hom.   *De homine (Summa de creaturis II)*, ed. S. C. A. Borgnet, Paris 1896 (Opera Omnia, 35);

Über den Menschen. Lateinisch-deutsch, H. Anzulewicz and J. R. Söder, Hambourg: Felix Meiner Verlag, 2004.

sum. theol.   *Summa theologiae*, ed. P. Iammy, Lugduni 1651 (Opera omnia, 18);

Summa theologiae, ed. S. C. A. Borgnet, Paris 1895 (Opera omnia, 33).

in Sent.   *Commentarium in Sententias,* ed. S. C. A. Borgnet, Paris 1894 (Opera omnia, 28).

Alc.   Alcuinus

rat. an.   *De ratione animae,* PL 101, 639 A-650 C.

Alex. Halen.   Alexander de Hales

gloss.   *Glossa in quatuor libros Sententiarum,* ed. PP. Collegii S. Bonaventurae, Firenze: Quaracchi, 1952.

q. ant.   *Quaestiones disputatae 'antequam esset frater',* ed. PP. Collegii S. Bonaventurae, Firenze: Quaracchi, 1960, voll. I-III.

sum. theol.   *Summa theologica,* ed. PP. Collegii S. Bonaventurae, Firenze: Quaracchi, 1924-1948.

Andr. Sun.   Andreas Sunonis filius

hexaem.   *Hexaemeron,* ed. S. Ebbesen – L. B. Mortensen, Hauniae, 1985 (Corpus Philosophorum Danicorum Medii Aevi, 11. 1).

Ans. Cant.   Anselmus Cantuarensis

monol.   *Monologion,* ed. F. S. Schmitt, Stuttgart: Friedrich Frommann Verlag, 1968 (S. Anselmi Opera Omnia, 1).

de uer.   *De ueritate,* ed. F. S. Schmitt, Edinburgh: Nelson, 1946 (S. Anselmi Opera Omnia, 1).

Ans. Laud.   Anselmus Laudunensis

sent.   *Sententiae seu flores sententiarum,* in O. Lottin, *Psychologie et morale aux XIIe et XIIIe siècles,* vol. V: *Problèmes d'histoire littéraire: l'école d'Anselme de Laon et de Guillaume de Champeaux,* Gembloux: Duculot 1959, pp. 9-188.

Arist. Aristoteles

an. post.   *Analytica posteriora* (Bekker 24a-70b), *Translatio Iacobi*, ed. L. Minio-Paluello – B. G. Dod, Bruxelles-Paris: Desclée De Brouwer, 1968 (AL 4. 1), pp. 1-107.

de an.   *De anima* (Bekker 402a-435b), *Translatio nova*, ed. R.-A. Gauthier, in Thomas Aquinas, *Sentencia libri de anima*, Roma-Paris 1984 (EL 45.1);

Translatio vetus, ed. M. Alonso, in Pedro Hispano, *Obras filosoficas*, vol. III, Madrid: Instituto Luis Vives de Filosofia, 1952.

mem.   *De memoria* (Bekker 449b-453a), ed. J. Siwek, in Aristoteles, *Parva Naturalia Graece et Latine*, Roma: Desclée - Editori Pontifici, 1963, pp. 128-168.

metaph.   *Metaphysica* (Bekker 980a- 1093b), *Translatio vetus*, ed. G. Vuillemin- Diem, Bruxelles-Paris: Desclée De Brouwer, 1970 (AL 25. 2), pp. 7-275.

somn. et vig.   *De somno et vigilia* (Bekker 453b-458a), ed. J. Siwek, in Aristoteles, *Parva Naturalia Graece et Latine*, Roma: Desclée - Editori Pontifici, 1963, pp. 170-204.

Ps. Arist. Pseudo-Aristoteles: Alfredus de Sareshel (Alfredus Anglicus)

motu cord.   *De motu cordis*, ed. C. Baeumker, Münster: Aschendorff, 1923 (B. G. Ph. M., 23.1).

Aug. Augustinus Hipponensis

an. quant.   *De animae quantitate*, ed. W. Hörmann, Wien: Hoelder-Pichler-Tempsky, 1986, CSEL 89, pp. 131-231, PL 32, 1035-1080.

c. Adim.   *Contra Adimantum*, ed. J. Zycha, Vindobonae 1892, CSEL 25. 1, pp. 115-190, PL 42, 129-172.

civ.   *De civitate Dei*, ed. B. Dombart – A. Kalb, Turnhout: Brepols, 1955, CCSL 47-48, PL 41, 13-804.

c. Faust.   *Contra Faustum*, ed. J. Zycha, Vindobonae 1891, CSEL 25. 1, pp. 249-797, PL 42, 207-518.

conf.   *Confessiones*, ed. L. Verheijen, Turnhout: Brepols, 1981, CCSL 27, pp. 1-273, PL 32, 659-868.

en. Ps.   *Enarrationes in Psalmos*, ed. E. Dekkers – I. Fraipont, Turnhout: Brepols, 1954-1956, CCSL 38-40, PL 36, 67-1966.

ep.   *Epistulae*, ed. A. Goldbacher, Vindobonae: Tempsky, 1895-1911, CSEL 34, 44, 57, PL 33, 61-1094.

gen ad litt.   *De Genesi ad litteram*, ed. J. Zycha, Wien: Hoelder-Pichler-Tempsky, 1894, CSEL 28. 1, pp. 1-435, PL 34, 245-486.

imm. an.   *De immortalitate animae*, ed. W. Hörmann, Wien: Hoelder-Pichler-Tempsky, 1986, CSEL 89, pp. 101-128, PL 32, 1021-1034.

Io. ev. tr.   *In Iohannis evangelium tractatus*, ed. R. Willems, Turnhout: Brepols, 1954, CCSL 36, pp. 1-688, PL 35, 1379-1970.

nat. et or. an.   *De natura et origine animae*, ed. C. F. Vrba, J. Zycha, Wien: Hoelder-Pichler-Tempsky, 1913, CSEL 60, pp. 303-419, PL 44, 475-547.

ord.   *De ordine*, ed. W. M. Green, Turnhout: Brepols, 1970, CCSL 29, pp. 89-137, PL 32, 977-1020.

praed. sanct.   *De praedestinatione sanctorum*, PL 44, 959-992.

serm.   *Sermones*, ed. G. Morin, Roma: Typis Polyglottis Vaticanis, 1930

trin.   *De Trinitate*, ed. W. J. Mountain, Turnhout: Brepols, 1968, CCSL 50-50A, PL 42, 819-1098.

Ps.-Aug.   Pseudo - Augustinus

spir. et an.   *De spiritu et anima*, PL 40, 788-789.

Auer.   Averroes Cordubensis

in De an.   *Commentarium magnum in Aristotelis De anima*, ed. F. S. Crawford, Cambridge-Massachusetts: The Mediaeval Academy of America, 1953.

Auic.   Avicenna

can.   *Liber Canonis*, ed. Venezia 1507 (repr. Hildesheim: Olms, 1964*)*.

de an.   *Liber de anima seu sextus de naturalibus, Traduction latine médiévale*, ed. S. Van Riet, Louvain – Leiden: Peeters - Brill, 1968-1972 (Avicenna Latinus).

metaph.   *Metaphysica: Liber de philosophia prima siue scientia diuina, Traduction latine médiévale*, ed. S. Van Riet, Louvain: Peeters, 1977 (Avicenna Latinus).

Auicebr.   Avicebron (Ibn Gebirol)

Fons vitae   *Fons uitae ex arabico in latinum translatus ab Iohanne Hispano et Dominico Gundissalino*, ed. C. Baeumker, Münster: Aschendorff, 1891-1895 (B. G. Ph. M., 1. 2-4).

Bern. Clar.   Bernardus Claraevallensis

de conver.   *Ad clericos de conversione*, ed. J. Leclercq - H.-M. Rochais, Roma: Editiones Cistercienses, 1974 (Sancti Bernardi Opera, 4), PL 182, 833 B-856 D.

Boeth. Boethius

c. Eut. Contra Eutychen et Nestorium, c. 3, ed. C. Moreschini, Monaco: Saur, 2005 (Bibliotheca Teubneriana); PL 64, 1337 – 1354.

in De int. In Aristotelis De interpretatione, PL 64, 293 D-640 A.

in Cat. In Categorias Aristotelis, PL 64, 159 A-294 C.

in Isag. In Isagogen Porphyrii, ed. G. Schepss – S. Brandt, Wien 1906, CSEL 48.

int. Anal. Interpretatio Analiticorum Posteriorum Aristotelis, PL 64, 711 C-910 C.

Bonav. Bonaventure

in Sent. Commentarium in IV libros Sententiarum, ed. PP. Collegii S. Bonaventurae, Quaracchi 1885-1889.

Calc. Calcidius

comm. in Tim. Commentarius in Timaeum CCXXVII, ed. P. Jensen – J. H. Waszink, London: Warburg Institute, 1962 (Corpus Platonicum Medii Aevi, 4).

Cass. Cassiodorus Vivariensis

de an. De anima, PL 70, 1279 D-1320 C.

Claud. Mam. Claudianus Mamertus

de stat. an. De statu animae, ed. A. Engelbrecht, Vindobonae 1885, CSEL 11.

Cost. Costa ben Luca

diff. an. et spir. De differentia animae et spiritus, ed. C. S. Barach, Innsbruck 1878.

Ps.-Dionys. Pseudo – Dionysius Areopagita

cael. hier. De coelesti hierarchia, edd. G. Heil - A. M. Ritter, Berlin: W. de Gruyter, 1991 (Corpus Dionysiacum, 2);

De caelesti hierarchia, ed. P. Chevalier in *Dionisiaca. Recueil donnant l'ensemble des traductions latines des ouvrages attribués au Denys de l'Aréopage*, 2 voll., Brugge: Desclée de Brouwer, 1937, pp. 725-1039, PG 3, 120-369.

div. nom. De divinis nominibus, ed. B. R. Suchla, W. de Gruyter, Berlin 1990 (Corpus Dionysiacum, 1);

De diuinis nominibus, ed. P. Chevalier in *Dionisiaca. Recueil donnant l'ensemble des traductions latines des ouvrages attribués au Denys de l'Aréopage,* 2 voll., Brugge: Desclée de Brouwer, 1937, pp. 1-561, PG 3, 585-984.

Dom. Gund.   Dominicus Gundissalinus

de an.   *Tractatus de anima,* ed. J. T. Muckle, "The Treatise De Anima of Dominicus Gundissalinus", *Mediaeval Studies* 2 (1940), pp. 23-84.

de un.   *De unitate,* ed. P. Correns, Münster: Aschendorff, 1891 (B. G. Ph. M., 1.1).

Duns Scotus   Ioannes Duns Scotus

quodl.   *Quaestiones quodlibetales* in *Petri Tatareti Lucidissima commentaria, siue (vt vocant) Reportata, in quatuor libros sententiarum, et Quodlibeta Ioannis Duns Scoti, in tres priore libros nusquam antehac typis excussa, ab innumeris erroribus expurgata,* Venetiis 1583 (exempl.: *Padova, Biblioteca del Seminario Vescovile, 500.ROSSA.SUP.D.3.-10.5*).

Gilb. Pict.   Gilbertus Pictaviensis

in C. Eut.   *Expositio in Boecii librum Contra Euticen et Nestorium,* in *The Commentaries on Boethius by Gilbert of Poitiers,* ed. N. M. Häring, Toronto: Pontifical Institute of Mediaeval Studies, 1966.

gl. ord.   *Biblia Latina cum Glossa Ordinaria,* ed. Adolph Rusch, Strassburg 1480-81, repr. Turnhout: Brepols, 1992.

Greg. Naz.   Gregorius Nazianzenus

in Theoph.   *In Theophania (Oratio* 38), ed. A. Engelbrecht, Vindobonae et Lipsiae 1910, CSEL 46.1, SC 358.

Guill. Altissiod.   Guillelmus Altissiodorensis

sum. aur.   *Summa Aurea,* ed. J. Ribaillier, Roma: Editiones Collegii S. Bonaventurae ad Claras Aquas Grottaferrata, 1982.

Guill. de Alv.   Guillelmus de Alvernia

de an..   *De anima,* ed. B. Le Feron, in *Opera omnia. Supplementum,* ed. F. Hotot- B. Le Feron, Orléans-Paris 1674 (repr. Frankfurt a. M. 1963).

Guill. de Conch.   Guillelmus de Conchis

gl. super Plat.   *Glosae super Platonem*, ed. E. A. Jeauneau, Turnhout: Brepols, 2006, CCCM 203.

Guill. Mar.   Guillelmus de la Mare

correct.   *Correctorium Fratris Thomae*, in P. Glorieux, *Les premières polémiques thomistes: Le Correctorium Corruptorii "Quare"*, Kain: Le Saulchoir, 1927.

Guill. de Tocco   Guillelmus de Tocco

yst. S. Thom.   *Ystoria Sancti Thome de Aquino*, ed. C. Le Brun Gouanvic, Toronto: Pontifical Institute of Medieval Studies, 1996.

Ps.-Herm.   Pseudo Hermes

vig. quat. phil.   *Liber viginti quattuor philosophorum*, ed. F. Hudry, in *Hermes latinus* III, 1, ed. P. Lucentini, Turnhout: Brepols, 1997, CCCM 143 a.

Hieron.   Hieronymus

in Math.   *Commentarium in Matheum*, ed. D. Hurst - M. Adriaen, Turnhout: Brepols, 1969, CCSL 77.

Hil. Pict.   Hilarius Pictaviensis

tract. super Ps.   *Tractatus super Psalmos*, ed. J. Doignon, Turnhout: Brepols, 2002, CCSL 61a.

Hugo de S. Caro   Hugo de Sancto Caro

in Sent.   *Commentarium in Sententias*, ed. W. Breuning, *Die hypostatische Union in der Theologie Wilhelms von Auxerre, Hugos von St. Cher und Rolands von Cremona*, Trier: Paulinus Verlag, 1962, pp. 334-87;

Commentarium in Sententias, ed. W. H. Principe, *Hugh of Saint- Cher's Theology of the Hypostatic Union*, Toronto: Pontifical Institute of Mediaeval Studies, 1970, pp. 163-243.

q. de an.   *Quaestio de anima*, ed. M. Bieniak, "Una questione disputata di Ugo di St.-Cher sull'anima. Edizione e studio dottrinale", *Studia antyczne i mediewistyczne* 2 [37] (2004), pp. 168-184.

Hugo de S. Vict.   Hugo de Sancto Victore

didasc.   *Didascalicon*, ed. H. Buttimer, Washington: The Catholic University Press, 1939.

sacr.   *De sacramentis*, PL 176, 173 A-618 B.

Ps. Hugo de S. Vict.   Pseudo Hugo de Sancto Victore

   sum. sent.   *Summa sententiarum*, PL 176, 43 A-174 A.

Ioh. Blund   Iohannes Blund

   tract. de an.   *Tractatus de anima*, ed. D. A. Callus - R. W. Hunt, London: Oxford University Press, 1970 (Auctores Britannici Medii Aevi, 2).

Ioh. Dam.   Iohannes Damascenus

   fid. orth.   *De fide orthodoxa* (gr.), ed. B. Kotter, in *Die Schriften des Iohannes von Damascos*, ed. Byzantynisches Institut der Abtei Scheyern, II: *Ekdosis akribes tes orthodoxu pisteos - Expositio fidei*, Berlin: De Gruyter, 1973; *De fide orthodoxa, Translatio Burgundionis*, ed. E. M. Buytaert, Louvain-New York: Franciscan Institute Publications, 1955, PG 94, 789-1228.

Isid. Hisp.   Isidorus Hispalensis

   diff.   *Differentiae*, PL 83, 9 A-98 A.

Ioh. Rup.   Iohannes de Rupella (Jean de La Rochelle)

   sum. de an.   *Summa de anima*, ed. J.-G. Bougerol, Paris: Vrin, 1995.

   tract. de div.   *Tractatus de divisione multiplici potentiarum animae*, ed. P. Michaud-Quantin, Paris: Vrin, 1964.

Macr.   Macrobius

   in somn. Scip.   *Comentarii in Somnium Scipionis*, ed. J. Willis, Leipzig: Teubner, 1970.

Nemes.   Nemesius Emesenus

   nat. hom.   *De natura Hominis*, ed. M. Morani, Leipzig: Teubner, 1987; *De natura Hominis, Translatio Burgundionis*, ed. G. Verbeke - J. R. Moncho, Leiden: Brill, 1975 (Corpus latinorum commentariorum in Aristitolem graecorum, Suppl. 1).

Nic. Amb.   Nicolaus Ambianensis

   ars cath.   *Ars fidei catholicae*, ed. M. Dreyer, Münster: Aschendorff, 1993 (B. G. Ph. Th. M., N. F., 37), pp. 76-120, PL 210, 595 A-618 B.

Petr. de Barro   Petrus de Barro

    q. de illo verbo. *Quaestio de illo verbo: "Faciamus hominem ad imaginem et similitudinem nostram"*, ed. P. Künzle, *Das Verhältnis der Seele zu ihren Potenzen; problemgeschichtliche Untersuchungen von Augustin bis und mit Thomas von Aquin*, Freiburg: Universitätsverlag, 1956, pp. 229-231.

Petr. Lomb.   Petrus Lombardus

    sent. *Sententiae in IV libris distinctae*, ed. PP. Collegii S. Bonaventurae ad Claras Aquas, Roma 1981;

    sent., ed. 1916 *Sententiae*, ed. PP. Collegii S. Bonaventurae, Ad Claras Aquas 1916.

Philipp.   Philippus Cancellarius

    q. de ymag. *Quaestio de ymagine et similitudine nostra*, ed. N. Wicki, *Die Philosophie Philipps des Kanzlers: ein philosophierender Theologe des frühen 13. Jahrhunderts*, Fribourg: Academic Press, 2005, pp. 171-178.

    qq. de incarn. *Quaestiones de incarnatione*, ed. W. Principe, *Philip the Chancellor's Theology of the Hypostatic Union*, Toronto: The Pontifical Institute of Mediaeval Studies, 1975, pp. 158-188.

    sum. de bon. *Summa de bono*, ed. N. Wicki, 2 voll., Bernae: Editiones Francke, 1985.

Phil. Alex.   Philo Alexandrinus

    quod deter. *Quod deterius potiori insidiari soleat*, ed. I. Feuer, Paris: Les Éditions du Cerf, 1965.

Plato

    Phaedo *Phaedo* interprete Henrico Aristippo, ed. Minio-Paluello, London: Warburg Institute, 1950 (Corpus Platonicum Medii Aevi, 2).

    Tim. *Timaeus*, ed. J. H. Waszink, London: Warburg Institute, 1975 (Corpus Platonicum Medii Aevi, 4).

De pot. an. et ob.

Anonymus, *De potentiis animae et obiectis*, ed. D. A. Callus, "The Powers of the Soul. An Early Unpublished Text", *RTAM* 19 (1952), pp. 131-170.

Prisc.   Priscianus

inst.   *Prisciani grammatici Caesariensis institutionum grammati-*
carum libri XVIII, ed. M. Hertz – H. Keil, in *Grammatici*
Latini, vol. II-III, Leipzig: Teubner, 1855-1859 (repr. Olms,
Hildesheim 1961).

Rab. Maur.   Rabanus Maurus

de an.   *Tractatus de anima*, PL 110, 1109 B-1120 C.

Rich. de S. Vict.   Richardus de Sancto Victore

trin.   *De Trinitate*, ed. J. Ribaillier, Paris: Vrin, 1958.

Rich. de Mediav.   Richardus de Mediavilla

in III Sent.   *Sacre theologie doctoris eximij Ricardi de Mediauilla in*
tertium Sententiarum questiones solidissime, per Lazarum
Soardum Impressum Venetijs 1509, die xxij Septembris
(exempl.: *Padova, Biblioteca del Seminario Vescovile 500.*
ROSSA.SUP.AA.6.-8.3).

Rol. Crem.   Rolandus Cremonensis

sum.   *Summa* III, ed. A. Cortesi, Bergamo: Edizioni Monumenta
Bergomensia, 1962.

Sim. Torn.   Simon Tornacensis

sum.   *Summa*, ed. M. Schmaus, "Die Texte der Trinitätslehre in
den Sententiae des Simons von Tournai", *RTAM*, 4 (1932), pp.
60-72.

Steph. Langt.   Stephanus Langton

de pers.   *De persona*, ed. M. Bieniak, *CIMAGL* 77 (2006), pp. 95-109.

q. de hom.   *Quaestio de homine assumpto, et utrum Christus sit duo*, ed.
L. O. Nielsen – S. Ebbesen, "Texts Illustrating the Debate
about Christology in the Wake of Alexandeer III's 1177
Condemnation", *CIMAGL* 66 (1996), pp. 229-240.

in Sent.   *Commentarius in Sententias*, ed. A. M. Landgraf, *Der*
Sentenzenkommentar des Kardinals Stephan Langton,
Münster: Aschendorff, 1952 (B.G.Ph.Th.M., 37.1).

sum.   *Summa*, ed. S. Ebbesen - L. B. Mortensen, *CIMAGL* 49 (1985),
pp. 37-224.

sum. Duac.   *Summa Duacensis (Douai 434)*, ed. P. Glorieux, Paris: Vrin
1955.

Thom. de Aquino   Thomas de Aquino

in Sent.   *In Sententias*, ed. EP, in Bologna: Edizioni Studio Domenicano, 2000.

sum. c. gent.   *Summa contra gentiles*, Roma: Typis Riccardi Garroni, 1926, EL 14.

sum. theol.   *Summa theologiae*, Roma 1888-1903, EL 4-11.

qq. de an.   *Quaestiones disputatae de anima*, ed. B.-C. Bazán, Roma-Paris 1996, EL 24. 1.

resp. de art.   *Responsio de 108 articulis ad magistrum Ioannem de Vercellis*, in *Opuscula Theologica* I, ed. R. A. Verardo, Roma: Marietti, 1954.

sent. De an.   *Sentencia libri De anima*, ed. R.-A. Gauthier, Roma-Paris 1984, EL 45. 1.

Thom. de Vio   Thomas de Vio (Cajetanus)

in Sum. theol.   *Commentarium* in Thomas de Aquino, *Summa theologiae*, Roma 1888-1903, EL 4-11.

Vigil. Taps.   Vigilius Tapsensis

de unit. Trin.   *De unitate Trinitatis*, PL 42, 1156-1172.

(D) STUDIES

Aiello, A., "La conoscenza intellettiva dell'individuale: note alla soluzione di Guglielmo de la Mare", *Acta philosophica* 9 (2000), pp. 5-31.

d'Alverny, M.-T., *Alain de Lille, Textes inédits, avec une introduction sur sa vie et ses oeuvres*, Paris: Vrin, 1965.

Angelini, G., *L'ortodossia e la grammatica. Analisi di struttura e deduzione storica della Teologia Trinitaria di Prepositino*, Roma: Università Gregoriana Editrice, 1972.

Antl, L., "An Introduction to the "Quaestiones Theologicae" of Stephen Langton", *FS* 12 (1952), pp. 151-175.

Arnold, J., *Perfecta Communicatio. Die Trinitätstheologie Wilhelms von Auxerre*, Münster: Aschendorff, 1995 (B. G. Ph. Th. M., N. F., 42).

Barber, M., *The Cathars. Dualist Heretics in Languedoc in the High Middle Ages*, London-New York: Longman, 2000.

Bartkó, J., *Un prédicateur français au Moyen Âge: les Sermons modèles de Hugues de Saint-Cher (1263)*, Veszprém: Pannon Egy. K., 2006.

Bataillon, L.-J., Dahan, G., and Gy, P.-M., eds, *Hugues de Saint-Cher († 1263), bibliste et théologien,* Turnhout: Brepols, 2004.

Bataillon, L.-J., Bériou, N., Dahan, G., Quinto, R., eds, *Langton, Étienne, Predicateur, bibliste et théologien, Colloque international 13-15 septembre 2006, Paris, Centre d'études du Saulchoir, EPHE-CNRS,* Turnhout: Brepols, forthcoming.

Bazán, B.C., "Pluralisme de formes ou dualisme de substances?" *Revue Philosophique de Louvain* 67 (1969), pp. 30-73.

Bazán, B.C., "The Human Soul: Form *and* Substance? Thomas Aquinas' Critique of Eclectic Aristotelianism", *AHDLMA* 64 (1997), pp. 95-126.

Bernardini, P., "La dottrina dell'anima separata nella prima metà del XIII secolo e i suoi influssi sulla teoria della conoscenza (1240-60 ca.)", in *Etica e conoscenza nel XIII e XIV secolo,* ed. Zavattero, I., Arezzo: Dipartimento di Studi Storico-Sociali e Filosofici, 2006.

Bertola, E., "Alano di Lilla, Filippo il Cancelliere e una inedita "quaestio" sull'immortalità dell'anima umana", *Rivista di Filosofia neo-scolastica* 62 (1970), pp. 245-271.

Bertola, E., "Le fonti medico-filosofiche della dottrina dello «spirito»", *Sophia* 26 (1958), pp. 48-61.

Bianchi, L., *La filosofia nelle università: secoli XIII-XIV,* Firenze: La nuova Italia, 1997.

Bieniak, M., "Una questione disputata di Ugo di St.-Cher sull'anima. Edizione e studio dottrinale", *Studia antyczne i mediewistyczne* 2 [37] (2004), pp. 127-184.

Bieniak, M., "The *Sentences* Commentary of Hugh of St.-Cher", in *Mediaeval Commentaries on the* Sentences *of Peter Lombard. Vol. 2,* ed. Rosemann, P., Leiden: Brill, 2010, pp. 111-148.

Bieniak, M., "Filippo il Cancelliere ed Ugo di St.-Cher sull'anima umana" in *L'origine dell'Ordine dei Predicatori e l'Università di Bologna. Atti del convegno (Bologna, 18-20 febbraio 2005),* ed. Bertuzzi, G., Bologna: Edizioni Studio Domenicano, 2006, pp. 105-117.

Blaise, A., *Dictionnaire latin-français des auteurs chrétiens,* Turnhout: Brepols, 1954.

Bougerol, J.-G., "Introduction", in Jean de la Rochelle, *Summa de anima,* Paris: Vrin, 1995.

Brachtendorf, J., *Die Struktur des menschlichen Geistes nach Augustinus. Selbstreflexion und Erkenntnis Gottes in "De Trinitate",* Hamburg: Felix Meiner, 2000.

Brachtendorf, J., ed., *Gott und sein Bild. Augustins De Trinitate im Spiegel gegenwärtiger Forschung,* Paderborn: Schöningh, 2000.

Brady, I., "Remigius – Nemesius", *FS* 8 (1948), pp. 275-284.

Brenet, J.-B., "Introduction", in Guillaume d'Auvergne, *De l'Âme (VII, 1-9)*, Paris: Vrin, 1998, pp. 7-83.

Breuning, W., *Die hypostatische Union in der Theologie Wilhelms von Auxerre, Hugos von St. Cher und Rolands von Cremona*, Trier: Paulinus Verlag, 1962.

Callus, D.A., "The Powers of the Soul. An Early Unpublished Text", *RTAM* 19 (1952), pp. 131-170.

Casagrande, C., Vecchio, S., eds, *Anima e corpo nella cultura medievale. Atti del V Convegno di studi della Società Italiana per lo Studio del Pensiero Medievale, Venezia, 25-28 settembre 1995*, Firenze: SISMEL edizioni del Galluzzo, 1999.

Catalogue général des manuscrits des bibliothèques publiques des départements de France. Bibliothèque de Douai, 1878, vol. IV.

Cillerai, B., "Agostino: la memoria centro dell' 'actio animae'", in *Atti del Convegno "Tracce nella mente. Teorie della memoria da Platone ai moderni", (Pisa 25-26 settembre 2006)*, ed. Sassi, M., Pisa: Edizioni Scuola Normale Superiore, forthcoming.

Cillerai, B., *La memoria come* capacitas Dei *secondo S. Agostino: unità e complessità*, Pisa: ETS, forthcoming.

Cipriani, N., "Memory", in *Augustine Through the Ages: An Encyclopedia*, ed. Fitzgerald, A., Grand Rapids, Michigan: Eerdmans Publishing Company, 1999, pp. 563-564.

Colish, M.L., "The Pseudo-Peter of Poitiers Gloss", in *Mediaeval Commentaries on the Sentences of Peter Lombard. Vol. 2*, ed. Rosemann, P., Leiden: Brill, 2010, pp. 1-33.

Contenson, P.-M. de, "Avicennisme latin et vision de Dieu au début du XIIIe siècle", *AHDLMA* 26 (1959), pp. 29-97.

Cullmann, O., *Immortality of the Soul or Resurrection of the Dead? The Witness of the New Testament*, London: Epworth Press, 1958.

Dales, R.C., *The Problem of the Rational Soul in the Thirteenth Century*, Leiden - New York: Brill, 1995.

Degl'Innocenti, U., *Il problema della persona nel pensiero di S. Tommaso*, Roma: Libreria editrice della Pontificia Università Lateranense, 1967.

Diem, G., "Les traductions gréco-latines de la Métaphysique au Moyen Âge: Le problème de la Metaphysica Vetus", *Archiv für Geschichte der Philosophie* 49 (1967), pp. 7-71.

Dod, B.G., "Aristoteles Latinus", in *The Cambridge History of Later Medieval Philosophy*, ed. Kretzmann, N., Kenny, A., Pinborg, J., Cambridge: Cambridge University Press, 1982, pp. 45-79.

Doucet, V., "A travers le manuscrit 434 de Douai", *Antonianum* 27 (1952), pp. 531-580.

Doucet, V., "Prolegomena", in Alexander de Hales, *Summa theologica* III, Quaracchi: Editiones Collegii S. Bonaventurae, 1948, pp. XI-LVII.

Druart, M. T., "The Human Soul's Individuation and its Survival after the Body's Death: Avicenna on the Causal Relation between Body and Soul", *Arabic sciences and philosophy* 10. 2 (2000), pp. 259-273.

Duvernoy, J., *La religion des cathares,* Toulouse: Privat, 1976.

Ebbesen, S., Mortensen, L.B., "A Partial Edition of Stephen Langton's *Summa* and *Quaestiones*, with Parallels from Andrew Sunesen's *Hexaemeron*", *CIMAGL* 49 (1985), pp. 25-224.

Ebbesen, S., "Addenda to Gertz Commentarius", in Andreae Sunonis filii *Hexaemeron*, ed. Ebbesen, S., Mortensen, L.B., Hauniae, 1988 (*Corpus Philosophorum Danicorum Medii Aevi* 11. 2), pp. 445-449.

Emery, K., "*Quaestiones, Sententiae* and *Summae* from the Later Twelfth and Early Thirteenth Centuries: The Joseph N. Garvin Papers", *Bulletin de philosophie médiévale* 48 (2006), pp. 15-82.

Erismann, Ch., "Alain de Lille, la métaphysique érigénienne et la pluralité des formes", in *Alain de Lille, le Docteur Universel. Actes du XIeme Colloque intérnational de la Société Inernationale pour l'Etude de la Philosophie Médiévale, Paris 23-25 octobre 2003*, ed. Solère, J. L., Vasiliu, A., Galonnier, A., Turnhout: Brepols, 2005.

Faes de Mottoni, B., "Les manuscrits du commentaire des Sentences d'Hugues de St. Cher", in *Hugues de St-Cher, Bibliste et Theologien*, ed. Bataillon, L.-J., Dahan, G., and Gy, P.-M., Turnhout: Brepols, 2004, pp. 273-298.

Fichtenau, H., *Heretics and Scholars in the High Middle Ages, 1000-1200*, tr.. Kaiser, D. A, Pennsylvania: The Pennsylvania State University Press, 1998.

Filthaut, E., *Roland von Cremona O. P. und die Anfänge der Scholastik im Predigerorden. Ein Beitrag zur Geistesgeschichte der älteren Dominikaner,* Vechta i. O.: Albertus-Magnus-Verlag der Dominikaner, 1936.

Fisher, J., "Hugh of St. Cher and the Development of Medieval Theology", *Speculum* 31 (1956), pp. 57-69.

Fries, A., "Zur Problematik der "Summa theologiae" unter dem Namen des Albertus Magnus", *Franziskanische Studien* 70 (1988), pp. 68-91.

Fries, A., "Zum Verhältnis des Albertus Magnus zur "Summa theologiae" unter seinem Namen", *Franziskanische Studien* 71 (1989), pp. 123-137.

Froese, V., "Body and Soul: A Selected Annotated Bibliography", *Direction* 37. 2 (2008), pp. 243–247.

Gauthier, R.-A., "Le traité De anima et de potenciis eius", *Revue des sciences philosophiques et théologiques* 66 (1982), pp. 3-55.

Gauthier, R.-A., "Notes sur les débuts (1225-1240) du premier 'Averroisme'", *Revue des sciences philosophiques et théologiques* 66 (1982), pp. 321-374.

Gauthier, R.-A., "Préface", in Thomas de Aquino, *Sentencia libri De anima*, Roma-Paris 1984 (EL 45.1).

Ghisalberti, A., "L'esegesi della scuola domenicana del sec. XIII", in *La Bibbia nel Medio Evo,* ed. Cremascoli, G., Bologna 1996.

Gillon, L.-B., "La noción de persona en Hugo de San Caro", *Ciencia Tomista* 64 (1943), pp. 171-177.

Gilson, E., *History of Christian Philosophy in the Middle Ages*, New York: Random House, 1955.

Glorieux,P., *Répertoire des maîtres en théologie de Paris au 13. siècle*, Paris: Vrin, 1933.

Glorieux, P., "Les 572 Questions du manuscrit de Douai 434", *RTAM* 10 (1938), pp. 123-157, 225-267.

Glorieux, P., "La Summa Duacensis", *RTAM* 12 (1940), pp. 104-135.

Glorieux, P., "Somme "Quoniam homines" d'Alain de Lille", *AHDLMA* 28 (1953), pp. 113-364.

Glorieux, P., *La «Summa Duacensis» (Douai 434). Texte critique avec une introduction et des tables,* Paris: Vrin, 1955.

Grabmann, M., *Forschungen über die Lateinischen Aristoteles - Übersetzungen des XIII. Jahrhunderts*, Münster: Aschendorff, 1916 (B. G. Ph. M., 17. 5-6).

Grabmann, M., *I divieti ecclesiastici di Aristotele sotto Innocenzo III e Gregorio IX*, Roma 1941.

Gracia, J.J.E., *Introduction to the Problem of Individuation in the Early Middle Ages*, München – Washington: Philosophia Verlag - Catholic University of America Press 1984.

Gründel, J., *Die Lehre von den Umstanden der menschlichen Handlung im Mittelalter,* Münster: Aschendorff, 1963 (B. G. Ph. (Th.) M., 39. 5).

Hadot, P., "L'image de la Trinité dans l'âme chez Victorinus et chez saint Augustin", in *Studia Patristica*, VI, Berlin: Akademie-Verlag, 1962, pp. 409-442.

Häring, N.-M., "The Commentary of Gilbert, Bishop of Poitiers, on Boethius' Contra Eutychen et Nestorium", *AHDLMA* 21 (1954), pp. 241-357.

Harris, M.J., *Raised Immortal: Resurrection and Immortality in the New Testament*, Grand Rapids: Eerdmans, 1985.

Haskins, Ch.H., "A list of text-books from the close of the twelfth century", *Harvard Studies in Classical Philosophy* 20 (1909), pp. 356-376.

Hasse, D.N., *Avicenna's "De anima" in the Latin West. The Formation of a Peripatetic Philosophy of the Soul 1160-1300*, London: The Warburg Institute, 2000.

Heinzmann, R., *Die Unsterblichkeit der Seele und die Auferstehung des Leibes; eine problemgeschichtliche Untersuchung der frühscholastischen Sentenzen- und Summenliteratur von Anselm von Laon bis Wilhelm von Auxerre*, Münster: Aschendorff, 1965 (B. G. Ph. Th. M., 40, 3).

Heinzmann, R., "Das Verhältnis von Leib und Seele in Verständnis der Frühscholastik", *Theologie und Philosophie* 49 (1974), pp. 542-547.

Hess, C.R., "Roland of Cremona's Place in the Current of Thought", *Angelicum* 45 (1968), pp. 429-477.

Imbach, R., *Quodlibeta. Ausgewählte Artikel - Articles choisis*, Freiburg: Universitätsverlag, 1996.

Javelet, R., *Image et ressemblance au douzième siècle. De Saint Anselme à Alain de Lille*, Strasbourg: Éditions Letouzey & Ané, 1967.

Jüssen, G., "Wilhelm von Auvergne und die Transformation der scholastischen Philosophie im 13. Jahrhundert", in *Philosophie im Mittelalter. Entwicklungslinien und Paradigmen*, ed., J. Beckmann - L. Honnefelder, Hamburg: Meiner, 1987, pp. 141-164.

Jüssen, G., "Aristoteles-Rezeption und Aristoteles-Kritik in Wilhelm von Auvergne's Tractatus "De Anima"", in R. Työrinoja - S. Ebbesen - S. Knuuttila, *Knowledge and the Sciences in Medieval Philosophy. Proceedings of the VIII International Congress of Medieval Philosophy (S.I.E.P.M.)*, Helsinki: Luther-Agricola Society Series, 1990, pp. 87-96.

Kaeppeli, Th., *Scriptores Ordinis Praedicatorum Medii Aevi*, 4. voll., Roma: Ad Sanctae Sabinae - Istituto Storico Domenicano, 1970-1993.

Kalka, R., "Définition de la personne chez saint Thomas d'Aquin", *Journal Philosophique* 6 (1986), pp. 1-30.

Köhler, T.W., *Grundlagen des philosophisch-anthropologischen Diskurses im dreizehnten Jahrhundert: die Erkenntnisbemühungen um den Menschen im zeitgenössischen Verstandnis*, Leiden – Boston: Brill, 2000.

Kohler, J., "Ut Plato est individuum. Die Theologischen Regeln des Alain de Lille über das Problem der Individualität", in *Individuum und Individualität im Mittelalter*, ed. Aertsen, J.A., Speer, A., Berlin-New York: Gruyter, 1996, pp. 22-36.

Kramp, J., "Des Wilhelm von Auvergne "Magisterium Divinale"", *Gregorianum* 1 (1920), pp. 559-562.

Künzle, P., *Das Verhältnis der Seele zu ihren Potenzen; problemgeschichtliche Untersuchungen von Augustin bis und mit Thomas von Aquin*, Freiburg: Universitätsverlag, 1956.

Landgraf, A.M. , *Introduction à l'histoire de la littérature théologique de la scolastique naissante*, Montréal – Paris: Institut d'études médiévales - Vrin, 1973.

Lefèvre, G., *Les variations de Guillaume de Champeaux et la question des Universaux: Étude suivie de documents originaux*, Lille 1898.

Lenzi, M., *Forma e sostanza. Le origini del dibattito sulla natura dell'anima nel XIII secolo*, Doctorate dissertation, sup. Maierù, A., Università di Salerno, 2004-2005.

Libera, A. de, "Logique et théologie dans la *Summa "Quoniam hommes"* d'Alain de Lille", in *Gilbert de Poitiers et ses contemporains. Aux origines de la Logica Modernorum : Actes du 7ème Symposium européen de logique et de sémantique médiévales, Poitiers, Centre d'études supérieures de civilisation médiévale, 17-23 juin 1985*, ed. Jolivet, J., Libera, A. de, Napoli: Bibliopolis, 1987, pp. 437-469.

Libera, A. de, "Des accidents aux tropes", *Revue de Métaphysique et de Morale* 4 (2002), pp. 509-530.

Lipke, S., "Die Bedeutung der Seele für die Einheit des Menschen nach De homine", in *Albertus Magnus. Zum Gedenken nach 800 Jahren: Neue Zugänge, Aspekte und Perspektiven*, ed., W. Senner, Berlin 2001, pp. 207-219.

Loos, M., *Dualist Heresy in the Middle Ages*, trans. I. Lewitová, Praha: Akademia, 1974.

Lottin, O., "Quelques "Questiones" de maîtres parisiens aux environs de 1225-1235", *RTAM* 5 (1933), pp. 79-95.

Lottin, O., "Un petit traité sur l'âme de Hugues de Saint-Cher", *Revue neoscolastique de philosophie*, 34 (1932), pp. 468-475.

Lottin, O., "Roland de Crémone et Hugues de Saint-Cher", *RTAM* 12 (1940), pp. 136-143.

Lottin, O., *Psychologie et morale aux XIIᵉ et XIIIᵉ siècles*, 6. voll., Grembloux: Duculot, 1942-1960.

Lovejoy, A., *The Great Chain of Being: A Study of the History of an Idea*, Cambridge: Harvard University Press, 1961.

Lynch, K., "Some "Fontes" of the "Commentary" of Hugh of Saint Cher: William of Auxerre, Guy d'Orchelles, Alexander of Hales", *FS* 13 (1953), pp. 119-146.

Lynch, K., *The Sacrament of Confirmation in the early-middle scholastic period, I*, New York: St. Bonaventure, 1957.

Masnovo, A., *Da Guglielmo d'Auvergne a S. Tommaso d'Aquino*, vol. III: *L'uomo*, Milano: Vita e pensiero, 1945.

Mayaud, P.-N., ed., *Le problème de l'individuation*, Paris: Vrin, 1991.

McGinn, B., *The Golden Chain. A Study in the Theological Anthropology of Isaac of Stella*, Washington D.C.: Cistercian Publications, 1972.

Merle, H., "Aptum natum esse. Aptitudo naturalis", in id., *Glossaire du latin philosophique médiéval*, Bruxelles, Union Académique Internationale, 1982, pp. 122-139.

Michot, J.R., *La destinée de l'homme selon Avicenne. Le retour à Dieu (ma'ad) et l'imagination*, Leuven: Peeters, 1986.

Minio-Paluello, L., "Le texte du «De anima» d'Aristote: la tradition latine avant 1500", in *Opuscula. The Latin Aristotle*, Amsterdam: Hakkert, 1972, pp. 250-276.

Minio-Paluello, L., "Nuovi impulsi allo studio della logica : la seconda fase della riscoperta di Aristotele e di Boezio", in *La scuola nell'Occidente latino dell'alto medioevo, vol. II*, ed. Centro italiano di studi sull'alto medioevo, Spoleto 1972.

Miramon, Ch. de, "La place d'Hugues de Saint-Cher dans les débats sur la pluralité des bénéfices (1230-1240)" in *Hugues de Saint-Cher († 1263), bibliste et théologien*, ed. Bataillon, L.-J. , Dahan, G., and Gy, P.-M., Turnhout: Brepols, 2004.

Moore, P.S., *The Works of Peter of Poitiers, Master in Theology and Chancellor of Paris (1193-1205)*, South Bend: Publications in Mediaeval Studies, 1936.

Morenzoni, F., Tilliette, J.-Y., eds, *Autour de Guillaume d'Auvergne († 1249)*, Turnhout: Brepols, 2005.

Motta, B., *La mediazione estrema. L'antropologia di Nemesio di Emesa fra platonismo e aristotelismo*, Padova: Il Poligrafo, 2004.

Mourant, J.A., *Saint Augustine on Memory*, Villanova: University Press, 1980.

Muckle, J.T., "Isaac Israeli's Definition of Truth", *AHDLMA* 1 (1933), pp. 5-8.

Nielsen, L.O., *Theology and Philosophy in the Twelfth Century. A Study on Gilbert Porreta's Thinking and the Theological Exposition of the Doctrine of the Incarnation during the Period 1130-1180*, Leiden: Brill, 1982.

Niermeyer, J.F., *Mediae latinitatis lexicon minus*, Leiden: Brill, 1976.

O'Daly, G., *Augustine's Philosophy of Mind*, Berkeley: University of California Press, 1987.

Osborne, Th., "Unibilitas: The Key to Bonaventure's Understanding of Human Nature", *Journal of the History of Philosophy* 37. 2 (1999), pp. 227-250.

Paravicini Bagliani, A., *Cardinali di curia e 'familiae' cardinalizie dal 1227 al 1254*, 2 voll, Padova: Editrice Antenore, 1972.

Pegis, A.C., *St. Thomas and the Problem of the Soul in the Thirteenth Century*, Toronto: Pontifical Institute of Mediaeval Studies, 1934.

Pegis, A.C., "The Separated Soul and Its Nature in St. Thomas", in *St. Thomas Aquinas: 1274-1974. Commemorative Studies*, ed. A. A. Maurer, Toronto: Pontifical Institute of Medieval Studies, 1974, vol. I, pp. 131-158.

Portalié, E., "Abélard", in *Dictionnaire de théologie catholique I*, ed. A. Vacant, E. Mangenot, Paris: Librairie Letouzey-Ane, 1903, pp. 36-55.

PP. Collegii S. Bonaventurae, "Prolegomena", in Alexandri de Hales *Glossa in quatuor libros Sententiarum*, Firenze: Quaracchi, 1952.

Principe, W.H., *William of Auxerre's Theology of the Hypostatic Union*, Toronto: Pontifical Institute of Mediaeval Studies, 1963.

Principe, W.H., *Hugh of Saint-Cher's Theology of the Hypostatic Union*, Toronto: Pontifical Institute of Mediaeval Studies, 1970.

Principe, W.H., *Philip the Chancellor's Theology of the Hypostatic Union*, Toronto: Pontifical Institute of Mediaeval Studies, 1975.

Quinto, R., "Alanus de Insulis", in *Grundriss der Geschichte der Philosophie (Begründet von Friedrich Ueberweg). Die Philosophie des Mittelalters, Band 2: 12. Jahrhundert*, ed. Imbach, R., Ricklin,T., Basel: Schwabe, forthcoming.

Quinto, R., "Anselm von Laon", in *Grundriss der Geschichte der Philosophie (Begründet von Friedrich Uebeweg). Die Philosophie des Mittelalters, Band 2: 12. Jahrhundert*, ed. Imbach, R., Ricklin,T., Basel: Schwabe, forthcoming.

Quinto, R., "Stephen Langton", in *Mediaeval Commentaries on the* Sentences *of Peter Lombard. Vol. 2*, ed. Rosemann, P., Leiden: Brill, 2009, pp. 35-78.

Quinto, R., "Il Codice 434 di Douai, Stefano Langton e Nicola di Tournai", *Sacris Erudiri* 36 (1996), pp. 233-361.

Quinto, R., "Hugh of St.-Cher's Use of Stephen Langton", in *Medieval Analyses in Language and Cognition. Acts of the Symposium "The Copenhagen School of Medieval Philosophy", January 10-13, 1996*, ed. Ebbesen, S., Friedman, R. L., Copenhagen: Det Kongelige Danske Videnskabernes Selskab, 1999, pp. 281-300.

Quinto, R., "Le Commentaire des Sentences d'Hugues de St.-Cher et la littérature théologique de son temps" in *Hugues de St-Cher. Bibliste et Theologien*, ed. Bataillon, L.-J. , Dahan, G., and Gy, P.-M., Turnhout: Brepols, 2004, pp. 299-324.

Quinto, R., *"Doctor Nominatissimus". Stefano Langton († 1228) e la tradizione delle sue opere*, Münster: Aschendorff, 1994 (B. G. Ph. Th. M., N. F., 39).

Ribaillier, J., "Introduction", in Guillelmus Altissiodorensis, *Summa aurea*, Paris – Roma: Editiones Collegii S. Bonaventurae, 1987.

Rondeau, M.J., "Remarques sur l'anthropologie de saint Hilaire", *Studia Patristica* 6 (1962), pp. 197-210.

Rosemann, P., ed., *Mediaeval Commentaries on the* Sentences *of Peter Lombard. Vol. 2*, Leiden: Brill, 2010.

Schmaus, M., "Das Fortwirken der augustinischen Trinitätspsychologie bis zur Karolingischen Zeit", in *Vitae et Veritati. Festgabe für Karl Adam*, Düsserldorf: Patmos-Verlag, 1956, pp. 44-56.

Schmaus, M., "Die Texte der Trinitätslehre in den Sententiae des Simon von Tournai", *RTAM* 4 (1932), pp. 59-72.

Schmaus, M., "Die Trinitätslehre des Simon von Tournai", *RTAM* 3 (1931), pp. 373-385.

Schneyer, J.B., *Die Sittenkritik in den Predigten Philipps des Kanzlers*, Münster: Aschendorff, 1962-1963 (B. G. Ph. Th. M., 39.4).

Schneyer, J.B., *Repertorium der lateinischen Sermones des Mittelalters für die zeit von 1150-1350*, 11. voll., Münster: Aschendorff, 1969-1990 (B. G. Ph. Th. M, 43).

Schulthess, P., Imbach, R., *Die Philosophie im lateinischen Mittelalter: ein Handbuch mit einem bio-bibliographischen Repertorium*, Zürich: Artemis & Winkler, 1996.

Schulz, G., *Veritas est adequatio intellectus et rei. Untersuchungen zur Wahrheitsbegriff*, Leiden: Brill, 1993.

Sebti, M., *Avicenne: l'âme humaine*, Paris: Presses universitaires de France, 2000.

Sebti, M., "Une épitre inédite d'Avicenne, *Ta'alluq al-nafs bi-l-badan (De l'attachement de l'âme et du corps)*: édition critique, traduction et annotation", *Documenti e studi sulla tradizione filosofica medievale* 15 (2004), pp. 141-200.

Solignac, A., ""Memoria" dans la tradition augustinienne", in *Dictionnaire de spiritualité. Ascétique et mystique, doctrine et histoire*, vol. x, Paris: Beauchesne, 1980, pp. 994 b-1002 b.

Stegmüller, F., "Die neugefundene Parisier Benefizien-Disputation des Kardinals Hugo von St. Cher O. P.", *Historisches Jahrbuch*, 72 (1953), pp. 176-204.

Sweeney, M., "Soul as Substance and Method in Thomas Aquinas' Anthropological Writings", *AHDLMA* 66 (1999), pp. 143-187.

Tolomio, I., *L'anima dell'uomo: trattati sull'anima dal V al IX secolo*, Milano: Rusconi, 1979.

Torrell, J.-P., *Théorie de la prophétie et philosophie de la connaissance aux environs de 1230. La contribution d'Hugues de Saint-Cher*, Louvain: Spicilegium sacrum Lovaniense, 1977.

Van den Eynde, D., "Stephen Langton and Hugh of St. Cher on the causality of the Sacraments", *FS* 11 (1951), pp. 141-155.

Vanni Rovighi, S., *L'antropologia filosofica di San Tommaso d'Aquino*, Milano: Vita e pensiero, 1965.

Van Steenberghen, F., *Introduction à l'étude de la philosophie médiévale*, Louvain: Peeters, 1974.

Verbeke, G., "Introduction", in Avicenna, *Liber de philosophia prima sive Scientia divina. Traduction latine medievale*, I-III, ed. S. Van Riet, Louvain – Leiden: Peeters - Brill, 1977-1983 (Avicenna Latinus), pp. 1-46.

Verbeke, G., "Le «De anima» d'Avicenne. Une conception spiritualiste de l'homme", in Avicenna, *Liber de anima, Traduction latine médiévale*, IV-V, ed. S. Van Riet, Louvain: Editions Orientalistes, 1968 (Avicenna Latinus).

Walker Bynum, C., *The Resurrection of the Body in Western Christianity: 200-1336*, New York: Columbia University Press, 1995.

Warichez, J., *Les Disputationes de Simon de Tournai: texte inedit*, Louvain: Spicilegium sacrum lovaniense, 1932.

Wéber, H., *La personne humaine au XIIIᵉ siècle*, Paris: Vrin, 1991.

Wicki, N., "Introduction", in Philippi Cancellarii «Summa de bono», Bernae: Editiones Francke, 1985, vol. I, pp. 1*-66*.

Wicki, N., *Die Philosophie Philipps des Kanzlers: ein philosophierender Theologe des frühen 13. Jahrhunderts*, Fribourg: Academic Press, 2005.

Wielockx, R., *Zur «Summa theologiae» des Albertus Magnus*, «Ephemerides Theologicae Lovanienses» 66. 1 (1990), pp. 78-110.

Woleński, J., "Izaak Israeli i Tomasz z Akwinu o prawdzie", *Studia Judaica* 8 (2005), pp. 5-13.

Zavalloni, R., *Richard de Mediavilla et la controverse sur la pluralité des formes*, Louvain: Éditions de l'Institut supérieur de philosophie, 1951.

INDICES

INDEX NOMINUM

INDEX OF MANUSCRIPTS

DE WULF-MANSION CENTRE
ANCIENT AND MEDIEVAL PHILOSOPHY

Series 1

Series 3
FRANCISCI DE MARCHIA
OPERA PHILOSOPHICA ET THEOLOGICA
Editionibus curandis praeest R. L. Friedman

CORPUS LATINUM
COMMENTARIORUM IN ARISTOTELEM GRAECORUM